MENTAL HYGIENE
THE
DYNAMICS
OF
ADJUSTMENT

HERBERT A. CARROLL

Professor Emeritus of Psychology
University of New Hampshire

PRENTICE-HALL, INC.
ENGLEWOOD CLIFFS, NEW JERSEY

fifth edition

MENTAL HYGIENE

**THE
DYNAMICS
OF
ADJUSTMENT**

HERBERT A. CARROLL

MENTAL HYGIENE
THE DYNAMICS OF ADJUSTMENT
fifth edition

Printed in the United States of America

Library of Congress Catalog Card Number 69-19921

Current printing (last digit):

10 9 8 7 6 5 4 3

*Photographs by Herbert M. Rosenthal. Photograph on page 78
by Sue Rosenthal. Family Group, by Henry Moore, page 186,
courtesy of the Museum of Modern Art, New York.*

Prentice-Hall International, Inc., LONDON
Prentice-Hall of Australia, Pty. Ltd., SYDNEY
Prentice-Hall of Canada, Ltd., TORONTO
Prentice-Hall of India Private Ltd., NEW DELHI
Prentice-Hall of Japan, Inc., TOKYO

PREFACE

This new edition of *Mental Hygiene,* like those preceding it, has been written for college students with a limited background in psychology. Consequently, I have included some material on topics which are covered in detail in general psychology courses. A student can comprehend problems associated with the need for achievement only if he has some understanding of individual differences; he can understand the adjustment sequence only if he knows something about motivation and learning. In a few sections, then, mental hygiene material might be said to be encased in content which is basic to general psychology. Through this approach it is possible to fill in gaps in the student's background.

In this fifth edition I have reorganized the material to a considerable extent without departing drastically from the overall plan of the earlier editions. The chapters on motivation and on learning have been combined into a single chapter on the adjustment sequence and placed early in the book so that the student will better understand material which comes later. Also, in this edition the discussion of the need for emotional security is much more extensive. In earlier editions this was linked closely with the home, a subject now considered in a separate chapter. In addition to reorganization, much of the content has been revised and a great deal of new material added.

In writing this book I have drawn upon three sources: theory, research, and practical experience. With respect to theory I have been to a considerable extent eclectic, although I have leaned toward the phenomenological point of view. I have in many instances cited early theories and early conclusions arrived at through research, since it is obvious that the latest is not necessarily the best. For example, the insights of William James, Sigmund Freud, Alfred Adler, and, more recently, Carl Rogers are still useful.

Good research, past or present, on the psychology of adjustment is scarce. This subdivision does not yet constitute a body of science. I have not hesitated to draw upon experience, since much can be learned about mental health from actually working with disturbed individuals. Consequently, several case studies are included. Some of these are presented briefly and a few, including transcriptions from taped interviews, at greater length. Theory and research become more meaningful to the student reader when they are applied to actual individuals in real life situations.

I am indebted to Mrs. Helen Donaldson, one of my former graduate students, for her assistance in the preparation of this manuscript. I should also like to take this opportunity to express my thanks to all of my students over the past forty years, especially those whom I saw in counseling. I learned a great deal from them.

HERBERT A. CARROLL

CONTENTS

15

MENTAL HYGIENE
THE
DYNAMICS
OF
ADJUSTMENT

INTRODUCTION

Clinical psychology, which includes mental hygiene, is a combination of philosophy, science, and art. Those who work in this field function in accordance with certain philosophical premises that are difficult to test scientifically. For example, the practicing psychologist who is concerned with promoting human welfare may accept the Freudian assumption that all men are basically evil or he may accept the Rogerian assumption that all men are basically good and are striving to grow. Many clinical psychologists are scientists, since they are raising questions and testing their hypotheses through research. However, most of those who are active in the field do little or no research themselves; instead, they draw upon the studies done by others. This is not an unusual situation. Most physicians are not scientists—they are practitioners of the art of medicine. Professional psychologists who are working with individuals or groups apply to the problems at hand knowledge that has been gathered not only in psychology but also in sociology, anthropology, and biology. This application is an art, for art is *creative doing*.

In mental hygiene the emphasis is on prevention. *Prevention* in its broadest sense means both the establishment of those conditions that will further normal emotional life and the treatment of minor behavior disorders in order that serious mental disturbances may be avoided.

It is rather difficult to define "good mental health" and "poor mental health." A person with good mental health is not entirely free from anxiety and feelings of guilt, but neither is he overwhelmed by them. He is able to meet the usual problems of life with considerable confidence, and in most instances he can resolve them without serious damage to his self-structure. For the most part, he maintains his self-respect. Obviously, he is not always free from conflict, nor is he always emotionally stable. The range of normality is wide.

Unless the cause is organic, a person with poor mental health differs in degree, rather than in kind, from one with good mental health. His feelings of guilt may at times overwhelm him; his anxiety is not productive but frighteningly threatening. He sees no clear way to resolve his conflicts. He is usually unable to handle crises successfully, and this inability eventually robs him of his confidence and self-respect. In time, the threats from within and without may become so great that he develops a behavior disorder. This disorder, of course, can be of any degree of seriousness from very mild to very serious.

WHAT IS THE SCOPE OF THE PROBLEM?

The extent of the problems related to mental health is so great that a full-length book would be needed merely to present the statistics on frequency, causes, possible solutions, and cost. Moreover, in these rapidly changing times, it is likely that such material would be out-of-date in a very short time. For example, crime is rapidly increasing in America and the causes are not the same as they were ten years ago or even five years ago. Therefore, only a partial answer can be given in this introductory chapter to the question raised in the heading of this section.

After World War II, the American people became increasingly aware of the personal, social, and economic problems involved in the very considerable incidence of behavior disorders. This awareness has helped to provide better care for those who are mentally disturbed and a somewhat improved understanding and utilization of preventive measures. However, a great deal of confusion over the causes of behavior disorders and a hesitancy to face the fact that this is our greatest health problem still persist. At present, slightly less than one half of one per cent of our total population is in mental hospitals or institutions as resident patients. Approximately one half of all hospital beds in the United States are occupied by mental patients, and about half of these patients have a disorder called schizophrenia. In addition, it is well known that many persons suffering from serious behavior disorders never receive treatment of any kind. It is impossible to determine accurately the size of this last group, but it is very large. Not realizing that these individuals are mentally ill, families and friends often regard them as very difficult personalities who are failing in various aspects of living. Disturbed persons may break the law and go to jail rather than to a mental institution. They may become recluses. They may escape into alcoholism or drug addiction.

There are also persons who are recognized as mentally ill by their families and associates, but who receive no treatment for a variety of reasons. The community may lack appropriate facilities; they may not be able to afford treatment; or, in many instances, a combination of false pride and ignorance makes them afraid that they will lower their own and their family's status by admitting that they suffer from a mental disorder. Another group whose disorders have been recognized receives treatment from private practitioners outside hospital walls.

It is estimated that the total number of seriously disturbed persons who have been hospitalized is approximately the same as the number of those who have not. In addition to those who are not receiving needed institutional care, there are many who, although their behavior is neurotic, are only partially handicapped. One can only guess at the prevalence of this kind of disorder. Certainly, there are more neurotics than psychotics—probably about three times as many. There are even more who have emotional maladjustments not sufficiently acute to be termed neuroses.

We have been looking at the statistics in the preceding paragraphs from a cross-sectional point of view; in other words, they represent the situation as it is today in the total population of the United States. What if we take a longitudinal point of view and consider the entire life span instead of one moment in time? It is estimated that one of every twenty persons will eventually be admitted to a mental hospital and another one in twenty will be at least temporarily incapacitated by a psychotic episode, although not hospitalized, at some time during his life. In other words, it is estimated that ten per cent of our children will, at some time in the course of their lives, suffer from a temporary or a permanent psychosis. The number who will be neurotic, for at least a time, is much greater. In addition to these two groups, there are those who, though they never resort to psychotic or neurotic behavior, experience periods of emotional turmoil which are very threatening.

What are the most frequent behavior disorders among those who are hospitalized? Year after year, from one fifth to one fourth of first admissions are persons with schizophrenia. Schizophrenia does not mean split personality. It means, rather, the separation of the person from reality. He has escaped from the real world, which has overwhelmed him, into an unreal world of fantasy and distorted perceptions. Because schizophrenic patients usually are rather young when admitted to hospitals and have a relatively low death rate, those who are not discharged tend to accumulate from year to year; hence, as was indicated earlier, they make up approximately half of the resident populations of mental hospitals.

At what age is a serious behavior disorder likely to develop? The three most crucial periods appear to be late adolescence, middle age, and old age. Functional psychoses such as schizophrenia are most likely to appear in youth, and organic psychoses such as cerebral arteriosclerosis are most likely to appear in old age.

In the light of these facts how can we account for the considerable indifference and even hostility of the American people toward those persons who are emotionally disturbed and even toward those who are treating them? This attitude springs largely from fear: fear for ourselves, fear for the members of our family, and fear of those who are psychotic. Fear is caused primarily by lack of knowledge, and the public has very little knowledge of the nature of behavior disorders, their causes, or their treatment. Not so very long ago we had a somewhat similar attitude toward physical disorders.

When we are afraid we usually do one of two things—run or fight. The public has to some extent reacted to the threat of emotional disturbances in both ways. It has run away by pretending that the problem is not as serious as it is, by being apathetic to conditions in our mental hospitals, and by being unconcerned about the need for funds for extensive research on diagnosis and treatment. When the problem becomes personal—say, a member of the family has become psychotic and needs to be hospitalized—there is a marked tendency to "put him away" and forget him if possible. The fighting reaction frequently results in ridicule. Ridicule is directed at the disturbed person and at the professional men and women who are working in the field of mental health.

In recent years a relatively new kind of fighting reaction has developed—the accusation by an individual or by a group that those who disagree with the opinions held by that individual or group are "sick." A term frequently used is "paranoid." The dangers inherent in this distortion, brought about by a limited understanding of the nature and causes of behavior disorders, are obvious. Great as the mental health problem is in the United States and important as it is to deal with the problem vigorously, we should always remember that at any given time approximately ninety per cent of our people are in good mental health. This includes not only conformists but also nonconformists, those who swim with the tide and those who swim against it. Conformity is not synonymous with good mental health; neither is nonconformity synonymous with poor mental health. Refusal to accept all or most of the current mores may actually be evidence of self-actualization. Emotionally disturbed persons need help, but the best mental hygiene approach for the emotionally healthy is to permit them to develop their potentialities with a minimum of interference.

"Americans View Their Mental Health"

In 1955 the United States Congress authorized the Joint Commission on Mental Illness and Health to conduct a study of the mental health of the nation and to present to Congress, the United States Surgeon General, and the governors of the several states a report of its findings and its recommendations for possible federal and state mental health programs. The Joint Commission on Mental Illness and Health is a multidisciplinary nonprofit organization representing thirty-six national agencies concerned with mental health and welfare. In 1960 this Commission published its fourth volume, entitled *Americans View Their Mental Health*. The co-authors and their assistants

. . . interviewed 2,460 Americans over the age of twenty-one living at home, selected so as to be representative of the total population in such characteristics as age, sex, education, income, occupation, and place of residence. Transients and all individuals in hospitals, prisons, or other institutions at the time were excluded. The interviewed group therefore constituted an accurately proportioned miniature of the "normal," stable, adult population of the United States.[1]

The cooperation of the selected subjects was excellent; only 8 per cent refused to be interviewed. The respondents talked freely and frankly.

Dr. J. R. Ewalt, director of the Commission, says in his introduction to this volume:

In general effect, the Gurin-Veroff-Feld monograph supports the community surveys showing a high prevalence of persons with various psychiatric or psychological illnesses or maladjustments as determined through psychiatric diagnosis of symptoms. . . . Nearly one in four adult Americans says that some time in life he has felt sufficiently troubled to need help. One in seven sought it.

This summation in itself indicates a rather high degree of self-perception and willingness for Americans to admit that they have weaknesses and problems, although they do not always identify the psychological aspects of their difficulty, and often see it as organic or external to themselves. Whether perceived as psychological problems or not, their troubles all appear to have a mental or emotional component, requiring understanding of the behavior of themselves and others.

The study additionally provides one of the first pieces, if not *the* first, of convincing evidence that public education in mental health principles during the present generation has increased general understanding of the human mind. It is still unclear what media and kinds of information are most effective, but it is clear that the younger, better educated group—the ones who have been exposed to the most mental health information in school or in their personal reading —have much greater recognition of the psychological nature of many of their problems and, hence, more appreciation of the mental health professions as a resource when help is needed.[2]

[1] G. Gurin; J. Veroff, and S. Feld, *Americans View Their Mental Health* (New York: Basic Books, Inc., Publishers, 1960), p. xi.
[2] *Ibid.*, pp. xxv–xxvi.

Perhaps the most significant statement in the preceding quotation is that up to one in four, or approximately 25 per cent of adult Americans, stated that they had at one time or another been so disturbed emotionally that they felt that they needed help. It should be kept in mind that this is from the longitudinal rather than the cross-sectional point of view.

The sources of happiness and unhappiness, as stated by the respondents in the survey, are summarized in Table I.

TABLE I[3]

Comparison of Sources of Happiness and Unhappiness		
Reasons	Sources of happiness	Sources of unhappiness
Economic	29%	27%
Children	29	7
Marriage	17	5
Other interpersonal sources	16	3
Job	14	11
Respondent's health	9	7
Family's health	8	5
Independence; absence of burdens or restraints	8	0
Personal characteristics (and problems)	2	13
Community, national, and world problems	0	13
Miscellaneous	12	4
Not happy (unhappy) about anything	5	18
Not ascertained	2	2
Total	*	*
Number of people	(2460)	(2460)

* Indicates that percentages total to more than 100 per cent because some respondents gave more than one response.

The data in Table I indicate, as the authors point out, that persons who are not seriously maladjusted tend to externalize their problems. They stress economic and material matters as sources of unhappiness and play down inadequacies in the self, including personal conflicts and feelings of guilt. An understanding of the internal problems, which in the majority of cases have been at least superficially externalized, would presumably be achieved only

3 *Ibid.*, p. 24.

through psychotherapy. The authors in commenting on the reasons for unhappiness say:

> Although most of the responses are not personal in the sense of involving self-questioning and self-blame, they do tend to be self-oriented. The causes for concern are, in most cases, limited to factors that have an immediate effect on the individual. Problems that have a community or national or world locus are mentioned by only 13 per cent of the population. . . . In their day-to-day living, people are actively concerned with the things that affect them in immediate and tangible ways, and problems of broader and more general concern tend to sink beneath the level of immediate awareness.[4]

Later in the volume the authors present a summary of the reasons why persons who felt that they needed help with their emotional problems did not try to get it. Slightly more than 25 per cent believed that they could eventually have solved their own problems without professional assistance, while about 20 per cent did not know where to go. A considerable number were deterred by shame. This was a very important factor among those who lived in small towns, where the percentage was 25. Only about 7 per cent thought that professional treatment would be of no help, and an even smaller number were concerned about the expense.

This study points up clearly the extent of the mental health problem among noninstitutionalized persons. It also shows how necessary is an increased dissemination of knowledge concerning the nature and causes of emotional problems.

THE MENTAL HYGIENE POINT OF VIEW

Mental hygiene, as was pointed out earlier, is concerned primarily with prevention. It seeks to create the kind of personal and social environment which furthers sound mental health. An important part of this environment is the set of attitudes held by the individual and by the social group of which he is a member. In fact, sound mental health is best understood as a point of view. This point of view includes:

[4] *Ibid.,* p. 28.

1. Self-respect and respect for others.

2. Understanding and tolerance of one's limitations and the limitations of others.

3. Understanding of the fact that all behavior is caused.

4. Understanding the drive for self-actualization.

Self-Respect and Respect for Others

A person who likes himself is usually mentally healthy. Conversely, a strong dislike of one's self is a typical symptom of maladjustment. A psychologist conducting a series of brief diagnostic interviews would do well to include the following questions: (1) Do people like you? (2) Do you like people? (3) Do you like yourself? If answered honestly, the responses would reveal the extent or lack of the person's social and emotional adjustment. The normal individual feels that he is an accepted member of a social group, that he is liked by the members of that group, and that they, in turn, are liked by him. In response to the third question, he will say, "Sure," or, "I never thought about it," or, "Well, I'm not conceited."

The maladjusted person reacts quite differently. His expression may become bitter, or he may break into tears. His comments may be as follows: "No, I've never had any real friends. I like people, but they don't seem to want me around. Do I like myself? No. There are times when I hate myself."

Mental hygiene emphasizes building up rather than tearing down another's ego It stresses tolerance and praise as opposed to blame and punishment, the positive rather than the negative approach; it respects the dignity of the individual.

These principles can be practiced in many ways. The teacher should exclude sarcasm and fear as weapons of control. The parent should be lavish with encouragement and help his child capitalize on his gifts, small or great. The foreman or manager should seek to find out why the employee is not doing satisfactory work and then try to make necessary adjustments. The army officer should know that morale does not spring from fear of authority but from the realization that a job has been done well. Since loss of self-respect underlies the great majority of emotional disorders, it follows that any experience which bolsters one's feeling of worth is an aid in preventing maladjustments.

Tolerance of Limitations

A cardinal principle of mental hygiene is that the realities of life must be seen clearly and, to a considerable extent, accepted. A person must also accept himself as he is. To struggle against realities is to court a mental breakdown. The well-adjusted person has learned to capitalize on his assets and to accept his limitations.

Many boys and young men who are poor athletes fight this fact instead of accepting it. Instead of concentrating on their intellectual or social gifts, they devote themselves to the hopeless task of becoming outstanding athletes. It is desirable—even admirable—for a person to try to improve himself as long as he keeps his goals within reach. It is undesirable, sometimes tragic, for a person to try desperately to achieve success in a field in which he has little ability.

In school and college, intellectual limitations are rarely faced honestly by either student or teacher. It is important for an individual's mental health that he know approximately what his mental level is. If it is relatively low, he must adjust to that condition. Teachers and professors should recognize that certain students in their classes possess limited mental capacity and should never be expected to do more than they are capable of doing.

"Know thyself" is sound mental hygiene, though difficult to achieve. It is even more difficult to know others, for the facts of individual differences make the situation extremely complex. No two persons, not even identical twins, are ever exactly alike. Every human being, although he has much in common with his fellows, is unique in the patterns of abilities and limitations which he possesses. However, in spite of the difficulties involved, the person who respects and accepts himself usually respects and accepts others. He does not reject a member of his family or one of his friends because of differences in behavior or points of view. He is not contemptuous of those who are less intelligent or whose moral standards or religious convictions differ from his.

Behavior Is Caused

In any science it is necessary to accept causation. Nothing just happens. There are reasons for everything, including human behavior.

Jane is afraid of dogs. Why? Bill is afraid of the dark. Why? Louise is getting low grades in college. Why? Angela is unpopular on campus. Why? Jim has a severe headache two or three times a week, but the doctor says nothing is wrong with him. Then why does his head ache? Philip has been stealing articles of clothing in the high school. Why? Mary cannot concentrate on her studies. Why? John becomes so tense during examinations that he can hardly read the test questions. Why?

It is usually impossible to identify all significant causes of a specific act, but they are always there. The counselor, knowing that behavior is determined, never blames an individual. He would no more criticize a person for being neurotic than a doctor would criticize a patient for suffering from cancer. The psychological point of view requires that behavior problems be treated objectively. It has little in common with the moralistic point of view.

The moralistic attitude toward adjustive difficulties is still widely held. According to this view, every individual is morally responsible for his behavior. In the extreme moralistic attitude, the individual who commits an antisocial act is judged guilty of willful wrongdoing. He has sinned and must be punished. If he becomes depressed, he is told to snap out of it. If he spends a great deal of time in daydreaming, he is considered lazy. If he develops a neurosis, he is likely to be blamed for it. Such blame almost invariably intensifies the variant's belief that he is inferior, and so makes him more instead of less neurotic.

It is desirable for a well-adjusted person to act without dwelling on the causes of his behavior. When, however, a person is emotionally maladjusted, or is becoming so, it is wise for him to ask why. The first step in reducing tension is to discover what causes the tension. To ignore the condition, to pretend that it does not exist, will intensify the disorder.

A person is responsible for his acts in the sense that the "I" is a composite of his physical organism, experiential background, and the goals which are one product of that organism and background. Hence, an individual determines what decision to make or what act to perform, but he does so in the light of the immediate situation and in the long shadow of past experiences.

As Combs and Snygg point out:

> From the point of view of the behaver himself behavior is caused. It is purposeful. It always has a reason. Sometimes the reasons are

vague and confused, in which case his behavior is equally vague and uncertain; sometimes the meanings are extremely clear and definite. But everything we do seems reasonable and necessary at the time we are doing it. When we look at other people from an external, objective point of view, their behavior may seem irrational because we do not experience things as they do. Even our own behavior may, in retrospect, seem to have been silly or ineffective. But at the instant of behaving, each person's actions seem to him to be the best and most effective acts he can perform under the circumstances. If, at that instant, he knew how to behave more effectively, he would do so.

From the point of view of an observer who knows the location of an exit, the behavior of a fire victim rushing back again and again to a jammed door is completely unreasonable. From the point of view of the victim in those circumstances, it is the most reasonable thing he can do because the door is the closest approximation to an exit he can find. However capricious, irrelevant, and irrational his behavior may appear to an outsider, from his point of view *at that instant*, his behavior is purposeful, relevant, and pertinent to the situation as he understands it.[5]

Drive for Self-Actualization

Human behavior is dynamic. Every person is urged on throughout his life by desires which must be satisfied. He is never completely at rest. His life is a constant struggle for food, warmth, achievement, affection, sex satisfactions, recognition, and economic and emotional security. It is also a constant struggle for self-actualization. He recognizes the need or purposefulness in his life. He must be working toward certain goals, the achievement of which provides him with a feeling of adequacy.

A basic assumption held by most scientists is that all living organisms possess a drive for growth. Each organism tries not only to maintain itself but also to mature and to gain as much as possible from its environment within the limitations set by that environment and by the structure of the organism. Every organism also has within it the seeds of destruction, death, and decay.

Since human beings, with their high level of intellect, can make decisions and look to the future, it is not surprising that they are

---

[5] A. W. Combs, and D. Snygg, *Individual Behavior*, rev. ed. (New York: Harper, & Row, Publishers, 1959), pp. 17–18.

vitally concerned with what Maslow calls self-actualization. They drive forward in their search for fulfillment of their potentialities. The struggle is both painful and rewarding but, with possibly some exceptions, the rewards are more than worth the pain.

It is important that the family, the school, and the broader society in which the individual lives provide, insofar as is possible, opportunities for individual growth and development. If parents recognize the existence of the need for self-enhancement, they will provide the child with a safe environment in which he can reach out in many directions. Teachers will do the same, realizing that if the conditions are right, children and young people will welcome the opportunity to learn. Community, state, and national leaders should be aware that physical security is not enough. Above and beyond that everyone needs the psychological security which comes from self-actualization. This important topic will be developed in greater detail in later chapters.

THE
ADJUSTMENT
SEQUENCE

An extensive discussion of motivation and learning, important though they are in psychology, is unnecessary in a book on mental hygiene. However, the reader (especially one who has not taken a course in general psychology) should be provided with a brief introduction to these topics. There are many theories of motivation and learning, and a vast amount of research material is available. The matter in this chapter has been selected largely because it has significance in mental hygiene.

Motivation is a general term covering goal-seeking behavior growing out of the existence of needs. This behavior is directional. It is toward a desired goal, but it may also be away from a situation which is unpleasant for the individual. The activity of the organism in its goal-seeking behavior results in varying degrees of learning, because through activity behavior is modified to a greater or lesser degree, and any modification or change which comes about through a response to a situation can be defined as learning.

Some of the theories and principles of motivation and learning become especially meaningful to the student of mental hygiene if they are considered within the context of the adjustment sequence which is as follows: *motivation—frustration and/or conflict—emotional tension—response—tension reduction—effects.* It should be noted that the same sequence is followed in learning to be maladjusted as in learning to be well adjusted. Each of the steps in the adjustment sequence will now be considered in some detail.

MOTIVATION

All behavior, whether desirable or undesirable, normal or abnormal, is the result of causes, usually of a number of causes intricately interwoven. In other words, all behavior is motivated. A student may be earning average grades because he has average (college) intelligence, because he does not study very much, because he prefers to devote his time to social activities, because he experiences emotional blocks during examinations, because he resents authority as represented by his instructors, because he wishes to disappoint his parents who expect him to be an honor student. A novelist may write a book because he feels that he has something important to say, because for him this is a form of catharsis, because he is a recluse and experiences companionship with his imaginary characters, because he needs the royalties, because there is a discrepancy between his ideal self and his real self—and in his writing he can express his ideal self. A surgeon may use all the skills at his command because he is eager to save the life of the patient, because he wishes to impress his colleagues, because he is a perfectionist, because he enjoys manipulating the instruments of his profession, because he likes to have power over another human being, because he has a strong desire to prove to himself and others that he is a better man than his father, who was a great surgeon. A physicist may have chosen his field because he was interested in science, because he wished to advance the frontiers of knowledge, because the laboratory provided an escape for him from human relations, because it offered him an opportunity to sublimate his destructive urges, because being a scientist would give him prestige. A psychotic patient in a mental hospital may be there because his parents overprotected him in childhood, because he had deep feelings of guilt over sexual experiences in adolescence, because his level of aspiration was too high and he was never able to achieve the goals which he had set for himself, because he had certain personality characteristics which caused him to be rejected by his own age group, because he experienced several emotional shocks in childhood, because he had learned over a period of years to feel inadequate in real life situations and so had escaped into a world of fantasy.

The examples that could be given of interrelated multiple causes of any form of complex behavior are almost numberless. These causes vary not only from individual to individual, but also within the same individual. Yet, in spite of the variation in configurations of the many groups of stimuli, both internal and external, that result in a certain response, it is possible to identify, at least tentatively, the drives or needs common to all human beings. It is even possible, at least theoretically, to give a monistic explanation of behavior—to reduce all of the drives or needs to a single motivating force.

Although psychologists agree that all behavior is motivated, they disagree on the source, nature, and number of the activating forces. They even disagree on what labels to use. A few, notably psychoanalysts, have retained the concept of instincts. A much larger number prefer the term *drive*. In recent years, the word *needs* has achieved considerable popularity.

Instincts

Early in the present century it was generally assumed that the primary motivating forces in human behavior were instincts. For example, McDougall stated in his *An Introduction to Social Psychology* in 1926 that the essential motivating powers of all thought and action are innate. He listed several specific instincts such as flight, curiosity, pugnacity, reproduction, and acquisition. McDougall's books, especially the one just mentioned, had a profound effect on psychological thinking.

Unfortunately, the term *instinct* has been used with a variety of meanings. The classic definition is that interest is an organized and complex pattern of behavior which is characteristic of a given species in a specific situation. It is unlearned and, more or less, inflexible. Instincts defined in this manner are nonexistent among human beings; at least, none has been scientifically demonstrated. In human beings all complex patterns of behavior are affected by learning. Even among lower animals, instinctive activity is influenced by environment. Learning takes place, and variability in the patterns of behavior results. There is a great difference between the point of view that man's social needs, as well as his physical needs, are part of the very hereditary nature of mankind and the view that man's social needs are learned from the culture in which he is reared and that even the satisfactions of his physical needs are markedly affected by his culture.

There are a few modern psychologists who prefer not to discard the concept of instincts but to modify the definition. For example, Maslow argues for what he calls "instinctoid needs." These needs, he believes, have an instinctual basis, but the manner in which they are satisfied depends to a very considerable extent on learning. Instead of changing the definition of instinct and so adding to the confusion of what has always been a highly theoretical concept, it is more profitable to discard the term altogether as it relates to human behavior. Thinking in terms of a dichotomy between instinct and learning leads us to the same impasse that blocked progress for so long in the heredity-environment controversy over intelligence. It is wiser to think in terms of an inherited structure interacting with its environment. It should be mentioned again that the nature of the inherited structure is very important. The family cat has inherited the kind of structure that predisposes it to certain activities and at the same time limits what it can do. It can catch mice, it can climb trees, but it cannot talk and it cannot read a book. Human beings have inherited the kind of structure which makes it possible for them to walk, to drive automobiles, to experience sex satisfactions, to communicate with others through the use of words, and to plan for the future. But they cannot grow to be fifty feet tall, they cannot live on grass, they cannot solve problems that are beyond their limitations. The behavior of all living things is determined by the nature of the inherited structure and the environment in which it lives and has lived. To call such behavior *instinctive* or even *instinctoid* is an over simplification.

Drives or Needs

The terms *drive* and *need* have almost completely supplanted the older concept of instinct. These two relatively new terms are more flexible than *instinct,* since when combined with motives they include the effects of learning and of social inheritance as well as of biological inheritance.

A *drive* is an aroused reaction tendency that sets up activities in the organism and sustains them. It increases the individual's general activity level. The drive is great or small, depending upon the strength of the stimuli. Drives are usually divided into two categories, primary and secondary. The primary drives are physiological, and the secondary drives are social.

Need has a meaning which is very similar to drive. It represents a lack that results in an imbalance, upsetting the individual's optimum equilibrium. This lack arouses activity in the organism. It is a goad to action.

Motives

A need, as was stated in the preceding section, is a general want or lack. It gives rise to one or more motives. A *motive* is a rather specific process which has been learned. It is directed toward a goal. For example, a man may be hungry and needs to eat. The organism having been aroused, he goes to the pantry and makes himself a sandwich. He may have a need for achievement so he goes to college and while there actively pursues a number of specific motives, such as studying for an examination or doing a laboratory experiment with care. The number of motives is very great; the number of needs is small, so small that some theorists reduce them to one.

Four Explanations of Motivation

Psychologists have given considerable attention to the very difficult problem of discovering what are the fundamental drives or needs. They have provided us with many classifications, ranging from Murray's list of thirty-seven to Combs's and Snygg's one. While at first glance it may appear that no agreement had been reached, a closer study indicates that most of these opinions have much in common. A brief description of four representative theories follows.

Freud   Probably no man has ever been more of a storm center in the field of psychology than Sigmund Freud, the Viennese physician who founded psychoanalysis. The contributions which Freud has made to our understanding of the dynamics of personality are of lasting value. He reached his conclusions through clinical experience and at all times showed a marked willingness to modify those conclusions on the basis of new evidence. To a considerable extent it is because of these changes made by Freud throughout the course of his long life that he has been so generally misunderstood. The writer is basing this discussion on Freud's *Outline of Psychoanalysis,* since this is his last book and a final summary of his views.

Freud was a dualist. He based his theory of motivation on the existence of instincts. He says:

> The forces which we assume to exist behind the tensions caused by the needs of the id are called *instincts.* They represent the somatic demands upon mental life. . . . They are the ultimate cause of all activity. . . . It is possible to distinguish an indeterminate number of instincts and in common practice this is in fact done. For us, however, the important question arises whether we may not be able to derive all of these various instincts from a few fundamental ones. We have found that instincts can change their aim (by displacement) and also that they can replace one another—the energy of one instinct passing over to another. This latter process is still insufficiently understood. After long doubts and vacillations we have decided to assume the existence of only two basic instincts, *Eros and the destructive instinct.*[1]

Freud states clearly, then, that the two instincts, "Eros and the destructive instinct," are "the ultimate cause of all activity." What does he mean by Eros, and what does he mean by "destructive instinct"?

Eros is the life or erotic instinct. It includes all sexual impulses as well as the urge for self-preservation. The destructive instinct, on the other hand, represents the desire to destroy even to the extent of destroying one's self through death. "The function of the life instinct or Eros," explains Brill, "is to produce life by uniting single, living particles or germ cells, while the task of the death instinct is to cause the living organic matter to revert to its former lifeless or inorganic state."[2]

It is difficult to accept destructiveness, including self-destructiveness, as a basic primal force. As a matter of fact, Freud himself stresses the life instinct, and in stressing it underscores the pleasure

---

[1] Sigmund Freud, *An Outline of Psychoanalysis,* trans. James Strachey (New York: W. W. Norton & Company, Inc., 1949), pp. 19–20.
[2] A. A. Brill, *Lectures on Psychoanalytic Psychiatry* (New York: Alfred A. Knopf, Inc., 1946), p. 275.

principle. He states that "the power of the id expresses the true purpose of the individual organism's life,"[3] and later "the id obeys the inexorable pleasure principle."[4] *Id* is a dynamic concept referring to unlearned basic drives which obey nothing but the pleasure principle. Thus *pleasure principle,* in turn, is the concept that physiological and mental tensions lead to behavior that will bring maximal pleasure. In conformity with the pleasure principle, the individual desires direct and immediate gratification. The pleasure principle operates with relatively little blocking in the infant. The adult, however, finds it necessary to exercise restraint. In recognition of this, Freud developed the reality principle which states that the individual forgoes immediate gratification of a libidinal desire in order to avoid pain and in order to achieve greater pleasure at some time in the future. The reality principle is subordinate to the pleasure principle. It is merely a brake applied as lightly as possible.

Freud is occasionally classed as a monist; the statement is made that he regarded the need for sexual gratification as the one great driving force of man. Although he does not oversimplify to this extent, it is nevertheless true that he placed great emphasis upon the role of sex needs in human behavior. It is the hard core of the life instinct. Used in a broad sense, it is the essence of pleasure. The importance which Freud gave sex resulted, as would be expected, in violent attacks upon his views. Adults were especially incensed by his theory concerning infantile sexuality. Freud maintained that the human being experiences sex satisfactions from birth on, although these satisfactions in infancy and childhood are generalized, pleasure being obtained from stimulation of all the erogenous zones, such as the lips, the nipples, and the anus. In the course of normal development, sex interests become relatively specific and lead to heterosexual relationships and the reproduction of life.

Freud is still such a controversial figure that it is difficult to evaluate his work. He has contributed much to our understanding of personality. He has stimulated a great deal of experimentation, and the effects of his influence can be found in the office of every therapist. His position regarding motivation, however, is weak at a number of points, three of which will be noted here. His view

3 Freud, *op. cit.,* p. 19.
4 *Ibid.,* p. 109.

of instincts was so narrow that he resorted to the questionable concept of sublimation to explain the rich variety of human activities. It would seem, also, that he overemphasized the importance of sex, especially the importance of the influence of early sex experiences upon adult behavior. He gave little or no attention to present motivation as a causal factor in the development of a neurosis or a psychosis. Finally, he ignored man as an organism with social needs, placing his emphasis instead upon the instinctual and biological needs. This basic error probably resulted in part, at least, from Freud's early training as a physician. Even in our own day physicians are prone to stress instincts and heredity and to overlook the considerable potency of environmental factors.

Adler   Alfred Adler was a student of Freud's, but in 1912 he broke away from his mentor and founded a school of individual psychology. Adler was a monist. Because of his emphasis on the struggle for superiority, it has frequently been stated that he maintained that the single basic drive is the will to power. Actually, according to Adler, security represents the basic drive, whereas the attempts to achieve superiority are merely means of achieving the security goal.

> Our civilization makes important contributions to the determination of the goal. It sets boundaries against which a child batters himself until he finds a way to the fulfillment of his wishes which promises both security and adaptation to life. How much security the child demands in relation to the actualities of our culture may be learned early in his life. By security we do not consider only security from danger; we refer to that further coefficient of safety which guarantees the continued existence of the human organism under optimum circumstances, in very much the same way that we speak of the "coefficient of safety" in the operation of a well-planned machine. A child acquires this coefficient of safety by demanding a "plus" factor of safety greater than is necessary merely for the satisfaction of his given instincts, greater than would be necessary for a quiet development. Thus arises a new movement in his soul life. This new movement is, very plainly, a tendency toward domination and superiority. Like the grownup, a child wants to outdistance all his rivals. He strains for a superiority which will vouchsafe him that security and adaptation which are synonymous with the goal he has previously set for himself.[5]

[5] Alfred Adler, *Understanding Human Nature*, trans. Walter Beran Wolfe (New York: Greenberg Publisher, Inc., 1927), pp. 23–24.

Further, Adler states "it is the feeling of inferiority, inadequacy, insecurity, which determines the goal of an individual's existence."[6]

A closer examination of the preceding quotations will help us understand Adler's point of view. Note that he believes simple security from danger is not enough; the individual requires a margin of safety. He achieves this margin of safety through domination and superiority. In other words, the struggle for achievement and status is really an outgrowth of the fundamental need for security. The struggle, however, is more dramatic than the basic need itself and has many more practical implications for human beings. Adler was a practical man interested in the application of his theory. Consequently, he deals so extensively with the will to power that it appears as though that were the basic need.

According to Adler, the fight against feelings of inferiority and insecurity (terms which he frequently uses interchangeably) begins early in childhood. He says "the goal toward which every human being's actions are directed is determined by those influences and those impressions which the environment gives to the child. The ideal state, that is, the goal, of each human being, is probably formed in the first months of his life."[7] During this early period the individual sets up a purposive life plan as a means of compensating for his feelings of insecurity. This feeling of insecurity is associated with real or imagined physical defects. Since no human being is ever physically perfect, it is relatively easy to find a blemish. The handicap may be as simple as a small birthmark or it may be a major one such as physical deformity. Adler stresses the significance of physical size in the family circle. The young child, because he is small, feels insecure in the presence of his parents and older siblings. The very fact that they tower over him creates in him a feeling of inferiority and so, in turn, intensifies his desire to dominate.

Although Adler stresses the struggle for superiority, he is not favorably disposed toward it. He says:

When we question how we can most advantageously oppose the development of the striving for power, this most prominent evil of our civilization, we are faced with a difficulty, for this striving begins when the child cannot be easily approached. One can begin to make attempts at improvement and clarification only much later in life.

6 *Ibid.*, p. 72.
7 *Ibid.*, p. 23.

> But *living* with the child at this time does offer an opportunity to so develop his social feeling that the striving for personal power becomes a negligible factor.[8]

Adler goes on to say:

> An uninhibited striving for power is capable of producing degenerations in the psychic development of the child, an exaggerated drive for security and might, may change courage to impudence, obedience into cowardice, tenderness into a subtle treachery for dominating the world. . . . Education affects the child by virtue of its conscious or unconscious desire to compensate him for his insecurity, by schooling him in the technique of life, by giving him an educated understanding, and by furnishing him with a social feeling for his fellows. All these measures, whatever their source, are means to help the growing child rid himself of his insecurity and his feeling of inferiority.[9]

The preceding statement is sound mental hygiene. All children feel insecure to some extent and many of them compensate for that feeling of insecurity by an excessive emphasis on achievement. A family and school situation which provides emotional security as well as opportunities for success does much toward helping the child to develop normal patterns of behavior.

Maslow   Maslow's theory of motivation is, as he says, "in the functionalist tradition of Dewey, and is fused with the holism of Wertheimer, Goldstein, and Gestalt psychology, and with the dynamicism of Freud and Adler."[10] While he is not a phenomenologist in the sense that Combs and Snygg are, he nevertheless shares many of their theories. The following brief discussion of Maslow's theory is based on his article, "A Theory of Human Motivation,"[11] which was later expanded into a book, *Motivation and Personality*.

Maslow stresses that the individual should be viewed as a whole. The total person is motivated, not just a part. To be sure, for prac-

---

8 *Ibid.,* p. 73.

9 *Ibid.,* p. 74.

10 A. H. Maslow, *Motivation and Personality* (New York: Harper & Row, Publishers, 1954), p. 80.

11 A. H. Maslow, "A Theory of Human Motivation," in *Psychological Review,* L (1943), 370–96.

tical purposes one must think in terms of certain needs or of specific motives, but actually it is the total organism that is stirred to activity. Maslow accordingly emphasizes that any motivated behavior can satisfy many needs at the same time. In other words, an act is multi-motivated.

Maslow proposes the concept, "hierarchies of prepotency." By this he means that a need of higher order does not appear until a more prepotent need has been satisfied. A need that has been satisfied is no longer a need; therefore, the satisfaction of one need releases the individual to try to satisfy other needs. A person is dominated not by his satisfactions but by his wants.

Although emphasizing the wholeness of the individual, Maslow proposes five sets of basic needs. Arranged on a scale from lowest to highest these are: physiological needs, safety needs, love needs, esteem needs, and the need for self-actualization. He says:

> These basic goals are related to each other, being arranged in a hierarchy of prepotency. This means that the most prepotent goal will monopolize consciousness and will tend of itself to organize the recruitment of the various capacities of the organism. The less prepotent needs are minimized, even forgotten or denied, but when a need is fairly well satisfied the next prepotent ("higher") need emerges, in turn, to dominate the conscious life and to serve as the center of organization of behavior, since gratified needs are not active motivators.[12]

Maslow goes on to point out that usually a person is partially rather than completely satisfied, or, to state it in reverse, he is usually partially unsatisfied in all of his needs. Partial satisfaction, then, is a normal state of affairs to which most persons learn to adjust. If, however, the individual's frustration—resulting either from incomplete satisfaction of basic needs or from a breakdown of his defenses—is too great, then he experiences psychological threat. Maslow says "with a few exceptions all psychopathology may be partially traced to such threats."[13]

Maslow, as was noted earlier, places self-actualization at the top of his hierarchy of needs. This need, he says refers "to man's desire for self-fulfillment; namely, to the tendency for him to become ac-

12 *Ibid.*, p. 395.
13 *Ibid.*, p. 396.

tualized in what he is potentially."[14] It seems to this writer that self-actualization might very well be looked upon as the sole motivating force, and the psychological, safety, love, and esteem needs as parts of it.

It is difficult to differentiate Maslow's *self-actualization* from Rogers's *drive for growth* or Combs's and Snygg's *need for adequacy*. It will be seen from the following discussion of the theory of motivation presented by Combs and Snygg that there is at least a considerable overlap in the two points of view.

Combs and Snygg Combs and Snygg point out that psychology has had two general frames of reference. The older of these is the external approach to human behavior. Within this frame of reference, psychologists observed their subjects in various situations and tried to explain the subjects' behavior in terms of the situation to which they were reacting. On the basis of these observations, the causes of behavior were assigned to those aspects of the environment to which the subjects were responding. The authors emphasize the importance of the contributions that have come from this kind of approach, especially with respect to the prediction of normative behavior. They then speak of the second main frame of reference which is called the perceptual or the phenomenological approach. They say:

> This approach seeks to understand the behavior of the individual from *his own* point of view. It attempts to observe people, not as they seem to outsiders, but as they seem to themselves. People do not behave solely because of the external forces to which they are exposed. People behave as they do in consequence of how things seem to them . . . behavior in this frame of reference is seen as a problem of human perception. *This perceptual view of behavior is the frame of reference of this book.* [15]

Phenomenology is a technical term for the philosophical method which was introduced into psychology by Husserl in 1900. It emphasizes direct experience and the form that such experience takes. The phenomenal field is the entire universe, including the

14 Maslow, *Motivation and Personality,* pp. 91–92.
15 A. W. Combs, and D. Snygg, *Individual Behavior,* rev. ed. (New York: Harper & Row, Publishers, 1959), p. 11.

self as it is experienced by the individual at the time of action. "It is each individual's personal and unique field of awareness, the field of perception responsible for his every behavior."[16]

The following example given by Combs and Snygg indicates clearly the highly personal nature of each individual's field of perception.

> Several years ago a friend of mine was driving a car at dusk along a western road. A globular mass, about two feet in diameter, suddenly appeared directly in the path of the car. A passenger screamed and grasped the wheel attempting to steer the car around the object. The driver, however, tightened his grip on the wheel and drove directly into the object. The behavior of both the driver and the passenger was determined by his own phenomenal field. The passenger, an easterner, saw the object in the highway as a boulder and fought desperately to steer the car around it. The driver, a native westerner, saw it as a tumbleweed and devoted his efforts to keeping his passenger from overturning the car.[17]

Combs and Snygg present as a basic postulate "All behavior, without exception, is completely determined by, and pertinent to, the perceptual field of the behaving organism."[18] This statement is in agreement with the point of view concerning causality expressed in the first chapter of this book. All behavior is caused. To the behaver himself, the reasons for his behavior are impelling ones at the time the response is made. No matter how irrelevant the behavior may appear to an outsider, from the point of view of the behaver it is pertinent to the situation as he sees and understands it. It is reality to him. At the instant of action the field is organized with reference to the needs of the behaver and the means by which he is trying to satisfy them. The need or needs become the focal point of the phenomenal field. This gives to behavior its meaning, direction, and consistency.

What, according to Combs and Snygg, is the basic human need? In the first edition of *Individual Behavior* it was defined as the preservation and enhancement of the phenomenal self. The phenomenal self is a part of the phenomenal field, but it is that part of

16 *Ibid.,* p. 20.
17 *Ibid.,* p. 20.
18 *Ibid.,* p. 20.

the field which the individual experiences as being characteristic of him. It is the I—the physical self, the experiencing self, the re-membering self, the goal-seeking self. It is the self which is respond-ing at a given time to all of the characteristics of the phenomenal field of which he is aware. This phenomenal self is driven on throughout life by the need to preserve itself. However, the pres-ervation of the self as it exists it not enough; since human beings are aware of the future, they are impelled to strengthen themselves against that future. This point of view is strikingly similar to that presented by Adler, who stated that the individual strove for superi-ority, not merely to achieve immediate security but to build up a reserve as well.

In the revised edition of *Individual Behavior,* Combs and Snygg rephrased their definition of man's basic needs as follows:

> We can define man's basic need, then, as a need for adequacy. It represents in man the expression of a universal tendency of all things. It is expressed in man's every behavior at every instant of his ex-istence. Asleep or awake, each of us is engaged in an insatiable quest for personal adequacy. This quest may find its expression in a wide variety of behavior aimed, in one form or another, at the maintenance or enhancement of our perceptions of personal worth and value. Other authors have spoken of this need as a need for self-actualization, or self-realization. In the field of psychotherapy this need has been described as a need for growth . . . whenever we refer to man's basic need, we mean that *great driving, striving force in each of us by which we are continually seeking to make our-selves more adequate to cope with life.*[19]

This need (adequacy) has two principal characteristics: the maintenance of the self and the enhancement of the self. In main-taining the self, it is of course necessary to preserve internal physical equilibrium. The physiological needs must be satisfied. If one or more of these needs is frustrated to any considerable extent, the person experiencing the frustration concentrates almost exclusively upon their satisfaction. In our society, however, the emphasis for most persons is not on keeping alive but on maintaining one's per-ception of the self. "From birth to death the maintenance of the

[19] *Ibid.,* p. 46.

phenomenal self is the most pressing, the most crucial, if not the only task of existence."[20] The individual is vitally concerned with preserving his self as he perceives that self. In accordance with this need he selects from his perceptual field those aspects which are meaningful for him, those which reinforce his picture of himself. This principle holds for those with a negative self-concept as well as for those with a positive self-concept. For example, there is the case of a brilliant undergraduate student who came to the Counseling Service because of an overall feeling of inadequacy. He was convinced, among other things, that he was below average intellectually. The counselor, thinking to reassure him, gave him an intelligence test and found that he was at the 99th percentile for college students. However, when he gave this information to the counselee, it was immediately rejected with the statement that this was not so, that the counselor had scored the test incorrectly in order to make him, the counselee, feel better.

In spite of the reaction of the counselee, which was a manifestation of his desire to preserve his picture of himself, it should be noted that he had come in for counseling because he felt inadequate. On the one hand, he wished to maintain the self; on the other hand, he wished to enhance the self. This is the kind of conflict which many persons, perhaps most, experience. In psychotherapy it is seen in its clearest form. The client clings to his phenomenal self because it is the only reality he knows and he is afraid to give up any part of it. At the same time he feels the need to be more adequate, to grow, to be able to deal more effectively with life. No matter how well adjusted he may be he still strives to build for the future.

As Combs and Snygg point out, each person's perceptual field has both stability and fluidity. It has a high degree of stability because it is, to a considerable extent, organized and predictable. This organization and predictability provides the individual with security. Hence, he tries to maintain it. At the same time the perceptual field is fluid. It is constantly changing, thus making changes in behavior possible. In the well-adjusted individual there is a nice balance between stability and fluidity. He knows who he is and where he is going. Moreover, because of the fluidity of his field, many roads are open to him. The maladjusted individual, on the other hand, is living under so much threat that he concentrates on preserving

20 *Ibid.,* p. 45.

his self. His field is less fluid. There are fewer roads down which he can go. This is the rigidity so characteristic of seriously disturbed persons.

The theory of motivation presented by Combs and Snygg has much to commend it. Through their concept of the phenomenal self they succeed in bringing together a significant relationship among the stimuli of the immediate external situation, the memories of the past which bear upon this immediate situation, and the nature and condition of the physical self at the time that the situation is experienced. Their primary concern is with the behaver himself and with the need of that behaver to preserve and enhance himself. The behaver is not, on the one hand, merely going through life responding to his instincts nor, on the other hand, responding automatically to external stimuli. To be sure, his behavior is caused, but it is determined by the phenomenal field.

A question might be raised as to whether or not Combs and Snygg have given one need or two. They have answered this question by stating "Though the maintenance and enhancement of the self are two different words, this does not mean that man has two different needs. We express maintenance and enhancement as two different words, but both relate to exactly the same function—the production of a more adequate self. Both refer to man's striving to accomplish, like the rest of his universe, an adequate organization."[21]

For practical purposes the writer has subdivided the need for adequacy into four categories: the need for achievement, the need for status, the need for physical security and the need for emotional security. This is an arbitrary classification, to be sure, since no one of these needs exists in isolation. The individual always acts as a total personality. These four needs will be discussed at length in Chapters Four through Seven.

The preceding background material on motivation should aid the reader in understanding the first step in the adjustment sequence. In a specific situation there may be a single motive that initiates behavior. Usually, however, motivation is complex although one desire may be dominant. Whenever a motive or a number of motives stirs the individual from his relative complacency, the entire sequence is set in motion.

21 *Ibid.,* p. 45.

FRUSTRATION AND/OR CONFLICT

A frustration is the condition of being thwarted in the satisfaction of a motive. The thwarting may be largely the result of external (environmental) conditions, or it may be internal, arising primarily from the mental and emotional states of the individual. External frustrations are inevitable, for there are always certain factors in a person's situation which keep him from achieving fully the desires which he has. During an economic depression he may be deprived of the opportunity to earn a sufficient income to support his family. This condition is imposed upon him from without. The death of a wife or child may deeply disturb his feeling of emotional security. In time of war, millions of young men are abruptly shifted from civilian activities, which allow a considerable degree of independence and initiative, to a regimented form of life that for many is filled with frustrations. Many college students, especially freshmen, find the change from home and high school to the campus a difficult one to make because of the frustrations experienced in the new situation.

Internal frustrations, as the term indicates, come from within the individual. They result from an inability to satisfy a desire or need because of fear of the consequences, because of inhibitions, or because of conflicts. Internal frustrations represent a more serious threat to the personality of the individual than do external frustrations. If severe, they create considerable emotional tension with accompanying behavior disorders.

The fears, the inhibitions, and the conflicts which keep an individual from working to full capacity—and which even keep him from doing what he wants to do—have been learned and are now a part of the self. A college student may have an excellent intellect and may have conscientiously prepared for an examination, yet when he is taking that examination, his fear of failure inhibits his recall to such an extent that he cannot do as well as he is capable of doing. Another student who is socially inclined finds it impossible to enjoy himself at a dance. His inhibitions make it impossible for him to "let himself go," and at the end of the evening he feels frustrated.

In considering the phenomenon of frustration, it is important always to think in terms of degree. It is obviously impossible to divide people into two groups, those who are frustrated and those who are not, for all are frustrated to some extent. Often one hears that children should not be given everything they want—as though it is possible for someone to have everything he wants. The child, like the adult, is always somewhat frustrated. The problem is to try to prevent him from becoming so severely frustrated that he loses confidence in himself.

Some needs are more insistent than others, and the strength of a specific need varies from person to person. The frustration of an important need results in more serious consequences than the frustration of a minor need. Everyone must eat to live. Total frustration of the hunger need results in death. On the other hand, even though we may have a fairly strong desire to wear expensive clothes and to drive a high-priced car, we can get along without them.

Individuals vary considerably with respect to the extent to which they can tolerate frustration. An experience that is very disturbing for one person may be accepted calmly by another. One child of three may try again and again to build his pile of blocks, showing little or no exasperation when the steeple topples over. Another child of the same age explodes in a fit of anger at the first false move which destroys his handiwork. Frustration, whether external or internal, must always be interpreted in terms of the individual who is experiencing it.

Frustration-Aggression

Frustration results in aggression, and this aggression may be directed toward either the person or persons who have caused the frustration or toward a substitute or substitutes. Aggression may also be turned inward toward the self. Dollard *et al.* state the thesis as follows:

> . . . the occurrence of aggressive behavior always presupposes the existence of frustration and, contrariwise, the existence of frustration always leads to some form of aggression. From the point of view of daily observation, it does not seem unreasonable to assume that aggressive behavior of the usually recognized varieties is always traceable to and produced by some form of frustration. But it is by no means so immediately evident that, whenever frustration occurs,

aggression of some kind and in some degree will inevitably result. In many adults and even children, frustration may be followed so promptly by an apparent acceptance of the situation and readjustment thereto that one looks in vain for the relatively gross criteria ordinarily thought of as characterizing aggressive action. It must be kept in mind, however, that one of the earliest lessons human beings learn as a result of social living is to suppress and restrain their overtly aggressive reactions. This does not mean, however, that such reaction tendencies are thereby annihilated; rather it has been found that, although these reactions may be temporarily compressed, delayed, disguised, displaced, or otherwise deflected from their immediate and logical goal, they are not destroyed.[22]

Direct aggression is a normal method of maintaining self-esteem when frustrated. If a boy on the playground is made to feel ridiculous by a classmate, it is wholly natural for him to try to maintain his status by knocking the other boy down. If, however, he is afraid to respond as directly as this, the frustrations which he experiences in school may find an outlet through aggressive behavior at home. He may use his younger brother as a substitute and beat him severely, or he may behave belligerently toward his parents. He feels that he must do something to relieve the tension caused by the frustrations which he has experienced in another situation.

In discussing the role of violence in human behavior, Berkowitz[23] argues that "anger and learned habits separately or together create a readiness to act in a hostile manner," but if aggressive behavior is actually to occur there must be something about the present situation which arouses "present or past anger instigators." Berkowitz distinguishes between anger ("the emotional state resulting from a frustration presumably creating a readiness for aggressive acts") and aggression ("behavior whose goal is the injuring of some person").

Berkowitz agrees that to express anger is to feel better, but he claims this is no insurance against an attack on the same victim (or a similar one) at some future date. In fact, an aggressive act may actually serve to strengthen a habit of aggression. There is no easy

[22] John Dollard; N. E. Miller; L. W. Doob; O. H. Mowrer, and R. R. Sears, *Frustration and Aggression* (New Haven, Conn.: Yale University Press, 1939), pp. 1–2.
[23] Leonard Berkowitz, "Aggressive Cues in Aggressive Behavior and Hostility Catharsis," *Psychological Review*, LXXVII, No. 2 (1964), 104–22.

answer. To inhibit the anger may also serve to increase "the strength of any subsequent aggressive responses" and to "raise the level of tension experienced by the person."

When aggression is turned inward, it is more dangerous for the mental health of the individual than when it is turned outward. Instead of blaming another, the individual blames himself. A certain amount of self-criticism does no one any harm. Every person should know what his limitations are and accept them. Aggression toward one's self can, however, be carried to such extremes that eventually the self is destroyed—psychologically, as in schizophrenia, for example, or physically, as in suicide.

No individual can tolerate aggression toward himself for an indefinite period of time. Eventually he is forced into finding some form of escape. The following case illustrates the point.

F.D. was a college girl with wealthy and ambitious parents. Her mother had been graduated with honors from a well-known New England women's college. The daughter tried hard to do as well, but unfortunately she had an intelligence quotient of only 105. At the time she first asked for psychological help, she was very discouraged because she was on scholastic probation and was in danger of being dropped from college because of low grades. She blamed herself for her low academic standing, and found it impossible to accept the fact that one cannot expect to transcend his intellectual limitations. Moreover, she felt that she was a complete failure socially. No one seemed to like her. She was convinced that she was "no good." She hated herself and had done so for several years. There was little or no animosity toward others. All the considerable aggression which had developed from her severe frustrations was directed against herself. Eventually she committed suicide. Her self had become so despicable in her eyes that she concluded that it must be destroyed.

Conflicts

A conflict always involves thwarting, but it includes also the necessity of making a choice between two, or among more than two, types of behavior. An individual experiences some degree of conflict whenever he makes an adjustment. Often these conflicts are minor and temporary. If, however, a selection has to be made between two responses that are antithetical, the conflict may be severe and persistent. It is at this point that the symbolic processes play an important part. The material that the individual has learned, the experiences that he has had, and the adjustment habits that he has formed constitute the matériel for the battle.

Psychoanalysis stresses the importance of conflicts in the life of an individual. The forces involved have been labeled the *id*, the *ego*, and the *superego*. The id, according to Freud, "has no organization and unified will, only an impulsion to obtain satisfaction for the instinctual needs in accordance with the pleasure principle . . . the id knows no value, no good and evil, no morality."[24] At the other extreme is the superego, which Freud defines as "the representative of all moral restrictions, the advocate of the impulse toward perfection, in short it is as much as we have been able to apprehend psychologically of what people call the 'higher' things in human life."[25]

The id and the superego are forever at war. The results would certainly be disastrous if it were not for the ego, which acts as a mediator. The ego, as Freud says, has a hard time of it.

> Its every movement is watched by the severe super-ego, which holds up certain norms of behaviour, without regard to any difficulties coming from the id and the external world; and if these norms are not acted up to, it punishes the ego with the feelings of tension which manifest themselves as a sense of inferiority and guilt. In this way, goaded on by the id, hemmed in by the superego, and rebuffed by reality, the ego struggles to cope with its economic task of reducing the forces and influences which work in it and upon it to some kind of harmony; and we may well understand how it is that we so often cannot repress the cry: "Life is not easy." When the ego is forced to acknowledge its weakness, it breaks out into anxiety; reality anxiety in face of the external world, normal anxiety in face of the super-ego, and neurotic anxiety in face of the strength of the passions in the id.[26]

Although this vivid presentation of conflicts is overly dramatic, it contains a great deal of truth. The layman uses different terms.

[24] Sigmund Freud, *New Introductory Lectures on Psycho-Analysis*, W. J. H. Sprott, trans. (New York: W. W. Norton & Company, Inc., 1933), pp. 104–105. Copyright 1933 by the author. Reprinted by permission of the publishers.
[25] *Ibid.*, p. 95.
[26] *Ibid.*, pp. 109–10.

He speaks of base desires which he has and which he curbs because of his conscience. Conscience is an attitude, a set of values that has been learned. It stems from fear of punishment and desire for social reward. Conscience frustrates many a personal need and precipitates innumerable conflicts.

Conflicts are not limited to incompatibility between a person's desires and his conscience. They also represent an interaction between the self and present and past experiences. Most of these experiences are attractive or repellent in varying degrees; there are some which are neutral because they have little or no significance for the individual. Since in the light of his experiential background the individual reacts either positively or negatively to a motive or a number of motives, it follows that there are three kinds of conflicts: approach–approach, avoidance–avoidance and approach–avoidance.

Approach-Approach   In an approach–approach conflict a person is faced with the problem of making a choice between two positive goals. Usually this is not a very difficult task and the amount of emotional tension involved is slight. An example of this type of simple conflict would be trying to decide on a beautiful summer day whether to go to the beach or to the golf course. To be sure, there are times when it is very difficult to choose between two desirable courses of action. A young woman, for example, may be devoted to her family and at the same time be in love with a man who is not acceptable to her parents. She is drawn toward her parents by strong affectional ties and at the same time is drawn toward the man she loves. It is obvious that this kind of situation can create considerable emotional tension.

Avoidance-Avoidance   Avoidance–avoidance conflicts are usually more serious than approach–approach conflicts. The individual is now caught in a situation where he must choose between two or possibly more negative courses of action. Because of the threat involved in such a situation he would prefer to do nothing or to find some means of escape. Usually if he does nothing about resolving the conflict the threat remains and tension builds up. He may after a while hit upon a way of escape—an escape that may be either constructive or destructive, normal or abnormal. For example, a soldier in battle may have to choose between his fear of death at the hands of the enemy or, if he does not do his part, the loss of the respect of his comrades in arms. He escapes both negative actions through a psychological paralysis of his legs. The resolution of avoidance–avoidance conflicts is of course not necessarily as extreme as in the preceding example; one or more of the adjustment mechanisms discussed in the following chapter may be utilized. If the avoidance–avoidance conflict is not too strong it is possible to accept from among the two courses of action the one which is less threatening and even to feel some sense of satisfaction in doing something well that originally you did not want to do at all. An example of this would be a student who does not wish to study and at the same time does not wish to incur the displeasure of his parents by becoming a dropout. He decides to put some real effort into his studying and is rewarded by high grades. The conflict has been resolved positively.

Approach-Avoidance   Approach–avoidance conflicts are characteristically the most serious of the three under discussion. This is especially true if the conflict is centered in one's relationship with another person who both attracts and repels him. He may be drawn toward this other person by dependency or by affection or even by love and yet at the same time he is repelled by him because of certain personality characteristics or, more seriously, because of fear or even hatred. When a person is drawn almost irresistibly toward a feared object or individual, the tension becomes unbearable.

EMOTIONAL TENSION

Emotional tension is a feeling of strain or suspense. It is a bodily response to the frustrations and/or conflicts which the individual experiences during the interim between motivation and a successful response. It therefore maintains the motive or motives present at the time; it serves as a drive for finding a solution.

There is considerable variation in the intensity of emotional tension. For example, a man who becomes thirsty and can satisfy that thirst almost immediately by pouring himself a drink of water has very little emotional tension. Obviously more tension occurs when a person is faced with a conflict situation that forces him to postpone a decision for days or perhaps weeks. An example of this would be a man devoted to his family who has been offered an excellent position as a traveling salesman but who, if he accepts the offer, will be able to be with his family only once or twice a month. He may have many sleepless nights before he decides what to do.

As was pointed out earlier, an approach–avoidance conflict is likely to bring about the most severe emotional tension. This is especially true where a considerable feeling of guilt is involved. If a person is motivated toward a kind of behavioral activity which he perceives to be wrong, evil, and degrading and the attraction of that behavioral act is so strong that he cannot rid himself of it, then the tension grows to a point where the bodily processes are seriously affected, the mental processes are confused, and the emotional state is chaotic. A person in this unhappy situation frequently finds his escape in a neurotic or psychotic reaction, or at times in suicide. Extreme emotional tension cannot be tolerated indefinitely. Some kind —any kind—of response becomes mandatory.

RESPONSE

The last three steps in the adjustment sequence—response, tension reduction, and effects—involve learning. A human being inherits his capacity for learning; he does not inherit behavior patterns, except for simple reflexes. He inherits a brain but he does not inherit information or mental associations. He inherits potentialities for adaptation, but the kind of adjustment mechanisms that he adopts is dependent upon the nature of the experiences which he has. Inheriting the power to use language, he may learn English, French, or Russian. Inheriting the power to think in mathematical terms, he may learn arithmetic, algebra, or geometry. Inheriting the power to develop emotional and social behavior patterns, he may learn confidence, control, and conformity, or he may learn to be afraid, to go to emotional extremes or to be antisocial. He can also learn to be neurotic.

Every individual is constantly adjusting, and every adjustment made is a modification of the patterns of learned behavior, resulting in a change, even though a minute one, in the personality of the individual—in what he is. When a new adjustment is made its nature will be considerably affected by the history of earlier adjust-ments, especially by the rewards or punishments which accompanied them. A specific behavioral act, then, must be interpreted not only in terms of the immediate situation, but also in terms of the be-havior resorted to in earlier situations.

An individual does not just act; he acts in accordance with the nature of his personality. There is a high degree of internal con-sistency in the behavior of every individual. Although one's personal-ity is constantly changing, one always remains more like himself than like anyone else.

We know that human beings learn. We know a great deal about the conditions which facilitate learning. We have some in-formation on how we learn. We can observe the changes in behavior when we have learned. We have, however, little or no knowledge of just what takes place in the nervous system during the learning proc-ess. In spite of the considerable amount of experimentation that has been carried on for more than half a century, we are still almost as much in the dark concerning the relationship between learning and nervous structure as we were before the experiments were made. Neither the neurologist nor the physiological psychologist can give specific answers to the question of how learning takes place. It may be, of course, that they will provide these answers for us at some time in the future. However, since learning is a process, it can be studied with considerable success without a complete understanding of the structural basis.

It was pointed out earlier in this chapter that there are several theories of motivation. There are also several explanations, prin-ciples, or laws of learning. A brief look at three of these, condition-ing, insight, and trial and error, follows.

The Conditioned Response

At the turn of the century, Pavlov, a Russian physiologist, noted that the dog on which he was experimenting responded with a saliva flow not only to the presence of food but also to such substitute stim-uli as the presence of the man who usually fed him or the sound of his approaching footsteps. As a result of this observation, Pavlov set up his famous experiment on conditioning.

A dog that was accustomed to serve as a subject for experimen-tation was harnessed to a table. An electric bell was then started and, after it had been ringing for a few seconds, food was placed in the animal's mouth. This procedure was repeated several times. Eventually a conditioned response was established, the dog responding with a flow of saliva to the ringing of the bell. A biologically inadequate stimulus had produced a response similar to one that would characteristically result from a biologically adequate stimulus.

That conditioning takes place in human beings is a matter of common observation. We speak of our "mouths watering" in anticipation of a good dinner. Babies learn to respond to the sight of a bottle because of its association in their minds with milk. The knee jerk or the reflex wink can be so conditioned that the response will result from a substitute stimulus. Many emotional responses can also be explained in terms of conditioning, especially if the response was learned during infancy or early childhood.

Watson succeeded in conditioning a child to be afraid of a white rat. When the rat first appeared, the child showed no fear but reached out to touch it. Then a steel bar was placed behind the child, and when he reached for the rat or when the rat was presented to him the bar was struck, making a loud noise. At the eighth trial, the bar was not struck, but by this time the child had become so conditioned that he responded to the rat by withdrawal and crying. The fear which he had of the noise from the bar being struck had become associated with the rat. He was now reacting emotionally to the substitute stimulus.

Eliminating Conditioned Responses   A conditioned response can be unconditioned. A common procedure is to set up a situation in which the fear object will become associated with a pleasurable experience. A conditioned response can also be eliminated by repeating the artificial stimulus without providing a reward for the response. Pavlov found that if an animal who had been conditioned to respond to the ringing of a bell by a saliva flow was subjected to a series of experiences wherein no food was given after the ringing of the bell, it ceased, after a few trials, to give the salivary response. Even an animal loses interest if you cry "wolf" often enough.

Traumatic Experiences   As was previously noted, conditioning involves stimulus substitution. In learning anxiety—and anxiety is at the immediate source of all functional behavior disorders—the individual who has experienced a trauma, which is the unconditioned stimulus, responds to the associated danger signal, which is the conditioned stimulus, in essentially the same way that he previously responded to the trauma. A traumatic experience is an emotional shock which involves at least a temporary disorganization of normal control. It is a shock because the resources of the individual are inadequate for successfully meeting the situation. The self is seriously threatened. For the time being, at least, the person sees little chance of maintaining his security. Environmental factors overwhelm him. Traumas are somewhat more likely to be experienced in childhood than in adult life, because the child, especially the infant, has had relatively little opportunity to learn enough about his environment to absorb the shock. What has been learned in past situations exerts a powerful influence upon the adjustment that is made to a present situation.

A person who has experienced a trauma to which he responded with extreme anxiety and accompanying emotional disorganization is likely to become confused concerning the actual causes of the effects. Associated stimuli become conditioned stimuli, and are, therefore, sufficiently potent to elicit an anxiety or even a panic response. For example, a young child who has been bitten by a dog may not only respond with fear a few days later to the presence of a dog but may also respond in the same way to the presence of a cat. After all, the cat, like the dog, has hair, four legs, and a tail. The child, lacking an adequate fund of learning, is unable to differentiate between the two.

An example of a more complex form of conditioning through trauma follows. One evening a father and mother left their four young children at home on their farm while they went to town to do some shopping. On their way back they saw in the distance that their house was on fire. Just as they reached the yard, the roof fell in and their four children were burned to death. The emotional shock was, of course, very great. The parents kept their sanity, but never afterward could the mother stand before a stove or cook over a fire, for such contacts with the agent which had destroyed her children invariably aroused the unbearable emotional reaction which she had experienced at the time of the initial shock.

Continuation of Conditioned Response   A conditioned response is strengthened through reinforcement and is weakened, though not destroyed, by nonreinforcement. According to Hull, need reduction is an essential basis for reinforcement. Pavlov's dog, it will be remembered, ceased to respond to the ringing of the bell with saliva flow when his hunger was not satisfied with food. A conditioned response, either adaptive or maladaptive, will continue, then, when it serves some purpose for the individual. Keeping in mind the basic security need, it is not surprising that the individual should respond to a situation to which he has been conditioned to regard as a threat with an attempt to escape. If, through new learning, he sees the situation as no longer threatening, the old response is replaced. Most adults have outgrown their childhood fears as the result of new information that has been acquired. They are able to substitute new modes of response for the earlier responses which are no longer necessary or acceptable as need satisfactions. On the other hand, some persons continue with maladaptive conditioned responses because these remain the only means of satisfying one or more needs.

Insight

Gestalt psychologists define insight as the sudden apprehension of meaning without reference to previous experience, such apprehension resulting in appropriate behavior. This is an extreme view of the meaning of insight. It would appear rather that insight results from experiences gleaned in earlier situations and from an immediate background of trial and error behavior. With human beings much of this trial and error learning resulting in insight is of a verbal nature.

Insight is the seeing of new relationships, the rearrangement of factors which were present all the time into a new pattern. The speed with which insight is achieved varies with the difficulty of the problem; the more difficult the problem, the longer the time needed. The degree of difficulty is related directly to the abilities which the problem solver can bring to bear upon it.

In psychotherapy a great deal of emphasis is placed on the importance of the achievement of insight. Perhaps the most important function of the therapist is to help his patient to see his problem in perspective. The maladjusted individual tends to concentrate on the specific frustration which he is experiencing. If he could succeed in integrating his present situation with his goals and with his past experiences, the current detail or details which had loomed so large would take their proper place as a minor part in the total pattern.

Köhler writes of the behavior of an ape in a frustrating situation. The ape, to be sure, was not neurotic, but there was a disruptive emotional reaction to his inability to reach a desired goal. He lacked the ability to organize into a meaningful pattern all the factors involved in the situation.

> Outside the animal's cage a banana is placed on the ground, beyond the reach of his arm. In a similar situation some days before the ape had used a stick as an instrument for the first time. He finds a stick to-day, too, but it is a rough thing. A branch projects from the side of the stick near the ape's hand. At first this branch does not operate as an obstacle because, when he reaches for the fruit, the ape holds his instrument accidentally in such a position that the branch is parallel to the bars of the cage and does not touch them. Presently, however, in order to change his place with regard to the fruit, the ape pulls the stick back into the cage. When he reaches for the fruit again, the branch hits a bar and the stick does not move in the direction of the fruit. The animal tries to overcome the difficulty by pushing hard and crudely a few times. Suddenly, however, and just after pressing forward with all his force, he pulls the stick back in the cage and bites the branch with the ferocity of anger. . . . When the ape is first directed completely toward the fruit, his reaching for it is determined directly in the manner we have described. To begin with, the obstacle in his way directly produces an increased effort in the same direction. But the ape can scarcely pull against the bar of his cage without localizing the place of the obstacle after a while by touch and, perhaps, by vision. He does not feel the obstacle in the direction of his main effort; he feels it in the locality of the branch. When an obstacle is experienced in our way we become angry by immediate determination, and our anger is an attitude directed toward or against the obstacle.[27]

As Köhler points out, in our emotional reaction to frustration, whether it be anger, fear, or discouragement, we tend to lose sight

[27] W. Köhler, *Gestalt Psychology* (New York: Liveright Publishing Corp., 1929), pp. 392–93.

of the goals toward which we are striving. The branch on the side of the ape's stick was but a tiny thing and yet, unless adjusted to, a very disturbing one. If the ape had been able to achieve insight into the total situation, the obstructing branch would have been a minor matter. If he had kept the branch parallel with the bars of the cage, as he did at first accidentally, he would have eliminated the nonintegrative factor in the total situation.

The development of insight is linked with reward and punishment. If the behavior resulting from insight is rewarding to the behaver he will tend to continue it. There can of course be erroneous insight. Behavior resulting from erroneous insight that appears maladaptive to the observer may seem adaptive to the behaver himself.

Trial-and-Error Learning

In trial-and-error learning, the learner tries various movements, apparently in a somewhat random manner and without a clear recognition of the connection between the movements and the desired results. The tentative movements that succeed are more frequently repeated in subsequent trials, and those that fail gradually disappear.

The first trial-and-error learning experiments were made by Thorndike at the turn of the century. The subjects of his early experiments were usually cats. Thorndike's work stimulated others to carry out a large number of similar experiments. Typically, the learner is confronted by a problem situation in which he has to reach a goal, such as food, or to achieve escape from an uncomfortable situation. For example, a hungry cat is confined in a box with a concealed mechanism operated by a latch. The problem the cat must solve is to open the door of the box by correctly manipulating the latch in order to gain access to the food that is outside. At first the cat shows a great deal of random behavior, such as dashing about inside the box, clawing, and biting. Eventually, the animal hits upon the correct response. The latch is moved and he escapes. Upon succeeding trials the time needed to make the correct response becomes shorter, although this reduction in time is slow and irregular. Eventually the correct response is stamped in.

It should be carefully noted that in the trial-and-error behavior just described, motivation on the one hand and reward and punishment on the other hand play important roles. Neither can be divorced from the learning process. The cat in the problem box is definitely motivated toward tension reduction through the satisfaction of a need, and the behavior that results in tension reduction through the satisfaction of that need is repeated. Moreover, there is avoidance of behavior that is not so rewarded.

In trial-and-error learning, as in insight, the degree of difficulty of the problem for the problem solver is important. If the problem is a simple one, the first move may be a correct response. For example, an adult who is given a puzzle which was designed for a young child will presumably put the pieces together correctly on his first trial. If, however, he is presented with a very complex puzzle he will undoubtedly make many false moves before he finally hits upon the correct arrangement of the pieces. In situations that have more personal significance for him and especially in situations where the conflicts are strong and the emotional tension considerable, he will almost certainly try out one solution after another. For example, a student with a relatively low intellectual potential is motivated to earn good grades in his courses. He responds by studying harder but his grades do not improve. He then takes an "I don't care" attitude but after a short time that makes him feel guilty. He tries rationalization and perhaps some of the other adjustment mechanisms but these fail to satisfy him. Finally, he goes to his parents and tells them that he is going to enlist in the Marines. It develops that this was for him a desirable response in that it reduced tension.

The final tension-reducing response which a person makes to a frustrating situation is of course not necessarily one that has long-term value for him. Instead of deciding to enlist in the Marines, the student in the preceding example might have concluded, on the basis of what appeared to be sound evidence, that the faculty of his college were plotting to fail him academically because they were fearful of his great intellect. This is a paranoid response and if used repeatedly leads to a psychosis.

TENSION REDUCTION

It will be remembered that the third step in the adjustment sequence, following motivation and frustration and/or conflict, is emotional tension, and that when emotional tension is present the individual seeks to reduce it. In most instances he eventually makes a response that brings about the desired results. An adjustment has been made and the motivated activity comes to an end. An adjustment is defined in terms of tension reduction. This adjustment may not be a good adjustment in the sense that the behavior adopted is socially acceptable or desirable, or, for that matter, desirable for the individual in the long run, but it does provide relief.

It would appear that tension reducing responses are more likely than not to be positive adjustments since in spite of the considerable extent of the mental health problem, the great majority of persons function adequately within the range of normality. Theoretically no value judgment should be made on an adjustment; practically, it is done all the time. For example, it would be difficult to argue that a neurotic or psychotic adjustment was a desirable one for the individual to make, and psychotherapists try to help the client to find a better response. Philosophy cannot be kept completely out of science, especially not in the case of psychology. Values are not absolute. They are subject to change and are particularly subject to exceptions. For example, physicians believe that it is better to be alive than dead. Usually this is true, but in some instances it is better to be dead than alive. For example, there is the case of an old man who had just had an operation for incurable cancer. When he complained about the pain he was experiencing his doctor replied, "Stop grumbling. I saved your life, didn't I? You had rather be alive than dead, hadn't you?" The patient responded with an emphatic "No."

In general, a good tension-reducing response is one which satisfies the individual's needs in a manner which furthers his growth and adds, perhaps ever so slightly, to his self-actualization. It is integrative, in that it is comfortably incorporated into the self-structure. It is a positive contribution to the development of an adequate self, not only for the present but also for the future.

In general, a poor response, even though it does reduce tension, is one that closes doors, that inhibits the growth of the individual. It retards the process of self-actualization. Even though it is immediately satisfying, it has a crippling effect on the personality over a period of time. Usually it is nonintegrative. An exception is the paranoid individual who is better integrated than most normal persons; however, he is severely handicapped by his delusions of persecution and grandeur. Obviously a poor response is a neurotic or psychotic adjustment. Yet the individual making it holds on to it because it is less threatening than whatever it was that brought on intolerable tension and anxiety.

No person always makes good responses and no person always makes poor responses. In both normal and abnormal behavior there is a mixture of the two. If most of the responses made not only reduce tension but also facilitate growth, it is easy to tolerate a relatively small number of inadequate adjustments. It is also important to note that a person whose growth is drastically limited by poor responses still makes many adjustments that are positive.

EFFECTS

The last step in the adjustment sequence, *effects*, is associated with the future as well as with the immediate present, since individuals tend to repeat responses that have led to tension reduction. The completed adjustment sequence becomes a part of the individual's experience. It is now a factor that must be reckoned with as the individual works out responses to new adjustments. The law of effect, or what was later called by Hull the law of primary reinforcement, is at work.

Law of Effect

According to the law of effect, as stated by Thorndike in his early work, when a particular response brings satisfying results the connection is strengthened; when the particular response brings dissatisfying results the connection is weakened. Over a period of time, the individual selects that kind of behavior which is rewarded by a satisfying state of affairs, and he avoids or eliminates that kind of behavior which is punished or carries in its wake an annoying state of affairs.

As it was originally stated, the law of effect gave approximately equal emphasis to reward and punishment. Later experiments, however, showed that the effects of the two were by no means equal, reward being much more potent. This is not to say that punishment has no effect on learning. The effect is there, but it is more indirect than at first was thought. Thorndike himself modified his early point of view concerning the importance of the role of punishment, stating in 1932 that whereas annoyers do affect learning, the extent to which they take away strength from the connection is in no way comparable to the way in which a satisfying aftereffect adds strength to it.

While reward is more effective than punishment in influencing the direction of behavior, the time factor must not be overlooked in evaluating the relative potency of these two stimuli. The prospect of immediate punishment will frequently exert a greater influence upon the action taken than will the prospect of a distant reward. The converse, of course, is also true. The prospect of an immediate reward will exert a greater influence on the action taken than will the prospect of a distant punishment. The time factor in reward and punishment is especially significant in child training and in the understanding of neurotic behavior. The young child is unwilling to forego immediate satisfaction in order to avoid distant punishment. He also shows little interest in accepting immediate deprivation in order that he may achieve a distant reward. In somewhat similar fashion the maladjusted person, who is characteristically immature, prefers the behavior which is rewarding in that it reduces tension for the time being, even though he knows that at some time in the future there will be punishing aftereffects. The drug addict resorts to his drugs, the alcoholic to his liquor, and the hysteric to his pains because the immediate result—escape—is satisfying. Either reward or punishment is most effective when it is closely associated in time with the behavioral act.

The affective intensity of a reward or punishment also influences the extent to which future behavior is affected. An intense experience creates a stronger connection than a relatively mild experience. In certain instances, a reward or punishment can be so strong that it is dominant over a number of weaker connections. An example of this is the traumatic experience discussed previously. In such an instance, the emotional shock is so great that the individual experiencing it is affected for a long time, perhaps throughout his life.

SUMMARY

The adjustment sequence is: *motivation–frustration* and/or *conflict–emotional tension–response–tension reduction–effects*. There is general agreement that all behavior is motivated. However, there is lack of agreement concerning the nature and number of the forces which activate behavior. Four of the many theories of motivation were discussed at the beginning of this chapter. Motivation is accompanied and followed by frustration and/or conflict which may be brief and inconsequential or long and threatening. This situation is accompanied and followed by emotional tension which, although it may be pleasant for a time, becomes a drive in itself since tension must be reduced eventually. The tension pushes the individual on to make a response. If the response is a conditioned one, characteristically it will be made quickly. The response may also be an insight; the individual suddenly perceives how the frustrating aspects of his problem can be made to fit into a meaningful pattern. Trial and error responses are frequently made until in most instances the individual hits on one which provides a solution. When an adjustment which is satisfactory for the individual is made, there is a reduction of tension. The response which is rewarding in that it reduces tension carries with it important effects and such responses are repeated in similar situations in the future. The first three steps in the adjustment sequence are all aspects of motivation; the last three steps are aspects of learning.

ADJUSTMENT MECHANISMS

chapter 3

All adjustments made by human beings could be considered adjustment mechanisms. However, it is customary to use a more limited definition of the term. An adjustment mechanism is a device resorted to in order to achieve an indirect satisfaction of a need so that tension will be reduced and self-respect maintained. Since frustrations are experienced by everyone and since everyone is compelled to maintain his ego, it follows that everyone makes use of adjustment mechanisms. They are our protection against the impact of a not always friendly environment; they are to some extent a buffer between the experiences of the present and those of the past. They provide an important part of the resiliency which every individual needs; without them, flexibility would be impossible. They are usually desirable, but in some instances can be unethical for the individual and undesirable for society. They lead to behavior disorders only when carried to extremes.

Because adjustment mechanisms are selected rather arbitrarily from the context of adjustments in general, there is disagreement among psychologists on how many there are. The writer has decided upon eleven to discuss in this chapter. Neurotic and psychotic adjustments will be explained later.

The principal mechanisms of adjustment are:

Compensation

Identification

Rationalization

Projection

Attention Getting

Negativism

Intellectualizing

Isolation

Daydreaming

Regression

Repression

COMPENSATION

Compensation as a mechanism of adjustment is usually defined as the exaggeration of a desirable trait to reduce a feeling of inferiority caused by an undesirable trait. Some psychologists have used the term to describe the extra effort put forth by an individual to achieve along lines where he is most defective. Another form of compensatory behavior is seen in the domineering person whose belligerence is merely a device for covering up an attitude of inferiority.

Compensatory behavior is a form of aggression turned outward. It represents active resistance against frustration. It is a fighting attempt to maintain the ego, and is frequently a powerful motivating force in achievement. According to Adler, compensation is the principal reason why certain men become great. Demosthenes utilized the mechanism of compensation when he forced himself to become a great orator in spite of an early speech defect. Napoleon's drive for power probably had its source in part in an early feeling of inferiority concerning his short stature and slight, rather feminine build. In more recent history, we have the example of a neurotic Hitler and a club-footed Goebbels throwing the world into a cataclysm of war, thus vitally affecting the future of mankind. During that same war a president who was a victim of infantile paralysis sat in the White House.

Literature abounds with character studies in which a defect, especially a physical defect, is compensated for by active aggression.

In Shakespeare's *Richard the Third,* for example, Gloucester speaks as follows:

> But I, that am not shap'd for sportive tricks,
> Nor made to court an amorous looking-glass;
> I, that am rudely stamp'd, and want love's majesty
> To strut before a wanton ambling nymph;
> I, that am curtail'd of this fair proportion,
> Cheated of feature by dissembling nature,
> Deform'd, unfinish'd, sent before my time
> Into this breathing world, scarce half made up,
> And that so lamely and unfashionable
> That dogs bark at me, as I halt by them;
> Why, I, in this weak piping time of peace,
> Have no delight to pass away the time,
> Unless to see my shadow in the sun
> And descant on mine own deformity;
> And therefore, since I cannot prove a lover,
> To entertain these fair well-spoken days,
> I am determined to prove a villain,
> And hate the idle pleasures of these days.
> Plots have I laid, inductions dangerous,
> By drunken prophecies, libels, and dreams,
> To set my brother Clarence and the King
> In deadly hate the one against the other:
> And if King Edward be as true and just
> As I am subtle, false, and treacherous,
> This day should Clarence closely be mew'd up,
> About a prophecy, which says, that G
> Of Edward's heirs the murderer shall be.
> Dive, thoughts, down to my soul: here Clarence comes.

Compensatory behavior is always based upon feelings of inadequacy. These feelings of inadequacy, however, are not necessarily caused, as Adler believes, by physical defects. They can and do result from frustration of any one of the four major needs. A college student may feel inferior because his need for status on campus has been frustrated, and he may compensate for that feeling of inferiority by boastful talk and belligerent bearing.

Such a student was referred to his university counseling service by the dean of men. He had for some time been a boisterous trouble-maker on campus. Before the end of the first interview, he was telling the psychologist about his shyness and his fears. His belligerent behavior was merely an attempt to maintain his self-respect.

Substitution

Frequently an individual who has become convinced of his inferiority in one kind of activity will give up trying to succeed along that line and concentrate on another activity. If such a substitution is made on a trial-and-error basis, the individual may find that he has merely changed his emphasis from one weakness to another. If, however, he has considered his personality and his opportunities carefully, preferably with the help of an experienced counselor, he has an excellent chance of achieving the success that he needs by concentrating his efforts on an activity in which he is superior. It is important for every person to give more attention to his gifts than to his defects. If he finds that he has been trying unsuccessfully to excel in a trait in which he is inferior, it is sound mental hygiene for him to shift his attention to an ability in which he is superior.

Transferred compensations are very frequently adopted by college students. The young man with little athletic ability who goes out for football and baseball during his freshman year and finds that he is not equal to the kind of competition which he meets, drops his ambition to be a gridiron or diamond hero and focuses his attention upon scholastic achievement. This example would probably be more often true if stated in reverse, the student substituting athletic for academic success. Many a high-ranking college woman owes her graduation honors to her social inadequacies as a freshman. Frustrated in her need for social success, she compensated for her failure in that area by leaning heavily on her intellectual gifts.

Sometimes an individual who is actually inferior in a large number of traits or abilities changes at random from one activity to another, hoping that eventually he will hit upon one in which he can be successful. He tries athletics, but his motor coordination is poor, and he fails. He tries to succeed in his studies, but his intellectual capacity is inferior, and he fails again. He makes a bid for popularity, but his personality characteristics are such that he is unacceptable to his peer group. With each new failure his feeling of inferiority deepens. It begins to seem to him that whichever way he turns he faces an impassable barrier. Out of this situation a severe psychoneurosis or a psychosis may develop.

Compensation Through One's Children

Parents frequently attempt to compensate for their own failures through their children. An ambitious mother, frustrated in her desire for a career, may bring pressure upon her daughter to forego marriage and to enter one of the professions. A man who wanted to be a doctor but who finds himself at fifty a high-school teacher of biology may attempt to force his son to enter the medical profession. This type of compensatory behavior frequently creates serious problems for the children. Often, of course, the young person possesses the interests and abilities which make it possible to satisfy both his parents and himself.

Development of Peculiar Abilities

An interesting variety of compensation is found in the individual who adjusts to the frustration of a basic need by perfecting himself in some ability where the chances of success are great because competition is slight. This behavior is seen in its most dramatic form in the achievements of the idiot-savant (who, actually, is neither idiot nor savant). The idiot-savant is always a person with relatively low mentality, usually at the moron level, who has, combined with his low intellectual status, a strong drive for attention and success. Unable to compete successfully with normal individuals in typical activities, the idiot-savant concentrates upon a limited skill. After years of drill, for example, he may be able to multiply three-place numbers by three-place numbers with accuracy and with ease. He can succeed in this specific task much better than his intellectual superiors, and the satisfactions which come from this success are great.

Normal individuals frequently resort to compensation through the development of peculiar abilities. Any unusual kind of hobby can be included in this classification. An individual who spends a great deal of time and money in collecting old coins, for example, may be doing so to relieve tension resulting from the frustration of the need for status. Such hobbies as these are valuable for the individual; they help him to maintain his ego.

Sublimation

Sublimation is a psychoanalytic term used to designate the conversion of psychic energies, which are basically sexual in nature, into nonsexual interests, such as art, sports, or scientific research. In recent years sublimation has taken on a broader meaning. It is used now to include activities substituted for all kinds of frustrations. An individual may sublimate any deep disappointment or thwarting through devoting himself to an activity which is socially approved. Often he gives an excessive amount of time to his work, for his work provides him with a means of escape. The individual who works day and night, who thinks of almost nothing but his job, and who continues this behavior over a period of years, is essentially as maladjusted as the person who resorts to alcoholism. Each is making extreme use of an escape mechanism. An important difference between the two, however, is that the person whose work affords him relief from tension is making a positive adjustment. Through sublimating in this way, he may eventually make a considerable contribution to society. It is entirely possible that many of our great scientists, by fighting their frustrations in the laboratory, have both saved themselves and enriched mankind.

IDENTIFICATION

Identification is a mechanism of adjustment by which the individual establishes a strong emotional tie with another person, a group of persons, or an institution, and then achieves his satisfactions, at least in part, by proxy—by basking in reflected glory. He draws his strength from the strength of others—he is a Boswell to a Samuel Johnson.

The mechanism of identification is in some degree universally used. The infant identifies himself with his mother; the growing boy draws heavily upon his father's strength. When two boys in a heated argument, not quite daring to fight, shout at one another, "My father can lick your father," each is attempting to increase his own courage and to bolster his own ego by thinking of himself and his father as one.

A college student who is unsure of himself may become closely attached to another student who is confident and poised. Often it happens that a group of such uncertain individuals will gather around a central figure who can do the things that they would like to do if they felt more adequate. As it is, they are quite content to be satellites.

The members of the family of a famous person usually identify themselves closely with him and so increase their own feeling of importance. Moreover they realize that others are going to make the same association. This is usually helpful both financially and socially. Many men in politics have used their identification with a famous person as a stepping stone to power. Augustus would never have become the first Emperor of Rome if he had not been identified by Romans with the slain Julius Caesar. Napoleon III made the most of his blood connection with the great Napoleon Bonaparte. Robert and Edward Kennedy profited by being brothers of the assassinated President John F. Kennedy. At a lower level wives of deceased public figures have been elected to succeed them not because of their qualifications but because of identification.

On a larger scale, a community derives considerable satisfaction from having a great man as a citizen. The individual members of that community, through the mechanism of identification, are made to feel more important than they would otherwise. They share in the great man's successes. Colleges and universities lean heavily upon the fame of certain of their alumni. There are colleges whose present prestige rests largely on the fact that a hundred years ago or so men who were students on their campuses eventually became eminent.

Identification is usually made with the town or city or state or nation in which the person lives. If he takes pride in the location of his residence, his feeling of worth and importance is enhanced. He feels a part of whatever his town or city or state represents. It may be something as insignificant as the size of the state; it may be success by proxy in living in a city which has a winning baseball or football team.

Innumerable examples could be given of identification. It is one of the most satisfactory of the adjustment mechanisms.

Guilt by Association

Identification is usually thought of as a desirable mechanism which is accompanied by a feeling of well-being. However, it can be negative instead of positive. When it is negative tension is increased. A child may feel ashamed and guilty because his father has committed some sex crime. A citizen of a gangster-ridden city may, because of his identification with that city, experience some feelings of guilt over the situation. Frequently large groups are affected by what is called mass guilt. This was true of the citizens of Dallas, Texas, after the assassination of President Kennedy in that city. Only one man committed the crime but they felt, without rational justification, that they were somehow involved.

For various reasons, a person may be ashamed of his nationality or race or he may be ashamed of his country and his government. Many a German still carries psychological scars because of the atrocities committed by Hitler and others during the Nazi regime.

RATIONALIZATION

Rationalization is the process of devising socially acceptable reasons for a socially unacceptable act or an opinion deemed blameworthy by the individual. It is a defense adjustment which helps the individual to maintain or even to enhance his image of himself. After much practice in rationalizing the individual may succeed in misleading himself as well as others concerning the true causes of his behavior.

All of us rationalize to some extent. The child soon learns that if he can think up a reason for his behavior that is satisfactory to his parents or to his teachers he escapes punishment. The boy on the playground starts a fight. The principal of the school appears unexpectedly and demands an explanation. The boy responds quickly. "He hit me first." The other boy says vehemently—and truthfully—"I did not. He hit me first." How is the principal to know which boy is rationalizing and which one is not?

A high-school girl arrives home two hours later than was expected. Her mother is disturbed and asks for an explanation. The girl says that she had to stay after school in order to make up some work in algebra. That satisfies her mother. The girl does not say that only half an hour was spent on the algebra and the remaining time in the company of a boy of whom her mother does not approve.

A college student fails an examination. His need for achievement is strong, and he wanted very much to pass it. Instead of admitting that his intelligence was inadequate to the task or that he had not thoroughly prepared for the test, he argues that the questions in the examination were unfair or ambiguous, or he may claim that he was not feeling well.

The use of rationalization is not limited to children and young people. Adults frequently offer the noblest of reasons for behavior which is actually motivated by selfish desires. Government leaders may maintain that their program is for the social good of all, when actually its objective is to bring more power to them. The game of thinking up acceptable reasons is played by everyone. The parents of a high school senior boy may be on the verge of deciding to send their son to Harvard. They cannot afford the cost of his expenses there and he does not have a scholarship. It would be much more practical financially for him to enter the state university. Their real reason for wishing him to go to Harvard is the social prestige that it would give them in their community. However, they do not admit this to themselves or to their friends. Instead they say that the state university is a country club and that the faculty is second-rate; or they say that the boy should be at a university in another section of the country. Their rationalizations may have some element of truth in them as rationalizations usually do. However, the point is that they are not giving the real reason for the decision.

A wholly rational man does not exist. Nearly all reasoning is colored by emotional factors that impel us to rationalize in order that our actual behavior will appear in a better light in our eyes and in the eyes of others.

Sour Grapes

The sour grapes mechanism is a form of rationalization. A person unable to obtain what he wants maintains that he did not want it anyway. He adjusts to frustration by denying the existence of any desire to attain the original goal. A boy fails to win a place on his school football team. Instead of accepting the fact that he was not a sufficiently good player, he says that he did not want to play anyway.

A young man falls in love with a girl and she rejects him. He reacts by saying that he never really cared for her and that he wouldn't have married her anyway because she did not measure up to his standards.

PROJECTION

Even though projection is considered here as a separate mechanism of adjustment, a good case could be made for presenting it as a form of rationalization. For that matter, there is some overlap among all of the adjustment mechanisms.

The term *projection* is used in three ways: (1) the placing of blame on an incidental and irrelevant and imaginary cause; (2) seeing in others the major personality defects which the individual himself possesses; (3) placing the blame for failure on others.

It is said that during World War II British flyers often placed the responsibility for engine trouble on "gremlins." The child who says that her table manners are bad because she has a sore finger is making use of projection. The boy who trips on the leg of the chair and then accuses the chair is using the same mechanism. The mechanic who blames his failures on his tools, and the businessman who maintains that certain errors were not his but his stenographer's are trying to escape responsibility through projection. Many if not most superstitions fall within this category. It is tension-reducing to believe that the cause of a misfortune which you have had was the black cat which ran in front of you or the crack in the sidewalk that you stepped on or the ladder that you walked under or the mirror that you broke.

This first way of using projection is usually harmless. The second one may also be harmless but it is more likely than the first to be a step toward a behavior disorder. When a person uses projection in this manner he is trying to escape from his feeling of guilt by convincing himself that his fellows are indulging in the same kinds of behavior which he himself has either indulged in or would like to. If he is belligerent he sees belligerence in others; if he has homosexual desires he convinces himself that many of those whom he knows experience similar urges. If he has cheated on examinations and feels guilty about it he says that most students cheat. A humorous example is the old lady who frequently reprimanded young people for using cuss words. In periods of delirium during her last illness she shocked the hospital staff by the color and violence of her language.

The third kind of projection, placing the blame for one's failures on others, is used to a considerable extent by normal persons. When it has some basis in fact and is not resorted to excessively, it helps a person to maintain his confidence and self-respect. The projection becomes a delusion when there is no basis in fact for the belief that others are to blame (which can extend even to the point of believing in a conspiracy). A college student, for example, complained that certain of his professors were "out to get him." It developed that the young man had ambitions to become a great physicist. As a matter of fact, part of the time he thought that he already was a great physicist. He was convinced that the members of the Physics Department were envious of his attainments and that they were trying to keep him from conducting an original piece of research in which he was interested because they were fearful that he would outshine them. His failure to achieve high grades was their fault, not his own. He had rationalized his lack of success to a point just short of psychosis. In this instance, as in all cases of excessive use of rationalization or projection, there was a belief that had to be maintained no matter what the cost.

ATTENTION GETTING

Attention getting, as the phrase indicates, is any kind of behavior resorted to by a person as a means of making others notice him. Sometimes it is approval that he desires, but he may also accept disapproval. What he is seeking primarily is to become at least for a little while the center of attraction so that he can feel significant and important.

This adjustment mechanism is used at an earlier age than any of the others. The infant cries as a means of letting others know that he needs to have something done for him. It is his only method of communicating with adults. He uses it frequently and should obtain as often as possible a rewarding response.

As the child grows older he makes use of a wide variety of attention getting devices. At the age of two or three he may interrupt adult conversation with long stories of his own; he may bring out some of his toys and enter into a period of noisy play; he may ask for a drink of water or for something to eat; he may ask irrelevant questions; he may fall down and pretend that he is hurt. For a small child these attention getting devices are usually well within the range of normality. It is difficult for adults to know how often they should respond positively and how often and at what times they should ignore the youngster.

Later when the child is in school he continues to use this adjustment mechanism, as every teacher knows. He may insist on telling about something that has happened at home; he may be noisy; he may ask a great many questions; he may start a fight. As in earlier years most of his efforts to gain attention are normal; they can of course be extreme enough to indicate an excessive amount of thwarting.

The adolescent also uses attention getting devices. He is half child and half man and characteristically is rather unsure of himself. Being uncertain, he is torn between wishing to be ignored on the one hand and wishing to be the center of attraction on the other hand. If conformity has not worked successfully for him he may try nonconforming behavior as a means of establishing himself as an individual. There is the example of the college freshman who went to a formal dance barefooted. He won a great deal of attention by this device. Most of the hippies of the sixties were probably trying to make others notice them because of their beards and bizarre clothes.

Attention getting adjustments are used to some extent throughout adult life. More often than not these are normal. Sometimes they are extreme enough to be called eccentricities. Occasionally they are abnormal. A large number of examples could be given. There was an English professor who always carried an umbrella, rain or shine. His students concluded that anybody who was as eccentric as that must be a genius. There was the man who fainted at Yankee Stadium and was carried out by the ushers. When the ushers returned, a baseball fan who had observed the episode asked one of them how the man was getting along. "Don't worry about him," replied the usher. "He comes here at least once a week and does the same thing." For a brief time by the simple device of fainting the man could shift the attention of a large number of persons from the baseball game to himself. An extreme case is the man who goes to the top of a tall building and tells those below that he is going to kill himself by jumping off. He may really mean it or he may, because of the intensity of his frustrations and conflicts, be trying in desperation to gain attention.

NEGATIVISM

Negativism is aggressive withdrawal. There is considerable overlap between this adjustment mechanism and attention getting since it is frequently used as a technique for gaining attention. It manifests itself in various forms such as refusal to eat, refusal to speak, refusal to cooperate, refusal to obey commands, and at times in doing the exact opposite of what has been requested.

Used within limits, negativism is a normal, even a necessary, form of adjustment. The young child of two or three, surrounded by authoritarian figures and limited in his ability to communicate with them, often uses negativism as a means of establishing himself as an independent person. If not used to excess this is desirable. Parents should be free to admit that at times the child is right and they are wrong. To be sure, if the child is too frequently rewarded for his negativistic behavior this kind of response will be reinforced and will carry over into later years.

Although negativism characteristically reaches its peak at the ages of two and three, it is frequently used during adolescence and for much the same reasons. The adolescent in trying to establish himself as an adult defies his parents and sometimes his teachers in order to prove to them and to himself that he is as important as they are and knows as much if not more than they do. Again, as in childhood a little of this is desirable; it is an important part of the process of growing up. However, if it is used excessively growth is restricted since there is a large element of withdrawal in negativism.

Extreme negativism is sometimes used by college students. Such students are against nearly everything. They fight their courses and their instructors. One brilliant college girl, for example, found it very difficult to take examinations. A glance at the questions was sufficient to arouse in her a feeling of rage. Then, even though she knew most of the answers, she would write very briefly or nothing at all, throw the examination on the instructor's desk, and leave the room. Afterward she would wonder why she had behaved in this manner, for she really wanted a good scholastic record.

Another college student wished to find out why she could not wash dishes when she was at home. She said that she wanted to help her mother, and did in other ways, but she could not bring herself to wash the dishes. A series of interviews revealed that the girl's parents had been somewhat sadistic in their treatment of her. She had been made to feel inferior since early childhood and had been frequently whipped because of her poor work around the house. Over a period of time she had come to associate physical punishment with washing dishes. She feared the strap, but she feared even more the complete loss of her self-respect. She discovered that in one way she could foil her tormentors. Nothing could make her do this one specific task. When her major adjustment problems were resolved through psychotherapy, the marked negativism disappeared.

This adjustment mechanism is used to some extent by adults. It is a frequent cause of friction between husbands and wives. If it is used a great deal by the husband, for example, he is said to be stubborn. It is used by men in their business or professional relationships. Often it is difficult to know whether such a man is negativistic or an independent thinker, for negativism as a means of adjustment can become very complex. For example, did Justice Holmes, the Great Dissenter, disagree again and again with most of the members of the Supreme Court of his day because of the logic and sincerity of his convictions or was he unconsciously fighting his father, the brilliant Oliver Wendell Holmes who had dominated him for the first forty years of his life? And what about a United States senator who is frequently in the position of being a minority of one? Is he a self-actualizing nonconformist or is he making excessive and complex use of negativism?

INTELLECTUALIZING

As a mechanism of adjustment, intellectualizing is an escape from threat into words. Long words or stilted phrases may be substituted for short words and simple phrases which have ugly connotations for the individual. In extreme instances, as in some patterns of schizophrenic behavior, the words become a tossed salad which have little or no meaning for the listener but probably do have some significance for the person using them.

Intellectualizing is frequently used by those who are very intelligent. Scientists sometimes carry the terminology of the laboratory into their social groups and into their families. It not only brings them attention but also provides an escape from feelings of inadequacy in home and social situations. It may be that the academic writer or speaker who makes simple material complex and complex material incomprehensible is intellectualizing in order to hide his lack of understanding.

Intellectualizing is frequently used by clients in psychotherapy as a technique for avoiding threatening words and experiences. They may use euphemisms or circumlocutions or they may talk at length about matters which have little or no relationship to the problems which are disturbing them. A case who exemplifies this is the young college instructor who came to the writer for professional help. During the first interview he talked at length about various philosophical theories. This continued for two or three interviews when he shifted to an attack on big business, especially public utilities. Later he shifted again, this time to politics. Finally it became necessary to tell him that he was escaping into intellectualism as a means of avoiding coming to grips with whatever it was that had created anxiety in him. Eventually he was able to talk about his boyhood and adolescence.

It developed that his parents were members of a small religious sect. They forced him to go with them to the meetings of the group. The boy was most disturbed when these meetings were held on street corners and he was the object of jibes and insults from his peers. After the meetings he would sneak home by back alleys wishing to avoid anyone of his own age group. These experiences and many other related ones, including a growing antagonism between his father and himself, undermined his self-respect. Eventually the response which he found most satisfying was intellectualizing. This adjustment, although it provided some tension reduction, was nevertheless a form of escape. As psychotherapy proceeded he came to understand this and made considerable progress in reducing anxiety and in re-organizing his self-image.

ISOLATION

Isolation is a withdrawal response. It is closely related to intellectualizing and daydreaming. Isolation, however, is usually thought of as a removal of one's self physically from a tension producing situation.

Isolation, like all of the other adjustment mechanisms, with the exception of repression, is a desirable, even necessary, kind of response. It becomes a maladjustment only when used to excess. Even then, in some instances, it makes possible the maintenance of relatively good mental health.

Though gregarious, human beings need a certain amount of seclusion. The young child should be provided with many opportunities to play by himself. If possible, he should have his own room containing his clothes, his toys, his books, and his furniture. These become a part of his phenomenal self. His room is a place to which he can go when he feels that he must escape for a while from trying to cope with a tension producing environment. In a few years, as an adolescent, he will have even greater need to be by himself at times. Again, his own room can be a haven. In later years a man likes to have his "den," or goes fishing or hunting. The woman, too, should have a room in the house to which she can go for periods of relaxation in isolation. There is the story of the old farmer of seventy-five who was asked why he was so healthy. He replied, "When Martha and I were married we agreed that whenever we got into a fight she would go to the kitchen and I would go outdoors. Well, sir, because of that agreement I've spent most of my life outdoors and that is why I am so healthy."

Isolation as a response to frustration and conflict can be so rewarding that it becomes generalized. The young child refuses to play with other children of the same age; the grade school child keeps by himself on the playground and withdraws into as much isolation as possible in the classroom; the adolescent shuns group activities and perhaps even avoids his parents when he can. An example is the high-school girl who was brought to a clinical psychologist by her mother. Nearly every day after she returned home from school she went to her room and locked the door. She refused to appear for dinner but would go to the pantry for something to eat after the other members of the family had gone to bed. This behavior had continued for some weeks. Eventually the girl told the psychologist how much she feared and had always feared her dictatorial father.

He was a threat to her confidence and security and her response to that threat was to keep out of his way. Moreover she tended to use the same kind of adjustment in other threatening situations.

A person who uses isolation excessively in childhood and youth is gradually limiting his ability to cope with his personal and impersonal environment. By running away he reduces tension, but he deprives himself of opportunities to learn how to deal with difficult situations. He is fostering inflexibility and so making it more and more difficult for him to function successfully as an adult.

Excessive use of isolation is a danger signal. It may lead to a serious disorder, especially if it is coupled with too much daydreaming. These two adjustment mechanisms are characteristics of the backgrounds of some forms of schizophrenia. However, it should not be concluded that every isolate is either a psychotic personality or rapidly becoming one. Many examples could be given of adults who keep their social contacts at a minimum and yet remain well within the range of normality.

The basic reason for resorting to isolation is that it provides at least a temporary escape from tension. The same is true of course of the other mechanisms of adjustment. The causes of the tension vary with the individual and his environment. It may be that he is physically handicapped and feels so inadequate when he is with other children that he prefers to withdraw. It may be that he is gifted intellectually and prefers to play with imaginary companions who understand him better than do real boys and girls. It may be that he feels frustrated and defeated in the classroom because he cannot achieve the academic goals set by his teachers and by his parents. It may be one or more of a thousand things that make him feel inadequate in the company of others. He would like to grow but he is afraid to try.

DAYDREAMING

Daydreaming is a satisfying imaginative fulfillment of desires. It is an escape from the difficulties of real life into a realm where all obstacles to success can be ignored or effectively surmounted. It provides relief from frustration and conflict.

Daydreaming as a mechanism of adjustment is used by everyone. It is a form of mental and emotional relaxation. It is essentially pleasant and restful. It can, and usually does, have much the same effect upon the mind that an afternoon nap has upon the body. Daydreaming, then, is wholly normal and desirable, becoming detrimental only when indulged in excessively.

An individual may turn to daydreaming in order to satisfy a need which he is unable to satisfy in real life. If, for example, he desires popularity but is not well liked by his peer group, he may imagine himself, in his daydreams, as the center of an admiring throng, and so, for a time, be happy. If he is an ambitious but low-ranking student, he may let his mind wander during a classroom lecture to a happier future in which he sees himself as a successful man. If he feels insecure in his relationship with his parents, he may dream of the day when he will have his own home—a home filled with peace and understanding. In this manner he escapes temporarily from the strain of the present.

Types of Daydreams

It has been pointed out before that every individual is constantly striving to maintain his ego. It is not surprising, therefore, that the hero motive daydreams are customarily classified into the conquering-hero type and the suffering-hero type.

In the conquering-hero type of daydream the individual sees himself as confident, poised, successful. He has achieved this mastery without the exertion that would have been necessary in a realistic situation. He pictures himself as a great football player making a spectacular touchdown run while thousands applaud him in a frenzy of admiration. He sees himself as a great musician holding an audience spellbound. He pictures himself performing an act which requires great courage, such as saving someone from drowning or from a fire.

The writer held a series of interviews with a college student who spent several hours a day imagining himself as a combination of Plato and Jack Dempsey. The young man was extremely ambitious to achieve outstanding intellectual success. He was frustrated in this by relatively low mentality. He wanted also to be a great athlete but was poorly equipped physically. Instead of accepting himself as he was, he turned to daydreaming as a means of achieving his goals. In this imaginary realm there were no external checks on his progress. He could be what he wanted to be.

The suffering-hero type of daydream is frequently resorted to by the individual who pities himself. It also involves an element of masochism. It is a type of daydream rather frequently indulged in by children. The child who feels that he is being mistreated at home may imagine himself as seriously ill or even dead. His cruel parents are heartbroken. Why hadn't they treated him better? The suffering-hero or martyr type of daydream is somewhat more dangerous than the conquering-hero type. It is a form of aggression turned inward, even though it is to some extent satisfying to the individual who resorts to it.

Shaffer and Shoben,[1] in *The Psychology of Adjustment*, report a study on the extent of daydreaming among normal people. In this study, "A questionnaire was administered to a group of undergraduate college students and, a few years later, to a somewhat older group of graduate students. Twelve types of common daydreams were described and questions were also asked about worry, about repeated or systematic daydreams, and about other types in general. A full description of each variety of fantasy was read to the students, who responded by indicating if they had *ever* had that sort of daydream, and whether they had done so *recently,* within the past thirty days or so. The questionnaire was anonymous." There were 64 men and 131 women in the undergraduate group with a median age of twenty-one and 83 men and 112 women in the graduate group with a median age of twenty-eight. The results of the study are shown in Table II.

It can be seen from Table II that many kinds of daydreams appear frequently. "The average person reported that he had experienced about twelve or thirteen types of daydreams in his life, and about four or five types within the past thirty days. There were no conspicuous differences between the undergraduate and graduate groups, although they were questioned at different universities." It is significant that nearly fifty per cent of the subjects reported that they had had repeated or systematized daydreams during the recent past. The results of the study show, as Shaffer and Shoben point out, that "daydreaming is a common experience of normal people."

Even though a moderate amount of daydreaming is normal, it can be carried to extremes. If in real life deep frustrations persist

[1] L. F. Shaffer, and E. J. Shoben, Jr., *The Psychology of Adjustment*, rev. ed. (Boston: Houghton Mifflin Company, 1956), pp. 205–6.

TABLE II

The Occurrence of Types of Daydreams Among Two Groups of Students								
Type	Percent of students reporting each type							
	Ever?				Recently?			
	Undergrad.		Grad.		Undergrad.		Grad.	
	M	W	M	W	M	W	M	W
1. Physical feat	91	60	96	58	30	3	13	2
2. Physical attractiveness	89	95	94	96	34	63	17	56
3. Mental feat	88	92	89	90	48	42	47	61
4. Vocational success	100	98	99	93	81	69	78	64
5. Money or possessions	100	97	94	95	69	66	51	52
6. Display	78	76	90	83	22	16	19	19
7. Saving	89	63	90	66	14	5	14	8
8. Grandeur	67	48	63	39	11	7	6	0
9. Homage	81	72	81	66	16	13	24	18
10. Sexual	97	96	96	89	74	73	63	71
11. Death or destruction	39	44	60	46	9	9	10	9
12. Martyr	70	79	64	62	9	15	10	12
13. Worry	92	89	87	91	45	56	49	50
14. Other types	63	53	52	51	30	20	24	23
15. Repeated daydreams	89	93	83	87	48	51	36	47
Median number of types	13	12	13	11	5	5	4	5

for the individual he may learn to depend more and more upon autistic thinking. From this may develop hallucinations and eventually, perhaps, schizophrenia. The individual has leaned so heavily upon his imaginary satisfactions that he now has difficulty in differentiating between the real and the unreal. The amount of time and energy devoted to daydreaming will be brought within the normal range only when the individual is able to satisfy his needs in reality.

REGRESSION

Regression is a form of adjustment involving a retreat from the complexities of the present to an earlier and simpler form of behavior. The individual who utilizes this mechanism is convinced that he is incapable of overcoming the difficulties in his immediate situation. He remembers that when he was younger he was happier and more successful. Why not return, then, to that more fortunate period of his life?

The desire to regress is present at times in everyone. It is affected somewhat by the factor of selective forgetting, which results in what has been called the "old oaken bucket" delusion. With the exception of the very earliest memories, pleasant experiences are on the whole remembered longer than unpleasant experiences. Middle-aged adults think of their childhood as being much happier than it actually was. It is easy to see why such an adult occasionally wishes that he were young again. Perhaps he may even pretend for a while that he is. Although it is a manifestation of temporary regression, it is entirely normal for a woman to play with dolls occasionally, or for a man to enjoy his son's Christmas toys as much, or perhaps even more, than his boy does.

One has only to observe the behavior of old graduates at commencement time to realize how strong the desire to regress can be. They are trying for a few days to recapture the glow of youth. Most of them have forgotten the unhappy experiences of college life. They no longer remember the long hours of study or the social frustrations which they experienced. Instead, they recall those things which were pleasant and exciting.

The desire to regress frequently is strong in college freshmen. For many young people, college presents a number of difficult adjustment problems. If the student feels incapable of solving these problems, he may develop a strong desire to return home. There life was simpler; there he could feel safe; there he could depend upon his parents to make difficult decisions for him. Occasionally, college students, especially if they are encouraged to do so by their parents, capitulate to this desire. Such behavior, of course, does not necessarily initiate the permanent establishment of regressive habits. In his next effort to break away from home the individual may be successful.

The person who resorts to the mechanism of regression is introverted, nonsuggestible, and lacking in self-confidence. Because his thoughts are turned in upon himself, he finds it difficult to make new friends and to adjust to new situations. Usually he is not open to suggestions. He does not take kindly to ideas which are at variance with his frame of reference. He has little or no interest in seeking out new experiences. In fact, because of his lack of confidence in himself, he tries to avoid new experiences. He feels secure only in old and tried situations. Unsure of himself, he is fearful of expressing emotion toward a new acquaintance or in a new situation.

The regressive personality is constantly looking to the past, for he distrusts and fears the future. To some degree, this attitude of mind is common to us all. The past has known values, and we feel safer with that which we know. We do not know what the future holds for us. Consequently it does not satisfy our need for safety but does challenge our spirit of adventure. The regressive personality does not want adventure. Fearing to face what lies ahead, he tries to turn his back on the future.

In serious cases of regressive behavior the individual retreats so successfully that he loses touch with reality and believes that he is once more a child. The condition is rather frequent in schizophrenia, especially in hebephrenic schizophrenia, and will be discussed in some detail in the chapter on psychotic adjustments.

REPRESSION

Repression is an adjustment mechanism by which thoughts and experiences which threaten the individual's self-structure are excluded from conscious awareness. In Freudian terms, repression is the effort to force such thoughts and experiences into the unconscious. Even though Freud introduced the concept of repression, it is not necessary to assume the existence of an unconscious reservoir as a depository for repressed material, since this form of adjustment can be explained in terms of selective forgetting.

The multitudinous experiences which a person has as he goes through life can be divided roughly into three categories: (1) those which are acceptable and can be incorporated into the self structure; (2) those which have little or no significance and are therefore ignored or quickly forgotten; (3) those which are perceived as threatening and are faced with anxiety or are repressed in an attempt to escape from anxiety. Experiences which are comfortably assimilated promote personality growth. Those which have little or no meaning for an individual are innocuous. Obviously there are a great many of these. For example, a man may drive twenty miles a day from his home to his office for ten years without remembering the number of the route that he used part of the way. Or a college student may sit through a dull lecture for an hour and walk out of the classroom without remembering anything that the instructor said.

Repression may be a deliberate and conscious process or it may be an involuntary mechanism which keeps threatening material from entering consciousness. Very little is known about how this is accomplished neurologically, but it is an observable phenomenon that is seen frequently in psychotherapy. Much if not most of the repression used by normal persons is knowingly done. A thought or a wish or a fantasy which the individual deems unworthy of him or which, more seriously, threatens his self-concept is thrust aside. He tries not to think about it and, if he is successful, represses it. With practice he learns how to inhibit the recall of unwelcome material. This, of course, includes behavioral acts which he regrets. "It wasn't like me," he says. "How could I have done it?" After a while he may really convince himself that he didn't do it. In other words, he is denying the existence of some of the realities of his life.

It will be remembered from the discussion of motivation in chapter two that everyone is constantly trying to maintain and enhance his phenomenal self. Therefore, he may deny the existence of positive characteristics or of socially acceptable experiences, if these do not fit into his self-image. For example, a beautiful woman may be convinced that she is ugly, an intelligent man that he is below average, or a popular adolescent that he is disliked. Repression of this kind of material is more likely to be found in severely maladjusted persons than in relatively well adjusted persons.

Repression is the least satisfactory of the adjustment mechanisms since it is nonintegrative. Its use may provide a temporary escape from anxiety, but over a period of time it usually creates anxiety. Yet it is used by everyone to some extent. Repressed desires, fantasies, and experiences constitute a burden, sometimes light, sometimes heavy, which each human being carries. For some the burden becomes too heavy and responses are made to the strain which may be neurotic or psychotic. Such persons need professional help. In psychotherapy, properly handled, a relationship develops between the therapist and the client which reduces tension and loosens inhibitions, thus making it possible for the client to bring into conscious awareness material previously repressed.

What has been repressed? The answer to this question is hard to come by. The therapist does not know and usually the client does not know until recall is made possible. It is a mistake to assume that repressed material always has sexual connotations although this happens often because of the taboos which surround sex in our culture. The only certainty is that whatever it is that has been repressed was a threat to the client's perception of himself. A few scattered examples selected from the writer's files follow. It should not be assumed from these that the repressed experience mentioned was the sole cause of the behavior disorder. In each instance, however, it was a significant one.

A young woman was having marital difficulties and became so depressed that she attempted suicide. She had repressed a lesbian experience which was satisfying and so increased her feeling of guilt. A professional man was a drug addict. He had repressed his hatred for his father who had been dead for many years. A Korean war veteran stuttered badly, especially when he tried to use certain words. He had repressed the guilt-ridden experience of being responsible for the wreck of a plane of which he was the pilot, causing the death of a member of his crew. A World War II veteran was suffering from generalized anxiety. He had inhibited the recall of a time when an ammunition dump which he was guarding blew up, killing several civilians. A widow was still mourning for her husband eight years after his death. She had forgotten how sharply she had criticized him shortly before he died. A man had lost the use of his right arm. He had repressed all memory of the time when his wife was insulted by another man and he did not have the courage to defend her. A college student had developed symptoms of a schizophrenic reaction. He had not been aware for years that when he was a boy he frequently asked his older brother to tie him up and beat him. A college girl had a compulsion to take five baths every day. She was very religious and had repressed the experience of swearing at her pastor. A young woman was afraid of crowds, especially in a large room or auditorium. She had inhibited recall of the time when as a young child she had forgot her lines in a school play and ran off the stage panic-stricken.

SUMMARY

Adjustment mechanisms are responses which provide indirect satisfactions. They reduce tension at least temporarily and usually help in maintaining self-respect. They are used in varying degrees by everyone. Adjustment mechanisms are not separate entities; each one overlaps one or more of the others. This accounts in part for the lack of agreement among psychologists in labeling and defining them. In this chapter, eleven have been considered: compensation, identification, rationalization, projection, attention getting, negativism, intellectualizing, isolation, daydreaming, regression, and repression. Compensation is the exaggeration of a desirable trait to reduce the feelings of inadequacy caused by an undesirable trait. It takes many forms, such as compensating for one's failures through the successes of one's children, by the development of peculiar abilities, or by sublimation. Identification is the establishment of strong emotional ties with another person, a group of persons, an institution, a state, or an inanimate object or objects. Usually identification is a desirable adjustment mechanism. When used wisely it enhances one's feeling of worth. Rationalization is the process of devising personally and socially acceptable reasons for an unacceptable thought or act. An interesting variation of rationalization is the sour grapes mechanism. Projection is used three ways: placing blame on an incidental or imaginary cause; seeing in others one's own personality defects; and placing the blame for failure on others. Attention getting is any kind of behavior resorted to by a person as a means of making others notice him. Negativism is aggressive withdrawal. It is used most frequently at the ages of two and three and during adolescence. Intellectualizing is an escape from threat into words. It is used frequently by those who are very intelligent. Isolation is usually thought of as a physical withdrawal from tension producing situations. Daydreaming is escape from the difficulties of real life into a world of fantasy where one's desires can be fulfilled in imagination. Regression is a retreat from the complexities of the present to an earlier and simpler form of behavior. Repression is a form of selective forgetting. It is nonintegrative and the least desirable of the adjustment mechanisms.

THE NEED
FOR
ACHIEVEMENT

chapter 4

Human beings do not exist in a vacuum; they exist in an environment. If they are to survive they must learn how to master those segments of their environment which are significant for them. This is so obvious it is a truism. There is no valid evidence that the need for achievement is inherited. There is, however, a wealth of evidence that from birth—or for that matter from conception—the individual is in a constant struggle to gain at least some control over part of his environment. Moreover, he is not content to achieve merely enough to preserve himself in the immediate present. He tries to build up a reserve against the future.

Achievement also possesses considerable social significance. A child born into our society learns very early in life that success brings reward. Reward enhances the self and so makes the self feel more secure. Techniques for satisfying the need for achievement can be seen all around us: in the young child as he struggles to build his pile of blocks; in the college student as he tries to earn an "A" in a course; in the research worker as he toils painstakingly to solve a difficult problem; in the inmate of an institution for the mentally retarded as she takes great pride in a basket she has woven or a rug she has braided. Everyone old and young is driven on throughout his life by the need to achieve. It is essential to one's mental health that this need be satisfied.

In his quest for achievement the individual will of course succeed at times and fail at times. When he fails he experiences a feeling of frustration. If he is a normal human being, however, the feeling of frustration is accompanied by a recognition that he must adjust to those factors in his environment which he cannot master. The individual who finds it difficult or impossible to make such adjustments will pile frustration upon frustration, failure upon failure, as he faces a wall which he can neither break through nor climb over. Instead of accepting the fact that there are certain things which he cannot do, that there are certain elements in his environment which he cannot conquer, he concentrates upon these and so denies himself the satisfaction which he would gain by giving his major attention to the achievement of goals which are within his reach.

The need for achievement must be satisfied frequently if an individual is to be well adjusted. Conversely, if the need for achievement is completely or for the most part frustrated over a long period of time, the individual will inevitably become maladjusted. One's goals should be obtainable. Repeatedly to attempt the impossible, habitually to reach for the stars, is to court a neurosis or psychosis.

INDIVIDUAL DIFFERENCES

Success must always be defined in terms of the goals that the individual has set for himself. These goals, in turn, should be selected in the light of the abilities possessed by the individual who is trying to achieve them. An ambition that is reasonable for one man may be quite unreasonable for another. It is laudable for the gifted track athlete to attempt to run the mile distance in less than four minutes; it would be ridiculous for the typical college man to try it. It is praiseworthy for the intellectually superior student to work for high honors; it is tragic for the very dull student to make a similar attempt.

Since the nature and extent of one's ambitions should be dependent on the abilities which the specific individual possesses, it is necessary, before we consider further what happens when the need for achievement is frustrated, to touch briefly on the basic facts concerning individual differences. Special attention will be given to differences in intellectual capacity and in academic achievement, since these are areas which are of particular interest and of considerable importance to college students.

The Normal Frequency Surface

Whenever height, intelligence, emotional stability, or almost any such trait or ability is objectively measured, the scores, if obtained on a large, unselected group, will be distributed over a surface which closely approximates the normal probability curve. (See Figure 1.)

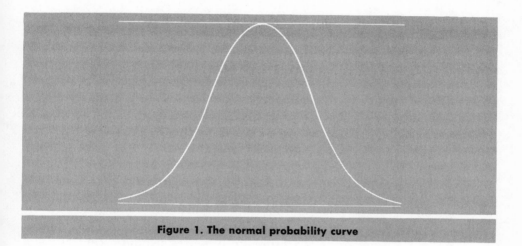

Figure 1. The normal probability curve

It can be seen from Figure 1 that the scores pile up around a central point, at the same time spreading away in either direction in steadily decreasing numbers. A distribution of scores rarely follows the normal probability curve exactly, but if the number of cases is large, it will closely approximate it.

Casual observation makes it easy for us to use as an example the distribution of height. We know that the number of American men who are five feet five is very much smaller than those who are five feet eight, and, in turn, the number of those who are five feet eleven is also very much smaller than those who are five feet eight. It is also obvious that the number below five feet four and over six feet is extremely small. It is not, however, quite so obvious to the layman that a similar situation exists with respect to intellectual capacity. (See Figure 2.)

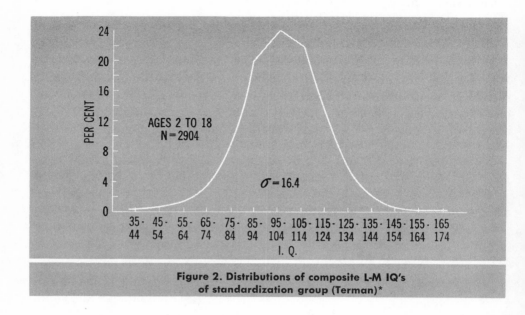

Figure 2. Distributions of composite L-M IQ's of standardization group (Terman)*

Figure 2 represents a distribution of the intelligence quotients of 2,904 individuals on whom the Terman-Merrill revision of the Stanford-Binet test of intelligence was standardized. In this figure, as in Figure 1, there is a piling-up of scores around a central point and a gradual tapering-off from that central point to the right and to the left. Average intelligence is represented by an intelligence quotient of 100. On the Stanford-Binet test, the standard deviation is 16, which indicates that roughly two thirds of an unselected group will fall between intelligence quotients 84 and 116.

If we were to measure the intellectual capacity of college students, the distribution of the obtained scores would also approximate the normal frequency surface. However, the mean, the standard deviation, and the range would be quite different from the ones noted in Figure 2. The average intelligence of college students is approximately 120. This mean varies somewhat, of course, from

1 L. M. Terman, and M. A. Merrill, *Measuring Intelligence* (Boston: Houghton Mifflin Company, 1937), p. 3.

college to college. The number of college students with below-average intelligence—that is, with an intelligence quotient of less than 100—is very small. These are important facts for a student to consider as he evaluates his academic success. To be an A student in high school is one thing; to be an A student in college, quite another. The degree of competition must always be kept in mind in judging one's success.

It is difficult for most persons to understand the facts concerning the distribution of intelligence. Instead of thinking in terms of the probability curve they proceed on the assumption that there are three groups: those who are feebleminded, those who are normal, and those who are geniuses. They know from observation that the feebleminded and genius groups are small and the normal group is large. They tend to believe that any differences within the normal group can be eliminated through effort and education. Many even think that if the conditions are right those who are mentally retarded can be made normal. The phrase "wiping out illiteracy" is often heard even though those who are seriously retarded and most of those who are moderately retarded can never learn to read or write. Because of this lack of understanding of the nature of individual differences great pressure is frequently put upon students to achieve at a level which is far beyond their intellectual capacity. For example, an adolescent with an intelligence quotient of 80 is not mentally retarded, but at the same time he does not have the intelligence to compete successfully with an equally well motivated adolescent who has an intelligence quotient of 115. The fact that intelligence is relative is also often overlooked. If at some time in the future a way should be found to increase the intellectual capacity of human beings, presumably all would profit by it. If so, society would become more complex and those at the bottom of the distribution would still be mentally retarded and those at the top geniuses.

Elementary Statistical Concepts

It may be that some of the terms used in the preceding comments are rather confusing to those students who have not been introduced to statistics. A brief description of a few elementary statistical concepts follows; an extensive treatment of these and other techniques can be found in any book on statistics in psychology or in education. An understanding of mental hygiene problems growing out of frustration of the need for achievement cannot be gained without full appreciation of the facts of individual differences; the facts of individual differences cannot, in turn, be understood without some knowledge of statistics.

Measures of Central Tendency   A measure of central tendency is the single score which best represents an entire series of scores. For example, if you knew that the average intelligence quotient of the students on your college campus was 120, and you were asked to guess the intellectual level of a student whom you had never met and knew nothing about, your best guess would be 120. The chances are more favorable that he would be at or near that point than that he would fall at, for example, 105 or 160.

The two measures of central tendency which are used most frequently are the mean and the median. The arithmetic mean is equivalent to the common average. The median is equivalent to the midscore of an uneven number of scores, or the midpoint of an even number of scores. Space will not be taken for a discussion of the computation of these and other measures; it will be enough for our purposes to consider how they should be interpreted.

In finding the common average, full weight is given to each score in the series. For instance, if we wish to find the average of the scores 17, 6, 4, 2, 1, we add these, divide the total by 5, and find that the average is 6. Each score, including the extremes 17 and 1, are given their full values. As a result, the average is the same as the second highest score in the distribution. The arithmetic mean, likewise, gives full weight to each score.

If we wish to find the midscore of this series, we would count up from the bottom or down from the top, once the scores had been arranged in order of size, and would find that 4 represented the middle of the distribution. This is two points lower than the common average. It does not give full value to extreme scores—in this case, the 17. Each score is counted as one.

Measures of Variability   In mental hygiene, we are primarily concerned with the individual case. In many instances, however, it is helpful to use a measure of central tendency as a point of reference. It is helpful, also, to know the facts concerning the variability of a series of scores. A measure of variability reveals the degree to which the scores in a distribution tend to cluster around the point of central tendency. Of these measures, the one seen most frequently in scientific literature is the standard deviation, usually represented by the Greek letter σ (sigma).

The standard deviation is found by obtaining the differences between the several scores and the mean of these scores, squaring these differences, and then finding the square root of the sum of the squares divided by the number of cases.

If the scores are distributed over the normal frequency surface, 68.26 per cent, or approximately two thirds, will fall within the limits of $\pm 1\sigma$. There is practical certainty that all of the scores will fall within the limits of $\pm 3\sigma$. For example, if a large representative sampling of children is examined with the Terman-Merrill revision of the Stanford-Binet test, the mean intelligence quotient will be 100 and the standard deviation of the distribution of intelligence quotients will be 16. This means that 68.26 per cent of the group falls between intelligence quotients 84 and 116, while there is practical certainty that no one will have an intelligence quotient below 52, or intelligence quotient above 148. Statistically it would be expected that there would be only three such cases out of a thousand. In actual practice, the number is slightly larger.

Another measure of variability is Q, or the semi-interquartile range; that is, one half the distance between Q_3 and Q_1. Q_3 is that point in a distribution of scores, arranged in order of size, below which 75 per cent of the cases fall; Q_1 is the point below which 25 per cent of the cases fall. Therefore, if $Q_3 = 80$ and $Q_1 = 60$, $Q = \dfrac{80 - 60}{2} = \dfrac{20}{2} = 10$. Q is a counting measure of variability. It is frequently used with the median, the counting measure of central tendency.

Correlation   It is often important, in trying to solve problems that arise in the field of personal guidance, to know the degree to which measured variables are associated. For example, is there any relationship between neurotic tendency and introversion? Between intelligence and emotional stability? Between scholastic achievement and success in later life? Procedures have been worked out by mathematicians which make it possible to state in mathematical terms the degree to which the relationship between two measured variables exists. Coefficients of correlation so obtained are always subject to a certain amount of error. Such errors result from a number of factors, including the nature of the two distributions of scores, the adequacy of the instruments used, the efficiency with which those instruments were handled, and the extent of the sampling upon which the conclusions are based. A coefficient of correlation, unless it represents a perfect negative or positive relationship, which it rarely does, provides no exact information concerning an individual case. It must always be interpreted in terms of probability. Moreover, it cannot be dogmatically stated that a certain coefficient of correlation is either large or small, because it must always be interpreted in the light of the problem which is being studied.

Coefficients of correlation range in size from minus 1.00 to plus 1.00, minus 1.00 representing perfect negative relationship and plus 1.00 perfect positive relationship. Zero represents chance correlation. The great majority of correlation coefficients appearing in psychological studies are positive, a result, in part, of the fact that good things tend to go together—that an individual who is superior in one trait is more likely than not to be superior in all others.

It is important to keep in mind that a coefficient of correlation does not of itself prove causation, although it may suggest the possibility that one variable has exercised considerable influence upon the other. For example, there is a correlation of .50 between siblings with respect to intelligence. It does not follow from this that a low level of intelligence in an older child has caused the younger brother also to be low in intelligence. An important causal factor in the background of both children is the intellectual capacity of the parents. That there is a high correlation between neurotic tendency and introversion does not of itself mean that possession of introvert traits causes one to become neurotic. Knowledge of the degree of relationship existing among the several human abilities which can now be measured provides good background for self-understanding and for work in the field of guidance. Such knowledge, however, must be used with considerable care, for what is true in terms of central tendency may not be true in terms of the individual case. A doctor, for example, may know that a certain set of symptoms indicates the presence of a certain disease in 85 per cent of all cases. However, he must be constantly aware of the fact that his patient may be one of the remaining 15 per cent. It is desirable to be able to think in terms of central tendency, variability, and correlation, but when one is dealing with human beings, one must never lose sight of the individual case.

Percentiles   There is one more measure which should be mentioned before we complete this glance at statistical measures. This measure is the percentile rank. As the word *percentile* indicates, the interpretation of each score in a distribution of scores is on a percentage basis. Percentile ranks range from zero to 99.99 plus. There can be no percentile rank of one hundred, since no member of a group could possibly score higher than 100 per cent of a group of which he is a part.

Zero percentile represents the lowest score, a point below which no one falls. A percentile rank of 50 represents the median of the group, a point below which 50 per cent of the cases fall. It is customary to define percentile rank in terms of "percentage lower." Percentile ranks must always be interpreted in terms of the group upon whom the ranks were determined. For example, a college freshman is told that he has a percentile rank of 90 on the intelligence test which was given to his class at the opening of the college year. If the percentile ranks were based upon the distribution of scores earned by that class, then this student's percentile rank of 90 means that 90 per cent of his class fall below him in intellectual capacity. It does not mean that 90 per cent of all college freshmen in the United States fall below him. It does not mean that 90 per cent of the general population fall below him. It means merely that 90 per cent of his own class fall below him. If the same examination had been given to a sampling of the general population of eighteen-year-olds, he would have earned a much higher percentile rank, probably 98 or 99. If the same test had been given to a sampling of college graduates and he had taken it with them, he would have rated well below the 90. It is important for the individual always to keep in mind the abilities of the different groups with whom he associates himself. His own abilities are relative, higher in one group, lower in another.

By way of example, we can trace the career of Donald, who had an intelligence quotient of 120. He attended grade school in a New England village. The size of his class ranged, through the eight years, from 30 to 40. Since he was the brightest boy in the group, his parents and teachers tended to overrate him. They were convinced that he would be a great success in college, and an outstanding professional man.

When Donald went to high school in a much larger adjoining town, he was a little surprised and disturbed to discover that he was no longer the brightest student in his class. An intelligence quotient of 120 was still relatively very good, but there were a number of children who rated higher. Donald was still well above average, however, and, being a diligent boy, he succeeded in earning excellent grades; but at the end of his four years in high school he was not valedictorian—not even salutatorian. His parents were troubled and accused the boy of not working hard enough. They were still convinced that he was a young genius because of what he had accomplished in grade school and blamed his inability to achieve high scholastic honors on lack of drive.

Donald then went to college where he began to compete with a much more select group than those with whom he had been associated in high school. Here, with respect to intellectual capacity, he was average, instead of superior, as he had been in high school, or the best in his class, as he had been in grade school. His grades during his freshman year were all B's and C's. He began to think of himself as a failure. His parents could not understand why their brilliant son was not doing better work in college. They blamed it on his lack of ambition, his lack of interest, and, at times, on a growing belief that precocity leads to early decline; that the bright child grows up to be a dull man; that the morning-glory folds early in the day.

However, Donald kept on working hard, puzzled, frequently discouraged, wondering why he was not able to achieve the academic goals that he and his parents had so confidently expected him to reach with ease. He and they completely overlooked the fact that as he changed from grade school to high school and from high school to college the quality of his competition changed. His intellectual capacity, in terms of IQ, had not appreciably altered. His achievements were not dimmed by anything within himself, but by the shadow of increased competition.

After Donald had finished his undergraduate work in college he went on to medical school, having barely achieved the undergraduate average required for entrance. In medical school the competition was greater still. Instead of being average for his class he was now in the lowest fifth, and before the year was over he was dropped because of poor work.

In terms of percentile rank the boy rated approximately as follows in the four different classes of which he had been a member: grade school, 99; high school, 82; college, 50; graduate school, 16.

Intelligence Tests

In the preceding pages the term *intelligence quotient* has been used rather frequently. Since a person's intellectual level is an important fact to be considered in setting up goals, especially those which are academic, brief consideration will now be given to the nature of intelligence and how it is measured.

The Nature of Intelligence   The exact physical basis of intellectual activity is still unknown. It is presumably a function of the entire organism, with the central nervous system, particularly the cerebral cortex, playing the most important part. Since the physical basis of mental capacity is not clearly understood, it is necessary to measure intelligence indirectly—to observe and record how a mind works on standard problems under controlled conditions. The problems which are set for the individual in an intelligence test are designed to sample the various aspects of intellectual behavior. Abstract intelligence at the human level is manifested primarily through ability to use symbols. This is why intelligence tests are so heavily weighted with number concepts and verbal material.

Intelligence has been defined in various ways. Binet describes it in terms of adaptation; Terman, in terms of the ability to use abstractions; Woodworth, as the adaptation of what one has learned to novel situations; and Munn, as demonstrated ability in the use of symbolic processes. Perhaps the most frequently used definition is "the ability to learn." It should be noted that the kind of intelligence which is measured by intelligence tests is abstract. An intelligence quotient does not provide a basis for an evaluation concerning an individual's mechanical ability or social aptitude. In intelligence testing, the psychologist sinks shafts at various critical points in order to discover the relative ability of an individual to use number and verbal symbols, to comprehend spatial relationships, to carry on inductive and deductive reasoning, and to handle other similar complex mental processes.

Assumptions Underlying Intelligence Tests   Two of the most important assumptions underlying intelligence testing are (1) that the person taking the test has had approximately the same opportunity to become familiar with the kind of material included in the test as had those upon whom the test was standardized; (2) that the person taking the test is doing the best of which he is capable. Environment, including education, has some effect upon test scores. It is one of the factors which makes the standard error of an IQ as large as it is. In certain instances, such as when a foreign-language is used in the home, environment becomes so important that a highly verbal test is unsuitable for use.

The second fundamental assumption holds special interest for clinical psychologists. Many individuals are incapable of doing their best in a test situation because of emotional blocks. For such persons a group test is usually worthless, and an individual test has value only after the psychologist has succeeded in establishing sufficient rapport with the examinee so that inhibiting emotional tension is reduced to a point where it does not seriously affect responses. Emotional tension manifests itself on an individual test through a considerable scatter of correct answers. This results from the fact that the person taking the test may experience occasional blocks on questions which are relatively easy and yet be able to think clearly on some questions that are relatively difficult. He may also experience inhibitions with respect to certain kinds of questions, such as those which measure number ability, and yet feel confident on other kinds of questions, such as those which sample verbal ability.

Interpretation of Intelligence Test Scores   An intelligence quotient is found for an individual by dividing his mental age by his chronological age. The mental-age concept was first introduced by Binet, a French psychologist, in 1908, when a revision of the 1905 Binet-Simon Scale appeared. A person's mental age is determined by comparing his intellectual behavior in a test situation with the intellectual behavior of the group upon whom the test has been standardized. If his responses are at the eight-year level, as determined by the acual performance of typical eight-year-old children, he is said to have a mental age of eight. If his chronological age is also eight, then he has an intelligence quotient of 100. If, however, he has a chronological age of 10, then his intelligence quotient is 80. Even though he is ten, he has not yet gone beyond a level of eight years in mental development.

An intelligence quotient must always be interpreted in terms of the test used. For example, a Stanford-Binet IQ and a Wechsler IQ do not mean the same thing. Two of the important reasons for variations in meaning are differences in the variability of the groups upon whom the tests were standardized and the difficulty of the tests at the upper levels. If, for example, two intelligence tests have mean IQs of 100 but one has a standard deviation of 15 and the other 12, then 115 on one test equals 112 on the other, since these two IQs would both be at plus one standard deviation on the continuum. Some group tests have what is called a "low roof." This makes it impossible for a really brilliant child or adult to demonstrate how well he could do if he were sufficiently challenged. There are certain group tests in which it is impossible for a junior or senior high school student to earn an intelligence quotient above the 130's. Chronological age also affects the interpretation of intelligence quotients. For example, a brilliant person can earn a much higher intelligence quotient on the Stanford-Binet test as a child than he can as an adult.

An intelligence quotient should always be considered as a *range* on a scale rather than as a *point* on a scale. Every IQ is accompanied by a standard error which indicates the degree of its variability. For example, if the standard error of an intelligence quotient of 100 is 4 then the chances are two out of three that the person who has earned an IQ of 100 on this test has a true IQ which lies within the limits of 96–104. Practical certainty, however, is not achieved until the limits are extended to 88–112. Another way of interpreting this standard error is to point out that on a retest it would not be at all surprising if the individual earned an IQ that varied by several points from the first IQ. The intelligence quotient is *relatively*, not *absolutely*, constant. One would not expect it to remain exactly the same from test to test.

Care should always be taken not to overrate or underrate the importance of intelligence as measured by intelligence tests. For example, if an individual has an intelligence quotient of 35 it is clear that he cannot profit from schooling of a verbal kind. He will never be able to make use of the symbols taught children in the primary grades. If a person has an IQ of 60 he is incapable of comprehending the linguistic, mathematical, and scientific subjects customarily taught in high school. If his intelligence quotient is less than 100 it is unlikely that he will be able to do college work. Young people with IQs below 120 would experience difficulty in graduate school. Intelligence, of course, is only one of the determiners of success, but it is an important one, especially in those activities that depend upon the ability to handle symbolic processes. Although the correlation between intelligence and scholastic achievement on the high school and college levels is low, there is a minimum IQ below which an individual cannot expect to succeed.

The University of New Hampshire Counseling Service prepared for the members of the faculty a mimeographed report which dealt with the relationship between scores earned on the American Council on Education Psychological Examination and the grades achieved by an entire freshman class. The data are presented in stanine groupings. To obtain stanines, the base line of the distribution of scores is divided into nine equal parts. If the distribution is a normal one, the following frequencies will be included in the nine areas of the normal probability surface: first stanine, 4 per cent; second stanine, 7 per cent; third stanine, 12 per cent; fourth stanine, 17 per cent; fifth stanine, 20 per cent; sixth stanine, 17 per cent; seventh stanine, 12 per cent; eighth stanine, 7 per cent; ninth stanine, 4 per cent.

In the Counseling Service report, the grade point averages were divided into four categories: 0–1.3; 1.4–1.8; 1.9–2.9; 3.0–4.0. The lowest category represents a danger zone; the second one, a border zone; the third, a safety zone or average achievement; and the fourth, outstanding achievement or honors work. Table III, taken from the report, contains some interesting and significant statistics.

An examination of Table III shows that freshmen who were in the top 4 per cent of their class intellectually (ninth stanine) did extremely well. Forty-six per cent, or nearly half, were in the 3.0–4.0 classification. However, there were 7 per cent who were in the 1.4–1.8 group representing borderline achievement. This indicates that intellectual capacity by itself is no guarantee of academic success.

TABLE III

Relationship Between Stanine Position on ACE and Grades Earned by
a Freshman Class at the University of New Hampshire

Grades	0–1.3	1.4–1.8	1.9–2.9	3.0–4.0	With-drawals	Total
Actual distribution	16%	19%	45%	14%	6%	100%
Stanine						
9*	0%	7%	46%	46%	0%	100%
8*	3	7	44	41	6	100
7*	7	18	43	25	7	100
6	11	20	47	18	4	100
5	15	18	55	9	3	100
4	16	19	49	9	7	100
3*	30	23	33	3	11	100
2*	25	28	42	2	4	100
1*	43	17	28	0	12	100

* Percentages within starred stanines are significantly different from those in "Actual distribution."

The 4 per cent who were in the first stanine (low intellectual capacity) did very poor work as would be expected. Forty-three per cent, or nearly half, were in the 0–1.3 category. Not a single student in this group was in the 3.0–4.0 classification. However, 28 per cent or slightly more than one fourth were doing average college work. It must be remembered that these 4 per cent had at least average intelligence when compared to the general population. College students constitute a relatively homogeneous group intellectually.

The 20 per cent in the middle stanine achieved grades which were quite close to the actual total distribution. Fifty-five per cent or slightly more than half were where they would be expected, that is, in the 1.9–2.9 category. However, 15 per cent were on the verge of failure. Obviously, it is easier to make more accurate predictions for students at either intellectual extreme than it is to predict for the average student.

The data in the preceding table make it clear that intelligence is not the sole factor in academic success or, for that matter, in success after graduation. It is important, to be sure, but diligence and emotional stability play their parts, too. It is also important to remember that college students are a select group intellectually. Approximately half of them have intelligence quotients over 120, and the number who fall below an intelligence quotient of 100 is extremely small.

Individual Intelligence Tests   Individual intelligence tests are much more satisfactory than group tests for measuring the mental ability of emotionally disturbed individuals. In a test situation with one person the psychologist has an excellent opportunity to establish rapport and so to reduce tension which causes blocking of recall and concentrated thought. It is very difficult to do this in administering a group test. Moreover, in an individual test situation the examiner, if he fails in his efforts to reduce tension, can at least observe its presence and note that because of it the test score is presumably lower than it would have been had the tension not been present. In a group test it is almost impossible to identify those who are not doing their best because of strain.

The most widely used individual intelligence tests are the Stanford-Binet, revised in 1960, and the two developed by Wechsler—the Wechsler Adult Intelligence Scale (WAIS) and the Wechsler Intelligence Scale for Children. Brief consideration will be given to the WAIS.

The person administering the WAIS records not only the scores, but also any significant behavior characteristics manifested by the examinee during the test period. In order that he may know what is expected of him, the subject is always told that he is taking an intelligence test. The examiner attempts to reduce the resultant anxiety by telling him that the test is not being given primarily to determine an intelligence quotient but rather to obtain information on his strengths and weaknesses. The subject is allowed to finish whatever he starts, even though he exceeds the time limit. This is a sound procedure, since the interruption of an activity before it is completed or before the subject wishes to abandon it is likely to increase tension and so affect the subject's performance on the remaining items.

Wechsler IQs are interpreted somewhat differently from Stanford-Binet IQs. Wechsler presents the following classifications:

TABLE IV

Intelligence Classification of WAIS IQs—Ages 16 to 75 (actual)[2]		
Classification	IQ	Percentage included
Defective	69 and below	2.2
Borderline	70–79	6.7
Dull-normal	80–89	16.1
Average	90–109	50.0
Bright-normal	110–119	16.1
Superior	120–129	6.7
Very superior	130 and above	2.2

In counseling, it is important to know not only a person's crude intelligence quotient, but also how well his intellectual capacity is functioning in specific situations. The WAIS provides a means of checking on the impairment of such functioning; it can be used as an aid in diagnosing behavior disorders. If there is a considerable difference between the verbal and performance IQs, an analysis of the subtests should be made to discover the specific sources of that difference. Since the characteristics of certain tests are associated with certain clinical groups, such an analysis may provide the psychologist with valuable diagnostic information.

Variations in Ability Are Wide

Variations in a single trait—physical, mental, or emotional—are very large. One baby at birth may weigh five times as much as another. One man may be a third taller than another, and in extreme instances, twice as tall. One child in a sixth-grade class may be at the second-grade level in reading ability, while another child in the same class may be able to read as well as a typical high-school senior. And so it is with all forms of academic achievement.

Human beings obviously differ widely in intelligence. Contrast, for example, the behavior of a severely retarded person with that of a genius such as Einstein or John Dewey. The severely retarded person cannot walk, cannot use words meaningfully, cannot dress himself, cannot feed himself. At the opposite pole stands the genius

2 D. Wechsler, *The Measurement and Appraisal of Adult Intelligence,* 4th ed. (Baltimore: The Williams & Wilkins Co., 1958), p. 42.

whose mental capacity is so great that he seems almost to transcend the usual limitations of the human mind.

A similar picture presents itself with respect to emotional stability. At one extreme stands the individual who is calm, poised, well-controlled in almost every situation—the sort of person said to have ice-water in his veins. At the opposite end of the distribution stands the psychotic individual who has lost control over his behavior. In fact, he is so exceptional it is not at all strange that earlier generations were convinced that such persons were inhabited by evil spirits.

With respect to the four fundamental needs of all human beings, it is important to keep in mind that the variations in the strength of these needs are considerable. One man may be consumed by insatiable ambition, while another, perhaps even a member of the same family, may be easygoing, casual, lazy. One man may have a very strong desire to be in the limelight, to get acclaim from his fellows, while another is much happier when he is alone and unnoticed. One man may be confident and another insecure. One man may possess relatively strong physiological drives which in another are relatively weak.

Differences in Abilities Are Usually Quantitative

When a human ability is measured, the differences in that ability are usually quantitative rather than qualitative. There is a continuity of scores from the lowest to the highest. For example, men are neither tall nor short in the sense that tall men and short men represent qualitative differences. Differences in intelligence are also quantitative. If one were to compare two-ten-year-old boys, one of whom had very low intellectual capacity and the other very high, the difference would appear so striking that it might appear on the surface that the two differed qualitatively. However, if the mental capacities of ten thousand ten-year-old boys were measured, the resultant scores would constitute a continuous series, and, as in the case of height, the gradations would be very fine.

A similar situation probably exists with respect to emotional stability. It is unscientific to classify human beings into a dichotomy: the sane and the insane. If a large representative group of individuals of college age were measured for emotional stability, the distribution would approximate the normal curve.

At the extreme right of the distribution are those who are exceptionally well adjusted. This small group includes those few individuals who meet nearly every crisis calmly. Their breaking-point is very high. Just below them will come those who are very well adjusted—individuals who meet life's problems and solve them with relatively little difficulty. In the center is the large average group to which the majority belongs. Individuals in this group experience frustrations and conflicts, disappointments and emotional disturbances, but they usually succeed in finding socially acceptable means of reducing tension. Below the average group are those who are emotionally maladjusted. Persons in this group experience considerable tension. In serious cases this tension is persistent. In this group fall those who have made excessive use of the mechanisms of adjustment which will be discussed in later chapters. They may be exceedingly self-conscious or withdrawn or negativistic. Many of them are in need of psychotherapy. Below this group are those who are suffering from an acute neurosis. At the extreme left of the distribution are those individuals who are psychotic.

Causes of Individual Differences

Identifying and isolating the causes of individual differences is difficult and complex. When a child is conceived, heredity has determined that he shall be a human being, equipped with the organs that are characteristic of human beings. The structure of the organs which he possesses has been determined at the time of the union of the parental germ cells. In the nuclei of these cells are chromosomes consisting of genes which are the determiners of heredity. It is known that a number of genes in combination are involved in the determination of even a simple characteristic of the individual organism. Geneticists are in no position at the present time to explain the combination which determines a complex organ like the brain. Moreover, the problems relating to detailed explanations of the inheritance of a single individual are complicated by the fact that he is the product, not only of the parental germ cells, but also of the germ cells of all the generations which produced his parents.

Studies of the relative potency of heredity and environment with respect to mental capacity have in the main followed four lines of attack: (1) Family histories of mentally deficient individuals; (2) family histories of mentally gifted individuals; (3) the extent of similarities between twins; and (4) the effect of a changed environment upon intellectual status.

Inheritance of Mental Deficiency   Feeblemindedness runs in families. This is not in itself proof that subnormal mentality is biologically inherited. A contributing factor to the intelligence of children of feebleminded parents is their social inheritance. It is impossible to evaluate accurately the effect upon a person of the presence of feebleminded adults in the home. Moreover, the socioeconomic status of parents of feebleminded children is usually low, and this may exercise some influence. On the other hand, there are many feebleminded children who are born into homes in which the intelligence and the socioeconomic level of the parents are above average.

No final conclusion can be given concerning the relative contributions of heredity and environment to feeblemindedness. The indications are, however, that of the two, heredity is much more important.

Inheritance of Mental Superiority   When studies of intellectually gifted children and of adult geniuses are made, a situation similar to that with respect to feebleminded children is found. Mental superiority runs in families, but it is impossible to disentangle the complex interacting effects of heredity and environment.

The most famous study of a family of geniuses is the one made by Winship and Davenport of the descendants of Richard Edwards, who was an eminent lawyer. His wife, Elizabeth Tuthill, possessed a brilliant mind. Their son was the father of Jonathan Edwards, who married Sarah Pierpont. Among the descendants of these two over a period of two hundred years were a number of distinguished individuals, including twelve college presidents, two United States senators, and one Vice-President of the United States.

Galton concluded, as a result of his studies of the families of geniuses, that great mental capacity is inherited. From his investigations he formulated his law of ancestral inheritance. According to this law a child inherits one half of his mental capacity from his parents, one fourth from his grandparents, one eighth from his great-grandparents, and so on back through the generations.

The fact that genius runs in families is not final proof that genius is entirely inherited. Gifted children tend to come from superior homes, having been reared in a superior environment. This environment undoubtedly contributes to some extent to their mental development. However, there are many instances of intellectually gifted children born into homes in which the parents and the socio-economic level were far below average. Again it is necessary to conclude that both heredity and environment have contributed to the mental capacity of the individual and that it is impossible to state in exact terms how important each influence has been.

Twins   The conclusions reached in a number of studies of twins are in agreement that identical twins are more alike than fraternal twins and that fraternal twins, in turn, are more alike than ordinary siblings. Identical (monozygous) twins have the same inheritance since they develop from a division of a single fertilized egg. Fraternal twins, on the other hand, are no more alike genetically than ordinary siblings. It is significant that the correlation between intelligence test scores of identical twins are consistently above .90, while for fraternal twins they characteristically run between .60 and .70. The typical correlation between intelligence test scores for ordinary siblings is .50.

Although the preceding correlations indicate the great importance of heredity in the determination of intelligence, it should be kept in mind that the environment of identical twins is more similar than the environment for siblings and probably even more similar than it is for fraternal twins, especially when the fraternal twins are not of the same sex. Evidently the greater likeness of fraternal twins in comparison with ordinary siblings is the result of environment.

An excellent method of studying the relative potency of heredity and environment with respect to intelligence is to examine the changes which take place in identical twins reared apart. One of the best of these studies was done by Newman, Freeman, and Holzinger.[3] The subjects for this study were nineteen pairs of identical twins who had been separated for a considerable period of time. The age at the time of separation ranged from two to six years and the age at the time of testing ranged from eleven to fifty-nine years. The greatest difference obtained in intelligence quotients was 24; the mean dif-

[3] H. H. Newman; F. N. Freeman; and K. J. Holzinger, *Twins: A Study of Heredity and Environment* (Chicago: University of Chicago Press, 1937).

ference for the nineteen pairs was 8.2. This is a somewhat larger difference than is found between identical twins living together and indicates a moderate effect of environment upon measured intelligence.

Effect of Changed Environment   There is considerable controversy over whether or not a radical change of environment will depress or increase the intelligence quotient of a child. The problem is difficult to solve because of the impossibility of controlling all the variables involved. To arrive at sound conclusions, it would be necessary to: (1) measure accurately the abilities of the individuals used in the experiment; (2) measure accurately the differences between the two environments being contrasted; and (3) measure accurately the impact of the particular environment upon the individual concerned, for environment must always be interpreted in terms of the person reacting to it.

Since in the studies made so far it has been impossible to meet these three requirements, it is not surprising that the conclusions reached are in disagreement. In general, however, the evidence indicates that a considerable change of environment produces only a very moderate change in measured intelligence.

Skodak and Skeels[4] studied a group of one hundred foster children for a period of thirteen years. These children were placed in foster homes for adoption before they were six months old. They were tested at ages two, four, seven, and thirteen. The true mothers of 63 of the children were given intelligence tests. Skodak and Skeels report an average intelligence quotient of 85.7 for this group and an average intelligence quotient for their children of 106 when these children were thirteen years of age. This represents a rather considerable difference which may be accounted for in part by the intelligence of the true fathers who were not tested. It is significant that the intelligence quotients of the children as measured by the 1937 Revision of the Stanford-Binet Intelligence Test when they were thirteen years of age correlated at .00 with the foster fathers' education and .02 with the foster mothers' education while the correlation with the true mothers' education was .32 and the cor-

[4] M. Skodak, and H. M. Skeels, "A Final Follow-up Study of One Hundred Adopted Children," *Journal of Genetic Psychology*, 75 (1949), pp. 85–125.

relation with the true mothers' intelligence quotient .44. It would appear from this study that although a favorable environment can improve measured intelligence to some extent, hereditary factors are more potent.

The preceding study and other similar ones indicate clearly that a child cannot exceed the intellectual potentialities which he has inherited. They also indicate that a good home environment begun early in life has a positive effect upon his intelligence, improving it moderately. It is significant that children reared in foster homes from infancy are closer to their own parents intellectually than they are to their foster parents, indicating that heredity is more potent than environment. The home and the school contribute a great deal to a child's intellectual development and emotional stability, but they do not make those who are mentally retarded average or those who are average superior.

Conclusion   Heredity and environment each contribute greatly to the physical and mental equipment of an individual and to his behavior. It is impossible at the present time to evaluate accurately the relative contribution of each. Obviously the two are interdependent. Heredity determines the capacities of an individual; environment determines the lines along which those capacities will be developed. Heredity provides the individual with his capital; environment determines how he will use that capital.

However much psychologists may disagree about the extent to which extreme changes in environment can affect one's intelligence quotient, or the exact extent to which heredity determines one's score on an intelligence test, there would be a consensus on the following points: (1) Definite limits to an individual's abilities have been set by his inherited nature; (2) environmental influences have some effect upon his physical development, a somewhat greater effect upon his mental development, and a very great effect upon his social and emotional development; (3) one's intelligence quotient remains *relatively* constant, the feebleminded remaining feebleminded, the average remaining average, and the gifted remaining gifted—with of course, occasional exceptions; (4) any changes in intelligence resulting from environmental conditions are most likely to result during infancy or early childhood; (5) there is considerable consistency in achievement insofar as academic work is concerned—those who do well in grade school are likely to do well in high school and later in college—allowing always for differences in degree of competition; and (6) every environment must be interpreted in terms of the individual reacting to it.

SUCCESS STRIVINGS

It is wholly necessary and normal for an individual to achieve—to control some segments, at least, of his environment. In fact, throughout his life he is in a constant struggle with his environment. The desire for achievement manifests itself in many ways, and the satisfaction of that desire is essential to the maintenance of sound mental health.

Since success is defined in terms of the goals which the individual has set for himself, it is important for every person to have an understanding of the nature and extent of his abilities and to adjust his goals accordingly.

The situation can be presented graphically as follows:

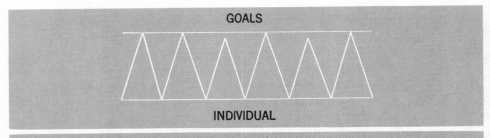

Figure 3. Success in attaining goals within reach of the individual

Here is an individual who has goals which are within reach and yet sufficiently high to provide a challenge. Much more often than not he achieves what he has worked for, and so has a feeling of confidence and well-being.

If his goals are far beyond his capacity to achieve, the following situation results:

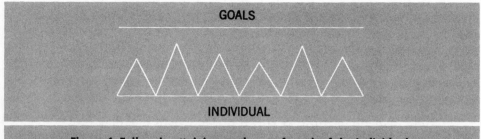

Figure 4. Failure in attaining goals out of reach of the individual

Here the individual reaches and falls back, reaches once more and falls back again. With each failure he loses a little more of his self-respect, a little more of the confidence which may once have been his.

Many examples could be given by an experienced college professor of what happens to college students when there are marked discrepancies between the abilities they possess and the goals they have set for themselves. A brief description of three rather typical cases drawn from the writer's files follow.

H.T. was a college junior who stood at the twentieth percentile for her class in intelligence. On the achievement test that she took as an entering freshman she rated as follows in terms of percentiles: English Mechanics, 47; Reading, 7; Mathematics, 12; Science, 8; Social Science, 30. Her ability to do scholastic work was obviously rather low. However, instead of being satisfied with C and D grades, H.T. worked hard for A's and B's, a level of achievement which was beyond her. She developed an attitude of inferiority. She became tense in class and was afraid to contribute to class discussions lest she make mistakes. Moreover she became very unsure of herself socially. In spite of the objective evidence she continued to refuse to believe that she was not capable of doing as well academically as the ablest students in her college.

D.H., a freshman, came to the Counseling Service in his college for assistance in resolving the tension that he experienced during examinations. This tension caused emotional blocks and made recall of information difficult and often impossible. Intellectually D.H. stood at the 41st percentile for his class, indicating that his intelligence was approximately average for college students. However, his ambitions were extremely high. He was convinced that he could become one of the country's great scientists. His father, a laborer who never went to high school, had urged his son repeatedly to improve the socioeconomic status of the family. D.H. tried so hard to achieve his and his father's goals that he did not do as well in college as he was actually capable of doing. His grades were predominantly D's. His poor scholastic work intensified his attitude of inferiority. He felt inadequate in a social group and believed that others disliked him. He resented this and frequently struck out verbally against his associates. He dressed meticulously and wondered why he felt it necessary to give so much attention to his appearance. It was, at least in part, a manifestation of his desire for attention and of his drive for perfectionism and also a substitute for his failure to achieve academically.

M.B., a freshman girl, was getting low grades, all D's and F's. She rated at the second percentile for her class intellectually. When she entered college she earned the following percentile ratings on a battery of standardized achievement tests: English Mechanics, 2; Reading, 4; Mathematics, 0; Science, 0; Social Science, 1. M.B. possessed not only ambition but also drive. She worked very hard studying far into the night. She was determined to make good in college, yet in spite of this conscientious effort, she eventually was dropped because of low scholastic standing. Her goals, although not extraordinarily high, were too high for her. She could not comprehend college course material.

In addition to knowing and accepting one's intellectual level it is often helpful in setting goals and in deciding on a vocation to obtain objective information from aptitude tests and interest inventories. College students frequently select a major for which they have little aptitude. For example, a young man may have decided to enter the medical profession because of family pressure, or because of the prestige of the M.D. degree. If his mentality is relatively low or if his scientific aptitude is slight, his misplaced ambition is frustrated. Another student with considerable aptitude in the linguistic field but with little mechanical aptitude may for various reasons decide to study to become an electrical engineer. He, too, may be frustrated and tense and perhaps does not know why. Assuming that there are no other important causes for the emotional difficulty, the solution for such individuals lies in goal reorientation; that is, in the selection of objectives which are in line with aptitudes and interests.

Usually a person's aptitudes and interests are similar, for we tend strongly to like to do the things that we can do well. Therein lies the principal value of vocational interest tests. There are a few individuals, however, who develop a strong interest in the fields for which they have little aptitude; they scorn concentration on work that is easy for them. In some cases this represents negativism; in others, it is the result of having been taught that the only worthwhile successes are those which one must struggle to achieve.

The number of special aptitude tests which are available is very large. In fact they cover almost every field, such as music, art, mechanics, medicine, law, nursing, etc. An aptitude test does not give a final answer to the question "What vocation should I enter?", but it does provide the person taking it with valuable information about himself.

The purpose of vocational interest inventories is not to measure interests in the several vocations directly but to compare the examinee's interests with those of the persons from the various occupational groups upon whom the test was standardized. For example, if an individual shows by his responses to the test items that his interests are similar to those which are characteristic of lawyers then it is assumed that at least insofar as interest is concerned the person should go into law. Interest inventories do not measure aptitude directly. Neither do they measure intelligence. They merely bring into focus the pattern of interests which the individual possesses.

The normal person accepts his limitations and functions within the framework provided him by nature and by training. The neurotic individual struggles against them. Feeling insecure, he may develop an abnormally strong desire for achievement as compensation for that feeling of insecurity. He tries to convince himself that he can become the master of any situation. His goals are superlatively high. Virginia Woolf has presented the emotional strain in an abnormal craving for success in the following passage:

> It was a splendid mind. For if thought is like the keyboard of a piano, divided into so many notes, or like the alphabet is ranged in twenty-six letters all in order, then his splendid mind had no sort of difficulty in running over those letters one by one, firmly and accu-

rately, until it had reached, say, the letter Q. He reached Q. Very few people in the whole of England ever reach Q. . . . But after Q? What comes next: After Q there are a number of letters the last of which is scarcely visible to mortal eyes, but glimmers red in the distance. Z is only reached once by one man in a generation. Still, if he could reach R it would be something. Here at least was Q. He dug his heels in at Q. Q he was sure of. Q he could demonstrate. If Q then is Q—R—Here he knocked his pipe out, with two or three resonant taps on the handle of the urn and proceeded. "Then R. . . ." He braced himself. He clenched himself.

Qualities that would have saved a ship's company exposed on a broiling sea with six biscuits and a flask of water—endurance and justice, foresight, devotion, skill, came to his help. R is then—what is R?

A shutter, like the leathern eyelid of a lizard, flickered over the intensity of his gaze and obscured the letter R. In that flash of darkness he heard people saying—he was a failure—that R was beyond him. He would never reach R. On to R, once more. R—

Qualities that in a desolate expedition across the icy solitudes of the Polar region would have made him the leader, the guide, the counsellor, whose temper, neither sanguine nor despondent, surveys with equanimity what is to be and faces it, came to his help again. R—

The lizard's eye flickered once more. The veins on his forehead bulged. The geranium in the urn became startlingly visible and, displayed among its leaves, he could see, without wishing it, that old, that obvious distinction between the two classes of men; on the one hand the steady goers of superhuman strength who, plodding and persevering, repeat the whole alphabet in order, twenty-six letters in all, from start to finish; on the other the gifted, the inspired who, miraculously, lump all the letters together in one flash—the way of genius. He had not genius; he laid no claim to that, but he had, or might have had, the power to repeat every letter of the alphabet from A to Z accurately in order. Meanwhile, he stuck at Q.[5]

It is clear that both cognitive and affective factors are involved in a person's level of aspiration. A person must have some comprehension of the difficulty of the task before him and of the relationship which exists between the difficulty of that task and his own abilities.

5 V. Woolf, *To the Lighthouse* (New York: Harcourt, Brace & World, Inc., 1927), pp. 53–55.

However, there is always some emotional involvement in this evalua-tion. The individual's expectations are raised or lowered by his hopes and fears. If the emotional involvement is great, there may be a lack of realism in the goals set.

When emotional learning and cognitive learning are not inte-grated, the individual's cognitive functions are impaired to some extent by his emotional functions. When this condition exists in an extreme form there is a consistent and significant difference between expectations and actual achievements. One of the purposes of psycho-therapy is to restore the necessary integration through insight. If adequate insights are achieved, intellectual and emotional acceptance of the situation results. In other words, the two are brought together at a realistic level.

SUMMARY

Human beings, like all other living organisms, live in an environ-ment which both sustains and threatens them. They must succeed in controlling certain aspects of that environment if they are to survive. The strength of the drive for mastery varies with individuals and with the culture in which he lives. His success depends to a considerable extent upon the abilities which he possesses. In this chapter differences in intelligence have been emphasized. Intel-ligence differences range all the way from the seriously retarded person whose intelligence quotient is close to zero to the genius who has an intelligence quotient of around 200. When obtained from a large unselected group, intelligence quotients are distributed over the normal probability surface so that the majority cluster around the average intelligence quotient of 100. This is a very significant fact, especially in a democracy, since average persons by sheer weight of numbers not only decide who will be elected to public office but also determine to a considerable extent the intellectual level of all aspects of the national life. Individual differences in intelligence result from a combination of heredity and environment. Each person inherits certain potentialities; these potentialities are in turn affected by the environment in which the individual lives from conception to death.

The need for achievement must be satisfied frequently. If the tension produced by it is to be reduced and mental health maintained, it follows that in order to obtain rewarding satisfactions a person's immediate and distant goals should be in line with the abilities which he possesses. He should have a thorough understanding of his assets and liabilities, capitalizing on the former and accepting the latter. If his level of aspiration is too low, he retards the process of self-actualization; if it is too high, he experiences more frustrations than he can tolerate.

THE NEED
FOR
STATUS

chapter 5

There is general agreement concerning the existence of the need for status, as noted in the classifications presented in Chapter Two. It is not always placed in a separate category. Certainly, it is closely related to the need for achievement and to the need for emotional security. However, for the purposes of a practical presentation of mental hygiene, it is desirable to list it as a separate need, keeping in mind always that no need actually stands by itself.

Since human beings are gregarious, human interrelationships assume considerable importance in the motivation of behavior. In order to maintain self-respect, a person must have the respect of others. When he behaves in such a way that approval results, he experiences a pleasant emotional state; when he behaves in such a way that he loses status, an unpleasant emotional state results. Desiring the pleasant emotional state, he becomes more and more conscious of what approval means to him. After a time, the need is learned and stays with him throughout his life. Insofar as he can, he plays the part that will bring acceptance and applause. He does so because he needs to "belong" and because his approved behavior enhances his feeling of personal worth.

CONFORMITY TO CULTURE PATTERNS

Since human beings live interdependently, each person is expected to behave in a manner acceptable to the culture patterns of his society. These patterns of behavior to which he must adjust are customarily classified into four categories: folkways, customs, mores, and taboos.

Folkways are the "correct" ways of behaving. Although they are subject to change, they sometimes continue for a considerable period of time. Though not vital, they usually assume great importance in the life of an individual, extending into all phases of his social life. Folkways vary from group to group, from community to community, and, of course, considerably from nation to nation. Although relatively insignificant in themselves, they are frequent causes of great mental distress. Few individuals can tolerate ostracism, yet some degree of ostracism will usually be imposed upon an individual who deviates considerably from his social group.

Customs are the *only* approved ways of doing things. They constitute a manner of thought and a way of life that has persisted in the social group for so long a time that any change in them seems unthinkable. Consequently, they are rarely questioned. It is customary to celebrate Christmas, and nearly every Christian conforms. Moreover, the day of celebration must be December 25. Customs are changed slowly, and always against considerable opposition. Many of the world's greatest thinkers have been put to death for challenging beliefs that had become customs.

The mores of a social order have even stronger emotional connotations than the customs of that order. The mores constitute a list of what an individual must do and what he must not do; of what is unquestionably right and what is unquestionably wrong. Although mores vary widely from culture to culture, they represent inflexible rules within a single culture.

In our society a child is taught from infancy what he must do and what he must not do. These teachings constitute the framework of his conscience, or, in Freudian terms, his superego. It is desirable, even necessary, for him to behave within that framework. However, if his concepts of right and wrong are too rigid and too logical, he will also find himself in conflict with his society. Even though he has been taught that he must not kill, he is expected to learn that in time of war it is his duty to kill. If he persists in the belief that was taught him in childhood he will be a pacifist, and his fellow-citizens may ostracize him for his consistency. A child is taught to tell the truth, but early in life he must learn to distinguish between "black" lies and "white" lies. He must learn that telling the truth is subject to infinite variations.

Taboos are basically the same as mores, although more specific and always negative. In our everyday life, we are constantly conforming to taboos, usually without giving thought to their desirability. A large number of taboos involve sex, urination, and defecation.

Group Code

Folkways, customs, mores, and taboos constitute an overlapping classification. They might well be grouped together under a single heading called a *group code*. Any individual within a certain group is expected to conform to the code by which that group lives. If he does not conform, he is subjected to ridicule, ostracism, or perhaps even to extreme punishment. Fortunately for them, the great majority of persons conform to their group code rather easily. Others, however, because of marked deviation from their group in intelligence, physique, interests, and so on, find it difficult to conform.

Adjustments to a Sequence of Group Codes   Every individual is to a considerable extent a product of the several groups of which he has been a member. Each has added to or subtracted from the frame of reference by which he lives. Because of the remarkable adaptability of human beings, most are able to weave into an integrated pattern the characteristics of the various group codes with which they have come into contact. A few, however, experience serious conflicts in trying to resolve antithetical aspects of the codes to which they are expected to conform. As an example, it will be helpful to note some of the major adjustments in behavior which one boy may have to make as he grows up.

In infancy he is expected to be cute. He is encouraged to show off. He becomes accustomed to having his demands met and to being the center of attention, especially if he is the first child in the family. When he is four a baby sister arrives. Now he must learn a number of difficult adjustments. He must, at this early age, discard a great deal of what has been taught him. Instead of being the center of attention, his place in the family becomes secondary. Instead of being encouraged to talk, he may now be told that children should be seen and not heard. When he asks for attention, he is likely to be urged to run along and play.

In another two years he is six. He now enters school, where a whole new code of behavior must be learned. His parents have taught him that he must always be truthful, but he finds that in the school group it is not always desirable to tell the truth about one's playmates. He has been taught by his parents to be generous, yet he encounters much selfishness among his classmates. He has been taught by his parents that he must keep clean and dress neatly, and yet he finds that most of the little boys in his group scorn both.

For some children, the first few weeks in school are almost a traumatic experience. They have to learn how to adjust to ridicule, if they are too large or too small, too bright or too dull, too aggressive or too shy. They have to acquire the very difficult trick of conforming both to the code of their parents and to the code of their playmates.

In three or four more years, the boy becomes a member of a gang, and the gang has its own code. The boy now learns that it is his duty to lie to protect the gang; that it is smart to steal from some people if you can get away with it; that deceiving the teacher is proof of cleverness; that destroying school property is all right if it is done in a certain way and at a certain time; and that one must fight to prove that he is not "yellow." To which code will the boy be loyal—to his parents' or to the gang's? How can he synthesize the two?

In a little while he reaches adolescence, and a whole new set of demands are made upon him. Where formerly he was expected to despise girls, he is now expected to like them. He must master the small talk of adolescence. He must learn all the ways in which a young man should behave toward a girl.

During this period he is living at home. His parents are urging one behavior pattern upon him, while his high-school crowd is expecting a somewhat different behavior pattern. His parents are urging him to earn high grades; if he does, he will lose status with his peers. His parents set one standard of behavior with respect to his relations with girls; his crowd sets quite another. Through it all, his parents remind him at one time that he is now grown up, and at another, treat him as though he were still a child. Is it any wonder that a great many behavior disorders develop from the conflicts of adolescence?

Eventually the boy goes on to college, where a new group code awaits him. During his freshman year he has several things to learn concerning social and moral behavior. Many aspects of the code of the new group of which he has become a member are in opposition to, or at least variations upon, the codes which he has previously learned. If he is flexible, he adjusts quickly. If he is rigid, he finds adjustment difficult. If the influence of his parents is still great, and if their standards of conduct are sharply at variance with those which he finds on the college campus, he will have many problems to resolve.

After finishing college, he assumes the responsibilities of adult life and identifies himself with groups which possess somewhat different codes than those to which he has become accustomed. If he becomes a doctor, he must assume the professional mannerisms of medical practitioners; otherwise, he will not win the confidence of his patients. If he becomes a college professor, he not only must conform to the moral and intellectual standards of his group, but must adopt their folkways, if he is to be accepted as one of them. If he goes into business, he must adjust to the mores of the men of the market place.

He will find that many things are expected of him as a husband and as a father. The community in which he lives will have standards to which a good citizen must conform. He must live in a house not too different from the other houses in his locality. He must furnish that house according to the customs of the time. He must have an automobile, and that automobile must be of a certain make—a symbol of his social and economic status in the community. He must dress as his associates dress. He must talk on topics that are acceptable to his group. He must avoid topics which are taboo.

Even when he dies, he must conform, or his family must conform for him. There must be a period of waiting for burial, preferably three days. There must be a religious service over his remains, and a tombstone must be erected over his grave. From birth to death and beyond, he is expected to conform to the demands of his culture. His society demands it, his need for status requires it.

ROLE-TAKING

The preceding discussion of the adjustments which must be made to a series of group codes as the individual lives through his life span demonstrates the importance of role-taking. As Shakespeare wrote:

> All the world's a stage,
> And all the men and women merely players:
> They have their exits and their entrances;
> And one man in his time plays many parts. . . .

One does not take a part in a play or in life without previously "learning his lines." Occasionally in a play and frequently in life he has to *ad lib,* but the seemingly impromptu remarks and behavior are offshoots of what has been learned in infancy and childhood. The nature of this learning process was discussed in some detail in Chapter Two.

The several statuses which the child must maintain are determined by his biological and social inheritance. If, for example, he is born a boy, he is expected in most instances to learn to play a boy's role. This statement is qualified by the phrase "in most instances" because occasionally a boy is expected to play a girl's role or a girl, a boy's role. This is frequently a cause of later homosexual behavior. During the early years the parents are powerful conditioning agents. The young child, needing status in their eyes, learns the behavior patterns that will bring it about. At first the learning process is largely one of conditioning, but as the child grows older, language becomes an important element in his role-taking and eventually he is able to solve many of his adjustment problems with respect to roles through the use of verbal symbols.

Cross-sectional View of Roles

It is clear that one plays many roles not only throughout his life but also in the course of a single day. Because of his considerable flexibility he is able to shift with surprising ease, even to change back and forth between seemingly contradictory roles. He can "praise the Lord and pass the ammunition" at the same time. The distraught and irritable wife and mother may, when guests arrive, become within the space of two or three minutes the poised and gracious hostess. The father may be the cold and ruthless dictator in his office at four o'clock and the kindly, affectionate parent at four-thirty. The college student changes his role many times in the course of a week. He behaves in one way when he is in class, in another when he is having a conference with his instructor, in another when he is on the football field, in another when he is in the dormitory, in another when he is out on a date, and in another when he is home for the weekend.

The fact that persons play so many diverse roles so successfully is at least part of the basis for the point of view of many sociologists that the individual is made up of a number of selves. Sorokin states the thesis as follows:

> . . . the individual has not one empirical soul, or self, or ego, but several: first, biological, and second, social egos. The individual has as many different social egos as there are different social groups and strata with which he is connected. These egos are as different from one another as the social groups and strata from which they spring. If some of these groups are antagonistic to each other, then the respective egos that represent these groups in the individual will also be antagonistic.[1]

In the preceding statement Sorokin overemphasizes the importance of the social group. He overlooks the fact that every person brings his total personality to each new group and that his variations in behavior as he goes from group to group are limited by his unique experiential background. Although a person's behavior is determined to a considerable extent by the nature of the group of which he is for a time a part, it is not determined entirely by that group. It should never be forgotten that all groups are made up of individuals. Human beings are flexible, but not completely flexible. There is a relatively fixed personality core which makes complete absorption by any one group impossible.

Conflicts between Roles   Since a person is expected to play so many varied roles, it is not surprising that the contradictory re-

---

[1] P. A. Sorokin, *Society, Culture, and Personality: Their Structure and Dynamics* (New York: Harper & Row, Publishers, 1947), p. 345.

quirements of these roles frequently result in conflict. There is some disagreement concerning the basic source of these conflicts. Is it to be found in contradictory social groups or is it to be found within the individual himself? Sociologists stress the former. For example, Sorokin writes:

> If the groups of an individual are in conflict; if they urge him to contradictory actions, duties, thoughts, convictions; if, for instance, the state demands what is disapproved by the church or the family, then the respective egos will be mutually antagonistic. The individual will be a house divided against himself, split by the inner conflicts. There will be no peace of mind, no unclouded conscience, no real happiness, no consistency in such an individual.[2]

Antithetical group requirements are, of course, important causes of adjustment difficulties. The real conflicts, however, lie not between the groups themselves but within the individual members of those groups. Each person brings to the group a self which he has acquired through learning, and the problem for that person is to synthesize what he has learned with what is expected of him by the group. If these two are sufficiently diverse, he may have considerable difficulty in bringing them together. His need for status impels him to conform, but at the same time what he has learned in the past may impel him with approximately equal force to reject. This is a conflict situation and can result in disorganization of behavior.

Longitudinal View of Roles

As has been previously noted, the roles that a person learns to play are determined to a considerable extent by such factors as his age, his sex, his intellectual capacity, and the socioeconomic status of his family. The mere awareness of growing older presents him with the necessity of successively identifying himself with new social groups and of learning his part in the activities of those groups. He has a role to get into a higher role as he matures. This role to get into a higher role, especially when the shift is made from a low socioeconomic level, frequently results in what might be called "role lag." The inability to play the desired new part successfully is, of course, frustrating and may cause the individual to withdraw into

2 *Ibid.,* p. 351.

fantasy where he can be whatever he wants to be, unhindered by reality.

Growing Older   There are a number of crisis situations in role-taking as the individual develops from infancy to childhood, from childhood to adulthood, and from adulthood to old age. Three or four of these will be mentioned as examples. The change from family life to school life at the age of five or six requires considerable new learning on the part of the child. He must now function as a member of the classroom group and as a member of the group on the playground. In clinical work it is found that many adjustment problems become serious at this point. Entering college is another important step in the lives of many individuals. College is a new and, in many respects, a different kind of world. It requires a number of adjustments on the part of the freshman. The role to be played in dormitory life is in itself a difficult one to master. The student who has not achieved flexibility in his earlier years experiences difficulty in his interpersonal relationships in college. The second most crucial period in the life of a college student is likely to be the second semester of his senior year, for at that time he faces the necessity of dropping the role of college student and of taking on the responsibilities of a wage-earner and a citizen. In later years, after a long period of productive activity, he retires from his business or his profession to play the very difficult role which is the lot of aged men and women. Although the strain resulting from playing these several successive roles is considerable, the majority of persons carry on more or less successfully to the end.

Hierarchy of Roles   Our society is a hierarchical structure. Hierarchies are present in all our institutions. A business concern has its president, its vice-president, and its lower-ranking officials. A university has its president, its deans, its professors, associate professors, assistant professors, instructors, and assistants. The Army has its commander-in-chief, its chief of staff, its generals, colonels, majors, and so on down to privates. Even the small American village has a social hierarchy. Such a system promotes competition for status. The ladder is there for all to climb. The top rung is short and has space for only a few; the bottom rung is long and accomodates many.

The desire to achieve prestige, status, or power is normal in our society when it is based on strength; that is, when the individual not only has the drive to achieve a higher status level but also has the ability to do so. Persons such as these were the ones who built the capitalistic system in the United States. The competition was ruthless at times but the results were astounding and on the whole constructive. Now that American society is becoming more and more socialistic there is less opportunity to achieve status through individual strength and productivity. However, the need is still present but since it rests on weakness and personal insignificance it is more likely to be satisfied in neurotic ways. The emphasis is placed on status symbols rather than on the actual achievement of status. An example of this is the young physician who said that the only reason why he went to medical school was so he could have M.D. after his name on his tombstone. He had very little interest in succeeding as a doctor and eventually committed suicide.

Status symbols have been used by human beings for a long, long time in all areas of life. Thousands could be listed from the past and from the present. Here are a few: the feathers in the headdress of an Indian chief; the crown worn by a king or queen; the academic robes of college professors; the priestly garb of the clergy; the beards and long hair of the beatniks; even the eccentric behavior of would-be writers and artists who do not have the ability to achieve but are trying to behave as though they had. The automobile one drives, the hotel one stays in, the restaurant one goes to, the clubs one belongs to, the house one lives in, the clothes one wears, the college one goes to, the city or state one lives in are all status symbols. It should not be concluded that the symbols are undesirable. They enrich the phenomenal field and frequently become a part of the phenomenal self. If they have been earned they represent rewards for actual achievements; if they have not been earned but are pretensions or if they become goals in themselves unrelated to ability and mastery they give little actual satisfaction to the individual. The feeling of weakness and insignificance may be temporarily assuaged, but in the long run it is intensified. The search for status when carried to extremes as a defense against helplessness and humiliation often results in a domineering attitude toward others.

Role Lag   Role lag is the individual's counterpart of society's cultural lag. When an old role cannot be completely abandoned and thus make way for a new role which is more appropriate for the present life situation, conflict results. It is doubtful if an old role can ever be fully abandoned; some residua remain. The lag becomes a source of serious conflict only when the residua are still such a potent part of the phenomenal self that they interfere to a marked extent with the acceptance of the new role.

Perhaps the best way to point up the significance of role lag and the conflicts that result from it is to present the material from an actual case. F.B. was a brilliant, sensitive college sophomore with sincere intellectual interests and with considerable artistic ability. As a boy he lived in the poorest section of a small city. His father, a very neurotic man, worked in a factory. The boy learned at a very early age to be ashamed of his superior mentality. A boy from such a home and such an environment was not supposed to be bright. Consequently he rejected intellectual achievement in order that he might comform to the role expected of him by his family, by his teachers, and especially by his peers. He took great pride in his ability to fight and became the best fighter in his gang. He was contemptuous of the boys who had good homes, good clothes, good manners, and good minds. He gained a great deal of satisfaction from being a problem to his teachers. He played his role well, and it brought him status with his peers.

World War II came along, and F.B. spent three years in the Army. Then, as a veteran, it was possible for him to go to college. Characteristics which now became desirable were the very ones he had rejected as a boy. It was important that he be, to some extent at least, intellectual. It was important for him to be at ease with men and women who were the prototypes of the boys and girls with good minds and good manners whom he had formerly scorned. He wanted to play this new part, but all of the old attitudes and patterns of behavior revolted against it. The conflicts kept him in a turmoil of confusion: "I want to get good grades; I won't." "I admire and respect my instructors; I despise them." "I wish I could be at ease with members of the faculty and with students; I don't want to have anything to do with them." "I wish I could talk freely with my intellectual equals; I wish I could be back with the gang and talking their language again." "I want to go ahead; I want to go back." "I know I have the ability to succeed; I am sure I am going to be a failure." "I feel terribly inferior; I was the best fighter in my school." "I wish I could live on campus; I can't bring myself to break away from home." "I can write better poetry than anybody else on this campus; everything I try to write is drivel." "Someday I should like to teach English in college; I should have been a boxer."

It took a long time for F.B. to establish himself in his new role. The attitudes which he once rejected had to be accepted, and the attitudes that he once accepted almost without question had to be modified or rejected. Integration and real satisfaction came only when he saw himself as an acceptable and contributing member of the very group which was once the antithesis of all that he stood for.

Role-Taking in Fantasy   Since human beings have the ability to make use of language, they can transcend the present in their role-taking. In fantasy they can change the past to some extent and shape the future to a considerable extent. They can pretend for a time that things are not what they seem to be. Used in moderation, fantasy is a desirable form of temporary escape.

Although role-taking in fantasy is a normal aspect of behavior, there are a few persons who use it to excess. The temptation is great to escape through verbal flights of fancy into a dream world where one can be everything that he wants to be, unfettered by the realities of his actual life situation. Our mental hospitals have many patients who found life so difficult and fantasy so satisfying that they turned to the latter as a permanent means of escape.

When a person cannot play a desired role in real life, it is not surprising that he should seek to play a comparable role in fantasy. The writer has selected from his files the case notes on and recorded interviews with a college man who had found reality so difficult that he spent several hours each day in an imaginary world. This young man has a brilliant mind, but his mental processes are blocked by anxieties which have been building up since early childhood. He feels very inferior, has deep feelings of guilt concerning his sex practices and desires, and is convinced that he is not acceptable to any social group. He is extremely ambitious but finds it impossible because of emotional tension to satisfy his ambitions either in the classroom or in social situations. He has tried hard to play his part in real life situations, but he is convinced that he has always failed. At the time he came to the author for help, he was giving so much time to role-taking in fantasy that he was concerned lest he leave the real world behind altogether. He was not psychotic, but there was danger of his becoming so. The following excerpt from one of the recorded interviews shows the appeal that the world of fantasy had for him.

*P.   Would you like to tell me a little about your ideal world?

*C.   Well, there is my conception—an absolute conception—of reality. In it success is merely a matter of knowing how to do something. It is not a struggle with chaotic matter that falls to pieces. It has more or less of an independent existence. It has meaning without the constant attention of the individual to make the thing stay together. It seems to me that everything in the world falls apart as we try to struggle for truth. . . . That seems to me to be about the essence of the conflict of my ideal world with the outer world. This ideal world is perfect in itself. It's just a matter of conforming with it and knowing how to get along with it,—not a matter of brute effort to force it to have some meaning. It is perfect and cannot be altered.

P.   If I have followed you correctly, the real world is a confusing world.

C.   That is as I find it.

P.   Yes.

C.   This other world, the abstract, the intellectual—I don't know what you'd call it. It's beyond my experience, but it is absolute and has significance. It has permanence to it. It is permanent. It is something you can depend upon. I have really experienced it only once or twice. . . . If there is such a world it is independent of me. It is not dependent on me to try to save it. It has already saved itself. It is something I can depend on and not something that is dependent on me.

P.   And you would like very much to believe that there is such a world.

C.   Yes.

P.   And you're striving to understand it and to identify yourself with it because that would make you feel safer.

C.   Yes. It would give me a sense of security.

P.   And that's the world that you escape into in your daydreams.

C.   That's the most satisfactory form of escape. (*Pause.*) I don't know whether you would call it escape or not. I call it reality so it couldn't be escape, could it?

P.   It is reality to you, then. That world is reality and what people ordi-

* P—Psychologist; C—Client.

narily call reality and what people ordinarily call the real world is unreality.

C.   Yeah. That's about it. I think it's logical. The thing is to forget about the unreal world, the world of the senses, then perhaps I could make a complete transference into the world of ideas which has purpose to it and get away from the shifting, unstable world.

The preceding dialogue points up the confusion of the person who is struggling to find his place and is not quite sure whether he wants it to be in the real world or in the world of fantasy. It should be noted that this young man is not quite certain as to which is the real world, he has lived in fantasy so much. In later interviews, he decided to accept the world of the senses and to forgo the world of ideas in which, as he said, there were no human beings as such. He could, however, very easily have taken a permanent role in his ideal world of fantasy and so have lost contact with reality.

MATERIAL FROM CASE STUDIES

A psychological theory or principle becomes most meaningful when it is brought down to actual cases. The individuals whose problems are discussed in the following pages were students whose principal difficulty, at least insofar as immediate causes are concerned, was the frustration of the need for status. It cannot be emphasized too often that there are always a number of causes of a behavior disorder. However, a clinical psychologist or psychiatrist will discover, in working with the patient, a few salient factors which rise above the others in importance. He will usually also find a dominant master cause which, if eliminated, will bring about a considerable reduction of tension. In each of the following cases there is an intensified need for status, the intensification resulting from the need's being unsatisfied for many varied reasons.

Religious Status

N.H. was a college freshman. She was a brilliant girl, rating in the top 10 per cent of her class intellectually. Her parents were fanatically religious, and her pastor very orthodox. In grade school and high school, N.H. had accepted the strict religion of her home without question. When she entered college, however, she became disturbed by some of the facts that she was learning in biology and sociology, and she was deeply troubled by the religious liberalism of her classmates.

When N.H. came to the writer for help, she was very tense. She explained that she still believed in the religion her parents had taught her, but that she needed friends and nobody seemed to want her company. Questioning revealed that she possessed a certain amount of missionary zeal and had been trying to convert some of the other students. Moreover, she sincerely believed in the taboos which she had been taught and which had become an important part of her frame of reference. This caused her to be concerned about the behavior of the other girls in her dormitory. Life to her was a very serious business, and her conviction was that it should be lived according to inflexible standards, largely made up of thou-shalt-nots.

Social Status of College

A freshman in a state university, J.T. was dissatisfied with his college. He longed to transfer to some private institution which would meet his intellectual and social standards. He had difficulty in making this transfer, however, because of his low grades. In intelligence he was at the sixtieth percentile of his class, but could not achieve to capacity because of ever-present tension.

J.T. came from a wealthy family. He had learned to overrate the importance of social success. Although he was proud of his family, he felt very insignificant and inferior. This was the result, in part, of long association with a domineering mother and a socially gifted older brother. J.T. had no interest whatsoever in girls. This was one reason why he wished to escape from a coeducational institution into a men's college. His smile, his walk, and the movements of his hands were all distinctly feminine. His interests, too, were feminine in nature. He was dimly conscious of homosexual urges, and this added to his feeling of inferiority.

On the Bernreuter Personality Inventory, J.T. rated at the ninety-ninth percentile in neurotic tendency, at zero percentile in self-confidence, at the ninety-eighth percentile in introversion, at the fourth percentile in submission, and at the ninety-ninth percentile in self-consciousness. The lack of self-confidence and the self-consciousness had played an important part in his social failures, and with each failure these had increased, as had the emotional strain under which he worked. His desire to transfer to a well-known men's college was motivated by the feeling that being a student in such an institution would provide him with a feeling of status which he knew he needed. He felt that by identifying himself with such an institution, his self-confidence would be restored.

Every individual is affected to some extent by the church, club, school, college, community, state, or nation of which he is a member. If, for example, the college in which he is enrolled thinks well of itself, regardless of the reason, then his own ego is bolstered by his association with it. On the other hand, if his college has developed an attitude of social or academic inferiority, then he, as a student, is likely to be affected by that attitude. This would be especially true if he himself felt somewhat inadequate. It takes a confident personality to rise above a home of poverty, a poor community, or a school of low standing. On the other hand, a weak individual is often carried along by a good family, a superior community, and a college with great traditions.

Superior Intelligence

Every group requires conformity of its members. Deviates of all kinds are faced with more difficult problems of adjustment than are average persons. Intellectual deviates are no exception to this rule.

J.F. was a brilliant college freshman standing in the top one per cent of his class. He had developed marked self-consciousness and a strong feeling of inferiority because he had known for years that he was different from the typical boy. He needed recognition, yet he had little desire to succeed along intellectual lines because in school he had been ridiculed for his superior mentality. He had great gifts which he was afraid to use. He could not achieve the status which he craved through the medium of athletics because he was not well enough equipped physically to excel in competitive games. He could not achieve it socially, for he was too self-conscious. Intellectual achievement had brought him nothing but misery.

J.F., in the course of a series of interviews, decided that it would help him if he tried to describe himself and the causes which had led up to his present tension, in writing. A few very revealing paragraphs from his statement follow:

> He thought differently than the rest. Perhaps it was a difference in IQ. Other students noticed the difference. He was taunted by the nick-

name "Professor." The immediate reaction was, of course, to pretend indifference. He found himself awkward in sports, and not so skilled as the other fellows. Being sensitive, he didn't want to display his inability, so he pretended not to care. He was interested in music. To many this was an unmasculine interest.

As young fellows became aware of the opposite sex, so did he. He found none who were interested in him. He never enjoyed himself with girls, because they weren't interested in him. With most fellows, he was tolerated; a few enjoyed him. He didn't seem to respond or act as they did. He was funny, wise-cracking, clowning, but there was something. . . .

Indeed there was! To this young fellow who thought a lot, life wasn't a very pretty thing. Why? For the reasons already listed. He wasn't a pal of the students, they called him or considered him "Professor"—and it hurt. It may even have established a subconscious reaction against success in studying hard, because he received derision instead of praise or prestige. He wasn't as natural in sports as the other fellows, so he thought he was inferior—and it hurt. He saw many other fellows with girls; he wasn't at ease with them, nor they with him, so he thought that he was one that girls wouldn't like—and that hurt. Fellows weren't eager over his company—so he was hurt again.

What is the result when a fellow experiences all this? He builds up a bad set of attitudes in which he knows he is inferior; he doesn't want to be, but can't seem to get away from it. And it tortured him day and night; it befogged his thinking, hampered everything he tried to do. He put up an amazing front intended to convince the world that he was happy. To some people he was a little queer, to others he was foolish. Some noticed that he was moody. A great camouflage! Underneath was a very unhappy, restive fellow.

Leadership

One becomes a leader of a group only when there is a close balance and interrelationship among the potential leader's characteristics, the group's characteristics, and the field in which the leadership is to be exercised. For example, a man running for Congress probably should not be too far above the crowd in intellect. Very superior mental capacity would be a handicap for him unless he had learned to use the language of the masses. On the other hand, to be a leader in a profession a man would necessarily have to be an intellectually gifted individual.

Adler maintains that the world's great men owe their eminent position to some psychic or somatic infirmity. According to this point of view, the strong drive for status which most leaders possess is a form of compensation for their defects. It is adjustment by aggression, but by a kind of aggression which is acceptable to their contemporaries, or at least to posterity. Through the success that they achieve as leaders their early feeling of inferiority is checked, or perhaps greatly reduced. It may even be lost altogether; motivation in later years is provided by the satisfactions which come from the consciousness of being a person of prestige.

On a college campus, personal frustrations are frequently the source of the need for leadership. These, however, are not usually of a very serious nature, for a really neurotic individual rarely possesses the poise essential to command the respect of others. The writer has held a number of counseling interviews with campus leaders. In every instance, a mild feeling of inadequacy was observed to exist behind the mask of poise and self-confidence. Each leader discussed his feeling of inadequacy very frankly, pointing out that he depended heavily upon the admiration of others in his struggle to maintain his ego.

F.C. was such a person. She was the outstanding social leader in her university. Her father, a very successful professional man, died when she was in grade school. His death resulted in a marked lowering of the economic status of her family. F.C., a proud and sensitive girl, found it difficult to accept the altered conditions. She adjusted by determining that she would be socially successful in spite of the handicaps under which she must work. She possessed many of the qualities of leadership, including a dominant personality. The prestige which she achieved as a leader almost completely eliminated the old attitude of inferiority, but she now stood in fear of the possibility of losing the satisfactions which come from leadership and which were at present the principal support of her ego.

SUMMARY

The need for status is closely related to the need for achievement and the need for emotional security. In order to satisfy this need it is necessary both to conform and to be individualistic. The pressure to conform comes from the several groups with which an individual is identified; the pressure to be individualistic comes from the person's drive for self-actualization. This situation is the source for much tension and many conflicts which persist in varying degrees from infancy until death. Fortunately the majority of persons are able to solve the problem at least partially by striking a balance between the two.

Most persons are sufficiently flexible to be able to play several roles and to maintain status in varying degrees in many groups. In the course of a week or even of a single day they shift their behavior to fit the varied situations at home, at work, and at play. Even though these changes in behavior are frequently considerable the core of the self structure of each individual remains relatively stable. However, when the longitudinal view of roles is taken changes will be observed not only in superficial behavior but also in basic personality characteristics. The latter are usually gradual. If the new roles which persons are expected to assume as they grow older are too threatening there may be a role lag, a desire or even a refusal to move on to the next stage or, if status is not being achieved in the world of reality, to achieve it in fantasy.

THE NEED
FOR
PHYSICAL
SECURITY

chapter *6*

The basic physical need is to maintain internal equilibrium. This need of an organism to maintain a constant state of functional balance among the different but interdependent elements and subsystems of the organism is called *homeostasis*. When, for any reason, the physiological processes are disturbed so that there is a state of imbalance, a physical need is said to exist. If this need is not satisfied, then the functioning of the organism is impaired. It is for this reason that we can speak of the need for physical security. Failure of the homeostatic processes is a threat to the organism.

The term homeostasis was first advanced by Walter B. Cannon in 1932. He stated that while the term *equilibria* could be applied to the constant conditions maintained within the body, the term homeostasis is probably better, since equilibria has come to possess a rather definite meaning in physics and chemistry. The term equilibria refers to relatively simple physicochemical states, while the term homeostasis refers to complex biological functions.

Human beings because of their highly complex homeostatic mechanisms are able to indulge in many activities apart from the direct struggle for survival. In this, they and all other mammals are much more fortunate than amphibians and reptiles. These latter, having simpler homeostatic processes than the mammal, are not nearly so independent of changes in the external environment. Since the amphibian cannot conserve his water content, he must remain in, or not stray far from, a watery environment. The reptile, being cold-blooded, takes on the temperature of his surroundings. If the environment is a cold one, he cannot help being sluggish. Man, of course, has much more freedom. His body temperature remains the same in cold as in hot weather.

All the cells of the body obtain their nutrients from the blood and lymph. These body fluids are remarkably stable chemically. The well-being of the cells and tissues depends upon this stability. Cannon has demonstrated that the blood tends to maintain rather constant percentages of water, sugar, salt, and calcium. The nervous system and the muscles use sugar almost exclusively for their source of energy. Thus it is readily apparent why the sugar content of the blood is an important factor in organismic activity. Oxygen, of course, is absolutely necessary for the homeostasis of the body. When there is an excess of carbon dioxide in the blood there is need for more oxygen. The excess of carbon dioxide brings about an increase in the acidity of the blood, and this increased acidity brings an increase in breathing by directly stimulating the respiratory centers in the nervous system. The autonomic nervous system is directly concerned with the maintenance of homeostasis. The sacral division of the parasympathetic system is involved in regulating the discharge of body wastes, the cranial division of that same system in regulating the digestive process and the absorption of food, and the sympathetic division in regulating such activities as promoting coagulation of the blood when the organism is bleeding. The endocrine glands also have many important regulatory functions in maintaining homeostasis.

Homeostasis is sometimes regarded as the only need of man. There is no question about its importance since a serious disruption of the physiological processes threatens or even destroys the life of the organism. However, excessive concentration on these physiological processes is likely to result in little or no attention being given to the psychological stimuli, which are potent causes of the disruption. The physiological state of an individual, to be sure, exercises a profound influence on his behavior. It is equally true that psychological factors exercise a profound influence on his physiological state. The two are constantly interacting. Obviously, organic drives are important. They are the source of a great deal of activity, but learned goals give those activities specific direction. It should be kept in mind that a man is a physical organism functioning in an environment to which he must adjust. The psychological adjustments that he must make are much more complex than those which are required of the lower forms of life. Some of man's physical needs, such as air, water, urination, and defecation, are satisfied at or near the automatic level. Consequently, they have relatively little significance for students of mental hygiene. The satisfaction of hunger and sex needs, however, involves much learning and a great many psychological hazards.

Everyone has experienced food hunger, although few of us have realized from personal experience how powerful a drive it becomes when one is denied food for a long time. In normal individuals hunger pangs are accompanied by contractions of the walls of the stomach. As time passes, these rhythmical contractions become more frequent, last longer, and are of greater strength. The individual experiencing them becomes restless, more active, and of course, more disposed to react to food. He feels a definite need and tries to satisfy it.

Obviously, a tremendous amount of human energy is devoted to the satisfaction of this single organic need. A considerable percentage of people are carrying on agricultural work, the major purpose of which is to provide food. Moreover, a principal drive to achievement is the necessity of earning enough money to pay the grocery bills. There can be no doubt that the need for food is a prime motivator of human behavior.

The physiological need which is most likely to be frustrated is sex. This is due in part to the fact that our culture has surrounded this drive with a large number of taboos. An individual normally wishes to give full expression to his desires. If satisfying a desire involves running counter to group restrictions, a certain amount of conflict inevitably results. Our society imposes inhibitions on the satisfaction of sex needs. These inhibitions constitute one of the most important causes of behavior disorders.

FOOD HUNGER

Although hunger is an organic drive, it has many social associations that, in turn, exercise considerable influence on the developing personality. This is especially true of children. Take, for instance, the problem of table manners. The hungry schoolboy of ten joins his family at the dinner table, thinking only of satisfying his hunger pangs. He eats too fast, he puts his fingers into his plate, he chews his food noisily, he spills some food on his clothes. His mother reprimands him. He feels frustrated, and perhaps irritated. His mother reprimands him again, and his digestive processes begin to slow down as a result of the tension he is experiencing; but he is so hungry that he continues to eat in a manner that is unacceptable to his parents. Finally, his father in exasperation orders him away from the table. Hunger has gotten him into trouble.

If this experience is repeated often—and in many homes it is—the boy may for a number of years, perhaps all of his life, associate the act of eating with a feeling of unpleasantness or with an attitude of antagonism toward those who are with him at the time. Or he may, because of the persistent frustrations connected with eating, develop certain undesirable mechanisms of behavior. It is significant that "the eating problem" is one that is frequently brought to the attention of psychologists dealing with the adjustment problems of children.

Once in a while fear becomes associated with eating. A girl of three suddenly found herself alone at the home dinner table with a group of strangers. Her mother was occupied in the kitchen at the time. The child screamed and demanded to be taken down from her high chair. This was done. She refused to eat anything that evening. The next morning, when placed at the table again, she took one look around, screamed in fear, and begged to be taken away from the table. The associations with the situation of the night before were strong enough to result in the same emotional reaction. Her behavior can logically be explained in terms of cues. A part of a former fear-producing situation was sufficient to bring about a similar response. This child refused to eat for two days, but finally, influenced by hunger and some reconditioning, she resumed her regular meals.

Occasionally a child resorts to refusing food as an attention-getting device. The child learns that his mother will be disturbed if he refuses to eat. He may even have learned that he can thus coerce his mother into granting certain demands. If used frequently and successfully, this adjustment mechanism may become an established habit, so that in later years the individual will actually be unable to eat or keep food in his stomach during a period of frustration and conflict.

Emotional tension occasionally manifests itself through a strong, almost compulsive, desire to eat a great deal more than is needed to satisfy hunger. The pleasure of eating is substituted for other pleasures which are desired but are unavailable. This was true of a college girl who went to a university clinic with the complaint that she could not refrain from asking for second, third, and sometimes fourth helpings at meals. It was not, she explained, because she was hungry, but because she could not stop eating. In her case the overeating manifested a feeling of insecurity. The person who over-eats because he feels insecure will very likely add one more cause of insecurity, namely, self-consciousness because he is overweight.

There have been a number of studies of feeding disturbances in children. Space will be taken here for a report on one made several years ago. Escalona observed the eating behavior of children, ranging from ten days to twenty-four months in age, for a period of twenty months. These observations were made at the Massachusetts Reformatory for Women where Escalona served as nursery psychologist. In this study, some of the causes of feeding disturbances in very young children are clearly revealed. The most frequent one was the lack of an atmosphere of emotional security in which the child could satisfy his food hunger. Escalona reports ten instances where infants less than a month old refused the breast, although there were no physical conditions present that made breast-feeding impossible. In eight of these cases the mothers were very tense, and this tension appeared to be disturbing to the infant. In six cases the babies were quite willing to be bottle-fed by someone else but refused to drink when the formula was presented by the restless, excitable mothers.

Concerning the importance of the emotional atmosphere in which the young child eats, Escalona makes the following statement:

> We have been impressed in the extreme to which children will go in starving themselves when the emotional difficulty is not discovered or cannot so easily be remedied. One girl of twelve months and a boy of twenty months refused food and drink for a long enough period seriously to impair their health, producing weight loss and general weakness. Both children vomited promptly when food was forced upon them. Both had undergone emotional traumata, one by

separation from a mother substitute and the other through unfortunate experiences in a foster home and subsequent radical changes
in his environment when he was returned to the nursery. Long after
they had re-established normal eating habits, both children tended to
relapse into rejection of food whenever they were even slightly disturbed emotionally. . . . It held true for the entire group that the
eating situation was a very sensitive indicator of the emotional atmosphere prevailing in the institution at large.[1]

Malnutrition

As Breckenridge and Vincent[2] point out, it is difficult to study the
relationship between malnutrition and intellectual and emotional
behavior because there are so many factors in the interaction of the
individual and his environment; in other words, it is difficult to
isolate the relationship. "Nevertheless," they say, "the effects of
undernutrition or malnutrition can be discernible in situations
which are complicated by poor physical environment and emotional
stresses and strains." Breckenridge and Vincent describe the behavior
of the subjects used in the Minnesota study on starvation. These subjects became increasingly ineffective in their daily living because of
undernutrition. "Men who had been energetic, even-tempered, humorous, patient, tolerant, enthusiastic, ambitious, and emotionally
stable became tired, apathetic, irritable, lacking in self-discipline
and self control." Their ambition was greatly reduced. They moved
about carefully. They cared little about their appearance. They
showed little interest in trying to be sociable and their interests became more and more narrow. At times they became depressed because of the frustration which they were experiencing in not being
able to do what they would like to do. "All sex feelings and expression virtually disappeared. All the time they were being dis-
tracted by hunger sensations and showing great concern about and
interest in food."

During the period when they were being rehabilitated and the
amount of their food was increased they recovered somewhat more
rapidly psychologically than they did physically. At first, the psychological improvement did not last because many had anticipated a

[1] S. K. Escalona, "Feeding Disturbances in Very Young Children," *American
Journal of Orthopsychiatry*, XV (1945), 79–80.
[2] M. E. Breckenridge, and E. L. Vincent, *Child Development* (Philadelphia:
W. B. Saunders Co., 1965), pp. 109–11.

quick and complete change. However, in time the behavior which had been characteristic of the group before the experiment began was reinstated. "The feeling of well-being increased the range of interest. The sense of group identity which had become strong dissipated as men began looking forward to making plans for their futures." It is interesting to note that in the Minnesota study the subjects' mental capacity did not change appreciably during the period of semi-starvation or when they were being rehabilitated.

Feeding Schedules for Infants

In years gone by mothers fed their babies when they were hungry. Eventually, however, this practice was dropped, and a feeding schedule was introduced, evidently the result, in part, of the growing influence of pediatricians, who found that the average infant needs to be fed every four hours. The fact that individual differences exist among infants as well as among adults was overlooked. Many babies need to be fed more or less frequently. The attempt to force all of them to conform to a time schedule which is average for the group results in considerable frustration of the need for physical security and of the need for emotional security. If, on the four-hour schedule, the child is supposed to be fed at two, for instance, he is expected to respond even though he is not hungry. If his hunger rhythms are such that he desires to be fed only once every five hours, he resists being fed at two because he is not hungry; the mother, believing that she is doing what is best for her child, has to resort to pleading or to force. Even an infant needs to have respect shown for his personality.

At the other extreme is the baby who needs to be fed more frequently than once every four hours. Perhaps his hunger rhythms cause him to desire food every three hours. Consequently, at one o'clock he is very hungry but he has to wait for an hour before the gap can be bridged between his own personal schedule and the time schedule of the average baby in whom he has no interest. In such a case the mother must listen to the child cry while she also waits for two o'clock. The whole experience is emotionally disturbing for both.

The infant should be given an opportunity to establish his own feeding schedule. If he is fed when he is hungry, in a brief period of time he will settle into a routine which is almost as fixed as one imposed upon him by an outside authority; moreover, it will be a routine which is in accord with his individual requirements. By allowing the infant to establish his own time schedule, the mother can save herself a great deal of anxiety and, more important, she can add greatly to her child's emotional security. By adding to his emotional security she is helping him to lay a sound foundation for later mental health.

SEX HUNGER

In our culture, the physiological need which is most often frustrated is sex. Sex behavior is surrounded by innumerable taboos. It is associated in the minds of many people with a feeling of shame. Because of this generally held point of view, it has been impossible for psychologists to study this phase of human behavior thoroughly.

Much of the freedom we have today with respect to the investigation of sex problems and instruction in sex hygiene we owe to Freud. Although Freud overemphasized the importance of the sex drive in human behavior, he did succeed, perhaps because of this overemphasis, in forcing a reluctant lay and professional world to recognize the fact that the satisfaction of sex needs, not only in adult years, but also in childhood, is essential to personality growth, and that frustration of these needs may result in distorted satisfactions and, perhaps, in serious behavior disorders. It was Freud who made it clear that sex desires do not appear abruptly at puberty, but are present from infancy.

The earliest phase of the individual's sex life is one of bodily satisfactions, especially satisfactions of the erogenous zones, the most highly sensitive of which, in very early childhood, is the mouth. This is an important reason why child psychologists emphasize the importance of breast feeding. In early childhood, autoerotic practices are normal.

As the child grows older, he enters what is frequently called the "homosexual period" (to use the word "homosexual" in a very broad sense). At this stage of development, his emotional attachments outside of the family circle are to those of the same sex. The girl's affections go to other girls, and the boy is devoted to his chums or to his gang. During this period boys tend to dislike and to despise girls, and girls tend to dislike and to envy boys.

When adolescence is reached, emotional attachments are normally shifted from those of the same sex to those of the opposite sex. Difficult adjustments have to be made during this period, and many young people fail to clear the hurdles. If the difficulties are too great, there may be regression to an earlier stage of development. This is more likely to be true if parental attachments remain strong.

In considering sex behavior it is important to keep in mind that all the individual inherits is a physical structure which predisposes him to sexual activity. What forms this activity takes depends upon learning. Hardy[3] expresses this point of view in an article on sexual motivation. He says, "it seems warranted to conclude that the overwhelming proportion of the variance in human sexual motivation and behavior is not explicable in terms of some biological need or tension, however conceived." Hardy gives eleven basic principles of motivation. Five of the eleven are as follows:

1. Motives are based upon learned expectations of an affective (hedonic) change.

2. For such an expectation to motivate behavior, the person must believe that some action (symbolic or overt) on his part helps or is required to bring about the desired affective change.

3. The confidence one places in a given affective expectation increases each time it is confirmed through having the affect follow or accompany the cues which arouse the expectation.

4. A family of expectations is a group of expectations which tend to arouse one another or to be aroused by a similar set of cues. Confirmation of one member of a family of expectations strengthens belief in other members of that family.

5. The perceived permanence or transience of the anticipated affective state is relevant in assessing the net effect of a given alternative.

After stating his principles of motivation, Hardy applies them specifically to sex. He postulates that certain conditions which are positive affectively "form the constitutional base for the elaboration of sexual appetite." In his discussion of childhood sexuality he points

[3] K. R. Hardy, "An Appetitional Theory of Sexual Motivation," *Psychological Review*, LXXI, No. 1 (1964), 1–12.

out that the sexual desires of children in American culture are very different from those of experienced adults because they do not have "the requisite background of affective learning." He says "there seems to be mounting evidence that extreme social deprivation in early childhood may produce pathological effects upon the development of normal heterosexuality, supporting the thesis that sexuality is in large part a derivative of experiential factors."

Later in this article Hardy discusses the development of sexual appetite in dating and courtship, pointing out the significance of initial tentative physical contact such as holding hands "generally originates in nonsexual motives." Positive effects from this initial activity can of course lead to more intimate physical relationships. "As erotic experiences are repeated," Hardy says, "the greater the association value of these cues to sexuality and the wider the range of cues to sexuality." In time, a large number of acts "may serve as sexual stimuli to the person with a history of arousal, while to the naïve person they have no such significance." Certain acts or situations can stimulate abnormal as well as normal sex behavior. In other words, the experiential background of the individual determines what is meaningful stimuli for him and what his sex objects and sexual behavior will be.

Autoerotic Practices

Autoerotic practices are varied. Only the most frequent one, masturbation, will be considered here.

A number of studies of the incidence of masturbation reveal that the practice is so widespread it can hardly be considered abnormal. The percentage for girls is around 60, for boys around 90. Girls usually begin masturbating at an earlier age than boys. Boys are somewhat more likely to continue masturbating into adult years than girls. Kinsey,[4] in an extensive study of human sexual behavior, states that ultimately 92 per cent of the total male population and 58 per cent of the total female population resort to masturbation which leads to orgasm.

---

[4] The two Kinsey reports, *Sexual Behavior in the Human Male* and *Sexual Behavior in the Human Female,* constitute the most extensive studies of human sexual behavior ever made and are an important source for facts concerning sex practices. This statement is valid even though Kinsey's subjects were volunteers and did not constitute a representative sampling of the human race or even of Americans. Generalizations from the study should, of course, be made with caution.

Masturbation can become a habit for a number of reasons. It may be merely a continuation of satisfying autoerotic practices carried on in infancy. It may develop from an attitude of inferiority, or from frustration in attempts at establishing heterosexual social relations. It may be learned from other children. It may be resorted to because of the need to release physiological tension. It may even be thought of as a kind of preparation for adult life.

Other etiological factors spring from our social customs. The adolescent boy or girl, having achieved sexual maturity, cannot satisfy his sex needs by means of the heterosexual relationships for which he is now ready. Marriage must not be thought of for several years. Fear of venereal disease and moral standards serve as restraints upon casual sex relationships before marriage. Faced with the impossibility of satisfying his desires, the individual frequently resorts to erotic daydreams and from these to masturbation.

Effects of Masturbation   There has been a tendency to exaggerate the harmful effects of masturbation. Boys and girls are frequently told that it will lead to feeblemindedness or insanity. There is no proof that, unless carried to great excesses, the habit will have any deleterious physical effects whatsoever. The individual may be harmed, however, by what he thinks about the habit. If, because of it, he develops a deep feeling of shame, he has built the foundation for an attitude of inferiority. If the individual persists in the habit even though he feels that it is shameful, a conflict between what he believes he ought to do and what he is actually doing may result in behavior disorders. It is not the habit, then, which is harmful, but what the individual thinks about the habit. Concerning this, Kinsey says:

> Millions of boys have lived in continual mental conflict over this problem. For that matter, many a boy still does. Many boys pass through a periodic succession of attempts to stop the habit, inevitable failures in those attempts, consequent periods of remorse, the making of new resolutions—and a new start on the whole cycle. It is difficult to imagine anything better calculated to do permanent damage to the personality of an individual.
>
> For several decades now, educators, clinical psychologists and psychiatrists, and some of the general medical practitioners have come to agree that the physical effects of masturbation are not

fundamentally different from the physical effects of any other sexual activity, and that any mental harm resulting from masturbation is an outcome of the conflicts introduced by the condemnation of the boy's activity. . . .

. . . For the boys who have not been too disturbed psychically, masturbation has, however, provided a regular sexual outlet which has alleviated nervous tensions; and the record is clear in many cases that these boys have on the whole lived more balanced lives than the boys who have been more restrained in their sexual activities.[5]

Homosexuality

Homosexuality is usually defined as sexual relationship between individuals of the same sex. In a somewhat broader sense it may be considered as a sexual attraction toward individuals of the same sex, even though no overt practices are involved. Homosexual behavior is much more widespread than is generally believed. Kinsey, in the extensive study previously referred to, provides detailed data which are summarized in the following quotation:

37 per cent of the total male population has at least some overt homosexual experience to the point of orgasm between adolescence and old age. . . . This accounts for nearly 2 males out of every 5 that one may meet.

50 per cent of the males who remain single until age 35 have had overt homosexual experience to the point of orgasm, since the onset of adolescence. . . .

58 per cent of the males who belong to the group that goes into high school but not beyond, 50 per cent of the grade school level, and 47 per cent of the college level have had homosexual experience to the point of orgasm if they remain single to the age of 35. . . .

63 per cent of all males never have overt homosexual experience to the point of orgasm after the onset of adolescence. . . .

50 per cent of all males (approximately) have neither overt nor psychic experience in the homosexual after the onset of adolescence. . . .

13 per cent of the males (approximately) react erotically to other males without having overt homosexual contacts after the onset of adolescence.

30 per cent of all males have at least incidental homosexual expe-

[5] A. C. Kinsey, *et al., Sexual Behavior in the Human Male* (Philadelphia: W. B. Saunders Co., 1948), pp. 513–14.

rience or reactions (i.e., rate 1 to 6) over at least a three-year period between the ages of 16 and 55. This accounts for one male out of every three in the population who is past the early years of adolescence. . . .

25 per cent of the male population has more than incidental homosexual experience or reactions (i.e., rates 2 to 6) for at least three years between the ages of 16 and 55. In terms of averages, one male out of approximately every four has had or will have such distinct and continued homosexual experience.

18 per cent of the males have at least as much of the homosexual as the heterosexual in their histories (i.e., rate 3–6) for at least three years between the ages of 16 and 55. This is more than one in six of the white male population.

13 per cent of the population has more of the homosexual than the heterosexual (i.e., rates 4–6) for at least three years between the ages of 16 and 55. This is one in eight of the white male population.

10 per cent of the males are more or less exclusively homosexual (i.e., rate 5 or 6) for at least three years between the ages of 16 and 55. This is one male in ten in the white male population.

8 per cent of the males are exclusively homosexual (i.e., rate a 6) for at least three years between the ages of 16 and 55. This is one male in every 13.

4 per cent of the white males are exclusively homosexual throughout their lives, after the onset of adolescence. . . .[6]

Public opinion to the contrary, homosexual relationships are much less frequent among women than among men. This is probably due in part to the fact that women characteristically have a less aggressive sex drive than men. Moreover, in our culture, an open show of affection between women is accepted. This relatively superficial outlet may be a factor in reducing the desire for more intimate relations. Concerning the extent of homosexuality among females, Kinsey says:

Among the females, the accumulative incidences of homosexual responses had ultimately reached 28 per cent; they had reached 50 per cent in the males. The accumulative incidences of overt contacts to the point of orgasm among the females had reached 13 per cent; among the males they had reached 37 per cent. This means that homosexual responses had occurred in about half as many females as males, and contacts which had proceeded to orgasm had occurred

[6] Kinsey *et al., op. cit.,* pp. 650–51.

in about a third as many females as males. Moreover, compared with the males, there were only about a half to a third as many of the females who were, in any age period, primarily or exclusively homosexual.[7]

It is clear from the preceding data that there is no heterosexual-homosexual dichotomy. Homosexuality, like other behavior traits, should be thought of in terms of degree. Certainly, as Kinsey has shown, a considerable percentage of human males have had actual homosexual experiences. It is especially important to note the considerable number of bisexuals; that is, those who find homosexual and heterosexual outlets equally satisfying. Sex hunger, like food hunger, has learned goals. The need initiates activity, but, as has been pointed out before, the direction that activity takes is dependent to a very great extent upon what the organism has learned.

Causation   Although there is a possibility that homosexuality is innate, it is significant that only a relatively small percentage of homosexuals possess secondary physical characteristics that are markedly feminine or masculine, as the case may be. It may be, of course, that some hidden dysfunction of the glandular system causes the abnormality in personality development. However, it appears much more likely that the behavior is psychogenic.

There are a number of factors in the life of an individual which might cause him to prefer individuals of his own sex to those of the opposite sex. One would be persistent failure during adolescence to establish satisfactory social and emotional heterosexual relationships. Occasionally homosexual interests result, for the girl, from a fear-producing experience with a man, or, for a boy, from his sense of failure in his first heterosexual experience. Such interests may, of course, be learned from satisfying relationships with an adult homosexual. They frequently develop from a cross-parent fixation. The following is an example.

A married man in his thirties experiences such a strong desire to be a woman that in the seclusion of his home he dresses completely in women's clothes at least once a week. He is both ashamed of this behavior and rewarded by it. He has very little interest in sexual relations with his wife but tries to persuade her to have relations with other men. If she would only do this he could identify

7 A. C. Kinsey *et al., Sexual Behavior in the Human Female* (Philadelphia: W. B. Saunders Co., 1953), pp. 474–75.

with her and experience vicarious satisfaction. He has had a few overt homosexual experiences, but these only partially fulfilled his needs.

As a child this man was very devoted to his mother, who was the only really significant person in his life. He hated and feared his father who was cruel and abusive. He said in one of the interviews with the writer that even now when he hears a man's footsteps in the apartment above his he trembles in fear. As a result of his early experiences he rebelled against being a man; he longed to be a woman. The fact that he could not was deeply frustrating.

In many instances a person has been taught to play the roles of the opposite sex. If he learns these roles thoroughly, when he reaches adolescence and the sex drive becomes strong, he will almost certainly find outlets in keeping with his self-perceptions. An example of how feminine identification, with resulting homosexual behavior, can be learned is a college freshman who was referred to the author because of his homosexual activities in his dormitory.

This young man was an invert interested in playing the feminine role only in sexual relations. He had almost no feelings of guilt about his behavior and no desire to change. In interviews with his parents it was learned that they had taught him female interests without realizing what they were doing. They had five children. The first child was a boy; that was fine. The second child was a boy; they were somewhat disappointed because they had wished for a girl. The third child was a boy; they were disappointed. The fourth child was a boy; they were deeply disappointed. Finally the fifth child arrived, and he was also a boy. They were told by their family physician that they could have no more children. The fifth child, who later became the college student under discussion, was treated by both parents as though he were the girl whom they had longed to have. The mother dressed him in girl's clothes until it was time for him to enter school. As he grew older she taught him how to sew and how to help with the housework. He rarely participated in the masculine activities of his father and his brothers. He learned his feminine roles so well that when he reached adolescence he carried his feminine image of himself into his sexual activities. Although he was a young man physically, he was a young woman psychologically.

Treatment   Homosexuality is both a social and a personal problem. How should it be treated socially? Should all persons who have committed a homosexual act be imprisoned? Our laws are very specific in classifying it as a criminal offense. If these laws were applied literally, and if all those who have indulged in homosexual behavior could be identified, it would follow that a least a third of the male population and an eighth of the female population would have to be isolated.

Obviously, institutionalization of all homosexuals is not feasible. Moreover, jailing a person because he has indulged in homosexual behavior is not likely to cause him to become more normal sexually. What should be done by society is an unanswered question. Possibly at some time in the future there will develop a better understanding of individuals who seek this form of sex outlet. With this increased understanding it should then be possible to attack the causes of homosexual behavior and so reduce the incidence.

Insofar as therapy with individuals is concerned, there is still a question as to how much can be done. The prognosis for adults who are past thirty years of age is very unfavorable. Usually the behavior patterns have become so fixed by that time that the individual has relatively little interest in changing or ability to change to heterosexual activities. Much can be done, however, with adolescents and with young people in their twenties. All learned behavior is subject to modification. Since the evidence indicates that homosexuality is learned, it follows that new sex goals, which are in the long run more acceptable both to the individual and to society, can be acquired. The fact that 37 per cent of the total male population have had at least some overt homosexual experience while only 4 per cent are exclusively homosexual throughout their lives is in itself proof that a considerable number of persons do change from homosexual to heterosexual activities. In the majority of cases such changes are made without the assistance of a therapist.

Dickey[8] studied adequacy feelings of 47 avowed homosexuals. Her subjects were volunteers ranging in age from 21 to 63 years with a mean of 34 years, who were assessed anonymously by means of self-rating questionnaires. Results indicated that those who rated high in feelings of adequacy tended to identify with masculine cultural norms. "Feelings of adequacy were associated with: job satisfaction, preference for leisure-time association with heterosexuals, idealization of the role of the typical heterosexual male, and identification

---

8 B. A. Dickey, "Attitudes Toward Sex Roles and Feelings of Adequacy in Homosexual Males," *Journal of Consulting Psychology*, XXV, No. 2 (1961), 116–22.

with the typical heterosexual male rather than with the typical homosexual male."

This study was not made with a random sample of homosexuals but, in this case, this seems to make the results more dramatic, for admitted homosexuals are, in effect, saying adequacy depends upon identification with the male role.

Heterosexual Relations

The problems involved in the gratification of heterosexual needs are extremely complex. For a very small number of persons a lifetime of celibacy provides a solution; for a larger number, but by no means the majority, monogamous marriage is sufficiently satisfying; for many, promiscuity is rewarding. However, all of these ways of dealing with sex hunger are far from being free of frustrations and conflicts. The celibate, unless he has an extremely weak sex drive, will almost certainly feel that he is missing one of the most important and pleasurable experiences in life. The married man or woman may find the spouse sexually unsatisfactory for a number of reasons. The promiscuous individual will probably find himself involved in many unhappy and perhaps guilt-ridden experiences.

In addition to reproduction the main purposes of sexual intercourse are the achievement of sensual pleasure and the expression of love. These purposes appear simple enough, but their fulfillment is a complex process. If sexual intercourse is carried through with a partner who satisfies the first purpose only, the rewards are usually fleeting and rather empty. If the intercourse is an expression of love but the partner is unresponsive or unskilled the act can be accompanied and followed by frustration and depression. Complete or at least nearly complete fulfillment comes when both purposes are fused into one with each partner in the sex act giving and receiving both sensual pleasure and love. It seems obvious that this is the healthiest kind of sex relationship.

There are many persons who are incapable of achieving the kind of peak experience which comes from combining sensual pleasure and love in sexual intercourse free from inhibitions and guilt. Excepting where there are physical abnormalities, heterosexual difficulties spring largely from fear or lack of competency. Our society insists on sex restraint. Intercourse outside of marriage is frowned upon. Many individuals, seeking to satisfy their sex needs but fearful of pregnancy or disease, resort to varied substitutions. Occasionally sex satisfactions are achieved through sadism or masochism. Sadism is a term applied to the behavior in which the individual achieves sex satisfaction through cruelty to others. This cruelty may be either mental or physical. Masochism is the achievement of sex achievement of sex gratification through suffering inflicted by another. Either sadism or masochism can, of course, take place between individuals of the same sex as well as between individuals of opposite sexes.

A feeling of personal inadequacy underlies many sexual maladjustments. It is one of the most important causes of frigidity in women and impotence in men. This feeling of inadequacy is usually accompanied by a sense of shame. If sexual maladjustments are to be reduced in number and in intensity, a healthier social attitude toward sex must be developed. Parents should talk about it frankly, giving their children whatever information they need. They should use care not to shroud the subject in mystery and not to distort it with feelings of disgust.

Premarital Intercourse

The subject of premarital intercourse will be considered as objectively as possible. This is not the place to render moral judgments, although it should be understood that the moral standards of the individual and the society in which he lives not only affect his sexual behavior but also how he feels about it.

A number of reasons have been given in support of premarital intercourse. The sex drive is strongest in men during the late teens and the early twenties. If abstinence from heterosexual relations is practiced during this period considerable frustration is likely to be experienced. As a result many may turn to substitutes such as masturbation or homosexuality. If premarital intercourse is indulged in, young people have an opportunity to learn from direct experience what is involved in sex relations. Moreover, if marriage is being considered by the partners in the sex act it gives them an opportunity to find out whether or not they are compatible in this area. This is important since sexual incompatibility is one of the main causes if not the main cause of unhappy marriages and divorce.

Many arguments are also advanced against premarital intercourse. In our society most young people have been taught that it is morally wrong. Therefore, if they indulge in it they must usually do so in secrecy and will likely experience feelings of guilt which may lead to disruptive anxiety. Then, too, in spite of the widespread knowledge of birth control methods, pregnancy may result. This can be a devastating experience for the two young people involved and for their families. If there is promiscuity in premarital intercourse many interpersonal problems will almost certainly exist involving jealousy, anger, resentment and probably even love and hate. Is the adolescent capable of handling this turmoil of emotions? Some of the experiences in premarital intercourse may be repulsive and the memories of these may carry over into marriage.

Extramarital Intercourse

Ours is a monogamous society, yet married persons, as the Kinsey studies show, are frequently polygamous in the sense that they have sexual relations with persons other than their marriage partners. There are arguments for and against such practices. A man may love his wife and so wish to continue with the marriage, but because she is inadequate sexually he turns to another woman—or to other women—for sensual pleasure. A woman may love her husband and her children and wish to keep her family intact yet because her husband is unsatisfactory as a sex partner she turns to another man—or to other men—to satisfy her sex needs. To be sure, there are many reasons other than sexual incompatibility which cause persons to resort to extramarital intercourse. Variety and a different kind of companionship are among these. However, much the same problems exist in extramarital intercourse as in premarital intercourse. Usually the activity is carried on in secret with accompanying guilt and anxiety and the interpersonal relationships can become very complex. Temporary pleasure is likely to be replaced by remorse. In many instances, of course, two families are broken up. If there are children in either or both families, the situation is especially difficult for them. In other words, extramarital intercourse is beset with many complications affecting the mental health of those involved.

College Students

Although college students constitute a select group intellectually and economically, they differ but little from the general population in their sex behavior. What difference there is appears largely in more varied heterosexual conduct. A research article by F. W. Finger[9] supports this statement as well as Kinsey's conclusions.

Finger, after some careful preliminary work in establishing rapport, asked 138 college men to fill out a questionnaire concerning sex beliefs and practices. Precautions were, of course, taken to insure anonymity. In spite of this, the results probably indicate the minimum rather than the maximum incidence of sex practices, especially homosexuality. Even when a person is assured that no one will be able to recognize his questionnaire, he is still somewhat reluctant to reveal experiences about which he has any guilt feelings. Of the 138 male students, 111 returned the questionnaire. The average age of the respondents was 19.4 years with a range of 17–23. All the subjects were unmarried.

Finger found in this study that 92.8 per cent of the 111 students responding had practiced masturbation leading to orgasm. This figure is not far removed from the 96 per cent for college graduates reported by Kinsey. Twenty-seven per cent of the group reported at least one overt homosexual experience leading to orgasm. This is lower than the 37 per cent reported by Kinsey. However, Kinsey found that college graduates are somewhat less likely than high school and grade school graduates to have resorted to homosexual behavior. Forty-five per cent of the group reported that they had had heterosexual intercourse. Forty-six per cent of this 45 per cent stated the frequency of such intercourse had totaled less than seven.

Finger also checked the questionnaire on the beliefs of the students concerning the frequency of various sex practices. He states the result as follows:

> To the question, "What percentage of men over 18 in the general population do you believe have masturbated sometime?" the answers ranged from 25 per cent to 100 per cent, with mean estimate 89.6 per cent. The average subject believed that 9.3 of his 10 best unmarried male friends had masturbated sometime, 7.3 of them within the past year. Only seven subjects recalled having been directly threatened with punishment for masturbation (one of them with castration), but 69 had at some time believed that harmful effects might result from the practice. The mean estimate of the proportion of homosexually experienced men in the general population was 21.5

[9] F. W. Finger, "Sex Beliefs and Practices Among Male College Students," *Journal of Abnormal and Social Psychology*, XLII (1947), 57–67.

per cent (range 1 per cent to 95 per cent); estimated incidence among the 10 best friends, 17 per cent (range 0 per cent to 100 per cent). The respondents estimated the incidence of non-virgin unmarried males over 18 to be 64.9 per cent in the general population, ranging from 25 per cent to 99 per cent, and estimated that 44 per cent of women entered into marriage with a history of intercourse.

The author of this article makes some additional observations of interest. He reports that those students who had experienced a certain form of sex gratification tend to impute to the general population, including their best friends, a greater frequency of that form of behavior than do those who had not indulged in it. This is a mechanism of adjustment called *projection*. Persons who have indulged in a kind of behavior that seems undesirable to them are likely either to believe that most other persons behave in the same way or to believe that they are the only ones who have behaved so abnormally. Finger also reports that although only seven of the responding students had ever been threatened with punishment for masturbation, 62 per cent stated that they had at some time believed that the consequences of the habit would be very harmful. Of the three forms of behavior studied—masturbation, homosexual acts, and premarital intercourse—all the subjects rated homosexual acts as the "most wrong."

The study by Finger was done in the late forties. It is difficult to say what the situation is now among college students. During recent years there has been a considerable loosening of the sex mores. It is not known whether this has resulted in more or less sexual activity, either normal or abnormal. It may be that there is less since there is a strong tendency to indulge in that which is prohibited. On the other hand, there may be more, partly because of increased knowledge of birth control and partly because venereal disease is no longer the scourge that it once was.

SUMMARY

The fundamental physical need is to maintain homeostasis. The frustration of one or more of the several specific organic drives disrupts to some degree the internal environment of the organism. The causes of such disruption are both physiological and psychological. The organic needs which have the most significance for students of mental hygiene are hunger and sex. It is important that both these needs be satisfied in an environment that provides a feeling of security. Of these two, sex frustrations and conflicts constitute the more serious cause of personality disturbances. Sex satisfactions in our culture are hemmed in by a considerable number of taboos. However, since the sex drive is a strong one and since the goals for that drive are learned, both males and females frequently become involved in sex practices that run counter to the requirements of their society.

THE NEED
FOR
EMOTIONAL
SECURITY

chapter **7**

In considering the need for emotional security it is desirable to have some knowledge of the autonomic nervous system, for this system plays an important part in emotional behavior. Emotional insecurity involves a denial of emotional satisfactions and accompanying this persistent denial is the prolonged presence of emergency emotion. These chronic tension states are harmful to the health of the organism.

Emotion and thinking are closely related. Persons suffering from chronic emotional tension perceive and think in a hyper-emotional setting that distorts the meaning of that which is being perceived or thought about. Those parts of the nervous system which deal with verbal and symbolic functions have an intimate relationship with the autonomic system. It is because of this relationship that we often respond to remembered embarrassments and anticipated or imagined crises with considerable emotional disturbance. Thus we worry about things about which we can do nothing and start being afraid long before the crisis is likely to occur. Emotional maladjustment exists when the sympathetic system is functioning out of a rational context; that is, when it is functioning on an emergency basis where it can serve no useful purpose.

In general the autonomic nervous system initiates adjustments within the body while the central or somatic nervous system—the brain and the spinal cord with their afferent and efferent nerves— initiates adjustment between the external environment and the body. The autonomic system innervates the visceral muscles, the glands, and the heart. The central system carries out both sensory and motor activities, whereas the autonomic system is almost exclusively a motor system. The motor part of the central system innervates the skeletal muscles such as those of the arms, the neck, and the legs. The central system can act very specifically; the autonomic system, particularly the sympathetic part, acts in a more general and diffused manner. The central and autonomic nervous systems are by no means independent of one another. The autonomic ganglia where the cell bodies of the autonomic nerves are located, though existing outside the central nervous system, are nevertheless connected with the spinal cord. Thus changes occurring in the brain and spinal cord can affect the autonomic nervous system.

The autonomic system has two parts, the sympathetic division and the parasympathetic division. The sympathetic division is connected to the middle region of the spinal cord while the parasympathetic division is connected either to the upper or cranial region of the cord or to the lower or sacral region. These two divisions work in the main towards opposite goals. The sympathetic system mobilizes the energy of the body for activities which involve effort whereas the parasympathetic system takes no part in such mobilization and works to conserve body energy. Therefore, when sympathetic activity has the upper hand, heart action is accelerated, perspiration increases, sexual and digestive functions are inhibited, and blood flows to the skeletal muscles. When the parasympathetic system is dominant, heart action is slowed, the pupils of the eyes are dilated, body heat is conserved, and sexual and digestive processes are stimulated. Most of the glands and visceral muscles receive innervation from both of these two divisions of the autonomic system. Thus one division may dominate at one time and the other at another time. Which division is in ascendency at any given time depends upon the nature of the emotional stimulation that the organism is receiving at that time.

Emotional behavior has both somatic and autonomic aspects. Hitting someone when angry and running when afraid are examples of somatic emotional behavior. The increase in heartbeat, the increase in perspiration, and the gasping for breath which accompany fright are examples of autonomic emotional behavior. It is the autonomic processes which give rise to the characteristic feeling tone of emotional experience. Emotional behavior is rather generalized in nature. According to Cannon's emergency theory emotion is to be considered as serving the purpose of mobilizing the energy of the body to meet the stimulus situation that is threatening it. It is the sympathetic system which is involved in mobilizing this body energy. It is this system that is active when one is afraid or angry. The pleasurable emotions which accompany the satiation of basic drives such as hunger and sex arise as the result of the activity of the parasympathetic system.

The term "emotional security" can better be described than defined. It must be thought of in terms of degree since it is doubtful that anyone ever feels completely secure. Emotion is always accompanied by some tension. Emotional security involves partial freedom from threat. It is a satisfying state in which the individual feels considerable peace of mind.

A high degree of emotional security is essential for physical and mental health. Persistent insecurity keeps the organism in a stirred-up state. Eventually such a disturbed condition may result in both physical and mental disorders. The body cannot tolerate indefinitely the strain placed upon it by the prolonged mobilization of energy resulting from excessive threat. In such a situation mental functions are also impaired; emotional blocks cause inhibitions and distortions. It is important that individuals, insofar as is possible, live in a climate which promotes a feeling of well-being.

SOURCES OF EMOTIONAL SECURITY

Obviously the need for emotional security is not a separate entity. A human being cannot be segmented; he must be considered as a total personality striving to preserve and enhance the self of which he is aware. For example, the striving for emotional security is always associated with the process of satisfying the need for physical security, the need for achievement, and the need for status. Persistent frustration of any of these needs results in disruptive emotional states. Stated positively, any experience which is pleasurable and satisfying and which fulfills even very slightly the basic need for adequacy results in a warm, comfortable feeling of safety and enhancement of the self.

There are several sources of emotional security. Four of these will be discussed in the following pages: (1) interpersonal relationships; (2) impersonal environment; (3) memories; (4) future prospects. The specific utilization of these sources by individuals varies with the personalities of those individuals and the environments in which they function.

Interpersonal Relationships

Human beings from infancy to old age find much of their emotional security from their relationship with others. Harry and Margaret Harlow[1] have written a significant article on social deprivation in monkeys. To be sure, as the Harlows point out, "research on non-human animals, even monkeys, will never resolve the baffling complex roles of various kinds of early experience in the development of human personality." However, in this study important conclusions were reached which might apply to human beings.

The Harlows observed the development of social behavior in rhesus monkeys at the primate laboratory of the University of Wisconsin. Monkeys, like human beings, have close attachments to their mothers and to their age mates. In the experiment some of the monkeys were deprived of all social contact for varying periods, some were raised without mothers but with a group of age mates and others with mothers but without age mates.

Fifty-six of the infant monkeys were separated from their mothers and each one was placed alone in a bare wire cage in a room where other infant monkeys were similarly housed and partially isolated. Each monkey could see and hear the others but any direct physical contact was impossible. It is interesting to note that from five to eight years later this group of monkeys exhibited many behavior abnormalities. They sat in their cages and stared into space or they circled their cages in a rigid, stereotyped way. Many of them had developed compulsive behavior similar to that seen in neurotic or psychotic human beings. This behavior was characteristically aggression toward the self rather than the more normal aggression toward others. An intensive study of six of these monkeys, then two

[1] Harry F. Harlow, and Margaret Kuenne Harlow, "Social Deprivation in Monkeys," *Scientific American* 207 (November 1962), 136–146.

years old, showed clearly that their sex behavior had been severely distorted by the two years of isolation in individual cages.

As a part of their overall study, the Harlows conducted an experiment on the emotional bond between mother and infant. One group of four monkeys was separated from their mothers at birth. Each one was supplied with a substitute mother in the form of "a welded wire cylindrical form with the nipple of the feeding bottle protruding from its breast and with a wooden head surmounting it." Sixty infant monkeys were given substitute mothers covered by terry cloth. It is not surprising that the Harlows found that the baby monkeys became strongly attached to the cloth mothers but had little or no attachment to the wire mothers.

In spite of the attachment for the cloth mothers which persisted after two years of separation the young monkeys so raised were socially and sexually abnormal. The cloth monkey substitute mother provided nourishment and a kind of warmth because of the cloth covering but of course it did not provide the emotional security which comes from the many aspects of a real personal mother-child relationship, including love.

The Harlows conducted a series of experiments on the relative importance of mother-infant relations and infant-infant relations in the development of rhesus monkey behavior and they found "that the mother-infant relation plays a positive role in the normal development of the infant-infant and heterosexual relations of the young monkey." They also found that the infant-infant affectional bond is very strong and can compensate successfully for mother deprivation. There were even indications that relationship with peers was more important than mothering.

The Harlow study with rhesus monkeys indicates clearly the great importance of personal relationships. In this respect, certainly, monkeys and human beings are alike. Social deprivation, especially in infancy and early childhood, not only leaves scars but also, if sufficiently severe, may result in later irreversible abnormal behavior. Food and impersonal comfort are not enough. Real emotional security, and with it normal behavior, comes from the give and take of positive relationships with others. Surrogate wire mothers, even though they produced food, were not satisfactory substitute mothers for the infant rhesus monkeys. For human beings institutions are not satisfactory substitutes for homes. An impersonal bureaucracy which provides financial aid for its citizens to meet their physical needs can provide little or no emotional security. The college or university which looks upon its students as so many IBM cards and which chooses their courses and their instructors for them electronically can expect and usually gets overt or covert rebellion. No one finds emotional security in being a number, a faceless nonentity lost in a sea of faceless nonentities.

Infancy and Early Childhood   The human infant goes through a long period of dependency on others. During the first few months of life, his mother is usually his main source, perhaps his only source, of emotional security. From his unverbalized relationship with her, from the warmth and care and love which surrounds him he draws his feeling of safety. He needs this emotional relationship as much as he needs food and physical care.

As he grows older, other avenues of personal relationships are opened up for him. These vary, of course, from family to family and from community to community. The father, the grandparents, the brothers and sisters and perhaps others outside the immediate family add variety and depth and scope to his emotional life and developing personality. Like the rhesus monkeys reported on by the Harlows, he needs some companionship with children of approximately the same age. Such associations have considerable value for him even though they are frequently marked by friction. He learns how to take care of himself in a variety of emotionally charged situations.

If, during infancy and early childhood, personal relationships have been unsatisfactory or practically non-existent, behavior disorders will almost certainly result from the deprivation and may handicap or even cripple the individual for the rest of his life. The feeling of insecurity in relation to others manifests itself in many ways. Three of these are: insatiable craving for affection, inability to accept affection, and disregard of the personalities of others.

It is understandable that such a person would develop an insatiable craving for emotional satisfactions. In later years, even though his friends give him a normal amount of attention, he feels that it is altogether too little. If he is married and his wife is really devoted to him he feels that she is not devoted enough. If he has children he tries to insist that they fix their affection solely on him. This excessive need for affection is comparable to excessive ambition described in Chapter Four. It remains forever unsatisfied. If carried on long enough it causes the individual to feel that he is completely alone in the world, that no one really cares for him. It is one of the important causes of suicide. Being starved for affection he usually finds it easy to fixate upon the psychiatrist or clinical psychologist to whom he may go for help and is for a time buoyed up by the interest and understanding shown by the therapist in his problems; but even that does not fully satisfy him. As long as he continues to feel emotionally insecure he will continue to crave more affection and understanding than it is possible for other individuals to give him.

The emotionally insecure person has lost his self-respect. He is convinced that he is unworthy of the devotion of others and so is unable to accept affection. This conviction of his unworthiness makes it impossible for him to believe in the sincerity of the love that may be shown him by the members of his family or by his friends. He feels that they must know him for what he is; and that being the case, they could not possibly regard him highly.

The socially deprived and thus emotionally insecure person is likely to concentrate on himself. When he is with a group he is so uncertain of his behavior that he finds it impossible to forget himself and concentrate his attention on the behavior and conversation of others. His fear of revealing himself sets up so high a barrier between him and others that those whom he meets cannot reveal themselves to him. Having shut himself off from his associates by his concentration upon himself he is able to develop but little understanding of the personalities of those about him. Concomitant with this lack of understanding is the disregard for the feelings of others. He asserts himself at the wrong time and then is likely to regret the disagreeable things he has said and done. He needs friendship but he irritates when he should please. All this can come about because personal relationships as sources of emotional security were inadequate during infancy and early childhood.

Later Childhood   Later childhood is being defined here as the years from six to twelve. This is sometimes called the middle childhood period and the chronological age range is admittedly set rather arbitrarily. For most children this is the period when they gradually break away from their parents as the principal source of emotional security and depend more and more upon new personal relationships, which can be very rewarding. Those children who found emotional security in their homes enter into their expanded and expanding world with confidence. They have learned that they can depend upon their parents for emotional satisfaction; therefore, they expect that their teachers and their schoolmates will add to rather than subtract from their feeling of safety and security. To be sure their expectations are by no means always fulfilled, but if a sound foundation has been laid in infancy and early childhood they can make the necessary adjustments unless the school situation is extremely threatening.

During the first two or three years of school life teachers can be and usually are an important source of emotional security. Young children see them as mother substitutes or perhaps as complements to their mothers. They are still dependent and draw upon the warmth and understanding of the teacher. They like to confide in her and have her do little personal things for them. If this new personal relationship with a stranger in authority is rewarding, there will be little or no objection to the limits which must be set on behavior in the classroom. Actually, children find considerable security in a well-structured, well-ordered school. Freedom which borders on chaos does not further self-actualization or provide a feeling of safety.

As children approach the middle period of the grade-school years parents and teachers, although remaining as sources of emotional security, gradually recede in importance and associations with other children become increasingly significant. With other children there is a mutual exchange of thoughts and emotions and a sharing of experiences at a very different level from the relationship with adults. If the child is accepted by his age group then this group, especially certain individuals within it, becomes a satisfying source of emotional security. Having a best friend or a pal or a buddy means a great deal to the child whose home ties are and should be weakening.

Many times, of course, a child is not accepted by his peers. This results in shutting off, at least temporarily, an important source of emotional security. He reacts to the frustration in one or more of many ways. He may revert to increased dependence on his parents; he may strive to become his teacher's pet; he may behave very aggressively toward other children; or he may withdraw into lonely isolation.

Adolescence and Early Maturity   Adolescence is characteristically the turbulent period in an individual's emotional life. In an affluent society such as ours he is still, to a considerable degree, and perhaps completely, dependent on his parents economically but they are no longer an important source of emotional security, except in cases of overprotection. Frequently his personal relationship with them is openly negative. His relationship with his teachers has also changed considerably from what it was in the lower grades. To be sure, he sometimes develops a strong attachment for one or two of them and finds this relationship rewarding, especially if he is treated as an equal. However, he tends to develop a strong dislike for the majority of his teachers whom he perceives as sources of frustration. Where does he go then for personal relationships which will make him feel safe and secure? Obviously he turns to his peers and he will go to almost any length to earn their approval and confidence.

For most adolescents, subgroup conformity is essential. There may be rebellion against adults and rebellion against the larger society but coupled with that is a willingness to go all the way with his group of peers. This includes dress, mannerisms, vocabulary, convictions, drinking, and perhaps even the use of drugs. The principal reason for this extreme response to group pressure in adolescence is that for a span of a few years the individual's greatest, and often only, source of emotional security in personal relationships is friends of his own age who, like himself, are making the difficult transition from childhood to maturity.

In late adolescence and early maturity there is a gradual loosening of the bonds with the peer group or groups. A clearer perception of the sex role develops and along with it increased dependence upon the emotional relationship with an individual of the opposite sex, a relationship which may eventually lead to marriage. There is also an easier relationship with older adults who in the course of normal development are no longer considered a threat but who are valued for their companionship. Also, during the early and middle twenties parents are rediscovered as real persons whose affection and friendship can once again be a source of emotional security, even though it is far less important now than it was in infancy and early childhood. During these years the individual is reaching out in many directions for meaningful personal relationships.

If during adolescence and early maturity positive relationships are meager or nonexistent, marked feelings of insecurity will almost certainly develop. Emotional deprivation during this period in life is an important reason why so many young people turn in desperation to schizophrenic adjustments. Emotional insecurity, like emotional security, exists in varying degrees. In a brief excerpt from a series of interviews, a young woman in her twenties tries to explain to a psychotherapist how she feels about her lack of personal relationships with others. She is not psychotic nor is she about to become so, partly because she can still depend upon her parents, but she is unhappy, confused, and insecure. The excerpt follows:

*C.   You're supposed to be happy, really happy, but I still get these awful moods. I always seem to have to depend on other people all the time to lift me out of my mood and cheer me up. I don't know whether that's good or bad. It doesn't seem as though you should have to depend on other people. Some people seem to have enough within themselves so that they are self-sufficient or happy or something. I'm always depending on other people. Other people joke and kid and laugh and try to cheer me up. It seems as though I always need someone else to depend on, to lift me out of my moods.

*P.   You depend on other people to support you and make you feel better.

C.   Yes. I'm dependent on other people emotionally and in every other way. Maybe it's the type of person I am; I don't know. I don't think I'll ever be a strong, positive personality. I guess I never will be. I'm sort of a dependent personality, but I should try not to need other people so much. I'll just never be a really self-sufficient person who just doesn't need other people. I wouldn't want to be, but it would be better to be a little bit different than I am.

P.   You really want to find strength within yourself.

C.   Yes, I've been lucky, I suppose. There always is somebody, a friend or somebody in my family but I always have that feeling that sometime I may be alone, when you've got to have that strength within yourself and I don't have any. But maybe I do. I have a certain philosophy and a certain religious faith. I've heard that people have a reserve that they don't even know is there until they have to call on it. A reserve of strength is there which you don't even know you have.

P.   And do you think you have it?

C.   I suppose so, but I have doubts about myself.

P.   And with those doubts you're afraid to test it.

      * C—Client; P—Psychologist

C. Yet when I am alone and have to be independent I find I can and that gives me a little more confidence, not depending on somebody else all the time for everything. After my mother has been away for a while I find that I can get along without her. I can cook the meals for my father and I can do the things that I have to do but I have that feeling when she goes—oh, I'm so lost—but after she's gone for a while I have that feeling—oh, I can get along without her—of course I'm going to have to some day. (Pause) . . . I know I should get away from home. I'm so afraid to but it would be the best thing, I know. . . . I feel as though I'm too dependent on my family for social life; I enjoy them very much. I have that feeling that I would just like to stay with them and never see anybody else or never do anything else. It's nice to have that relationship with your family but at the same time you shouldn't be so dependent on them.

P. Yes.

C. As I say I'd be perfectly willing to stay right under my own family roof and never go out but that isn't right, really. I guess I do feel comfortable in my own family. They accept me as I am and I don't have to pretend to try to be somebody I'm not or anything like that. On the other hand you can't depend so much on your family like that.

P. And so over the weekend you went out on a picnic and felt fairly relaxed.

C. I've got a wonderful family really. We all get along very well together. I enjoy my family very much but I can't be with them all the time.

P. A little extension of that feeling into other social groups would help, would it?

C. Well, with other people I'm just not myself. Your family accepts you just as you are. You can't expect other people to accept you as your family does.

The Adult Years   The chronological age range of the adult years exclusive of old age is flexible, varying with the individuals and with cultures. In our society it includes, roughly, the period between the early or middle twenties and the middle or late sixties. During this span of approximately forty-five years, normal healthy persons have a variety of meaningful personal relationships. Unlike the infant who is dependent primarily upon his parents and the adolescent who is dependent primarily upon his peer group, the adult finds his sources of emotional security in many individuals and in many groups.

These vary, of course, with the individual's socioeconomic status, his occupation or profession, and whether or not he is married. In general, men look to their wives and children, especially when the children are young, for affection and intimate love. They also depend upon their occupational associates or upon their professional relationships for friendship and emotional support. They also find satisfactions in church and community activities, in clubs and organizations, in fishing and hunting trips with friends, in their social occasions at home, and so on. In our present society the emotional satisfactions which come from personal relationships have much the same sources for women as for men, with some differences in emphasis. Women, characteristically, are more dependent upon their husbands and children as a source of emotional security. However, they too have their church and community activities, their clubs, and so on. Many also have work outside the home or careers which, as with men, provide fulfilling relationships.

The wide variety of personal associations during the adult years makes it relatively easy for an individual to be content even though one or more of the usual sources are non-existent. For example, a person can remain unmarried and still find personal relationships that are wholly adequate, or he may not be a "joiner" knowing that what he has at home and at work is all he needs. The flexibility and multiplicity of human contacts during adulthood make shifts and substitutions relatively easy. There are hazards, of course, but if there has not been too much deprivation during the years preceding maturity they do not usually constitute serious threats. However, if there have been serious deprivations during the formative years adult relationships are approached with temerity and rigidity and so may not become sources of emotional security but rather a series of tension-building threats. Under these conditions a crisis situation may precipitate a behavior disorder.

A crisis situation which will almost certainly arise at least once or perhaps several times during the adult years is the death of someone who is an important source of emotional security, such as a husband or wife, a child, a parent, or a close friend. The loss of the personal relationship results in bereavement. Very little research has been done on this important aspect of the emotional lives of human beings. There are many factors involved in the length and depth of the mourning. Obviously the closeness of the relationship with the deceased is fundamental. If there is remorse over what was done or left undone before the death occurred, the period of bereavement will be longer. The age of the person at the time of the loss is also important. In general, the hurt is less in later years, partly because by then the emotions have been dulled somewhat and partly because death now wears a familiar face. Those individuals who have a large number of personal relationships can usually turn rather easily, after a period of six or eight months, to those who are left as sources of emotional security. On the other hand, those who are dependent on just one or two are likely to feel that they are left with nothingness and may turn to suicide as an escape from unbearable grief. The intensity of bereavement indicates clearly the great importance of interpersonal relationships as a source of emotional security.

Old Age   Old age, like adolescence, is a difficult term to define in terms of calendar years. Two thousand years ago Cicero wrote that old age begins at forty-three. His definition was probably correct for his period and for many centuries thereafter. When old age begins early, the adolescent stage of development is relatively brief. At an age when in our society young men would still be undergraduate or graduate students, Augustus was marshalling the forces that would eventually make him emperor of Rome; George Washington was head of the Virginia militia; Alexander Hamilton was laying the foundation for a sound financial system for the United States of America; Napoleon was a general in the French army. In our present-day society, adolescence carries over into the twenties and old age is usually thought of as beginning at sixty-five. This is generally accepted as the age of mandatory retirement. It is the age when the majority of men and a much smaller number of women step over the arbitrary line between the productive years and the so-called golden years. To be sure, there are many exceptions. Dwight Eisenhower was in his late sixties when he served his second term as president. Winston Churchill was at the peak of his career after he had passed the age of sixty-five. Actually, there should be no definite chronological year set as the time when old age begins, partly because there are such wide individual differences and partly because aging is a gradual process.

In the later years, personal relationships continue to be a source of emotional security even though they are less significant and intense. The husband or wife is a needed companion but the children, now in their adult years and perhaps living far away, contribute much less to the emotional needs of their parents than they did when they were young. Grandchildren, if there are any, replace to some extent the sons and daughters. The circle of friends is gradually becoming smaller and smaller, especially for those whose professional associations no longer exist. This is not as serious a deprivation as it might appear to be, especially if the reduction in personal relationships is a gradual process.

There are two theories concerning the personal relationships and the work activities of aged persons: that they should remain as active as possible within their physical limitations and that they should disengage themselves, at least to a considerable extent. Actually these two theories should not be thought of as a dichotomy. Gradual disengagement is a necessity and should be welcomed. Most old people do not have the energy to participate in the kind of social life that was so rewarding for them in earlier years. Even visits by their children and grandchildren, while anticipated with pleasure, are concluded with relief. Many grandparents have been heard to say that it took them a month to recover from such visits. Personal relationships are needed, to be sure, but their keenness has been dulled by age. This is the time in life when other sources of emotional security, such as the impersonal environment and memories and, for some, even future prospects become more meaningful and satisfying.

The Impersonal Environment

In Chapter Four, the statement was made that environment must always be interpreted in terms of the individual reacting to it. An individual's impersonal environment is usually an important source of emotional security. However, like interpersonal relationships, it can constitute a threat. The impersonal environment includes everything which surrounds the individual throughout his life excepting, of course, his associations with other human beings. It should be noted that there is considerable overlap between that which is personal and that which is impersonal because of perceived and remembered associations. Our dependency on inanimate objects as a source of emotional security begins early in life. During late infancy and early childhood toys, stuffed animals, dolls, and so on are second only in importance to the relationship with parents. The little girl takes her doll to bed with her and the presence of the doll gives her a feeling of warmth and security. The little boy has a teddy bear or some other object which is an inseparable companion when he is alone.

It is desirable that the impersonal environment be rich in possibilities for a variety of attachments. Parents can never be quite sure what is going to appeal to a child. An example is a little girl a year and a half old who went to stay at her grandparent's home for a week. While there she had become fascinated by a woodbine leaf which lay against the porch screen. When her visit was concluded the only object which she was interested in saying goodbye to was this same leaf which she kissed wistfully.

As children grow older most objects which have been sources of emotional security are gradually replaced by new ones. What these will be depends, of course, upon the individual child and his surroundings. A gifted boy made a list of "the things that I think are buetiful" and which had special meaning for him. At the time he made the list, which he did not know would ever be seen by anyone else, he was eight years of age and was having some difficulty in his relationships with his peers. The following is an exact copy:

1. The other day I saw in a chicken dealer's truck a nice white rooster with black dots.

2. A paper atlas cover, all trimmed with gold and blue in the center.

3. The purple lilies with whitish yellow centers.

4. A red, white, and black handkerchief.

5. A chair with pretty flowers on it in sunset.

6. The waves dashing against rocks nicely set and not picked making wave breaker island.

7. The silver light on the ash tray in sunset.

8. The blue and gold saddle on my toy horse.

9. Lighting, which flashes so.

10. An almost cloudless sky with only a couple of fleecy clouds with inlets like the State of Washington.

11. Blue and pink plates mixed on a table.

12. My little pine's new growth. Its greener than all the rest and on it you see neither spider nor cocoon.

Adolescents usually concentrate so intensely on establishing and maintaining interpersonal relationships that they pay somewhat less attention to their impersonal environment than they did in childhood or will again in later years. When they are well into maturity material possessions become very important. The homes they rent or buy, the automobiles they own, certain pieces of furniture, and so on, become a part of themselves.

During late middle age and old age both men and women depend a great deal upon inanimate objects as a source of emotional security. Many even find such objects and other aspects of the impersonal environment more satisfying than personal relationships. The favorite chair, the comfortable room, the familiar house and grounds, antique pieces, pictures and articles that have been kept for many years as concrete reminders of pleasant experiences—all these and many more provide a feeling of safety that can never be found in "gilded playpens" for the old. There is satisfaction in caring for such objects, a task that can be performed with less strain than is involved in relations with other human beings. Those old people who can stay in familiar surroundings in daily contact with an impersonal environment which is part of themselves are fortunate.

For most persons, perhaps to some extent for everyone, natural scenery is a source of emotional security. Its meaning varies with individuals and with their geographical location. The sky, the ocean, the mountains, the lakes, the forests, the prairies, the fields, the parks, the trees, the flowers—one or more of these or many others which might be listed may have special significance for an individual, providing him with a feeling of protection; a kind of communion exists which is relaxing. This is true of persons of all ages although it is perhaps most important to those who are elderly. Through the years their attachment to certain aspects of their scenic surroundings has deepened and often has replaced to some extent the losses which they have experienced in personal relationships.

Memories

In mental hygiene and clinical psychology a great deal of attention has been given to memories, whether conscious or repressed, which have been threatening for the individual. Freud, Adler, Sullivan, and many others have laid much stress on the importance of early experiences with unhappy connotations. Relatively little attention has been given to the importance of memories which are sources of emotional security rather than of emotional insecurity. Every individual in the course of his life acquires a vast reservoir of memories of both kinds. If he is well integrated with a positive self-concept pleasant memories will predominate and constitute an important resource for him especially in his later years.

Supportive memories vary tremendously in variety and intensity. They may be associated with earlier personal relationships with objects, with books, with scenes, with travel or with a combination of these and other aspects of an individual's experiential background. Past achievements, especially for aged men, are especially important in maintaining a positive self image. Since pleasant memories provide a feeling of security it is not surprising that they are resorted to so often, especially when the present is rather threatening and the future is somewhat bleak.

Future Prospects

It was pointed out in earlier chapters that human beings have a strong drive for self-actualization. If they are relatively free from anxiety, future prospects constitute a source of emotional security. Working toward both immediate and distant goals is a rewarding experience even though there may be many obstacles which must be overcome. This is especially true during the period preceding middle age when optimism is characteristically at a high level. Children, if given the right home and school surroundings, like to learn; young people look forward to marriage and careers; mature adults, while enjoying the present, are working hard to establish for themselves a better and more secure future. The achievement of goals along the way is satisfying. The prospects that lie ahead remain alluring.

After middle age most persons are obliged to make many adjustments. Usually they are not as optimistic then as they were earlier. However, if they are sufficiently flexible, they begin to look forward to the last years of their lives as a time when they can shed many of their responsibilities and have enough leisure to do some of the things which they were not able to do earlier. They also develop new interests which fit their age and physical limitations. Some become amateur genealogists exploring their family histories and in so doing becoming identified to some extent with their ancestors. It is a tentative approach to an acceptance of the fact of death which in their old age they realize is now not far away. Many take pleasure in making detailed plans for that event. They make their wills and give oral or written instructions for the conduct of their funerals. Some even find a certain amount of security in contemplating tombstones and in selecting their own. An example of this is a woman in her late seventies who had inscribed on her tombstone the words "Mother sleeps well after life's fitful fever."

The fear of death is sometimes much overrated by persons far removed from it. Sir William Osler made a careful study of some 500 persons on their deathbeds. He stated that about 90 suffered bodily pain, 11 showed mental apprehension, two were positively terrified, one expressed spiritual exaltation, and one suffered bitter remorse. "The great majority gave no sign one way or the other; like their birth, their death was sleep and a forgetting" (quoted by Cowdry, 1940). Death is obviously a mystery for all; but for most it is apparently not a terrifying mystery.[2]

ANXIETY

In the preceding pages emphasis was placed upon the ways in which interpersonal relationships, the impersonal environment, memories, and future prospects satisfy the need for emotional security. These same sources can cause emotional insecurity with accompanying tension and anxiety. Anxiety is the apprehension which an individual experiences when his personality is threatened. It can be either constructive or destructive, depending upon the degree of the "apprehension" and the extent of the "threat." Normal anxiety is a reaction which is proportionate to the threat. It stimulates the individual to find ways of meeting the threat successfully. It is a stimulant for growth and development. An individual without some anxiety does not exist.

Whereas a limited amount of anxiety is essential for growth, an excessive amount is disrupting, frequently forcing the individual into building up neurotic or psychotic defenses. Extreme or neurotic anxiety, says May,

> . . . is a reaction to threat which is (1) disproportionate to the objective danger, (2) involves repression (dissociation) and other forms

[2] J. M. Brown; F. K. Berrien, and D. L. Russell, *Applied Psychology* (New York: The Macmillan Company, 1966), p. 175.

of intrapsychic conflict, and, as a corollary (3) is managed by means of various forms of retrenchment of activity and awareness, such as inhibitions, the development of symptoms, and varied neurotic defense mechanisms. It will be noted that these characteristics are related to each other; the reaction is disproportionate to the objective danger *because* some intrapsychic conflict is involved.[3]

The neurotic person never has a clear understanding of what is causing his anxiety tension. Consequently, responses are made with reference to the anxiety state itself rather than with reference to the actual cause of the anxiety. Initially these responses are characteristically trial and error in nature, but eventually the behavior that most effectively reduces the anxiety is selected and fixated by rewarding aftereffects, namely tension reduction. Thus, methods of behaving are resorted to, which immediately, although temporarily, reduce the anxiety. Such methods of adjustment not only fail to get at the source of the problem but also actually increase the anxiety for the period beyond the immediate present. Distant rewards are sacrificed in order to avoid immediate punishment.

Anxiety Is Learned

There have been a number of experiments with animals which demonstrate that anxiety is learned. Two examples of these will be presented here. The problem of learned anxiety among human beings will also be considered.

Miller[4] placed albino rats in a simple apparatus consisting of two compartments separated by a door. One compartment was white with a grid as a floor; the other was black without a grid. Before training, the animals showed no marked preference for either compartment. The rats were placed in the white compartment where they received an electric shock from the grid. They then escaped into the black compartment through the open door. After a number of such trials, the animals ran out of the white compartment even though they received no shock from the grid.

In order to demonstate that the animals had learned anxiety, they were taught a new adjustment without the use of further shock.

[3] R. May, *The Meaning of Anxiety* (New York: The Ronald Press Company, 1950), p. 197.

[4] N. E. Miller, "Studies of Fear as an Acquirable Drive: I. Fear as Motivation and Fear-reduction as Reinforcement in the Learning of New Responses," *Journal of Experimental Psychology*, XXXVIII (1948), 89–101.

The door, which had previously been left open, was now closed. The only way that it could be opened was by rotating a little wheel a fraction of a turn. This wheel was above the door. Under these conditions the animals, through trial-and-error behavior, learned to escape from the white compartment by rotating the wheel. Later the conditions were changed so that the door could be opened only by pressing a bar. This new adjustment was also learned. The learning of these new habits was definitely dependent upon the experience that the animals had had with moderately strong electric shock during the first stages of training. The state of anxiety had been created, and the animals were motivated by it to escape from a threatening situation.

Mowrer, in an earlier experiment, placed rats on a circular runway resembling a race track. It was enclosed by walls of transparent celluloid on either side; the floor was an electric grid. The rats were divided into three groups. Those in Group I were placed singly on the runway. A tone was sounded for five seconds, at the end of which time, if the rat had not moved out of the section where it was resting, an electric shock was applied. By moving to another section of the grid the rat escaped the shock. If, when the tone was presented, the rat moved immediately to another section of the grid, no shock was administered. For this group the tone-shock combinations were given regularly every sixty minutes.

The procedure for Group II was the same as for Group I, except that the tone-shock combinations were presented at three different intervals in random order. These intervals were 15 minutes, 60 minutes, and 105 minutes. The procedure for Group III involved tone-shock combinations every 60 minutes, but shocks without a preceding tone-warning were given between the 60-minute periods at 15-minute, 30-minute, and 45-minute intervals.

The animals in Group I learned the best, those in Group II next best, and those in Group III the poorest. Concerning this, Mowrer states:

> Speaking loosely, it may be said that the poorness of the learning obtained in the Group-II and Group-III animals was due to the fact that they were given less opportunity to "let down" between trials than were the Group-I animals. In other words, they were kept in a more or less chronic state of apprehension or suspense. In the

Group-II animals this was accomplished by "keeping them guessing" as to when each succeeding stimulation was to occur. In the Group-III animals, this element of uncertainty was presumably absent, but the stimuli came in such rapid succession that one stimulus had no more than occurred when the next one began to be "expected." In either case, conditioned reactions to the tone were relatively "unrewarding" in that little was gained in the way of anxiety-reduction when they occurred; whereas, in the case of the Group-I animals each response was followed by a relatively long, unvarying period of no stimulation, with correspondingly great anxiety-reduction.[5]

In the preceding experiment, the situation which made it possible for anxiety reduction to be achieved brought about the most learning. The response was reinforced by the anxiety reduction rewards. It seems probable that neurotic behavior, if it brings anxiety reduction, is therefore learned, regardless of how undesirable it may otherwise be. The experiment also brings out the fact that unpredictable punishment brings poorer learning than that which is predictable, and that too-frequent punishment brings the poorest learning. Applying this principle to human beings, if a child is sometimes punished for a certain act and at other times not punished for the same act, or if he is in a situation where he is repeatedly punished, then relatively little learning takes place. Instead, his anxiety is increased with accompanying tension and confusion. The basis has been laid for later neurotic or psychotic behavior, for eventually the individual must find some means of reducing the anxiety.

Although it is quite possible for an adult who has had a relatively normal childhood to become neurotic, in the great majority of cases of neurosis, there is an early history of anxiety and maladaptive behavior. All anxious children do not become neurotic adults, but most neurotic adults were anxious children. What are the factors in the childhood environment which lead to internalized conflict, to feelings of guilt, and to social immaturity? How is anxiety, the basis for later neurotic behavior, learned by children? Why does social and emotional development proceed harmoniously in some, whereas in others there is distortion and retardation?

In our society the world of the preschool child is typically the

[5] O. H. Mowrer, "Anxiety-Reduction and Learning," *Journal of Experimental Psychology,* XXVII (1940), 510.

family. From the time of birth, the infant is to a considerable degree dependant upon his parents. From them he achieves his basic personality structure. There are many possible relationships between the child and his parents, some desirable and some undesirable. They can be classified as follows:

Love (reward)—Wrath (punishment)
LOVE (REWARD)
WRATH (PUNISHMENT)
Love (reward)—WRATH (PUNISHMENT)
LOVE (REWARD)—Wrath (punishment)

LOVE (REWARD)—WRATH (PUNISHMENT)   In considering each of these five relationships between the child and his parents, the discussion of needs in Chapter Two should be recalled. It will be remembered that the child requires security. If he is denied security, he becomes anxious and the behavior to which he turns to reduce the anxiety will become fixated through the functioning of the law of effect. If the child experiences reward and punishment in approximately equal amounts at the hands of his parents, he is likely to become confused concerning his relationship with them. He feels insecure because their reaction to what he does is as likely to be wrath as love. He is emotionally dependent upon them, but he never knows when they will support him or when they will reject him. The situation is especially chaotic for the child when the reward or the punishment comes many hours, or perhaps many days, after the behavioral act. An erratic pattern in the distribution of love and wrath is very disturbing for the child. In such a situation he learns anxiety, and the anxiety, in turn, is likely to be accompanied by a feeling of guilt.

LOVE (REWARD)   If the relationship between the child and his parents does not include punishment, then the child is overprotected. Overprotection, as was pointed out in Chapter Four, can have very harmful effects. The child who is always rewarded, whose every whim is gratified, has little opportunity to learn to differentiate. It is unlikely that the parents can be overindulgent in dealing with the infant during the first few months of his life, but if overindulgence is continued the child will learn to expect too much from others. Such an approach by parents only delays the development of anxiety, for in later years the egocentric, pampered individual will find that he is inadequately equipped to handle his social relationships realistically. That will be the time when the anxiety will develop.

WRATH (PUNISHMENT)   At the opposite extreme is the *wrath* relationship between the child and his parents. Where there is continual wrath, punishment, and rejection with little or no love, reward, and acceptance, the child will certainly learn anxiety. The specific mechanisms of adjustment which he may use to reduce that anxiety are almost numberless. Of course he feels rejected. He may react to rejection by his parents by rejecting them himself. If he has no affection for them and his rejection of them seems wholly justified, he may generalize this principle which he has learned in his family relationships to society as a whole. He rejects society; he blames society, but he does not blame himself. This is an important basis of adult criminal behavior. It is also the foundation of psychopathic personalities.

LOVE (REWARD)—WRATH (PUNISHMENT)   A fourth relationship between the child and his parents is one in which there is some love and reward but a great deal more wrath and punishment. This relationship is conducive to the learning of anxiety early in life. The parents continue as love objects, but, at the same time, they constitute a threat to the child's security. In such a situation, the child is likely to develop an overly strong superego. Much of what he does is punished by his parents, so the child wishes he had behaved differently. Guilt feelings are likely to become strong. The child has experienced enough love from his parents to know what it is like and to desire more. It is very easy for him to be convinced—and probably he has been told this many times by his parents—that if only he had behaved differently he would have had more of their rewarding love. This situation is an important basis of neurotic behavior. As Mowrer very neatly states: "I believe the indications are that human beings fall victims of neurosis, not because of what they would do but cannot, but because of what they have done and would that they had not."[6]

LOVE (REWARD)—WRATH (PUNISHMENT)   The love-wrath rela-

[6] O. H. Mower, "Learning Theory and the Neurotic Paradox," *American Journal of Orthopsychiatry*, XVIII (1948), 596.

tionship between the child and his parents is the best. A preponderance of love gives the security necessary for normal growth, whereas the relatively small amount of wrath, appropriately applied, promotes desirable differentiation on the part of the child. This painful learning takes place in the secure environment of affection and acceptance. Anxiety is kept at a minimum; emotional and social maturity result. The child identifies himself with his parents and through them, in later years, identifies himself with his society. Through the medium of this kind of relationship his basic needs are satisfied, especially his need for emotional security and his need for status. He develops self-confidence, and it should be remembered that self-confidence, like anxiety, is learned.

Anxiety Is Repressive

Anxiety is an important cause of repression. This is especially true when it is associated with feelings of guilt. The person experiencing the anxiety wishes to forget the incident or incidents which caused it.

A person suffering from anxiety commonly follows one of two procedures in repressing it. He may substitute an acceptable cause for the real one and, in time, come to believe that the acceptable cause constitutes the actual source of his anxiety. The real cause becomes so thoroughly repressed that it is very difficult, if not impossible, for him to recall it. The second procedure does not involve substitutes. Instead, there is direct repression. Anxiety is present, perhaps very acute anxiety, but the individual has no conscious idea of what is causing it. This second method of repression is likely to result in more personality disintegration than the first.

The repressed causes of anxiety are often made accessible to a person through hypnotism. Inhibitions are weakened during the hypnotic trance, and forgotten experiences come more easily into consciousness. A certain student was working under considerable tension because of free-floating anxiety. He was anxious about his social relationships, about his academic work, about his future after he finished college—in fact, about almost everything. He knew that he was anxious, but he did not know why. In the course of therapy he was hypnotized. The following excerpt is taken from the dialogue which took place during the trance:

*C. I feel very, very small. I feel as though I were shrinking down into a very, very small space.

*P. Do you want to tell me a little more about that feeling?

C. It feels as though I'm getting very, very tiny. I see a sort of grey funnel with a black spot at the end of it. I see it now, but I have never seen it before.

P. Tell me more about that grey funnel.

C. All I can think of right now is the grey funnel with a black spot at the end of it.

P. How old were you when you saw it first?

C. I never saw it before. I've always seen things close in. I've never felt afraid. I haven't claustrophobia or anything like that. I just felt that I was shrinking along with everything else. The room is shrinking, but I am shrinking in proportion. I always feel a little close. I feel that way now. I feel as though my hands were very, very tiny. I think I've had that feeling just about all my life. I don't try to do it; it just comes. I don't try to get away from it. It comes any time. I'll be sitting reading and the book seems very, very small and my hands seem very, very small. It's just a feeling. Everything is very clear, but it is very, very tiny . . . my hands feel funny.

P. Think hard now, back as far as you can. Say back to the time when you were three years old. Can you think of any experience that you had then that made you very afraid?

C. Not afraid, but there was an experience that made me feel a little guilty. Not afraid, never afraid of anything. . . . I'm afraid of high places. I never mentioned that before. When I'm small and especially when I have my eyes closed, I'm afraid I'm going to topple forward and it's a long ways down. Funny, I've never felt exactly that way before. . . .

P. You're still in the trance. You're going deeper into the trance. You can recall clearly these things that happened to you when you were young.

C. I used to press my knuckles against my eyeballs and I could see spots. I could see spots, greys and greens and all colored spots. Patterns, very intricate colorful patterns. Greens, yellows at times, usually greens and yellows. Lines, greens and yellows.

P. Could you tell me more about that?

C. I can do it even today. (*Presses hands against eyes.*) First, when I press, I see a yellow blotch; then I see yellow blotches. I see a big, dazzling yellow thing in the middle. I see yellow spots; then I see—I see

* C—Client; P—Psychologist.

diagonals that come in from the outside. They come into a circle. Now they jiggle around. They bubble up in all different kinds of shapes. Very strange. Now I get that pattern again. It's like—oh, it's almost like scroll work. It's curly. It looks like a large number of tentacles. Now they are yellow on red. They are so thick they are like spaghetti, almost. There's that hole in the middle again. There always seems to be some pattern to the middle. Now it's a very reddish, orange color. It sinks down. Now there are two or three circles that seem to be jumping all around.

P. You're going deeper and deeper into the trance. Deeper and deeper. Deeper and deeper. Now, as you press your eyes what do you see?

C. Just green, green and yellow. There is jagged white lightning. Now I see something that I've seen a lot of times before. It's like a yellow floor. There are yellow tile; there are thin black lines along the side. There's a yellow blotch in the middle. Now it's brilliant white in the middle.

P. Can you tell me what it is?

C. Now it's green again. Every time I look I see something different. The shape that I see now is like a spiral. Now it's gone.

P. You're going deeper and deeper into the trance. Deeper and deeper. Deeper and deeper. Now try to see what the shape is. What is it the shape of?

C. It's black now with a yellow and white background. Now it's blue, grey. Now it's black. The only thing I can think of is cancer.

P. Tell me more about that.

C. It seems as though it could be cancer. Funny, I never thought about it that way before. There is that black thing with the tentacles and tentacles. The yellow and white is grey around the black center.

P. Is that associated with a person?

C. No.

P. Just a cancer. No person with it.

C. Everything goes so fast I don't have time to think about anything.

P. You're going deeper and deeper into the trance. Deeper and deeper. You're going to try now to think of associations with a cancer. Can you see a person with the cancer?

C. I can only think of my grandfather. He died of cancer. I was always supposed to be like my grandfather. They named me after him. I'm built the same.

P. How old were you when your grandfather died?

C. I was about nine, I think, I didn't know what cancer was then.

P. Did you think a great deal of your grandfather?

C. He was just a good joe that I always liked. I didn't want to be too near him because he used to blow cigar smoke into my face. He was being playful, but I didn't think it was very cute.

P. Tell me more about that.

C. He was very, very much a man. A strong farmer, he worked very hard, and he married three times. I remember sitting on his porch one time in a lightning storm. His third wife was afraid of lightning and she always wanted to hide under the bed. I remember him laughing about it. He couldn't understand how anyone could be afraid of lightning.

P. Did your grandfather suffer a good deal from the cancer?

C. I never saw him suffer. As far as I'm concerned there wasn't anything wrong with him when he died. I didn't see any signs of pain. I can't associate him with sickness. . . . I liked to go to my grandfather's farm. It was all quiet. I liked to see the trees and the sun shining through the green leaves. The leaves were such a deep green. Walking among them was like being under a canopy. The whole thing was like an old French painting. I thought of my grandfather as just part of it all. A man in a shirt walking up and down the path. I remember when I used to call co' boss and the cows came running. When my grandfather died I couldn't go to the farm any more—everything was all shot. I wouldn't recognize the place now. . . . As far as I'm concerned now, my grandfather was just a farmer, but when I was a boy he meant a lot more than that. The farm was something cool, water, pebbles in the brook. When I look at him now, he was a swell fellow, but I don't see him now as I did in childhood. Now he's just a dead grandfather who was a farmer.

P. How did you look at him in childhood?

C. I looked on him as a live grandfather who was a farmer, a part of the farm. I think of him as very powerful. A man with a whip in his hand. I think of him as a powerful animal, not cruel by any means. I think if a bull had jumped at him, he could have slapped him down. I think of him as pretty much of a figure.

P. Yet cancer was powerful enough to strike him down. Are you afraid of developing it yourself?

C. Yes, I'd say now that there's a good chance that I have it. I had a sort of hemorrhage yesterday morning and spit out two or three mouthfuls of blood. It bothered me a little bit, but I tried to push it off.

P. How recently has the anxiety about cancer been with you?

C. Oh, for a long time. I've read about it, and my grandfather died of it.

> I remember about a year after my grandfather died, I realized one night that I was going to die. I realized how little time a man has in comparison with what he doesn't have. I was panic-stricken. I was terrified. I started screaming and my mother came up. She tried to quiet me down. I was convinced and I am convinced now that you might just as well sit back and wait for death. . . . When I press my eyes I see stars and when I see stars I see death. When I see stars it's beautiful, but it is very definitely death. I think it's a beautiful way to think about it.

It can be seen from the preceding material that the student had repressed all memory of his grandfather's death by cancer and of his later panic reaction to the thought of death. As a boy he had identified himself with his grandfather, a powerful man who could slap down a charging bull. Yet mysterious death had come suddenly and not only struck down the boy's symbol of power but also taken from him his pleasant farm retreat. Undoubtedly there was some feeling of guilt associated with the anxiety, for a man is not supposed to be afraid to die. There had been several client-centered interviews with this young man before he was hypnotized. In no one of these was his grandfather ever mentioned; nor was there any mention of the later acute anxiety attacks concerning death.

Anxiety Inhibits New Learning

Mowrer has presented the view that a neurosis is not a learning excess but a learning deficit. He says, "The neurotic is an individual who has learned how not to learn."[7] He has learned how not to be socialized and so remains immature. He is like a machine with some of its parts missing. He cannot adequately handle the tasks of the immediate present because he is partially crippled.

The term *learning deficit* suggests—although Mowrer does not say this—that the neurotic person has not learned. Actually he has learned, up to a point. He has learned neurotic patterns of behavior, and these have become fixed because through them he was able in earlier years to reduce anxiety tension. The anxiety was learned first, and the relatively fixed maladaptive patterns of behavior were then learned as tension-reducing responses. However, assuming that in childhood the anxiety was only partially reduced through the adjust-

---

[7] Mowrer, "Learning Theory and the Neurotic Paradox," *op. cit.*, p. 605.

ment mechanisms used, the individual found himself caught in a trap. On the one hand, he continued with the undesirable responses because they brought him some relief; on the other hand, the continued anxiety made him afraid to try out new responses. The anxiety inhibited new learning. The anxious person always prefers to play it safe.

It is commonly observed that the normal child is relatively happy, flexible, and full of questions. He is very much interested in trying out new things. The maladjusted child is unhappy, rigid in his behavior, and is characteristically fearful of new situations. Why is he maladjusted, unhappy, and fearful? It would appear that it is because he has learned anxiety, and the anxiety in turn has inhibited the new learnings which must take place if he is to achieve emotional and social maturity. A characteristic symptom of a person who is close to schizophrenia is repetitive behavior or an inflexible daily routine. The repetitive or routine behavior provides a certain amount of safety for the individual. In following a set pattern he feels relatively secure. An example of this is the young man who is a gifted artist, but his anxiety has made him afraid to draw and to paint freely. Instead he sits for hours at a time drawing the same figure over and over again.

In a series of experiments with rats Maier has demonstrated the effect of presenting an insoluble problem to a rat, then forcing him to make some response. In these circumstances, the rat learns anxiety and his behavior becomes inhibited or stereotyped. The stereotyped responses are very specific. Those adopted by any given animal are repeated without variation for at least several hundred trials, without the animal's attempting even once an alternative.

Maier and Klee put a group of sixty rats through various experiences to establish position-reward and symbol-reward responses and also to establish position and symbol stereotypes.

All animals were then trained to form either a symbol-reward or a position-reward response, the character of which was different from the first response. Thus all animals were alike in that each had a rewarded response as a second response, but they differed in that part of them had stereotypes as their first responses and part had rewarded responses as their initial responses. After the second response was learned, all rats were treated alike in that the second response that had previously been rewarded was now punished on half the trials. Since the punishment was random it was impossible for the animal to learn a response that was adaptive in nature (i.e., a response that always led to reward and never to punishment). This is the condition which produces stereotypes.

During the 160 trials (10 trials per day) in this situation, 54 rats persisted in the second response that they had been trained to make, despite the fact that the reward aspect had been changed. Not only did these rats fail to alter their response, but 47 of them never made a single deviation in 160 trials. The remaining 7 rats made one deviation each in 160 trials.[8]

The stereotyped behavior of the rats in this experiment persisted even when by altering it they had the opportunity to obtain food easily. This is comparable to the behavior of human beings who, because of their anxiety, have sought security in neurotic or psychotic adjustments and by so doing have inhibited new learning.

SUMMARY

With the possible exception of physical survival, the need for emotional security is the most important of the four discussed in this and the three preceding chapters. Under certain conditions it becomes even more important than life itself. Human beings depend upon two principal sources for the satisfaction of this need: interpersonal relationships and the impersonal environment. Memories and future prospects are significant but less important. Positive interpersonal relationships during infancy and early childhood are essential for the development of a healthy personality. They loom large again during adolescence when acceptance by one's peers comes close to being a necessity. They continue of course to be important during the mature years and old age, although they diminish somewhat with the passage of time. Human beings also draw heavily upon their impersonal environments to bolster their feelings of security and safety. Each individual has a large number of inanimate objects and living but nonhuman things in his environment that have special significance for him. Memories, especially in old age, usually have a great deal of value as a source of emotional security, and future

---

[8] N. R. F. Maier, *Frustration: The Study of Behavior Without a Goal* (New York: McGraw-Hill Book Company, 1949), pp. 28–29. Copyright 1949 by McGraw-Hill Book Company. Used by permission.

prospects at any age can be wellsprings of motivation and satisfaction.

Anxiety results when the sources of emotional security are inadequate or predistorted. Anxiety is usually learned from early family relationships but it is often the result of later experiences. Mild anxiety is probably essential for growth but excessive or neurotic anxiety is repressive and inhibits new learning. The inhibition of new learning brings about rigid and immature behavior. The individual whose learning has been inhibited by anxiety is inadequately equipped to deal with his environment.

THE HOME

chapter 8

The home is a physical unit. It is a place where a few members of the human race live together in close association. It is also an economic unit where money is earned and saved and spent and where personal possessions are kept, possessions which as the years go by have considerable significance for the members of the family. The home is also a kind of emotional unit filled with such intangibles as love, hate, fear, anxiety, joy, anger, and sorrow. Although it is to some extent independent of the world outside it is nevertheless a part of the larger society. Its special potency lies in the fact that the child begins developing here and what happens to him during the most formative years of his life determines to a considerable extent his personality structure and eventually, to some degree, the structure of the society in which he will live as an adult.

FAMILY RELATIONSHIPS

When a child is born he knows nothing. All he inherits is a structure predisposing him to certain forms of activity and providing him with certain potentialities. The newborn infant usually begins life with a family. The human's period of infancy is a long one; in later

COLLECTION, THE MUSEUM OF MODERN ART, NEW YORK. A. Conger Goodyear Fund years as a growing child and as an adolescent he remains, to a considerable degree, intellectually, emotionally, and economically dependent upon his parents. As noted above, his experiences within the family circle determine in large measure the structure of his personality.

The good home satisfies the child's need for emotional security. It provides an atmosphere in which he can be himself. It is necessary for every person to know that there are those who care deeply for him, who accept him and like him for what he is. The child must be certain at all times that his parents love him and will continue to love him in spite of what he may say and do. They are his shield against the world that he does not understand. They are his protectors from the half-formed fears that he may have. They provide him with the feelings of contentment and of safety which are as necessary to his sound emotional growth as good food is to his physical growth. It is essential also that the child be certain that his parents care for each other. This does not mean that he should never overhear any disagreements between his parents, but it does mean that his emotional security depends upon his never doubting a strong affection between them.

If there is more than one child in the family, the parents bear the responsibility for making each one feel that he is important in his own right, that he is loved for his own sake. Parents should never make unfavorable comparisons among their children. Each should be praised for the abilities which he has and encouraged to develop them.

The need for emotional security is especially strong during the first few months of life. The importance of the relationship between the infant and his parents, especially his mother, during this period is emphasized by Ribble, who says:

> The groundwork for emotional development is laid in the first year of life. Babies are born with some capacity to respond positively to another human being. After the first week of life an infant fixes his gaze on the human face that approaches him, but not on any inanimate object. At four or five weeks the look is often followed by a smile or a gurgle. The hands of the child grope toward the feeder during the meal, and by four or five months there is a definite recognition of a familiar face. A charge of excitement through the entire

muscular system accompanies the smile of greeting. From this time on, definite seeking and reaching toward the most familiar person is seen. A basic relationship has been established. At this tender age it is not clearly love, but rather an expansive reaction to the satisfaction of need, a reaction which paves the way to loving—and also to the functions of perception and recognition.

An important way in which positive feeling reactions are stimulated in the child is in the care of his body. This includes feeding, bathing, dressing, and arrangements for sleeping periods. Here the parent naturally takes the active role. The skill and tenderness with which these activities are carried out contribute toward the child's first love feeling toward other persons who bring comfort and pleasure. This early care becomes to the small child a relational experience of great importance, even though to the busy parent it may soon become routine and perfunctory.[1]

Maslow and Szilagyi-Kessler conducted a study on the relationship between psychological security and the length of breast-feeding in infancy. They found that "the highest security scores were obtained by the groups who were breast-fed little or not at all and by those who were fed at the breast for over a year, a relatively long time in our culture."[2] At first glance it would appear from this study that breast-feeding was relatively unimportant. However, the writers point out that the children who were not breast-fed could not be, and that the mothers in the study indicated marked regret concerning this and tried to compensate to the child by additional affection. Breast-feeding or lack of it is significant for the child when it is a manifestation of affection or when it is a symbol of rejection. It is the affection or rejection, not the breast-feeding per se, which is important.

Identifications

The family provides the infant and young child with opportunities for identification with other human beings. The first significant relationship is usually with the mother, but as time goes on, the other members of the family group provide new understandings and

[1] M. A. Ribble, *The Personality of the Young Child* (New York: Columbia University Press, 1955), pp. 92–93.

[2] A. H. Maslow, and I. Szilagyi-Kessler, "Security and Breast-Feeding," *Journal of Abnormal Social Psychology*, XLI (1946), 84.

new emotional satisfactions for the child. He learns from them what the world he has been born into is like. The family circle is his universe in miniature. His experiences in this tiny universe largely determine his personality structure and his later adult attitude toward himself, others, and society in general.

Until recently the American home was not limited to one or two generations. It was a larger group, characteristically including grandparents and sometimes even uncles and aunts. This situation caused many problems, to be sure, but it did provide a wider range of choice for the growing child. If his mother was not satisfying his needs adequately he could turn to another significant adult, perhaps his grandfather or grandmother. Today this kind of identification is not easily available. Consequently, the parents carry a greater burden than ever before.

Expectancies and Goals

In the process of growing up within the family the child learns, among other things, what is expected of him in the present and in the future. In time these expectancies, which originally came from the significant persons in his environment, become his own. Seriously sought-after goals should be attainable. Occasionally, parents make the mistake of instilling expectancies that are not in keeping with their children's abilities. Clinicians working with college students frequently find that parental pressure for high social, athletic, or scholastic achievement is a major cause of marked emotional insecurity.

Parents who consider themselves failures sometimes try to compensate through their children. They plan great successes for them, usually in the field in which their own ambitions were thwarted. They then insist on these plans being carried out, regardless of the children's interests and abilities. For example, a man may have in his youth desired to be a physician, but circumstances made it impossible for him to achieve his goal. He now has a son in college. Here is his opportunity to succeed by proxy. The son is forced to take a premedical course, even though his real interest may be in languages or perhaps in a kind of work that does not require college training. If he is not interested in the vocation selected for him, conflict results, and either the son or the father, or both, is frustrated.

Rejection

It is commonly assumed that parents always love their children. Although probably the majority of parents care deeply for their offspring, there are a great many instances of rejection. Casual observation of families around us would produce a number of examples. Clinicians find it recurring frequently in the causal patterns of behavior disorders.

Rejection must be thought of in terms of degree, partial rejection being much more frequent than complete rejection. The parent often rationalizes partial rejection by maintaining that not granting the child's wishes is an excellent technique for building character. This argument is applied even in early infancy, when the child, who is having his first experience in facing the difficulties of life, should be receiving complete emotional support.

During the first years of life, sound character is built upon a foundation of emotional satisfactions rather than upon frustrations. A child who has been made comfortable and happy stands a much better chance of developing a positive, cooperative point of view than does the child who, very early in life, has developed the fear that he has lost, or may lose, his parents' love because he has behaved or is behaving in a certain way. There is the case of the young father who began feeding his infant son baked beans before he was a year old. He stoutly maintained that this was highly desirable, because it would so toughen the boy's digestive system that when he grew to be a man he would be able to eat anything. The argument that a strong character can be developed only through hard knocks in childhood is as unsound as the argument presented by this father.

In the later years of childhood, to be sure, the child should be guided into needed adjustments to the requirements of his culture. In providing this guidance, however, it should always be made clear to the child that his parents are sincerely trying to help him. He should never be made to feel that he is disliked by them because he does not wholly succeed in conforming to the standards which they wish him to acquire. Unfortunately this attitude is a difficult one for many parents to achieve. If the child continues to develop along lines which do not meet with their approval, actual dislike for him as an individual may develop.

There are, of course, a number of reasons why parents reject their children. Included among these reasons are physical appearance, marked difference in intelligence, moral standards, religious convictions, and interests.

If there are two daughters in the family, one beautiful and one homely, the parents may reject the homely one because they feel that she does not do them justice. Occasionally, to be sure, the beautiful one is rejected by the jealous mother. Many a child has felt that he has lost the love of his parents because he was overweight, and, on the other hand, many a son of an athletic father has been rejected because he was undersized.

A dull child born of brilliant parents is often emotionally rejected because of his scholastic inability. An example of complete rejection for this reason is that of the attorney who was convicted of killing his feebleminded son. Occasionally parents who are below average in intelligence will reject a child because he is too bright. Their envy of his intellectual attainments snuffs out the love which they once had for him. An example is that of the farm boy with an intelligence quotient of 150 who was constantly reminded by his parents that he would have to plan to go on to college, since he never would be able to earn a good, respectable livelihood with his hands, as his brothers and sisters could.

Moral and religious factors are frequent causes of rejection. We like to believe that a mother always stands by her wayward son. Often she does, but equally often she does not. Parents who are deeply religious frequently find it difficult to continue to love a child who questions their beliefs or who decides to change to another faith. Many young people have experienced the conflict involved in trying to decide between marrying a person of a different religious faith, on the one hand, and avoiding complete rejection by their parents, on the other.

Broadly speaking, two methods are used by parents in rejecting a child—withdrawal and aggression. Through the parents' withdrawal, the child is emotionally ostracized; he is made to feel that, although he is a member of the family, he is unwanted and is tolerated only as a matter of duty. Parents who use aggressive tactics usually rationalize their behavior. They maintain that the strict discipline which they are imposing upon the child, and the punishments which they are administering, are for his own good.

Overprotection

At the opposite extreme from rejection is overprotection. It is unlikely that a child can be overprotected during the first few months of his life. As he grows older, however, he must learn that his parents cannot constantly cater to him. Through the years of childhood he must gradually learn independence so that when he reaches the adolescent period he will find it relatively easy to make the necessary economic and emotional break with his family and to establish himself as an adult. Frequently parents, especially mothers, by being oversolicitous and by cultivating dependence in their children, make it difficult, if not impossible, for their children to establish normal relationships outside the family circle. Apron strings can become shackling irons.

Freudian psychology has made much of the fixation of one's affections upon a parent. Such a fixation is frequently noted in neurotic adults. Because of it, they may have found it impossible to establish normal heterosexual relationships. It is a frequent cause of celibacy and is often one of the causal factors in homosexual behavior.

Rejection, especially during the early years of life, robs the child of his parent's emotional support, which is essential to his well-being; overprotection, on the other hand, provides him with such a wealth of support that he finds it difficult to achieve emotional maturity and status as an independent, self-sufficient individual. "Unlimited and aimless permissiveness is not freedom for the child. Actually it interferes seriously with the course of his development, and, as a result, aggression continues with increasing vigor into the third and fourth years of life. By this time the child is seriously unhappy, because he is thoroughly disliked by members of his family and other adults and finds himself unable to win friends of his own age or to get along in a group."[3]

The wise parent steers a safe course between Scylla and Charybdis. He provides the growing child with the emotional security that he needs, and, at the same time, encourages him to develop those attitudes and relationships which will eventually lead to independence.

[3] Ribble, *op. cit.*, p. 68.

Broken Homes

If, because of death, separation, or divorce, a child loses one or both of his parents, he experiences an emotional crisis which may result in a marked feeling of insecurity. This is especially true of the school-age child who is old enough to feel the loss deeply and young enough to still be dependent upon both of his parents. It is usually easier for him to adjust to the death of one of his parents than to divorce. His emotional security is largely provided by the sure knowledge that his parents love each other. Their separation or divorce removes this support and may cause him to doubt whether real affection exists anywhere.

There has been a large number of studies on the effects of broken homes on children. The results indicate clearly that the child's emotional, social, and even intellectual development is likely to be affected. Torrance used 514 adolescent boys as subjects. These boys were enrolled at Georgia Military College. They came chiefly from the upper middle class. Of the total enrollment, 182 were from broken homes. Each of the 182 was paired with a boy who had the same intelligence quotient and was of the same chronological age but who was not from a broken home. Torrance found:

> The broken home group showed 2.4 times as many cases of retardation as the paired group, 1.8 times as many accelerated, 3 times as many cases of underachievement, 1.83 times as much overachievement, 2.1 times as many exhibited behavior problems, 1.3 times as many emotional problems, 1.3 times as many social problems, and 3.75 times as many health problems. There were 2.5 times as many in the paired group for whom no problems were recorded as in the broken home group.[4]

Torrance goes on to point out that the boy whose parents are separated or divorced is likely to have more problems than the boy whose parents are dead, indicating that there is a difference between deprivation and frustration. In many instances the boys' difficulties were found to have begun at about the time of the break between parents.

[4] P. Torrance, "The Influence of the Broken Home on Adolescent Adjustment," *Journal of Educational Sociology*, XVIII (1945), 360–61.

Madow and Hardy[5] used 211 neurotic soldiers as subjects of a study of the effects of broken homes. They found that 20.9 per cent of these neurotic soldiers came from families that were broken before the subjects were nine years of age, and 15.1 per cent when they were from nine to sixteen years of age. Thirty-six per cent, then, came from families that were broken before the soldiers were sixteen.

In the study conducted by the Joint Commission on Mental Health, referred to in Chapter One, a research team examined the effects of broken homes upon the later success in marriage and emotional stability of children coming from those homes. The authors give the following statistics on marital adjustments:

> While 15 per cent of the people from broken homes are currently divorced or separated from their spouses, only 5 per cent of the people from intact homes, and 9 per cent of the people from homes disrupted by death are currently divorced. There are differences as well among marital patterns of those who are presently married; people from divorced broken homes are distinctive in that 19 per cent of them as compared to 14 per cent of the group from death disrupted homes, and 8 per cent of the group of unbroken homes have been married and divorced prior to their current marriages . . . 68 per cent of the persons from divorced broken homes admit to some feelings of inadequacy of the spouse contrasted to 53 per cent for the other two groups; 60 per cent of those from divorced broken homes have had some problem in marriage contrasted to 40 per cent of the other two groups.[6]

In a summarizing statement the authors say:

> Two points stand out in these configurations of relationships. Persons from intact homes experience less general distress, greater marital stability, and fewer marital difficulties than persons from disrupted homes; and a home disrupted by divorce or separation has more evident effects than a home in which disruption has been caused by the death of one or both parents.
>
> The similarity of the responses of people whose parents died while they were growing up to those of respondents coming from intact

[5] L. Madow, and S. E. Hardy, "Incidence and Analysis of the Broken Family in the Background of Neurosis," *American Journal of Orthopsychiatry*, XVII (1947), 521–28.

[6] G. Gurin; J. Veroff, and S. Feld, *Americans View Their Mental Health* (New York: Basic Books, Inc., Publishers, 1960), pp. 247–48.

homes suggests that the effect of a broken home is more related to the nature of the disruption than to the fact of disruption. Divorce or separation implies that the failure of the parents' marital relationship was emphasized during the respondents' early experiences; death of a parent does not have this direct implication. Although any kind of separation deprives a child of having both parents available as models for the marriage relationship, this does not, in itself, seem crucial, as we examine the relationship between feelings of adjustment and early experiences in the home. It is the disturbed and disorganized marriage relationship, with all its potential effects on a growing child's development that seems to be the critical factor for this later adjustment.[7]

Data such as these indicate that there should be serious concern about the high divorce rate in the United States. A divorce is a disrupting emotional experience for the couple involved, but, even more important, it is likely to have very serious effects on that couple's children. Surely it is important that young people enter into marriage only after they have made it as certain as possible that the marriage will be a success.

Parental Discord

A home in which there is parental discord may have more serious ill effects on a child than a broken home. If the parents are incompatible and manifest their incompatibility by much quarreling, or even by violent disagreements, the child will probably be made to feel insecure. He may develop the fear that his parents are going to separate; perhaps he overhears that threat being frequently made. This anxiety, if present for a long period of time, may have a more lasting effect upon the child's personality than would a definite break from an intolerable situation. Moreover, there is always the danger that this specific anxiety may become generalized, so that the child is fearful of all the aspects of his future. An adult's anxiety neurosis frequently contains in its history a story of parental discord. If there is open antagonism between the parents, the child is caught between conflicting loyalties. To whom shall he give his support, his father or his mother? He may oscillate between the two, suffering under continual tension, or he may decide to join forces with one in opposition to the other. If the second course is taken,

[7] *Ibid.*, pp. 249–50.

deep resentment, even hatred, may develop. The experience will warp his personality and will make normal adult adjustments difficult. For example, if a son aligns himself with his mother against his father, he may develop what the Freudians call a "castration complex." He does not want to become a man because his father, whom he hates, is a man.

It is, of course, by no means inevitable that a child will develop behavior disorders because of friction between his parents. Many children succeed in adjusting to the situation, and in obtaining their necessary emotional satisfactions from outside sources. A large number of children, however, are seriously disturbed, at least temporarily, by excessive quarreling between their parents.

Relationship with Siblings

Adler has emphasized the importance of birth order in personality development. The only child is supposed to be spoiled because he has never had to compete with siblings for his parents' attention. The oldest child, having held the center of the stage for one or more years, is supposed to resent being partially replaced by a young brother or sister. The youngest child, the baby of the family, is supposed to be forever dependent. However, there is little evidence that birth order, in and of itself, is an important cause of behavior disorders.

Nevertheless, the relationships between siblings are very significant in personality development. Many children, as suggested earlier, feel inferior because their parents compare them unfavorably with their siblings. This can cause the child to compete with a brother or sister who is more gifted intellectually, physically, or socially than he is. Frustrated in these attempts, he may develop a defeatist attitude accompanied by a feeling of insecurity. This situation is somewhat more likely to develop between two children who are very close to each other in chronological age. Sometimes the younger tries to defeat the older; sometimes vice versa.

Perception of the self as inferior is learned. For example, a mentally inferior older brother is trying to do as well in school as a mentally superior younger brother. If the parents ignore the difference in innate mental capacity and frequently urge on the older boy with the argument that he ought to be ashamed because his grades are not as high as his brother's, an emotional disturbance may be initiated. Frequently, of course, the stimuli to compete come from nonparental sources.

In clinical work with college girls, the author has found that failure to compete successfully with a slightly older or slightly younger sister was often an important cause in the development of behavior disorders. A girl, for example, may lack confidence and poise, even self-respect, because for years she has been convinced that she is not as beautiful as her sister. This attitude is intensified if the sister takes pleasure in pointing out the girl's physical short-comings. Sometimes the competition is along social lines. Of two sisters, the one who is less likable, who is less popular with boys, who has not mastered the superficialities of small talk, may learn to feel more and more inadequate as time goes on.

Many other examples could be given of sibling rivalries and of the behavior disorders they sometimes cause. But suffice to say, from his earliest years each child should be taught that he need not try to emulate or to defeat his brothers and sisters, but should, rather, be satisfied with and develop those abilities which he does have.

Material from Case Studies   N.W. came to the counseling service with the complaint that she could not get along with her roommate. Since this is a very frequent problem among freshmen, on the surface it did not appear to be serious. However, in the second interview N.W. revealed considerable anxiety over an almost compulsive desire to kill the roommate. She said that sometimes she awoke in the middle of the night feeling the urge so strongly that she had difficulty in restraining herself. As time went on N.W. talked about her back-ground—especially her family relationships—slowly and painfully. The writer recalls that she usually brought her knitting to the inter-view. There were many long silences during which she found some degree of relaxation through the activity with her hands.

In the course of nearly sixty interviews it became clear that the principal source of N.W.'s serious personality difficulties was her family situation from earliest childhood to the present. Her father was a successful businessman and a pillar of the church. Her mother was narrow and strict. Both the father and mother were convinced that they knew what was best for their children. They expected model religious and moral conduct, and they insisted on exercising the privilege of selecting their children's vocations for them.

N.W. had two brothers and one sister, the brothers older than she, the sister younger. It so happened that these siblings met their parents' requirements without rebellion and consequently were fully accepted by them. N.W., however, was different. She was sensitive, artistic, and independent. The rest of the family were remarkably lacking in sensitivity and had very little appreciation of any form of aesthetics. As N.W. told the writer over and over, "I am the black sheep of the family." As a child, N.W. experienced difficulty with her parents when she expressed a dislike for Sunday school and church services. Sunday after Sunday she was forced to attend. When she rebelled she was severely beaten, and this physical brutality continued even into her college years. One Sunday when she was on her way to church after having been whipped for saying that she did not want to go, she burst out suddenly with angry curses against God and against her parents. This experience was not recalled until the thirtieth interview. She had such deep feelings of guilt concerning it that it had been repressed for a long period of time. The recall was painful for her; at first, all she could do was write on a piece of paper, "I have committed the unpardonable sin," and rush out of the office. Later she was able to talk about this experience objectively, and the recall and the catharsis proved to be a turning point in her therapy. The experience itself, when she was twelve years of age, was a different kind of turning point. Up until then she had fought against her parents' and brothers' rejection and against the hard and fast rules laid down for her to live by. After the outburst of profanity she began to withdraw, convinced now that she really was wicked and worthless. When she came in for counseling, rather serious personality disturbances were present. She was lethargic and somewhat unkempt. Verbal expression came haltingly; understanding, slowly and piecemeal. Some of the early outward signs of improvement were simple examples of positive behavior, such as the use of lipstick and rouge, a new hair-do, and better kept clothes. Eventually she achieved an excellent perspective of her experiential background and even drastically altered her perception of her parents. Instead of hating and fearing them she became sorry for them. N.W.'s early family training had laid the foundation of a distorted personality structure, but through psychotherapy she was able to make the needed modifications.

A college freshman, E.N., came to the counseling center in a state of considerable anxiety. The immediate cause of her distress was the fear that her grades for the semester would be unsatisfactory. On checking with her instructors, it was found that she was earning A's and B's in all of her courses.

In the interviews which followed, it was learned that E.N. had been brought up by foster parents. She did not know who her own parents were. Her first great shock with respect to her parentage came at the age of eleven when she was told for the first time that she was not the child of the couple whom she had always believed were her parents. For several days after having been told, she refused to believe the fact.

E.N. was a mentally superior girl, rating in the top quarter of her class intellectually. She was so lacking in self-confidence, however, that she worried a great deal about her scholastic work and was afraid that she would be dropped from college because of low grades. She felt insecure in social situations too and avoided groups as much as possible. She was troubled with insomnia, and had a rather poor appetite. Although she was ambitious, she was certain that she would be a failure. She faced the future with trepidation.

E.N. wrote an autobiography for the writer. The autobiography and the interviews clearly revealed the experiential background for her feeling of emotional insecurity. The situation in the family of her foster parents had been extremely difficult—so difficult, in fact, that it robbed the girl of her stability. A few passages from her autobiography follow:

> The problem that is before me now, that of dealing truthfully and objectively with my past, present, and future life, seems to be one at which I've been struggling always. Struggling is the suitable word in this instance, for all of life appears to be very much involved with struggle in order to make it worth living.
>
> Here at college, with so many people of my own age facing many of the same problems I do, there still is not enough inspiration for me. Seldom do I realize how uncertain all people must be about life and how concerned they are with their adolescent years. My many casual acquaintances don't ever appear to be so incompetent as I often feel. My independence and poise have gradually faded as I have begun to associate intimately with my own age group. Self-sufficiency and contentment have changed into a dependent attitude that causes me to seek out others constantly for companionship and

assurance. Yet there is the fear that perhaps I am not wanted or would not fit in. Then as I turn to myself I am again inadequate, for there remains no inner strength to spur me on.

I am constantly swimming about in life's ocean, frequently losing sight of all land and clinging to every passing straw. Now and then when I see the shore I cover great long distances and often float merrily on until the ever-dreaded wave of destruction sweeps me far off my course into a whirlpool of confusion and misery where I am alone with no glimmer of light to guide me onward. . . .

The past is a land where I still tread the ground but delicately. Shame, fear, sorrow, and yet pride are related to it.

At an early age I was made aware of constant friction between my foster parents, whom I believed to be my own until I was abruptly told that they were not.

Quarrels, actual fights, separations, desertions were common occurrences. I soon looked upon marriage as a horrid trap where one was caught for life. If all men were like my foster father, they were uneducated, irresponsible, immoral drunkards who had no backbone, and yet evoked a kind of pity.

At times my foster parents threatened to do each other bodily harm. One tells me to get the police or I'll be killed. The other begs me not to, and cries as hard as I do. I, loving them both with a child's pity, fearfully run out through the dark rainy streets to a corner where the familiar and frequently-sought blue uniform will follow me to the source of my worries. Disgrace falls heavily on us.

I was never allowed to visit other children's homes or play with their toys. I played alone in my own space or not at all. I joined in roller skating or hop scotch only on the sly because it would wear out my shoes. Sledding was considered much too dangerous for me. Throughout the elementary schools a doctor's excuse always eliminated me from gymnastics partly because of my heart condition, but largely because my foster parents didn't see any sense in physical education. . . .

In the end I made the great decision that I would leave home to room and board out in exchange for housework. By this time I had strongly sensed a different code of moral and ethical values. I wanted a clean, decent, honest, and happy home. The adjustment was not easy and took fully a year. It did not seem right that I should fully enjoy my new life, when to get it I had made others unhappy. Often as I ate I wondered if those who had for fifteen years provided for me had enough to eat. Though I could not bear to write to them because of their pleas to return, I felt the debt I owed them.

My independence and self-sufficiency were a help in my new house, but since it was not my home I felt insecure. If I burned the food or hurt the baby, would I be thrown out? Where could I go then? For two years this feeling grew steadily worse until the family moved away from the school from which I was to graduate in five months. An interested friend took me in for two weeks until I should find a place. She never has let go of me.

Even in her new home, E.N. continued to feel insecure. Having learned to expect tense situations in the family circle she was constantly overready to react. The changed environment helped, but it did not eliminate the anxiety which has been built up during the long years of emotional insecurity. Psychotherapy, involving catharsis and a series of insights, was needed before she was able to take positive action.

MARRIAGE

The family in our culture is founded upon monogamous marriage. If the family is to provide a child with the kind of environment which he needs for optimum development, it must be initiated by the union of a man and a woman who are well mated and who can live together congenially. Since marriage involves a close relationship between two persons for a long period of time, care should be taken to be as certain as possible that the several qualifications of a successful marriage are present. It is a relationship that should not be entered into hastily, for it involves far more than immediate satisfactions. It affects not only the emotional security of the marriage partners for years to come, but the emotional security of their children as well. One of the principal causes of maladjustment in children is the broken home or the home in which there is considerable friction.

A happy marriage is dependent upon a number of factors, many of which can be evaluated during the period of courtship. There are others that can be understood and adjusted to only after the marriage is an established fact. One of the latter is the handling of family finances, frequently a major marital problem. Marriage, of course, calls for a series of adjustments on the part of the couple who have contracted to live together and to work together. However there is greater likelihood that these adjustments will be made successfully if the couple is compatible at the outset. The most significant factors in compatibility are:

1. Maturity.
2. Similarity in interests and attitudes.
3. Similarity in religious beliefs.
4. Similarity in educational and cultural backgrounds.
5. Similarity in rate of living.
6. Similarity in attitudes toward sex.
7. Relationship with the parents of each.

Maturity

If one were to try to select the most important single factor in a successful marriage, that factor would be maturity. Obviously the degree of maturity is not determined by chronological age alone. Physical age, mental age, social age, and emotional age are as important. Other things being equal, the best chronological age for marriage is approximately twenty-five for men and twenty-two for women. At this time in life the typical individual has achieved a level of development where sudden changes of interests and attitudes are unlikely. Although habit patterns have been rather well established at this age, they have not become so set that the individual cannot adapt to new situations. He is still sufficiently flexible to make the adjustments necessary to married life. It should be remembered, of course, that the ages twenty-five and twenty-two represent central tendency. There are many instances of happy marriages on the part of much younger or much older persons.

Physical maturity is an important factor in marital readiness, although in our culture marriage usually is delayed for a considerable time after the individual has achieved puberty. We do not look with favor upon the marriage of fourteen-year-old children, yet the majority are capable of reproduction at that time. The age range for sexual maturity is considerable, being approximately seven to twenty for girls and nine to twenty-two for boys. A girl whose menstrual periods began when she was nine or ten is not only going to be more mature physically at sixteen than a girl who achieves puberty at fifteen, but the chances are good that she will also be more mature in other respects.

Should a man and woman of widely differing mental ages marry? Investigations reveal the fact that men tend to marry women who are less intelligent than themselves. What happens, then, to women with brilliant minds? Unfortunately for posterity a considerable percentage of them remain unmarried. However, from the point of view of marital happiness it is probably desirable that the man be somewhat superior to his wife. Our culture expects it; his need for status requires it. The difference, however, should not be great. Otherwise, the couple would lack common interests. A marriage can be successful if the wife is much abler intellectually than the husband, although the hazards involved are considerable.

Social maturity is closely related to emotional maturity. A socially mature individual understands social relations. He knows how to get along with others, including his wife and his family. He knows what is expected of him by society and conforms to a reasonable extent. He is ready and willing to accept the responsibilities that come with marriage and citizenship in the community. He is a socially dependable individual.

Perhaps the most important factor in maturity is the extent of emotional growth. A person may be twenty-five or thirty years of age and physically and mentally mature, yet have so little control over his emotions that his married life is made unhappy. A person who is emotionally mature has a reasonably objective point of view toward himself, his wife, his children, and the problems which inevitably arise in everyday living. He has worked out a philosophy of life, a frame of reference that makes it possible for him to avoid the daily or hourly crises which are characteristic of emotionally immature individuals. He depends upon present accomplishment for satisfaction of his mastery and status needs rather than upon the glory that may have been his when he was in high school or in college. He has an adult attitude toward sex, love, and marriage. He does not expect his wife to be primarily a mistress or a mother.

Similarity in Interests and Attitudes

It is important that a young couple consider carefully before marriage whether or not they have a community of interests and attitudes. Of these two, attitudes are more basic, for attitudes are the components of what is commonly called a "philosophy of life." A few of these attitudes will be considered briefly.

Is the couple mutually ambitious or does one have a strong drive for achievement and the other a desire for a comfortable, easy-going life? If it is the man who is intensely ambitious the situation is not quite so unfortunate, although his wife may resent the excessive amount of time that he spends on his business or professional duties. If it is the woman who is ambitious, she will almost certainly try to force her easy-going husband to heights that he has no desire to scale. Such pressure will inevitably result in friction.

Political convictions, if they are widely divergent, can be a source of conflict. It is difficult to see how one who is politically reactionary could live happily with one who is politically radical unless certain strong positive factors compensate for the difference. To be sure, it is not essential that the party allegiance of a married couple be the same, but it is important that the basic political beliefs be somewhat similar.

It is desirable that a couple be similar with respect to idealism or realism. If, for instance, the husband is idealistic and the wife grimly realistic, the husband will probably be frequently discouraged by his wife's lack of understanding. He will tend to feel that she does not see those things in life that are really worth while. He will eventually begin to wonder why he ever married such a materialistic person. On the other hand, the chances are very good that the realistic wife will be irritated by the idealistic attitudes of her husband. Many of his points of view will seem rather silly and to have little relation to the facts of life. She will frequently wish he would get down to earth, would see things as they actually are. It is hard to see how a lasting companionship built upon understanding and common goals could develop between an idealist and a realist.

Interests are, of course, closely related to attitudes. They include the innumerable activities of everyday life: attending movies, plays, and concerts, listening to the radio, watching television, club membership, community activities, church activities, social welfare drives, social activities with friends, social drinking, and so forth. It is too much to expect that a couple will have identical interests, but there should be a basic similarity present in the kind of things that they like to do. For example, if one enjoys card playing and the other does not, if one enjoys social drinking and the other does not, if one enjoys music and the other does not, and if one enjoys a large number of television programs and the other does not, the differences will make a close union between the couple difficult to achieve. On the other hand, if the couple enjoys discussing contemporary novels, if they both like to go to the movies frequently, if they both enjoy having friends in often and tend to like the same people, if they are both rather conventional, or if they both practice the same little family courtesies, a mutual identification is likely to develop.

Religious Beliefs

College students frequently raise the question: Should I marry a Catholic or should I marry a Protestant? If each member of the couple has accepted the doctrine of his church and is seriously trying to live by it, then the prospects of the marriage being a happy one are slight. Moreover, the attitudes of the respective parents of the couple are frequently important factors often leading to rejection of the son or daughter who marries outside the church. If such a marriage is entered into, there should be many compensating factors present.

If, on the other hand, the young couple take their religious beliefs lightly, even though they have been brought up in different faiths the chances of resultant friction because of religion are relatively small. Occasionally one member of the couple is quite willing to join the other's church. If this can be done without any great sacrifice of self-respect, the hazard involved is not great. It is best, however, to think the situation through very carefully before deciding to marry one whose religious beliefs are markedly different.

Educational and Cultural Backgrounds

Similarity in marital happiness is based to a considerable extent on little things. Relatively minor personal habits can be very irritating to a partner who has been reared in a social environment where meticulous care was taken to conform to certain taboos having to do with such matters as table manners and other social amenities. For example, a girl who has been brought up in a cultured family would have difficulty in retaining her love and respect for a husband who smacked his lips while eating, who used a toothpick in public, who did not shave every day, and who made frequent grammatical errors in conversation. In such a marriage the husband might well be equally irritated by a wife who considered these matters important and who was constantly trying to improve him.

Although similarity in intelligence is probably more important than similarity in educational background insofar as marital happiness is concerned, the latter has been found in a number of studies to be a significant factor. The extent of one's education is rather closely associated with status. Consequently, if one member of the married couple is a graduate of a college and the other has never finished high school, a superiority-inferiority relationship may develop. This is most likely to be true if it is the wife who has the more extensive educational background. Unless there are strong compensating factors present, there will be a tendency on the part of the husband to belittle his wife's education in order to build up his own ego and there will be a tendency on the part of the wife to envy her friends who have married well-educated and, perhaps, professional men. A common educational background, especially when combined with similar intellectual capacity, is a distinct aid to marital happiness. To be sure, marriages can succeed without this, but the safer course is to avoid a marriage in which there is a considerable difference in the educational backgrounds of the couple concerned. The more the married partners have in common the greater the likelihood of the success of their marriage.

Rate of Living

Similarity in rate of living is a significant factor in marital happiness. The speed with which one goes about his daily tasks is determined by both physiological and psychological factors. Some persons move, eat, think, and make decisions slowly and carefully. There is no intention here of suggesting a dichotomy with respect to rate of living, for individuals differ in this trait of personality, as in others, in degree rather than in kind. It is desirable for a married couple to be somewhat similar in rate of living, for a hare and a tortoise could hardly be expected to stay together for even two or three years, to say nothing of forty or fifty. A slow-spoken, phlegmatic husband would, unintentionally, be very irritating to a hyperactive wife. Differences in rate of living would enter into all phases of their life together. It would vitally affect their social relationships, their dinnertime conversation, their evenings together, and might to a considerable extent affect their sexual relationships.

Similarity in Attitudes Toward Sex

A successful marriage is, of course, based only in part upon satisfying sex relationships; nevertheless, sex relationships are essential to the happiness of the married couple. If they are not satisfactory, frustration and lack of security result. The studies that have been made of marriage make it clear that sex adjustment rates at or near the top among the problems faced by married couples.

The three factors most essential to satisfactory sexual relationships in marriage are: (1) knowledge; (2) relative lack of inhibitions; (3) similarity in the strength of the sex drive. Factual information concerning sex should be provided through sex education in our schools. This program should culminate in courses on marriage for high school seniors and for college students. In such a program, problems should be explored thoroughly and questions answered frankly.

Relationship with the Parents of Each

One excellent indication of emotional and social maturity is the extent to which the young person has emancipated himself from his parents. The truly adult individual has shifted his deepest affections from his parents to his spouse. He is no longer emotionally dependent upon those who have brought him up. As a mature person he looks upon his parents as friends. This new relationship is a sound one. He thinks a great deal of them, but he is not controlled by them. It is well for a young couple considering marriage to weigh carefully these parental relationships. A young woman who has a mother or father fixation and who insists on living at home, or at least next door, is not likely to become a good wife and mother. A young man who is still "Mom's little boy" is not very likely to possess the initiative and self-confidence which will make him a satisfactory husband and father.

Most of what a young man or young woman knows about family relationships has been learned from his or her own family circle. If the family relationship has been happy, there is an excellent chance that the young person will try to create the same kind of atmosphere in his own home. If, however, the family relationship has been unhappy, the young person is likely to carry the same patterns of behavior into his newly created family circle. Boys who have observed their fathers reacting angrily in the home may resent it at the time and vow that they will never behave in a similar fashion. Girls who have observed a complaining, nagging mother may decide that they will never act in this manner. However, if those are the patterns of behavior that they have learned through observation and imitation, the chances are all too good that son will be like father and daughter like mother.

SUMMARY

If life in the home is safe, if the developing child is experiencing warmth in his relationships with the members of his family, he is learning to feel secure in his later relationships and approaches them with confidence. If, on the other hand, marked insecurity is present within his family and he feels unwanted and unloved, then anxiety grows apace as the child learns to expect rejection and failure. The good home provides a permissive situation in which the child feels free to be himself and to reach out for new experiences. In it his personality is respected and the respect shown him eventually results in self-respect and in respect for others.

The success or failure of family relationships depends to a considerable extent upon the compatibility of the parents. Therefore it is important that young people carefully evaluate their similarities and dissimilarities before they enter into the marriage relationship. Love, although essential, is not enough. There should be a community of interests and attitudes. If the parents are congenial there is a strong likelihood that their children will be provided with the kind of atmosphere needed for optimum emotional development.

THE SCHOOL

chapter *9*

The two most important institutions in the life of an American child are the home and the school. The home has the responsibility of laying the foundation of the child's personality structure. By the time he enters school at the age of five or six he has an image of himself, but it is an image that is tentative and fluid. It can be altered considerably by the experiences which he has in school. During the first two or three years, especially, the teacher becomes a parent substitute for several hours of each school day. She is a very significant person in the child's life.

The principal goal of education is the development of adequate personalities. *Adequate personality* is not synonymous with *conformity;* it is much closer to *self-actualized.* Self-actualization is most likely to be achieved when a child is learning in a situation that is characterized by a great deal of challenge and relatively little threat. The teacher whose interest extends beyond subject matter to the total development of the children under her care provides an atmosphere of security and acceptance. She applies in practice the characteristics of the mental hygiene point of view discussed in the first chapter of this book.

A classroom atmosphere which makes a child feel safe, secure, accepted, and relaxed results in large measure from the attitudes held by the teacher. She should sincerely respect every individual in the group, regardless of his shortcomings. In other words, she accepts him as he is. She learns to know and to understand his limitations and adjusts her instruction accordingly. At the same time she helps him to grow because one of her functions as a teacher is to assist each child in developing his potentialities. Growth takes place where freedom exists. Growth is inhibited by excessive control. It does not follow from this that there should be no control. Extreme permissiveness is not only an unrealistic life situation but also confuses the child. He needs to have the classroom situation structured to some extent. He needs to know what the rules are and to expect to be punished when he breaks those rules. Many limits to human behavior are set in real life. It is important that the child learn to accept such limits. Actually, he feels more rather than less secure if he understands thoroughly what he can do and what he cannot do. Obviously, what is needed is a combination of freedom and control.

The child's freedom in the classroom is limited by the freedom of others. He must learn to respect the rights of his fellows. Freedom becomes license when every child is permitted to do whatever he wishes to. A case in point is a classroom in which an overly permissive teacher allowed each child to decide what he would do. As a result one youngster was learning how to type, another playing the piano, another singing, another trying to solve his arithmetic problems, another trying to read, another talking with a friend, and so on. Obviously in such an uproar no one was able to accomplish very much.

In addition to providing a classroom atmosphere in which the children can thrive, the teacher has the responsibility of identifying those who have emotional problems. Frequently she can deal with these problems herself. In such a situation some knowledge of mental hygiene helps, of course, but there are many sympathetic, understanding teachers who can assist a disturbed child through a difficult period by making it possible for him to identify with her and to confide in her. She should be a good listener, placing the emphasis on understanding, acceptance, and reflection rather than on advice-giving. Some children have no adults other than their teachers to whom they can go with their problems. It may be devastating if they cannot go to their teachers either. If the child's emotional disturbance is too complex for the teacher to handle he should be referred to a qualified counselor or therapist.

SCHOLASTIC ACHIEVEMENT

A knowledge of the facts of individual differences and a use of that knowledge in instructional procedures are essential to the teacher if she is to promote sound mental health in the children under her care. Although individual differences are not limited to the realm of the intellect, it is, nevertheless, especially important for the teacher to realize that her pupils are unequal in their intellectual potentialities. In a fifth-grade class, where the average chronological age is eleven years or a little less, there is likely to be a mental age range of from eight to fourteen. It may even be as great as from six to sixteen, or more. To set a common academic goal on a middle level for all to aim at is to frustrate the very dull and the very bright. Teachers usually adjust their instruction to the abilities of this middle group, although they occasionally set their standards so high that only the brightest can achieve.

The need for achievement is strong in every school child. The mental hygiene point of view requires that this need be satisfied, and it can be satisfied only when the scholastic goals set for him are within his reach. Instead of being concerned primarily with maintaining high standards, the school should be concerned with the vital problem of helping each student, at his own level, to increase his knowledge, to develop emotional stability, and to maintain his self-respect.

Children whose need for achievement is frustrated in the classroom adjust to the situation in various ways. It is to the credit of their flexibility that the educational process does not cause an even larger number to become emotionally maladjusted. Some of them make a fighting reaction and so become disciplinary problems. Others take an "I don't care" attitude, and still others resort to daydreaming. Usually there are only a few very conscientious children who do not resort successfully to protective methods of adjustment. Some, because of low mentality, cannot understand the material assigned to them to study, but they try their hardest and keep on trying—with failure as their only reward. After a few years of such hopeless efforts, the child's ego has been seriously damaged. There are children in our junior high schools with mental ages of nine or ten who are trying to comprehend algebra when they ought to be studying simple arithmetic. There are children in our senior high schools with reading ages of ten or eleven who are trying to comprehend Shakespeare when they ought to be studying a fifth-grade reader. It is imperative that the teacher know what the abilities of each child are and that she adjust her instruction to them rather than to arbitrary standards.

As has been pointed out, much is known about what psychological circumstances promote learning but far less is known about how learning takes place. In an excellent collection of research data Kidd and Rivoire[1] discuss some recent findings about learning in infancy and the pre-school years.

There are sex differences in perception from the beginning. Girls hear high tones best, boys low tones. Girls are more visually aware of their surroundings than boys but they seem less able to isolate details.

Both boys and girls become increasingly less able to learn foreign speech sounds. By age fourteen the ear seems attuned to speech sounds which seem correct. These sounds are difficult to modify. Though the foreign sounds can be heard it is difficult, if not impossible, to imitate them.

Up to age seven or eight a child understands only in terms of sight, hearing, touch, taste, and smell. Learning is strictly concrete. Little or no abstraction is possible.

Language is learned best in a close and lasting relationship with an adult. Studies show that the closer the relationship between child and mother the better the speaking and reading skills: in tests only children ranked first, brothers and sisters next, and twins last; in fact, twins were more likely than the other two groups to be somewhat retarded in speech development. Twins, of course, share the mother from the beginning.

These and other findings should be useful to parents and teachers in planning educational activities and judging results.

Intelligence Ratings

Information concerning the intelligence quotients and mental ages of pupils is valuable to the teacher if two requirements are met: (1) if the tests have been selected and administered by a trained person;

[1] Aline H. Kidd, and Jeanne L. Rivoire, *Perceptual Development in Children* (New York: International Universities Press, Inc., 1966).

(2) if the teacher knows how to interpret an intelligence quotient and a mental age. An intelligence quotient does not represent a final and exact index of a child's mental capacity. A test score is affected by a number of factors, including the emotional stability or instability of the person taking it. Moreover, an intelligence quotient should be considered as a range rather than as a point, for every such measure has a degree of error attached. The teacher should accept it with reservations; she should note whether or not it conforms to the child's school record and to her own subjective evaluation.

The question is often raised as to whether or not a child should be told what his intelligence rating is. He should never be given this information except by a trained counselor who will take the time to give an adequate explanation. To face reality is sound mental hygiene. Theoretically, it is desirable for every individual to know where he stands intellectually. There is, however, so much danger that an IQ score from a group test, or even an individual test, may be in error that it is desirable to have at least two ratings or preferably three, before a definite statement is made to the individual concerned. Even then the statement should be accompanied by qualifications.

Examinations

Examinations are an essential part of the educational program. It is the attitude toward examinations by teachers and by pupils that is important for mental hygiene. Teachers should not give the impression that examinations are being used as weapons, that they are something to fear. Instead, they should make it clear to their students that examinations are a means of helping both students and teachers to discover how much progress has been made in the acquisition of knowledge. They are devices which are used in a cooperative enterprise.

Unfortunately, the attitude toward examinations is frequently such that each test becomes a crisis in the child's life. His emotional reaction may be intense—so intense that he experiences emotional blocks which inhibit the recall of facts that he really knows. If he is a conscientious individual trying to master material that is too difficult for him, his concern over an examination may be so great that he cannot sleep the night before or the night after. Obviously such periods of tension do not further the mental health of the child.

Grades

Since most of our schools make use of grades, it is necessary to consider the question of healthy and unhealthy attitudes toward them. Teachers and pupils alike should take the point of view that grades are given for two practical reasons: (1) as an index to the quality of the work done; (2) as a basis for promotion.

The first of these reasons is subject to many qualifications. A grade in a single subject is by no means an accurate evaluation of the quality of the work done by the pupil. An average of a large number of grades is more reliable but still far from exact. The problem of the validity and reliability of grades has been carefully studied during the last quarter of a century. Investigators agree that the tests which are customarily used to measure the degree to which the student has achieved the objectives of the course are, on the whole, remarkably low in validity; that is, they do not measure what they purport to measure. The situation with respect to reliability is even worse; the grades given on an essay examination in history, for example, depend to a considerable degree upon who rates the paper and when he rates it. If the same paper is graded by a number of history teachers, there is a good chance that the grades given will range all the way from A to F. Even on a mathematics examination, the ratings are highly variable. Moreover, it has been found that a teacher does not give the same grades on a second or third reading of the same set of examinations. A great deal depends on how he happens to be feeling at the time.

If grades must be given as a basis for promotion, then a simple "passing" and "incomplete" plan provides the best system. If the school is convinced that in addition to this it needs to have a basis for the awarding of honors and scholarships, then a five-point system, A, B, C, D, and Incomplete, is acceptable. The percentage system should never be used, for it rests on the false assumption that grades are so exact that a teacher can differentiate between an eighty-nine and a ninety and that there is a goal of absolute perfection—100 per cent—that students should aim at. Obviously no pupil can do perfect work in a course; obviously the teacher himself does not know the material perfectly. Moreover, it is undesirable from the mental hygiene point of view for children to be taught to think in perfectionistic terms. Achievement in the classroom is always relative. A child's goal should not be perfection, or doing better than someone else, but should instead be to increase his own fund of knowledge in order that he may deal more adequately with his environment.

Grades, especially numerical grades, tend to stimulate competition. It is undesirable, both educationally and psychologically, for a child to feel that his principal reason for studying hard is that he may defeat someone else. Every school has observed examples of bitter competition for honors. The writer recalls an instance of two mentally superior high-school girls who fought for four years for the valedictory. The content of their courses was much less important to them than the percentage grades on their report cards at the end of each term. When they reached their senior year, the strain had already taken its toll in mental health. Eventually the final averages were announced. One girl came through with a 95.4 and the other with a 95.3. The one who lost the valedictory became very discouraged. Although she went on to college in the fall, her grades there were only average. Great harm had been done to the personalities of both.

What of the dull student who finds himself enmeshed in the grading system? Even though he does as well as he can, his report card is covered with D's and F's. Besides, he is likely to be constantly prodded by his teachers, who tell him that if he worked harder he could do better. Once in a while, of course, this statement is true; more often it is wholly false. The statement was made earlier in this chapter that every teacher should have an understanding of the facts of individual differences. If he does, he knows that there are many children in his classes who cannot do A, B, or even C work, no matter how hard they try. Why is it that the high-school physics teacher has not become another Einstein? Is it because he has not worked hard enough? The answer, of course, is that he does not have the mental capacity to achieve on that level. It is just as impossible for the dull child to understand plane geometry or to read Macbeth with appreciation. These are obvious facts, yet children are usually taught in the classroom as though these facts did not exist.

Even in these days, children are sometimes punished for not doing good work in school. From the mental hygiene point of view, failure is bad enough; failure accompanied by punishment for failing is even worse. The best stimulant for good work is success. The more often a child is successful, the better he will do. Therefore, the school should so plan its program that each child can experience a series of academic successes. This can be done only by taking his abilities into account and by encouraging him to set scholastic goals which are well within his reach. Failure is always at least temporarily disintegrating; persistent failure usually leads to serious behavior disorders. Success is a constructive experience; continued success usually leads to integration and to self-confidence.

PERSONALITY TESTING

Personality tests or inventories, especially the variety usually referred to as paper and pencil tests, are much less satisfactory than standardized achievement tests or intelligence tests. It is difficult to establish a high level of validity and reliability for such instruments. A test is valid when it measures what it purports to measure. If a test is to have validity there must be a standard which will provide a fixed point of reference. With respect to intelligence there is a fairly clear understanding of what constitutes intellectual behavior. By means of testing, it can be fairly accurately determined what intellectual potential actually exists at a certain age level. There are no comparable standards for such traits as dominance, or introversion, or antisocial tendencies. Behavior that would be antisocial in one group, for example, might be wholly acceptable in another.

A second difficulty in obtaining valid results on personality tests lies in the attitudes of the examinees. Individuals are much more hesitant about revealing their emotional problems and their adjustment difficulties than they are about demonstrating what they are capable of doing intellectually. When taking a personality test they are likely to feel that they must protect themselves. This they can easily do on a paper-and-pencil test by the simple device of answering the questions on the test in such a way that they will be placed in a favorable light. For example, if one is asked such questions as: "Do you pity yourself?" or "Do you feel inferior?" there is probably a strong desire to encircle the "No" rather than the "Yes" after the questions, even though the "Yes" represents the truth. A desire to maintain self-respect and to win the respect of others is usually stronger than the desire to be completely honest.

A third reason why personality tests are so often lacking in validity is that many of those taking them have so little understanding of themselves or are in such a state of confusion that they do not know the correct answers to the questions put to them. This is especially true of those persons with low mentality who cannot comprehend the meaning of the questions and also of those who are in such a disturbed state emotionally that they cannot think clearly about how they feel.

Reliability is as difficult to establish as validity. Personal behavior is both consistent and inconsistent, with some traits showing more consistency than others. Scholastic achievement, for example, is rather consistent. The traits measured by personality tests, although they show a degree of consistency, are much more inconsistent than the abilities which are measured by intelligence tests or achievement tests. A person is not always an introvert; neither is he always dominant. He varies from group to group and from time to time.

It is not to be concluded from this discussion that personality tests are wholly worthless. They have value in certain situations when used with discrimination. They should not be administered and interpreted by untrained personnel. Even counselors and psychologists should resort to them sparingly and with full knowledge of the technical, ethical, and mental health hazards involved.

Invasion of Privacy

The use of any test in grade school, high school or college is to some extent an invasion of privacy. However, there are very important differences between achievement tests and personality tests. Most students will readily admit that it is important for them as well as for their teachers to have an opportunity to communicate the extent of their knowledge of subject matter. Personality tests, on the other hand, are likely to be perceived by those tested as an invasion of their right to secrecy. The best personality tests or inventories when administered by experts reveal aspects of the core of the self which, in most instances, individuals do not wish to have revealed. Ruebhausen and Brim[2] discuss two aspects of the claim to privacy. The

[2] O. M. Ruebhausen, and O. G. Brim, "Privacy and Behavioral Research," *American Psychologist*, XXI, No. 5 (May 1966), 425–26. (Reprinted from November 1965 issue of the *Columbia Law Review*.)

first is the right to be let alone. This right is being violated in our schools much more now that in earlier years. Many teachers and counselors, armed with a wide variety of tests, may assume that every child needs to be fully evaluated even to the point where he becomes a psychograph rather than an individual. Often the final step is to try to make him conform rather than to actualize his potentialities.

The second aspect of the claim to privacy as stated by Reubhausen and Brim is the right to share and to communicate and also to withhold. The need to share has been discussed elsewhere in this book. Sharing and communicating with others is a very important part of emotional security, as was pointed out in Chapter Seven. Concerning the need to withhold, Ruebhausen and Brim say:

> Some things which we cannot face we therefore suppress. There are other facts or fears that, although not suppressed, we neither prefer to know nor wish to discuss. Then, too, there are ideas or beliefs or behavior that we are not sure we understand or, even if we do, we fear that the world may not. So to protect ourselves, or our processes of creativity, or our minority views, or our self-respect, all of us seek to withhold at least certain things from certain people at certain times. . . .
>
> The essence of privacy is no more and certainly no less than the freedom of the individual to pick and choose for himself the time and circumstances under which, and most importantly, the extent to which, his attitudes, beliefs, behavior, and opinions are to be shared with or withheld from others. The right to privacy is, therefore, a positive claim to a status of personal dignity—a claim for freedom, if you will, but freedom of a very special kind.

Personality tests or inventories administered in a school situation without the consent of the children taking them violates the right to withhold. These children are likely to feel threatened, a feeling which may persist over a period of years if they know that the results of the tests are filed in their cumulative records to be read by succeeding teachers. In 1968 the state of California enacted a law making it illegal to administer personality tests or inventories to any pupil from kindergarten through grade 12 without written permission from the parents or guardian of that pupil.

Personality tests and inventories are more damaging to the

mental health of children than subjective personality evaluations because of their assumed objectivity. Subjective evaluation is unavoidable and, within limits, desirable. A teacher working with a relatively small class learns a great deal about the personalities of those whom she is teaching and, incidentally, those whom she is teaching learn a great deal about her. The perceptive teacher who is really interested in the children in her classes knows after a few weeks or perhaps even after a few days which ones should be left alone, which ones need to talk with her about personal problems, and which ones are sufficiently disturbed to be referred to the school counselor or psychologist. There is no need for her to do any verbal prying or to resort to group personality testing.

DISCIPLINE

Disciplinary problems in the classroom develop from the frustration of one or more of the fundamental needs of the child. A child who responds to this frustration by outward aggression disturbs the class, the teacher, and possibly the principal. He becomes a disciplinary case. The child who responds by aggression against himself rarely becomes a disciplinary case, yet he experiences more personality impairment than the one who makes a fighting reaction.

The causes of misconduct, insofar as classroom conditions are concerned, are not hard to identify. Every child needs to succeed. If the academic tasks which have been set for him are too difficult, he feels frustrated. Frustration is uncomfortable, and he feels driven to do something about it. The something which he does may take the form of annoying the teacher, of mutilating his books or his desk, or of throwing various articles at his classmates. Denied the opportunity to satisfy his need for scholastic achievement, he strikes out against his environment. Adjustment of the course content to the abilities of the children being taught would solve many a disciplinary problem.

The child needs to have his abilities, whether small or great, recognized by his teacher and by his classmates. Some few individuals obtain full satisfaction from the knowledge that they have done well, but most persons desire that their contemporaries recognize their achievements. It enhances their feeling of personal worth. The desire for status does not necessarily mean that the individual expects to be outstanding. What he needs is the feeling that others like and respect him for what he is. The teacher who understands this emotional need will be as pleased with the minor classroom contributions as with the major ones. In class discussions she will encourage the dull and diffident student as much as the bright and confident one. She will not scorn the offer of the single talent because it is not ten times greater. She will never try to make any student in her class feel insignificant. She will be more lavish with praise than with criticism. She will help every student to maintain his self-respect.

The relationship between teacher and pupil should be such that the child is made to feel emotionally secure. The general atmosphere of the classroom should be relaxed and friendly. The teacher should understand the emotional needs of her pupils and should take them into consideration in the routine classroom work. She should resort to disciplinary measures only when such steps have to be taken for the good of the group. She should never use fear as a technique of control. To make a child feel emotionally insecure is to create, not eliminate, behavior problems.

A high-school girl was referred to the writer because she had refused to return to school. During the preceding year she had developed certain psychosomatic complaints, including faintness, a pain in her side, and frequent headaches. The following excerpts from the first of a series of recorded interviews indicates how helpless she felt in a threatening school atmosphere:

*P.   Would you like to tell me a little about the difficulties you have been having in school?

*C.   Well, I used to work about six hours on chemistry every night. I got C's before, so I wanted to get B's now and be on the honor roll. I had handed in my notebook and I got an A on that, and the teacher told me I'd been doing well on my tests, but when I got my report card it was a D. It was supposed to be a B, I guess. My home-room teacher had made a mistake, but I was so tired after working so long. . . .

P.   You worked so hard on it and you wanted so much to get a B. . . .

C.   I wasn't even thinking of getting a D in that. I thought I might get a D in history or something.

* P—Psychologist; C—Client.

P. And then when you got that D you just went home and felt very badly about it.

C. Yes.

P. Did you go back to school then?

C. No, I didn't.

P. And then this fall you tried to go back again. Would you like to tell me a little about that?

C. Well, the first time I came back, I was up in the science room taking notes that the teacher was giving me when all of a sudden a faint feeling came over me. I got kind of scared. I was afraid something would happen to me and I wouldn't be able to get home.

P. Yes. You felt very faint and were concerned about your health.

C. Yes. Yes, I didn't know what was going to happen to me.

P. Would you like to tell me a little bit more about how you felt?

C. I just felt like falling down. I stayed through the day, though. I didn't eat any lunch.

P. And then when you got home, did you feel any better?

C. It took me two or three months to come out of it. After a while I recovered and felt more like myself. I felt all right except when school was mentioned. I'm just afraid of it.

P. When school is mentioned, you feel afraid. Does it bring back that same faint feeling?

C. Yes. . . .

P. Doctor ———— told me that you felt there was something wrong with you physically. Do you want to tell me anything about that?

C. Well, sometimes I think I'm going to go out of my mind. When I have that faint feeling, I'm afraid I'm going to, and if I have any crack in my neck or anything, I'm afraid I have broken my neck.

P. Sometimes, then, you feel that you do have a crack in your neck.

C. Yes.

P. And that worries you a lot.

C. Yes.

P. And sometimes you feel that you're going out of your mind.

C. Yes, when I get excited or something I feel that way. My mind doesn't feel clear. I don't feel the way I should.

P. All confused.

C. Yes.

P. Have you felt that way for a long time?

C. Well, since I went to high school I have. If I had that feeling before, I can't remember it. . . .

P. Pretty hard for you to sleep sometimes?

C. Well, it is if I know school is coming up again the next morning.

P. When school is coming along, you worry an awful lot about it.

C. Yes, it makes me feel kind of sick all over. Food doesn't taste good to me or anything. I don't eat very much.

P. If you were going back to school tomorrow, for instance, what would you be thinking about during the evening or the night?

C. Well, I'd be thinking how I was going to feel and how the teachers were going to be, and if the subjects were going to be hard or not. I would wonder whether or not I could understand. . . .

C. Sometimes I want to get away from everything. Sometimes it is so strong that I think of killing myself.

P. Do you want to tell me when you are likely to feel that way?

C. Well, once in a while when I'm thinking about going back to school, and my mother tells me I have to go, I'd rather go down to the river and jump overboard or something, but I know that wouldn't be any help. It would just make my mother and father feel bad.

P. A pretty strong feeling, isn't it.

C. Yes. But my mother doesn't understand the reason why I can't go back. I want to go back to please her, but it's so frightening going back that almost anything would be better.[3]

THE TEACHER

The most important person in an educational institution or system is the classroom teacher, a rather obvious fact which is frequently overlooked by school administrators and by parents. Since she is so important; it is essential that she possess certain educational and personal qualifications. Rankin lists the following characteristics of effective teachers—"effective from the point of view of their good influence on the mental health of children in their care":

A teacher who likes children and youth. This is so fundamental and yet so simple that it seems almost unnecessary to state the fact.

[3] H. A. Carroll, "Motivation and Learning," *Fifty-fourth Yearbook of the National Society for the Study of Education*, Part II, pp. 64–66. Quoted by permission of the Society.

Fortunately, most teachers genuinely like children. Unfortunately, there are some who do not.

A teacher who is himself well adjusted and mentally healthy and thus exemplifies mental health for his pupils.

A teacher who is informed about what is known as to mental health in relation to education.

A teacher who understands the general course of the growth and development of children, and who can use varied techniques for getting to know individual children and their needs.

A teacher who provides a classroom climate conducive to mental health.

A teacher who helps individual pupils to meet their basic emotional needs.

A teacher who can identify children with serious problems and who knows how and where to refer them for help.[4]

A teacher should sincerely like children regardless of their shortcomings. This feeling toward children is essential to good teaching and absolutely necessary to the achievement of hygienic classroom relationships. If it is absent, the pupils know it, and their reactions are likely to be similar to those of children who have been rejected by their parents. Teachers who violate the principle of respect for personality are usually those who dislike some or all of those to whom they are giving instruction.

Closely related to interest is sensitivity to human relationships. It is difficult to explain exactly what is meant by this term. Rogers describes one who lacks such sensitivity as a "person who is quite obtuse to the reactions of others, who does not realize that his remarks have caused another pleasure or distress, who does not sense the hostility or friendliness which exists between himself and others, or between two of his acquaintances."[5] A person who is sensitive to human relationships quickly notes the reactions of others to himself and to one another. He responds to moods and knows how to adjust to them. It is important that the teacher possess this sensitivity. Without it, she will have little real understanding of the personalities of her pupils.

[4] P. T. Rankin, "Fostering Teacher Growth," *Fifty-fourth Yearbook of the National Society for the Study of Education*, Part II, p. 355. Quoted by permission of the Society.

[5] C. R. Rogers, *Counseling and Psychotherapy* (Boston: Houghton Mifflin Company, 1942), p. 254.

Perhaps the best way to find out what personality traits a teacher should have is to turn to the children themselves. Some years ago Witty[6] collected 14,000 letters from grade-school and high-school students on the subject "The Teacher Who Has Helped Me Most." He then analyzed the responses and listed the following traits in order of importance:

1. Cooperative, democratic attitude.
2. Kindliness and consideration for the individual.
3. Patience.
4. Wide interests.
5. Pleasing personal appearance and manner.
6. Fairness and impartiality.
7. Sense of humor.
8. Good disposition and consistent behavior.
9. Interest in pupil's problems.
10. Flexibility.
11. Use of recognition and praise.
12. Unusual proficiency in teaching a particular subject.

Witty follows this listing of positive traits with quotations from the children's letters. From these the author has selected one comment associated with each of the twelve characteristics.

1. Just being with her the first day gave me a happy and content feeling. I did not feel strange at all, but at home. Being with her makes me want to do all I can for her and everyone else, and myself, too.

2. She is a teacher that makes a fellow want to get up early and go to school and not play sick. If a fellow has a teacher like that, he can stand on his own feet.

3. He has lots of patience and explains everything thoroughly without getting mad if you don't understand it right away.

4. When teaching she brings in outside ideas and helps us to apply what we learn in our everyday lives.

5. We were all in the room when in walked a young-looking man

[6] P. A. Witty, "The Mental Health of the Teacher," *Fifty-fourth Yearbook of the National Society for the Study of Education*, Part II, pp. 311–16. Quoted by permission of the Society.

with a very pleasant smile. There was something about his voice and his smile that made me feel good clear down to my stomach.

6. She treats us all the same. She likes every one of us. You can tell it not by what she says but what she does.

7. I think Miss X likes to teach; she makes everyone laugh sometime during the day.

8. Do you know anyone who is never cross but always happy? That's my teacher.

9. It was not easy for me at school. My classmates did not like me as I was slow and sometimes tried to attract attention, thus upsetting everything. Miss X was kind and patient with me. She has explained over and over again why we do this or that. She has helped me to win the love of the other children.

10. He let us find out about many things. He helped us but we helped him too. That's why I like science.

11. School was just school until the fourth grade, but now it is so interesting I don't want to miss a day. You would have to know Miss X to get what I mean. You just want to do your best for her, because she is so good to all of us. She praises you when you deserve it.

12. Miss X didn't teach me to read—it was just like magic. Suddenly I could read out of my reader. She taught me and I didn't know it.

The following year 33,000 more letters were collected. From these, "sample letters were drawn at random, and the nature and frequency of undesirable characteristics were ascertained." They were as follows, arranged in order of rank:

1. Bad tempered and intolerant.

2. Unfair and inclined to have favorites.

3. Disinclined to show interest in the pupil and to take time to help him.

4. Unreasonable in demands.

5. Tendency to be gloomy and unfriendly.

6. Sarcastic and inclined to use ridicule.

7. Unattractive appearance.

8. Impatient and inflexible.

9. Tendency to talk excessively.

10. Inclined to talk down to pupils.

11.   Overbearing and conceited.

12.   Lacking in sense of humor.

Underlying all the characteristics in the preceding list is a threat to the status and security of the child. A comparison of the lists of positive and negative characteristics reveals clearly that the school child responds favorably to the teacher who practices the mental hygiene point of view in the classroom. He feels that she is a constructive force in his life if she respects his personality, understands his limitations, and creates an overall atmosphere of security.

Most American children spend from eight to twelve years or from 8,000 to 12,000 hours in the classroom. It is vitally important that during those years they be under the guidance of well-adjusted men and women. Everything possible should be done to attract well-integrated, intelligent individuals to the teaching profession and to make the conditions of their work such that their personalities will be strengthened rather than weakened.

COUNSELING

Counseling services should be available for children in every school system. How these services should be organized, what the personnel should be and what kind of assistance should be rendered is too broad a subject to be discussed at length in a textbook on mental hygiene. In large school systems, psychiatrists and clinical psychologists should be available for consultation and for individual psychotherapy with children who are seriously disturbed. In small school systems it is usually economically impossible to provide this kind of professional personnel; however, counselors with Master's degrees and teacher-counselors can do much in helping grade school and high school students with their emotional problems.

Since some of the broader aspects of counseling and psychotherapy will be presented in the last chapter, "Regaining Mental Health," the discussion at this point will be limited to a presentation of the material contained in Hobbs's[7] presidential address at the seventy-fourth annual convention of the American Psychological Association and printed in the *American Psychologist*

[7] N. Hobbs, "Helping Disturbed Children: Psychological and Ecological Strategies," *American Psychologist*, XXI, No. 6 (December 1966), 1105–15.

for December 1966. In this article Hobbs reports on a project for the reeducation of emotionally disturbed children in Tennessee and North Carolina. Two residential schools for such children were set up as a kind of laboratory "in which concepts of reeducation could be formulated and tried out." Funds were available for a training program for a small group of teacher-counselors. Each school was to have forty children ranging in age from six to twelve, to be subdivided into small groups of eight children each. Two carefully selected teacher-counselors were assigned to each group. Hobbs says "a teacher-counselor is a decent adult; educated, well trained; able to give and receive affection, to live relaxed, and to be firm; a person with private resources for the nourishment and refreshment of his own life; not an itinerant worker but a professional through and through; a person with a sense of the significance of time, of the usefulness of today and the promise of tomorrow; a person of hope, quiet confidence, and joy; one who has committed himself to children and to the proposition that children who are emotionally disturbed can be helped by the process of reeducation." Professional consultants were available to aid these teacher-counselors but they were the ones who carried the major responsibility for helping the children under their care.

The teacher-counselors in Hobbs's study were not psychotherapists. Hobbs believes that there is too much emphasis on individual psychotherapy as the best way of dealing with emotionally disturbed children. He is critical of excessive preoccupation with the intrapsychic life of the child, with the use of drugs, and with the separation of children from their families which are so often considered to be the "source of contagion." He prefers what he calls "a systems approach to the problem of working with a disturbed child." In other words instead of setting up "cure" as a goal he sees the problem as one of making a small social system work. Parents are looked upon not as sources of contagion but as responsible collaborators in the program. In addition to the home, the neighborhood, the school, and the community are also involved.

The effectiveness of the project is being carefully evaluated. Hobbs says:

The basic design for evaluating the effectiveness of the Re-ed schools involves observations taken at time of enrollment and repeated 6 months after discharge. Preliminary results present an encouraging picture. A composite rating of improvement, based on follow-up information on 93 graduates provided by all evaluators, gives a success rate of approximately 80%. We are in process of obtaining comparison data from control groups to determine the extent to which the reeducation effort is superior to changes that occur with the passage of time.

Detailed analyses show that mothers and fathers independently report a decrease in symptoms such as bedwetting, tantrums, nightmares, and school fears, and an increase in social maturity on a Vineland type check list. School adjustment as rated by teachers shows the same favorable trends. On a semantic differential measure of discrepancy between how the child is seen and parental standards for him, there is an interesting and dynamically significant difference between fathers and mothers. Both see the child as having improved. For fathers the perceived improvement results in lower discrepancy scores between the child as seen and a standard held for him. For some mothers, however, improvement results in a raising of standards so that discrepancy scores frequently remain high. This is not true of all mothers, but it is more frequently true of mothers than of fathers.

Underlying Concepts

Hobbs presents twelve concepts which underlie the process of reeducation in the two experimental schools. These concepts are applicable not only to the disturbed children in Hobbs's special setup but also to disturbed children in all schools and to a considerable degree to normal children as well.

Life Is to Be Lived Now   One of the characteristics of children is that they live in the present. Every hour of every day is important. They welcome involvement in meaningful living and in constructive relationships with other children and with adults. Disturbed children especially often find this involvement difficult, perhaps even frightening. Therefore it is important that they experience more successes than failures. The child learns from both, but he profits more from the former than from the latter.

Time Is an Ally   Time is a factor of great importance in the process of reeducation. "Several studies suggest that therapeutic intervention is not demonstrably superior to the passage of time without treatment in the subsequent adjustment of children diagnosed as emotionally disturbed. Treatment may simply speed up a process that would occur in an unknown percentage of children anyway." This is an important fact for grade school teachers to keep in mind, especially those teachers who tend to become overly concerned with minor adjustment problems. Hobbs says, "We try to avoid getting in the way of the normal restorative processes of life." It should be remembered that while most emotionally disturbed adults were emotionally disturbed as children, the great majority of emotionally disturbed children do not become emotionally disturbed adults.

Trust Is Essential   The emotionally disturbed child has learned to distrust adults since they are usually the cause of his difficulties. Because of past experience he assumes that they will hurt him in one way or another or, as was pointed out in Chapter Seven, be unpredictable in their relations with him—perhaps giving him a little love and then without warning withdrawing it. Such a child needs to be associated with one or more adults who are consistent and so can be trusted by him. This is an essential relationship quality in counseling and psychotherapy. The ability to inspire trust is also a characteristic of the good classroom teacher. Hobbs says, "I am confident of the soundness of the idea that some adults know, without knowing how they know, the way to inspire trust in children and to teach them to begin to use adults as mediators of new learning."

Competence Makes a Difference   In earlier chapters of this book, the need for achievement was stressed. Hobbs underscores this also in his discussion of competence. He says, "If a child feels that he is inadequate in school, inadequacy can become a pervasive theme in his life, leading to a consistent pattern of failure to work up to his level of ability. Underachievement in school is the single most common characteristic of emotionally disturbed children." He and his co-workers dealt with the problem of school achievement directly, helping the children learn school skills especially in areas where they had known defeat so often that they expected failure and were fearful of it. The school should be "a primary source of instruction in living."

Symptoms Can and Should Be Controlled   Usually counselors and psychotherapists emphasize the causes rather than the symptoms of behavior disorders. Hobbs believes that symptoms should be dealt with directly, pointing out that some are more crippling than others. The undesirable symptoms are those which alienate the child from those whom he needs as a source of security and of learning. He says, "There is much to be gained then from identifying symptoms that are standing in the way of normal development and working out specific plans for removing or altering the symptoms if possible. The problem is to help the child make effective contact with normal sources of affection, support, instruction, and discipline." This point of view is similar to the one which was discussed at length in Chapter Seven.

Cognitive Control Can Be Taught   In Hobbs's project on the reeducation of disturbed children there is a great deal of emphasis on personal problems and their management. Attention is focused on the present and the immediate future, not on the past and the distant future. "Children in a group are helped to consider what was good about the day just past, what went wrong that might be handled better tomorrow, and what was learned, especially in successes and failures in relationships among themselves." A by-product of this approach is the habit of talking things over with others, including members of the family.

Feelings Should Be Nurtured   It is unfortunate that emotions are so frequently downgraded at all levels in our educational systems from the primary grades to graduate school. Teaching without emotion is barren; learning without emotion is meaningless. It is especially important in working with disturbed children either individually or in groups to encourage the expression of feeling. Hobbs says, in connection with his study, "Anger, resentment, hostility are commonplace of course and their expression is used in various ways: to help some children learn to control their violent impulses and to help others give vent to feelings too long repressed." In his experimental groups companionship is encouraged but along with that the need to be alone is respected. Children need both.

The Group Is Important to Children   Group identification is important for emotionally disturbed children as it is for everyone else.

Each group in the Hobbs study "is kept intact for nearly all activities and becomes an important source of motivation, instruction, and control." Being a member of a group when it is functioning well or for that matter even when it is functioning poorly is, or at least can be, a constructive experience.

Ceremony and Ritual Give Order, Stability, and Confidence   The heading really tells the whole story here. Ceremony and ritual have a steadying effect on human beings. They have been used for centuries by barbarians and by civilized man. Children especially find ceremony and ritual, within limits of course, both exciting and stabilizing.

The Body Is the Armature of the Self   Perceptions of the body and the utilization of physical structure are an important part of a person's self-image and a significant factor in his mental health. Occupational therapy is based to a considerable extent on this assumption. Hobbs says, "We are intrigued by the idea that the physical self is the armature around which the psychological self is constructed and that a clearer experiencing of the potential and the boundaries of the body should lead to a clearer definition of the self, and thus to greater psychological fitness and more effective functioning."

Communities Are Important   Hobbs states that many of the children in his emotionally disturbed groups "come from families that are alienated or detached from community life." He stresses the importance of identification with the neighborhood or the town. The child and his family should be participating actively in community affairs. It would appear to be obvious that the neighborhood school can add much to a child's stability.

A Child Should Know Joy   The reader may be surprised to find the word "joy" mentioned in a research article in psychology since most psychologists appear to be fearful of using words or terms which have a positive emotional connotation. Hobbs says:

> We have often speculated about our lack of a psychology of well-being. There is an extensive literature on anxiety, guilt, and dread, but little that is well developed on joy. Most psychological experi-

ments rely for motivation on avoidance of pain or hunger or some other aversive stimuli: positive motivations are limited to the pleasure that comes from minute, discrete rewards. This poverty with respect to the most richly human of motivations leads to anaemic programming for children. We thus go beyond contemporary psychology to touch one of the most vital areas of human experiencing. We try to develop skill in developing joy in children. We believe that it is immensely important, that it is immediately therapeutic if further justification is required, for a child to know some joy in each day and to look forward with eagerness to at least some joy-giving event that is planned for tomorrow.

Comments

There are three reasons for having presented the article on "Helping Disturbed Children" in so much detail. First, Hobbs is one of the country's outstanding clinical psychologists and speaks with authority based on considerable research and long experience. Second, the teacher-counselor plan which he describes is one which could be used in a school system of almost any size. To be sure, it is just one method of helping emotionally disturbed children, but it is relatively inexpensive and evidently very effective. Third, the philosophy underlying the reeducation program as presented in the twelve concepts is applicable not only to emotionally disturbed children but also to normal children. A teacher who applied these concepts in her classroom would be doing a great deal to maintain or to improve the mental health of the children under her care.

SUMMARY

It is now generally recognized that the school should be concerned with the development of the whole child; his intellectual problems cannot be separated from his physical, social, and emotional problems. During his school years he should be given as much help in learning how to master social and emotional adjustments as he is given in learning how to play football or to read. The responsibility of the school is to educate total personalities. With respect to mental health, the school should seek to prevent behavior disorders through the utilization of healthful procedures and through the identification and treatment of those children who are experiencing serious adjustment difficulties. Sound mental hygiene attitudes should underlie all the activities of the school. The key figure in the achievement of these goals is the classroom teacher. She should have a deep interest in children and a real understanding of them and their problems. She should be able to promote in them a feeling of security and a sense of achievement.

THE COMMUNITY

chapter 10

The importance of attitudes in relation to mental health was stressed in Chapter One. The attitudes held by an individual are to a considerable extent a reflection of the attitudes held by members of his family and other significant figures in his experience; their attitudes in turn are to a considerable extent a reflection of the attitudes of the community and the larger society of which that community is a part. Attitudes, points of view, the values by which we live have been handed down from generation to generation, occasionally with major and frequently with minor modifications. They constitute our social inheritance and are fully as important as our biological inheritance. An important part of that social inheritance is the set of attitudes toward mental health that has retarded progress in the prevention and treatment of behavior disorders. These attitudes, however, are now being modified.

CHANGING ATTITUDES TOWARD MENTALLY DISTURBED PERSONS

Evidently human beings have always had a great need to understand themselves and the world—even the universe—around them. Evidently, also, the need for closure has been so great that answers had to be provided for unanswerable questions. When an event occurred mysteriously and with no apparent cause, such as a thunderstorm or an eclipse of the sun, special agents were created and made responsible for the mysterious happening. Mental illness was one of the events which defied rational explanation in terms of simple and observable cause and effect. Therefore it was logical in early societies to ascribe such abnormal behavior to the work of demons, witches, evil spirits, and unkind gods. Even today we have not wholly escaped from this attitude which has come down to us from early man.

Once an explanation for the causes has been made, the methods for handling the situation flow naturally from this and are largely determined by it. Deutsch reasons as follows about primitive and early beliefs in this area.

> Since mental diseases . . . are supernaturally induced, prophylaxis and cure are sought in magic. To ward off disease, talismans and amulets are worn, and other magic protective devices are utilized. Sickness is cured by exorcising the demon from the person possessed through incantation and prayer, through propitiation, cajoling, and even threats. On occasion, when the possessing demon is regarded as a corporal being, physical torture, such as squeezing or scourging the body, may be resorted to in driving him out.[1]

It is difficult to comprehend the vital part that belief in demons and witches played in medieval thinking. Since the religious leaders of those days saw the world as a battleground between good and evil, between God and Satan picturesquely and dramatically battling for men's souls, it was inevitable that persons would be on the alert to find out whose soul had been won by Satan (every soul, once won by Satan, constituted an increase in his forces, thus creating a greater threat to those still unpossessed). A fellow human thought to be possessed was regarded with suspicion, fear, and even hatred. The logical thing to do in such a situation was to take the individual to a priest who, as a representative of God, would try to cast the devil out of him and so return him to the side of the angels.

It was only a short step from this point to a belief in witchcraft, wherein the Devil persuaded certain persons to sell their souls to him in return for supernatural powers. Possessing these supernatural

---

[1] Albert Deutsch, *The Mentally Ill in America*, 2nd ed. (New York: Doubleday & Company, Inc., 1949), p. 2.

powers they could then cast all sorts of misfortune upon their enemies and so constituted a danger to the community. The popular belief in witches grew apace. During the period from 1450 to 1700, no less than 100,000 persons were executed as witches, according to Deutsch. Deutsch goes on to say that there is convincing evidence that large numbers of these persons who were convicted of witchcraft were actually mentally ill. He says,

> Of those who confessed voluntarily without the application of torture, and they constituted a large number, many reveal themselves unmistakably to us by their testimony as victims of various psychoses— dementia praecox, manic-depressive psychosis, paranoia, and a consuming desire for expiation. Too often did these unfortunate deluded individuals implicate other persons in satanic plots that existed only in their own fevered imaginations, and draw these persons to the stake with them. What percentage of the victims of the witch mania were mentally unsound is of course beyond calculation, but on the basis of the records it would seem no exaggeration to judge that they comprised at least one-third of the total executed.[2]

Witchcraft in New England is a familiar tale to Americans. Although it existed in the other colonies, it flourished most fanatically in the land of the Puritans. This is not surprising in view of Puritanism's narrow, rigid, repressive philosophy of religion and life. Even today we have not wholly discarded the Puritan tradition. The Puritans tended to regard any deviation in human behavior with suspicion. Since behavior disorders constitute deviate behavior patterns, it follows that emotionally disturbed persons were almost certain to be regarded as witches and punished accordingly.

Apart from the belief in witchcraft, attitudes toward those who were mentally ill were but a part of the broader attitude toward suffering in general: suffering was the punishment meted out to witches and inferior persons by a stern Deity. Emotionally disturbed persons were objects of contempt. They were weaklings, incapable of making right choices. If they could not help themselves, why help them? If they became an economic or a social problem, then they should be disposed of as quickly and as cheaply as possible. Those who were violently insane were regarded as criminals and imprisoned. Those who were harmlessly insane were regarded as un-

[2] *Ibid.,* pp. 20–21.

wanted paupers. Thus it became a common custom to force these persons to leave the community. Sometimes, instead of being made to leave town, harmlessly insane persons were auctioned off to the lowest bidders, who became responsible for their care. It is easy to imagine the kind of care which they received. Deutsch summarizes the care and treatment of mentally deranged persons in Colonial times as follows:

> . . . the mentally ill were hanged, imprisoned, tortured and otherwise persecuted as agents of Satan. Regarded as sub-human beings, they were chained in specially devised kennels and cages like wild beasts, and thrown into prisons, bridewells and jails like criminals. They were incarcerated in workhouse dungeons, or made to slave as able-bodied paupers, unclassified from the rest. They were left to wander about stark naked, driven from place to place like mad dogs, subjected to whippings as vagrants and rogues. Even the well-to-do were not spared confinement in strong rooms and cellar dungeons, while legislation usually concerned itself more with their property than their persons.[3]

It takes a great deal of time to modify any complex attitude held by a large group of people. This has been especially true of the attitude toward those human beings who have lost rational control of themselves. The emotional basis of the attitude appears to be a mixture of fear and contempt, with fear predominating. When we are afraid we usually do one of two things: run away or fight. Society has done both with respect to those who are mentally ill. For centuries we have tried to avoid the problem by pretending that it is not nearly so great as it really is. In individual families there persists a strong tendency to pretend that the relative who is developing a serious behavior disorder is really all right, that there is nothing wrong with him. When he does become psychotic, he is likely to be "put away" and forgotten so far as is possible.

The hostility to which we resort in time of fear is clearly manifest in our treatment of mentally disturbed persons through the centuries, although it is not so great now as it was in colonial times. One result of this mild change is better treatment of mental patients in hospitals. The history of the changing attitude toward treatment is an interesting one. In the 18th century, mental institutions were per-

3 *Ibid.*, p. 53.

ceived as agencies for confinement, not for cure. They were prisons of the worst sort. The attendants, many of them evidently sadists, were free to chain and to beat the inmates. Conditions in general were almost unbelievably bad, but even as the repressive, primitive tendencies of this period were at their worst, simultaneously, progressive forces, long in incubation, were reaching fruition. Vast upheavals were occurring on both sides of the Atlantic in concepts about nearly all areas of human activity and human relationships. The cry was raised for a more humanitarian approach toward those who were mentally ill. The professional approach to insanity was being radically influenced in Europe by the humane ideas of Pinel and Tuke. The former, in France, was noted for his principle of nonrestraint and his conviction that the mentally ill would respond favorably to kindness and trust and respect for their dignity as human beings. Tuke, in England, also believed that there was such a thing as improvement—that mental disorders could be cured. He and his fellow Quakers in York, England, founded an institution known as The Retreat in which they tried to set up positive group living arrangements. Consideration was emphasized; any form of terrorization was forbidden.

Back in the United States, Benjamin Rush, a member of the staff of the Pennsylvania Hospital in Philadelphia in the years just following the American Revolution, was contributing to the advancement of the trend toward more humane and intelligent treatment of insane persons. For example, he objected to the total lack of heating and ventilating facilities in the cells for the insane, pointing out that they would never get well as long as they were forced to live in such quarters. The popular belief at that time was that the insane were insensitive to heat and cold. This belief, partly responsible for the sanctioning of untold suffering, persisted for decades after Rush's time. Rush's work at Pennsylvania Hospital was very significant in that it symbolized the emergence of a new concept in America about mental patients: a public institution receiving the insane should not be thought of as a prison for malefactors but as a hospital for treatment. This represented a radical departure from the thinking of the past. Actual practice lagged far behind, and even today the concepts of the Middle Ages have not been fully discarded by the general public. However, slow progress was made. Popular opinion gradually changed to the point where public support was given to improved care of the insane. However, progress is usually characterized by advance and then retreat. The forward steps of the 18th century were to be followed by backward steps in the 19th century.

During the early part of the 19th century several new institutions for the insane were established. However, the establishment of these institutions had one effect which probably was not expected by the leaders of the movement for better care for mentally disturbed persons. The public, having exerted itself to bring into existence some housing facilities, now settled back with the feeling that the problem had been solved through their being able to hide away at the lowest possible cost the insane members of society. Actual treatment of the persons in these institutions was very limited or nonexistent, and little attention was paid to the large number of disturbed persons who were not institutionalized.

In the second quarter of the 19th century a belief in the curability of insanity, originating in England, swept across both England and the United States. Prior to that time the conviction was widespread, as it is among some groups today, that once a person became insane he always remained insane. Now reports were being made of 80 and 90 and even 100 per cent cures being achieved with large groups of patients. At first these unfounded claims produced positive results in that the public was stirred to build additional institutions and hospitals. It also resulted in a temporary shifting of the emphasis from custodial care to treatment. However, once the cult of curability had run its course it was followed by a period of reaction, the effects of which are still felt. The public, disillusioned by the exposure of the false claims concerning the ease with which insanity could be cured, became extremely pessimistic—returning to the point of view "once insane, always insane." This attitude persisted long after a sound basis for limited optimism had been established.

No discussion, however brief, of the changing attitudes toward the insane during the 19th century would be complete without some reference to the outstanding reform work of Dorothea Dix. Reform movements are usually characterized by a great deal of zeal, and this was true of the one led by Dorothea Dix, whose name is associated with the erection of more than thirty new hospitals for the care of mentally ill persons in the United States. Dorothea Dix campaigned ceaselessly for humane treatment for the insane. She and other reformers brought out into the open tales of cruelty and squalor. These so shocked the people that they brought pressure to bear upon their state legislatures to improve the situation through the building of new hospitals in which it was hoped that humane treatment would be available. These state hospitals were milestones in the history of the treatment of mentally disturbed persons.

At the end of the 19th century and at the beginning of the 20th the general public was on the whole either indifferent or actively hostile toward persons who were mentally ill and toward those who were trying to treat them. There was a popular unwillingness to send psychotic relatives to mental hospitals. If a person were sent, he found upon returning to his community that he carried with him the stigma of having been in a "madhouse." On the positive side, however, psychiatrists were beginning to build private practices outside the hospitals. There was an increase in the number of outpatient departments of psychopathic hospitals, and there was a marked increase in the output of theory and research relating to the treatment of mental disorders. It was during this period that Freud began the publication of his startling articles and books and that Clifford Beers launched his mental hygiene movement. *Prevention* was the principal goal of this movement and, associated with it, the removal from the popular mind of the idea that it was a disgrace to be or to have been mentally ill.

Beers, a Yale graduate, had spent three years in three different mental institutions, two private and one state hospital. Although he was psychotic, he was sufficiently in touch with reality to observe in detail the treatment, sometimes brutal, of the patients by doctors and attendants. He himself experienced personal abuse, such as being thrown about and choked. During one period he spent twenty-one nights and part of the days in a strait jacket. Beers was so disturbed by what he saw and by what he personally experienced that he decided to devote his life to exposing mental hospital conditions and to leading a reform movement. He began by writing a book, *A Mind That Found Itself,* which has become a classic in the field of social reform.

Beers succeeded in winning the support of some of the leading psychologists and psychiatrists of his day. Together they formed The National Committee for Mental Hygiene in 1909. This committee stimulated the establishment of mental hygiene and child guidance clinics and disseminated information about emotional disturbances to the general public. However, as a reform movement, it was not nearly so successful as Beers had hoped. In recent years the National Association for Mental Health has replaced the National Committee for Mental Hygiene.

What has the situation been in recent years, and what is it now? The answer is that, although progress has been and is being made, there is still a considerable lag. There are reasons for both optimism and pessimism. Since World War II, substantial gains have been made in the fight against mental illness. One measure of public support is the considerable increase in dollars spent in this area. For example, in 1956 Congress appropriated only 18 million dollars for the activities of the National Institute of Mental Health. By 1959 the appropriation had been raised to $53,400,000, and by 1961 to $100,-900,000. If a greater span of years is taken, going back to 1950 (the first year of the existence of the National Institute of Mental Health as a separate organization), the increase is from $8,700,000 in 1950 to the previously mentioned $100,900,000 in 1961. During this eleven-year span, the increase in the Congressional appropriation for mental health has been greater than increases in appropriations to combat either cancer or heart disease. This is due in part to the fact that in 1950 the National Institute of Mental Health received a relatively low proportion of the funds. In that year, $18,900,000 was allotted to fight cancer and $10,700,000 to be used against heart disease.

In addition to the considerable increases in appropriations by Congress for the use of the National Institute of Mental Health, there have been great increases in state and county appropriations for the hospital care of those suffering from severe behavior disorders. These increases are not nearly enough, but they do constitute a hopeful sign.

There are indices other than dollars spent which reveal recent gains.

Between 1956 and 1958, the number of physicians working in public mental hospitals increased from 45 to 57 per cent adequacy . . . an even more significant index is total professional patient care personnel in public mental hospitals (including physicians, registered nurses, social workers, psychologists, psychometrists, occupational therapists, and other therapists). Such personnel increased from 2.8

to 3.4 per one hundred patients between 1956 and 1958, the number of psychologists increasing from 65 per cent adequacy to 75 per cent; of registered nurses from 20 to 23 per cent; and of social workers from 36 to 40 per cent. . . . The professional man hours spent in mental health clinics by psychiatrists, psychologists and social workers rose from 116 to 147 per one hundred thousand population between 1955 and 1959.[4]

All of this is good. We have come a long way since the days of Bedlam and the witch hunts. It should not be forgotten, however, that we still have a long way to go. Mental health services still lag far behind the demonstrated need. Public response, although improving, is still relatively apathetic. One way of evaluating the response of the public is to look at the fund drive results of the ten largest national voluntary health groups (Table V).

It can be seen from Table V that among the ten leading drives mental health ranks eighth. During the ten-year period from 1950 through 1959, more than $437,000,000 was collected for polio as compared to $22,500,000 for mental health. To make another comparison, about ten times more was collected by the American Cancer Society than by the National Association for Mental Health. Why is this so? It is certainly the result in part, as was pointed out in Chapter One, of the basic attitudes toward persons with serious behavior disorders. There is still widespread fear, coupled with a belief that the situation is hopeless. Mental health, although receiving more favorable publicity than it did twenty or thirty years ago, still receives less attention in our newspapers and magazines than do the major physical disorders. Apparently the care and treatment of the mentally ill lacks broad popular appeal.

There are startling differences in the care provided in state, county, and city mental hospitals as compared with other types of hospitals. "The 1960 Guide Issue of The American Hospital Association journal, *Hospitals,* shows that two of every three of these [latter] hospitals are accredited according to the minimum standards of the Joint Commission on Accreditation of Hospitals, and that patient care costs them $31.16 per patient per day, a sum that helps support 2.3 employes per patient, but does not, of course, cover

[4] *Action for Mental Health,* Final Report of the Joint Commission on Mental Illness and Health (New York: Basic Books, Inc., Publishers, 1961), pp. 8–9.

TABLE V

Total Funds Raised Nationally in Ten Leading Voluntary Health Campaigns, 1950–1959
(in millions of dollars)[5]

Year	1 Polio	2 TB	3 Cancer	4 Heart	5 Crippled Children	6 Cerebral Palsy	7 Muscular Dystrophy	8 Mental Health[b]	9 Arthritis	10 Multiple Sclerosis
1950	30.8	21.0	13.9	4.1	5.8	1.0	—[a]	—[c]	0.7	0.18
1951	33.5	21.7	14.6	5.5	6.1	2.1	—[a]	0.7	1.0	0.19
1952	41.4	23.2	16.4	6.7	6.7	4.0	0.26	0.6	1.0	0.25
1953	51.4	23.8	19.8	8.5	7.7	6.4	0.6	0.7[A]	1.4	0.45
1954	65.0	24.0	21.7	11.3	8.1	8.2	4.0	1.7[A]	1.5	0.8
1955	52.5	24.6	24.4	13.6	8.5	7.5	3.9	2.4	1.8	1.3
1956	51.9	25.8	27.2	17.5	9.8	8.1	3.0	2.6	2.2	2.0
1957	44.0	26.3	29.6	20.5	10.3	8.4	3.7	3.8	2.4	2.3
1958	35.4	26.0	29.7	22.3	10.4	9.2	4.9	4.5	3.0	2.5
1959	31.3[E]	26.0	31.0[E]	24.0	10.3	9.5	4.6	5.5[E]	3.6	—[d]
Totals	437.2	242.4	228.3	134.0	83.7	64.4	24.96	22.5	18.6	9.97

SOURCE: Rough figures supplied by National Information Bureau for (1) National Foundation, (2) National Tuberculosis Association, (3) American Cancer Society, (4) American Heart Association, (5) National Association for Crippled Children and Adults, (6) United Cerebral Palsy Association, (7) Muscular Dystrophy Association of America, (8) National Association for Mental Health, (9) Arthritis and Rheumatism Foundation, (10) National Multiple Sclerosis Society.

[a] No campaign.
[b] Figures for 1951 and 1952 from National Information Bureau, for 1953–1959 from National Association for Mental Health.
[c] Not available, due to merger.
[d] Not available.
[E] Estimate.
[A] Approximate.
[5] Ibid., p. 15.

private doctor bills."[6] In contrast to this, the cost per patient per day in state, county, and city psychiatric hospitals is $4.44, a sum that helps support 0.32 employees per patient. To be sure, the care provided for mental patients in private hospitals and in hospitals operated by the Veterans Administration is much better. However, 80 per cent of hospitalized mentally disturbed persons are in state hospitals. "We still have a long, long way to go to provide healing care for the mentally ill of America."[7]

It is possible that within the next few years the following may be understood and accepted by the general public:

1. Behavior disorders, with the exception of the organic psychoses, are learned. They are not genetically transmitted, although certain potentialities or predisposing factors may be inherited. There is no proof that such a complex pattern of behavior as schizophrenia, for example, can be inherited. To be sure, both neurotic and psychotic behavior runs in families. Obviously, this is not conclusive evidence that such behavior is passed on to succeeding generations through the genes. It must be remembered that a person's social inheritance is as important as his biological inheritance. The kind of family in which he is reared and the larger culture in which he functions are extremely potent in determining whether he will develop a normal or an abnormal personality structure. There is a wealth of evidence that individuals learn behavior disorders in the same way that they learn normal behavior. In simple terms, their experiential background causes disturbed persons to make inaccurate and distorted responses to the problems of living. It is just as easy to learn that two plus two equals five as it is to learn that two plus two equals four. Predisposing factors, however, may be inherited. For example, a person who has inherited low mentality or physical abnormalities is off to a bad start. Such handicaps may give him a low threshold of resistance, rendering him more susceptible to behavior disorders. However, the important point to keep in mind is that neurotic reactions and functional psychotic reactions are learned. They are not disease entities. In the light of present knowledge there is no relevant organic pathology present.

2. Since behavior disorders (with the exception of the organic psychoses) are learned, they can be treated through psychotherapy.

[6] *Ibid.*, p. 18.
[7] *Ibid.*, p. 23.

The general public has difficulty in understanding what psycho-therapy is. In a broad sense, it includes all psychological or mental methods of treating behavior disorders. It is a learning situation in which the client is provided with an opportunity to make corrective adjustments in his perceptions of himself and of his environment. It is intellectual and emotional reeducation.

3. Like treatment for physical illness, treatment for behavior disorders should begin early. In general, the older the patient the less likelihood of success; also, the more severe the behavior disorder the less the likelihood of successful treatment. It is very important to identify children who are experiencing rather severe emotional difficulties and to provide professional treatment for them, just as we do for children with physical disorders. In the majority of such instances it is relatively easy to restore them to good mental health. To be sure, many disturbed children eventually learn satisfactory adjustments without professional assistance, but it is equally true that without this kind of help many become neurotic or psychotic.

4. Behavior disorders in a large number of cases can be pre-vented through the application of mental hygiene principles. It is especially important that these be applied in the school and in the home, the two institutions which exert the greatest influence upon the developing child. The child who is respected by his parents and by his teachers develops a positive self-image; the child who is under constant attack and threat develops a negative self-image— a long first step toward severe emotional difficulties. The child who has knowledge of his abilities and his limitations develops a realistic appraisal of himself. This is an important part of the foundation of a healthy personality.

5. Persons suffering from behavior disorders, even when they are psychotic, are still human beings possessing the same needs everyone else has. They feel, suffer, love, and hate. They respond to kindness and react against cruelty. They should not be outcasts. Rogers says,

> I think of one man with whom I have spent many hours, including many hours of silence. There have been long stretches when I had no way of knowing whether the relationship had any meaning for him. He was uncommunicative, seemingly indifferent, withdrawn,

inarticulate. I think of an hour when he felt completely worthless, hopeless, suicidal. He wanted to run away, wanted to do away with himself because, as he muttered in flat despair, "I just don't care." I responded, "I know you don't care about yourself, don't care at *all,* but I just want you to know that *I* care." And then, after a long pause, came a violent flood of deep, wracking, gasping sobs which continued for nearly half an hour. It was dramatic evidence of what all of us have learned—that behind the curtains of silence and hallucination, and strange talk, and hostility, and indifference, there is in each case a person, and that if we are skillful and fortunate we can *reach* that person, and can live, often for brief moments only, in a direct person-to-person relationship with him. To me that fact seems to say something about the nature of schizophrenia. It says something too about the nature of man and his craving for and fear of a deep human relationship. It seems to say that human beings are persons, whether we have labelled them as schizophrenic or whatever.[8]

6. Persons suffering from behavior disorders differ only in degree from normal persons. They have made excessive use of the same adjustment mechanisms used by normal persons to some extent. Every person has his breaking point; the sane and the insane, the normal and the abnormal are all brothers under the skin. There is no completely healthy person; neither is there a completely unhealthy person.

7. Behavior disorders, including some serious psychotic reactions, can be cured. In the light of present knowledge this statement, of course, does not apply to all persons suffering from behavior disorders. As with physical disease a number of qualifying factors must be taken into consideration, such as age, physical condition, personal environment, stage of development, nature of the disorder, and kind of treatment. It simply is not true that a person who has been institutionalized because of a psychotic episode remains psychotic for the rest of his life. A large number recover.

8. Psychiatrists, psychologists, and other professionally trained men and women have the same healthy, dedicated interest in their work as do other professional groups. If more rapid progress is to be achieved in the prevention of behavior disorders and in the care

[8] C. R. Rogers, "The Significance or Meaning of the Study to Date," *The Psychiatric Institute Bulletin* (The University of Wisconsin, Wisconsin Psychiatric Institute [mimeographed bulletin]). I, No. 10 (h), September 2, 1961, 4–5.

and treatment of those who have succumbed, there must be a change in the attitude of the public toward those who carry the main responsibility for doing the job.

9. To seek and to receive treatment for behavior disorders is nothing to be ashamed of. A person is no more responsible for deviations in his behavior than he is for deviations in the functioning of his body. He should seek treatment for such deviations with the same objectivity that he would seek treatment for physical illness. There has been considerable improvement with respect to this point during the last ten or fifteen years. Persons are now much less hesitant about seeking help in solving their emotional problems.

CONTRIBUTIONS TO BETTER MENTAL HEALTH

The increased understanding of the causes of behavior disorders and the greater realization of the importance of prevention and early treatment is resulting in specific community efforts to improve mental health. Many communities in which nothing definite has yet been done are asking such questions as: What can we do? Where do we start? To some citizens the most important goal is the improvement and expansion of clinic and hospital facilities; to others, more mental hygiene, both taught and applied in our schools, seems most urgent; or, increased recreation facilities seem an essential first step; or, a positive constructive religion is basic.

All of these are important. No one approach can be singled out as the only way to a solution of mental health problems. It is necessary to move ahead on all fronts simultaneously.

The Church

In most communities religion plays a conspicuous role, both in the lives of individuals and in the collective life of the community itself. The crucial question here is, of course, to what extent and in what way does the practice of religion contribute to mental health? Basically, religion is more emotional than intellectual. Its most powerful appeal is to faith, and faith carries many individuals through difficult periods of their lives. Religion satisfies, to some extent, the need for status, and it has not been wholly blind to physiological. needs. Its principal contribution, however, lies in satisfying the need for emotional security.

No individual is ever sufficient unto himself alone. Human nature is such that every person desires to be at least somewhat dependent upon another who is stronger than himself. A belief in God satisfies his desire. The individual feels secure because of the faith he has in a Supreme Being. His need is especially great if he has no fellow humans to whom he can turn. Moreover, worship, including prayer, is a form of catharsis, and catharsis is always good for one who is in trouble. Mental hygienists, far from being opposed to religion, welcome the positive contributions that religion can make.

Religion becomes a negative force when it stresses fear. Fortunately, in our present-day churches, much less is heard about Hell than used to be the case. When punishment for sins is stressed, the need for emotional security is frustrated. The individual is denied the basic satisfaction he seeks in religion. The church that understands human weakness, instead of condemning it, is a church which is building personality rather than destroying it. Individuals like to believe that they cannot be destroyed; religion offers them eternity. Individuals are puzzled about ultimate causes; religion offers them the answers. Above all, individuals need to lean against a power that is greater than themselves. Religion provides them with that power. Human beings need religion, but it must be a religion which fulfills their desires, if they are to grow in emotional strength.

Value Systems   Religious institutions have been associated with value systems. In fact, it is very doubtful if an organized system of moral and ethical values can exist for any considerable length of time without religious sanction. Throughout history, one of the most important contributions of religion, regardless of its kind, has been the value system which it has taught. To be sure, these values have frequently been viewed as absolutes. Concepts of absolute honesty, of absolute truthfulness, of absolute integrity, and of absolute purity have been set up as goals to work toward. No one can achieve the absolute, since for finite human beings nothing is ever perfect. However, few persons have taken the absolutist teachings literally. Instead, they have looked upon the values emphasized by the church as provisional absolutes, as goals to work toward without expectation of complete achievement. Viewed in this way, the value systems of the several churches have been very constructive forces in society and in the lives of individuals. Every human being has to have a value system by which he lives. It is essential for good mental health that his personal values are those which are most constructive for him, for his community, and for the larger society of which he and his community are a part. The churches in a community can help greatly in the prevention of behavior disorders through helping individuals to acquire those basic values which have proved their worth through the centuries.

The Clergy   To whom do individuals go in time of trouble? They are most likely to seek help from clergymen. This group ranks above physicians and considerably above psychiatrists and psychologists as a professional resource—a situation that provides an opportunity and a challenge to the clergy.

Pastoral counseling, then, is a very important activity in the mental health field. Protestant ministers are, generally speaking, better trained for this kind of service than Catholic priests or Jewish rabbis. They have, on the average, received more extensive instruction in clinical psychology, such instruction being offered in the great majority of Protestant theological schools. Possibly, in part, because of this training the Protestant clergyman finds it easier to take a psychological rather than a strictly religious point of view. However, this remains an obstacle even to many of the Protestant faith. It is difficult for the clergyman to play the moralistic role in his Sunday sermons and the psychological role with certain of his parishioners in the counseling relationship during the week.

The clergyman, because of his interests, is often especially well qualified to deal with emotional problems. He is much more concerned with human beings as personalities than as physical organisms. Unlike the physician who, because of his training, usually looks for physical causes of behavior disorders, the clergyman looks to the personal life of his parishioners. His warmth and understanding often bring about better results than would be achieved by the better-trained psychiatrist—unless that psychiatrist also has the same personality qualifications. It is a hopeful sign that many of the large churches in our urban areas have set up counseling centers. Frequently, psychiatrists and clinical psychologists, as well as churchmen, are on the staffs of such centers. This interdisciplinary approach has much to commend it. It is the kind of addition to the country's mental health facilities that should be encouraged.

The School

In a democratic society such as ours, the school is second only to the home in affecting the mental health of our children. The school in the United States is characteristically a responsibility of the community. This important institution provides the community with its best opportunity to foster good mental health. Ojemann lists the interactions which define the role of the community in the mental health of the school as follows:

1. If the school is to work "understandingly" with the child it must have a variety of background information about him. Some of these data may be supplied by various community agencies.

2. If teachers and administrators are to appraise the child objectively and guide him according to his needs rather than projecting their desires into his pattern of living, they will need opportunities for satisfying their own feelings of adequacy, personal worth, sex expression, and the like. The attitudes of the community may help or hinder them in this.

3. In developing its program to meet the demands of the growing personality the school may from time to time make changes in content and method. If these changes are not understood, the community cannot react intelligently toward them.

4. The out-of-school work required of the child should be within his range of ability. Sometimes, because of the difficulty of school materials, the child must be given patient help by his parents. Conditions in the community may pose unnecessarily complicated problems for the child.

5. It would help the school's mental-hygiene program if the community exemplified a "causal" approach in its relations with the child. How the child is treated by the police, the leader of the recreational group, the minister, the doctor, or his employer, if he works part time—the kind of relationships they demonstrate—influences his learning and the way he works and plays with others. . . .

6. The school is interested in helping each child learn constructive ways of working out his feelings of self-respect, adequacy, and other demands of the growing personality. These ways will vary with the special abilities of each child. If the community through its system of values and rewards and punishments gives approval to narrow and prejudiced attitudes, the work of the school may be largely undone. What the community rewards may seem more real to the child than what the school teaches.[9]

It is very important that the teachers in the school systems be fully aware of the mental health needs of the children in their care. This awareness can be furthered through formal courses in mental hygiene and through in-service training. Often teachers need to be stimulated by the counselors and psychologists in the school systems, by the administrative officers, and by the public.

Perhaps the best single medium for disseminating information concerning mental health and for taking steps to do something about the problem is the Parent-Teachers Association. Parent-teacher groups are organized to help the children in our schools. These organizations provide teachers and parents with the opportunity to get together to discuss the needs of the children and to plan and to support programs for meeting those needs. Frequently parent-teacher groups lose sight of their principal objective and become merely social gatherings or clubs. Where there has been a strong desire to do something for the children, this desire has often been translated into improving the facilities of the physical plant. This, of course, is desirable up to a point. Major attention, however, should be given to the less tangible personal factors. What are the qualifications of the teachers? Are they creating an emotionally healthy school atmosphere? Children spend a considerable portion of their lives from age six to age eighteen in the school situation. What happens during those thousands of hours greatly influences the child's mental health for good or for ill.

Parent-teacher groups should be interested in the extracurricular activities of the school. Are there enough—or too many? Do they

9 R. H. Ojemann, "The Role of the Community in the Mental-Health Program of the School," *Fifty-fourth Yearbook of the National Society for the Study of Education*, Part II, pp. 129–30. Quoted by permission of the Society.

provide emotional, intellectual, and physical outlets for all the pupils? Are they properly supervised? Are the playground facilities adequate, and—more important—are those for children in the lower and middle grades, especially, supervised with due regard for the needs of the shy and the retiring child, the nonathletic child, and the overly aggressive child? The playground, to some children, is a place of torment because of the unrestrained mental and physical attacks of some of their peers.

Parent-teacher groups should be interested in the curriculum of the schools, and they should acquaint themselves with some of the facts concerning individual differences. The parents in the group should learn from the teachers, and the teachers in the group should learn from the parents; both parents and teachers should be improving their understanding of children through reading and through a well-planned lecture program.

Child Guidance Clinics

The American people have come to recognize the importance of the work done by social welfare agencies throughout the country. Social workers have definitely established a place for themselves. In recent years an increased interest in health clinics has developed. This is partially illustrated by the present-day demands for socialized medicine, growing out of a widespread realization that the poor have a right to medical care.

There has not been, however, the same amount of interest in child guidance clinics. The need for such guidance centers is great, for the time to treat behavior disorders is when they are still in an incipient stage.

The time is rapidly approaching when communities will feel as great a responsibility concerning problems of mental health as they now do concerning problems of physical health. They will be willing to make as much effort to prevent the development of a neurosis or a psychosis as they now make to protect children against scarlet fever or diphtheria. They will not consider a mental disorder a disgrace but will provide the mental patient with as good care as he would receive if suffering from a somatic disorder. They will raise the mental and emotional components of human beings to a position of equality with the physical component.

The Joint Commission on Mental Illness and Health makes the following recommendation for community mental health clinics for children:

> Psychiatric clinics providing intensive psychotherapy for children plus appropriate medical or social treatment procedures should be fostered and, where they exist, expanded. The present state-aid program is insufficient to provide the needs in this area.[10]

The authors, in elaborating on their recommendations, state:

> Intelligent planning and guidance from a mental health clinic can do much in the rehabilitation of some children. Whereas the clinic occupied a pivotal position in the care of emotionally disturbed or mentally ill children, ideally it should be considered a part of a spectrum of community services, including special instruction for classroom teachers in the handling of emotional disturbances, special public school classes for emotionally disturbed children, day care school centers, the mental health clinic, resident schools (not only for the around-the-clock patient but also for day and night care), and children's units in general and mental hospitals.[11]

In summary, the program of any community mental hygiene clinic encompasses both prevention and treatment. If the clinic receives the active support of the organizations within the community, and especially of the parents, adequate measures for prevention can be taken. This involves primarily the education of teachers and parents in mental hygiene principles and a certain amount of limited group therapy for both. An adequate program for treatment requires machinery for the early detection of emotionally disturbed children and, of course, a suitable number of psychiatrists, psychologists, and social workers to handle the treatment. Certainly such a program is expensive, but over a period of years it would not cost nearly so much in dollars and cents, to say nothing of human misery, as it would to finance the care in mental hospitals of those persons who, without identification and treatment in childhood, would in adult years become psychotic.

10 *Action for Mental Health,* Final Report of the Joint Commission on Mental Illness and Health (New York: Basic Books, Inc., Publishers, 1961), p. 263.
11 *Ibid.,* pp. 263–64.

SUMMARY

The extent of the effort made by a community, a state, or a nation
to promote sound mental health and to care for persons who are mentally and emotionally disabled is vitally affected by the attitudes held
by the citizens of that community, state, or nation. In past centuries
the attitudes of the general public were largely negative, with occasional temporary shifts to positive points of view. During the 20th
century, as a result of the dissemination of increased knowledge,
there has been a gradual increase in public awareness of the importance of the problem of mental health and of a desire to do
something constructive about it. It now seems entirely possible that,
before the end of the century, Americans will be as objective about
mental health as they now are about physical health. With this increased objectivity will come not only a desire and a willingness to
obtain treatment from professionally trained men and women but
also increased emphasis on prevention in the home and in the school.

THE SELF:
What It Is
And
Where It Comes From

Interest in the self, in what it is and how it develops, is not a recent phenomenon. Early psychologists, such as William James, and many philosophers, novelists, and poets who preceded them were concerned with this vital subject. For example, Whitman wrote in his poem "Song of Myself":

> I have said that the soul is not more than the body,
> And I have said that the body is not more than the soul,
> And nothing, no God, is greater to one than one's self is.

Socrates stirred his listeners by his probing questions into the nature of the human soul. He tried to make them consider what they meant when they said "I" or "me." To some these were threatening questions, and eventually Socrates was required to drink the poison hemlock for asking them and others of like nature. Even today there are those who object to any exploration of the self. Francis Bacon believed that knowledge of one's self and of others is the first requisite for success in life. Spinoza wrote that man's happiness consists in the power of maintaining one's being.

William James, who was both a philosopher and a psychologist, discussed the "self" with great insight in his *Principles of Psychology*, published in 1890. Much of what he had to say three quarters of a century ago remains true today. James defined self as, "All that [one] is tempted to call by the name of 'me'."[1] He makes a distinction between the self as known which he calls the "me" and the self as the knower which he calls the "I." The following discussion will be limited to his presentation of the "me." He says:

> *In its widest possible sense,* however, *a man's Me is the sum total of all that he can call his,* not only his body and his psychic powers, but his clothes and his house, his wife and children, his ancestors and friends, his reputation and works, his lands and horses, and yacht and bank account. All these things give him the same emotions. If they wax away and die away, he feels cast down—not necessarily in the same degree for each thing, but in much the same way for all. . . . *The constituents of the Me may be divided into classes,* those which make up respectively—
> The material me;
> The social me; and
> The spiritual me.[2]

"The material me," as described by James, has many of the same characteristics as "the phenomenal self" which was discussed in Chapter Two. It includes one's body, the clothes that one wears, the members of one's immediate family, and one's home (including the objects in it). All these are part of the material self.

"The social me," according to James, is the recognition which one receives from his fellow human beings. James states that a person "has as many different social selves as there are distinct groups of persons about whose opinion he cares."[3] James does not mean by this statement that the several selves are completely different. Instead he considers them to be different sides of the single, relatively unified self which the individual shows as he goes from one group to another. This unity of the selves is of course not complete; rivalry and conflict exist. In a famous passage James wrote:

[1] W. James, *Principles of Psychology* (New York: Henry Holt and Company, 1890), I, 91.

[2] W. James, *Psychology, Briefer Course* (New York: Henry Holt and Company, 1892), p. 177.

[3] *Ibid.*, p. 179.

I am often confronted by the necessity of standing by one of my empirical selves and relinquishing the rest. Not that I would not, if I could, be both handsome and fat and well dressed, and a great athlete, and make a million a year, be a wit, a bon-vivant, and a lady-killer, as well as a philosopher; a philanthropist, statesman, warrior, and African explorer, as well as a "tone-poet" and saint. But the thing is simply impossible. The millionaire's work would run counter to the saint's; the bon-vivant and the philanthropist would trip each other up; the philosopher and the lady-killer could not well keep house in the same tenement of clay. . . . To make any one of them actual, the rest must more or less be suppressed. . . . So the seeker of his truest, strongest, deepest self must review the list carefully, and pick out the one on which to stake his salvation. All other selves thereupon become unreal, but the fortunes of this self are real. Its failures are real failures, its triumphs real triumphs, carrying shame and gladness with them. . . .

I, who for the time have staked my all on being a psychologist, am mortified if others know more psychology than I. But I am contented to wallow in the grossest ignorance of Greek. My deficiencies there give me no sense of personal humiliation at all.[4]

James does not develop the "spiritual me" as clearly as he does the "material me" and the "social me." By the spiritual self he means the central nucleus of one's inner or subjective being, the entire collection of the person's states of consciousness.

In spite of the great prestige of William James, most of his American contemporaries did not share his interest in the nature of the self. The subject was not considered an appropriate one for scientific investigation. However, during the early part of the 20th century, the concept was kept alive by a few writers such as Cooley, Mead, and Dewey. During the period since World War II, however, interest in the subject has been revived. Allport says:

In very recent years the tide has turned. Perhaps without being fully aware of the historical situation, many psychologists have commenced to embrace what two decades ago would have been considered a heresy. They have re-introduced self and ego unashamedly and, as if to make up for lost time, have employed ancillary concepts such as self-image, self-actualization, self-affirmation, phenomenal ego, ego-involvement, ego-striving, and many other hyphenated elaborations

[4] James, *Principles of Psychology*, I, 91.

which to experimental positivism still have a slight flavor of scientific obscenity.[5]

FOUR MODERN THEORIES

During the last two or three decades several major theories have been advanced to explain the development and organization of the self. Four of these will now be presented briefly; it will be seen that they have much in common.

Sullivan

Harry Stack Sullivan was a practicing psychiatrist. His theories were presented in a series of lectures rather than in books. He appears to have developed them as a means of explaining the process of psychotherapy. Consequently, there is a certain incompleteness, a situation that several psychologists and psychiatrists have tried to remedy through the publication of clarifying articles.

According to Sullivan, all individuals possess at birth the potentiality to become human. He postulates that from the disappointments and frustrations which the infant experiences during the early stages of life, the self emerges by way of the unique phenomenon of empathy. Sullivan's use of the term *empathy* in this context has a very specific meaning. It is a relationship which precedes language, is without cognition on the part of the infant, and is quite probably one-sided. He says:

> Empathy is the term that we use to refer to the peculiar emotional linkage that subtends the relationship of the infant with other significant people—the mother or the nurse. Long before there are signs of any understanding of emotional expression, there is evidence of this emotional contagion or communion.[6]

As part of his human equipment the infant has the ability to cry. Crying, according to Sullivan, is the universal tool of infancy and as the infant uses this magic tool he develops ability or power, because he soon recognizes by way of this empathic communion that

[5] G. W. Allport, *Becoming* (New Haven: Yale University Press, 1960), p. 37 (paperbound edition).

[6] H. S. Sullivan, *Conceptions of Modern Psychiatry*, 2nd ed. (New York: W. W. Norton & Company, Inc., 1953), p. 17.

crying causes a significant person to attend to him. From this ability or power there emerges another magic tool—the infant's expression of satisfaction. The baby has discovered that his mother is enchanted when he expresses his satisfaction by smiling at her. Thus we have a developmental sequence: the infant feels uncomfortable, dissatisfied; he cries and gets attention; he discovers his power; his dissatisfaction is relieved, and he shows this by an expression of contentment; his parent is delighted; he recognizes the delight and thereby discovers another power.

The basis of the self-concept, then, is found in the infant's potential to become human (a part of which is his ability to cry), from which he discovers powers by means of the phenomenon of empathy.

As the infant grows older, a self-system or self-dynamism gradually emerges. During this period the significant persons in the child's environment find it necessary to utilize certain restraints in the teaching of personal habits. The rewards and punishments which accompany this teaching are very important in the evolution of the self-system. Sullivan says:

> The self dynamism is built up out of this experience of approbation and disapproval, of reward and punishment. The peculiarity of the self dynamism is that as it grows it functions, in accordance with its state of development, right from the start. As it develops, it becomes more and more related to a microscope in its function. Since the approbation of the important person is very valuable, since disapprobation denies satisfaction and gives anxiety, the self becomes extremely important. It permits a minute focus on those performances of the child which are the cause of approbation and disapprobation, but, very much like a microscope, it interferes with noticing the rest of the world. When you are staring through your microscope, you don't see much except what comes through that channel. So with the self dynamism. It has a tendency to focus attention on performances with the significant other person which get approbation or disfavor. And that peculiarity, closely connected with anxiety, persists thenceforth through life. It comes about that the self, that to which we refer when we say "I," is the only thing which has alertness, which notices what goes on, and, needless to say, notices what goes on in its own field.[7]

Thus the self-system is built upon experiences of approval and disapproval. Sullivan says, in one of his most significant statements,

[7] *Ibid.*, pp. 20–21.

"The self may be said to be made up of reflected appraisals."[8] If these appraisals have been chiefly derogatory, then the self-image will be disparaging and hostile. If, on the other hand, the reflected appraisals have been chiefly positive and constructive, then the self which has experienced those appraisals will be confident and approving.

According to Sullivan, only those impulses which have been approved or disapproved are permitted into awareness. Those which have not been subjected to evaluation by the significant persons in the child's environment become dissociated from the self. The term *dissociation* is introduced to account for behavior which is not "noticed" by the individual. Sullivan states that

> . . . healthy development of personality is inversely proportionate to the amount, to the number, of tendencies which have come to exist in dissociation . . . if there is nothing dissociated, then whether one be a genius or imbecile, it is quite certain that he will be mentally healthy. . . . One might say that the larger the proportion of energy systems in a personality which act exterior to the awareness of the person, the greater the chances that he will meet some crisis in the interpersonal relations in which he cannot act in the fashion which we call mental health.[9]

Sullivan has added a great deal to our understanding of how the self develops. His emphasis on the importance of the empathic relationship between the child and his mother or a mother substitute is an important contribution. Certainly interpersonal relationships with significant persons are a powerful force in forming the self in both early infancy and later developmental stages. Probably the force is not as all-powerful as Sullivan believed. He was convinced that there was a developmental time for all aspects of emotional growth and if it did not occur then it never would. He said, "the person who has never known love or tenderness as a small child is permanently incapable of recognizing it or experiencing it in later years."[10] This represents a limited view of human potentialities. Emotional deprivation in infancy and childhood leaves scars, but it cannot (except possibly in very extreme cases) destroy a

---

8 *Ibid.,* p. 22.
9 *Ibid.,* p. 47.
10 *Ibid.,* p. 99.

basic emotion such as love or eliminate the drive for growth. One is impressed, however, with the kernels of truth in what Sullivan has to say. For example, when he states that "many become inferior caricatures of what they might have been,"[11] we know that to some extent this applies to everyone, although "inferior caricatures" is too strong a phrase. Each person in the process of self-actualization has been hampered to a greater or lesser degree by the culture in which he has lived and by the persons who have influenced his development.

Allport

In Allport's theory of "becoming," personality includes "all the regions of our life that we regard as peculiarly ours, and which for the time being I suggest we call the *proprium*. The proprium includes all aspects of personality that make for inward unity."[12]

The term *proprium* as used by Allport closely resembles the term *phenomenal self* or possibly even the self-concept as used by Combs and Snygg, whose theory will be discussed later. Although Allport lists eight aspects of the proprium, he does not intend that it be thought of as segmented. It is a unity, and these aspects are descriptive aids in understanding the development of the self. The eight aspects are: bodily sense, self-identity, ego-enhancement, ego-extension, rational agent, self-image, propriate striving, and the knower.

"The bodily *me*" is made up of the many sensations that exist within the organism. These physical sensations may be experienced keenly, slightly, or almost not at all. "The bodily sense," says Allport, "remains a lifelong anchor for our self-awareness, thought it never alone accounts for the entire sense of self, probably not even in the young child."[13] Organic sensations, then, are an important part of one's perception of self but they are only a part.

The sense of self-identity develops gradually as the child slowly learns to differentiate himself from his environment. Allport emphasizes the importance of social interaction in this process, but it would seem that interaction with the impersonal environment also helps the child to realize that he is a separate being. Allport believes that the infant has no sense of self-identity. This does not

11 *Ibid.*, p. 15.
12 Allport, *op. cit.*, p. 40.
13 *Ibid.*, p. 42.

come until the child has reached the age of four or five. When it has developed, it becomes all the proof one needs that one exists.

The third aspect of the proprium, ego-enhancement, means a number of things. It includes search for self, self-esteem, self-love. It is closely associated with the need for survival. It is basically the same as the concept of the "enhancement of the phenomenal self" which was discussed in Chapter Two.

"Ego-extension" involves bringing into the growing self persons and objects which possess emotional importance for the individual. Allport implies that this characteristic of the proprium comes after bodily sense, self-identity, and ego-enhancement. Certainly it follows bodily sense—and probably self-identity—but it is difficult to see how it comes later than ego-enhancement. A child as young as two years, for example, thinks in terms of "my doll"; certainly by the age of four or five when, according to Allport, self-identity (although still somewhat unstable) is achieved, the child has extended his sense of self to include all or most of those within the immediate family circle, as well as his favorite toys.

In adult years one's ego is extended to a wide variety of objects, persons, groups, values, and abstractions. The self has now become a broad, rich, varied, and complex organization of objects, persons, ideas, and convictions.

The ego or the "rational agent" in personality carries the responsibility of synthesizing inner needs with reality. Allport credits Freud with explaining how the rational ego utilizes defenses such as rationalization in order to reduce anxiety. However, Allport points out that the rational agent of the proprium "is capable also of yielding true solutions, appropriate adjustments, accurate planning, and a relatively faultless solving of the equations of life."[14]

The "self-image" aspect of the proprium includes both the self-concept and the person's aspirations for himself, or (to use different terms), the real self and the ideal self. Much growth takes place because of the existence of a self-image. One of the functions of this image is to link the present with the future.

Propriate striving is the term which Allport uses to label the motivational force of the proprium. "Propriate striving," he says, "distinguishes itself from other forms of motivation in that, however

[14] *Ibid.*, p. 46.

beset by conflicts, it makes for unification of personality . . . the possession of the long range goals, regarded as central to one's personal existence, distinguishes the human being from the animal, the adult from the child, and in many cases the healthy personality from the sick."[15] Allport states that striving always has a future reference. In fact, he stresses "future-directedness" and takes issue with those psychologists who explain present mental states in terms of past experiences. It is difficult to follow Allport here. Where does the striving with its future reference come from if not from the experiential background of the individual? Certainly a person's interests, expectations, and intentions are the products of his immediate and distant past.

The last aspect of the proprium, "the knower," transcends all the others. Allport says:

> We not only know *things*, but we know (i.e., are acquainted with) the empirical features of our own proprium. It is I who have bodily sensations, I who recognize my self-identity from day to day; I who note and reflect upon my self-assertion, self-extension, my own rationalizations, as well as upon my interests and strivings. When I thus think about my own propriate functions I am likely to perceive their essential togetherness, and to feel them intimately bound is one way of the knowing function itself.
>
> Since such knowing is beyond any shadow of doubt, a state that is peculiarly ours, we admit it as the eighth clear function of the proprium.[16]

Allport, in contrast with many other personality theorists, is concerned with the development of the healthy personality. In fact, he states that it is necessary for an infant to be normally endowed if he is to develop a sense of self. This point of view is open to criticism. Where is the line to be drawn between normal endowment and abnormal endowment? Does not the imbecile, or even the idiot, have a self—though it is limited? To be sure, "proprium" can be defined in such a way as to eliminate all those below a certain mental age. Allport does this when he states that self-identity is not achieved in the normally endowed child until he reaches the age of four or five.

15 *Ibid.*, pp. 50–51.
16 *Ibid.*, p. 53.

One of Allport's important contributions is his insistence that "all psychological functions commonly ascribed to a self or ego must be admitted as data in the scientific study of personality."[17] He is impatient with those psychologists who for so many decades have treated aspects of the total personality as though they were separate entities.

Diamond

Solomon Diamond postulates a dual process—the search for self and the defense of self—as the core of human personality. Each of these is an ongoing process throughout the life of the individual. He is constantly discovering new aspects of his self and is at the same time defending that self against threats of change. According to Diamond, self-discovery is achieved in two basic ways: through recognition and exploration of the body and through identification with and imitation of ideal persons.

The exploration of the body, although most revealing in infancy and early childhood, goes on throughout life. For example, the infant discovers his fingers and toes; the girl in early adolescence is very conscious of the development of womanly characteristics; the boy's perception of himself is affected by developing muscles; the aging woman observes new lines in her face; the aging man notes the deterioration of his physical vigor. The child, the adolescent, the adult—each observes his own body and the bodies of others in order to compare and evaluate himself.

The body image becomes such an important part of the self that most persons actually locate the self in some part of the physical organism. Diamond[18] cites a study by Horowitz, who asked a group of college men to give three answers to the questions: "If you had to locate yourself at some point that is you, where would that point be?" The most frequent answer was the head; the brain, the heart, and the eyes were given almost as often. Other answers included the face, the hands, and the genitals. It is interesting that late in the 19th century William James was concerned with this question and decided that his self was located most specifically in the muscular tension of his forehead.

17 *Ibid.*, p. 55.
18 S. Diamond, *Personality and Temperament* (New York: Harper & Row, Publishers, 1957), p. 223.

The same question was asked of a group of 54 students in a mental hygiene class at the University of New Hampshire. The results appear in Table VI.

TABLE VI

Physical Location of Self					
Number of Responses			Percentages		
Total	Women	Men	Total	Women	Men
Head, brain, mind	28	13	15	18.92	19.69	18.29
Face	15	4	11	10.135	6.06	13.42
Arms, hands	27	11	16	18.24	16.67	19.51
Sex organs	6	1	5	4.06	1.52	6.10
Eyes	13	5	8	8.78	7.57	9.76
Mouth, speech	7	3	4	4.73	4.54	4.87
Legs, feet	9	4	5	6.08	6.06	6.10
Hair	7	4	3	4.73	6.06	3.66
Chest, heart	15	11	4	10.135	16.67	4.87
Stomach	2	1	1	1.35	1.52	1.22
Inside head	3	2	1	2.03	3.03	1.22
Physical appearance, body	5	1	4	3.38	1.52	4.87
				7.43	9.09	6.10
Miscellaneous	11	6	5			
Totals	148	66	82	100.00	100.00	100.00

The sample in Table VI is very small. Moreover, in a class situation a few students may not have taken the question seriously. However, it is interesting to note that head, brain, and mind were regarded as the most likely location of the self, with arms and hands a close second.

Jourard and Remy used college students as subjects of a study of the differences between the sexes in variability of cathexis-responses to the body and to the self. They found that men tend to have a more highly differentiated self-concept than body image. The opposite is true of women. The authors suggest that

. . . among women the appearance of the body is an important determiner both of self esteem and of acceptability to others whereas among men the apperance of the body is of lesser relevance for these valued ends. Being more concerned than the men about their bodies, the women could thus be expected to make finer differentiations than the men with their body images.[19]

Although the process of discovering the body image is an important aspect of developing the self-concept, it may be that Diamond has overemphasized it. His second process of self-discovery through identification with and imitation of ideal persons is probably more important. He says, "We learn about ourselves not only by experiencing our own actions, but also by experiencing the actions of others, who serve as both mirrors and models for imitation."[20] Diamond maintains that it is desirable for the child to identify most completely with the parent of the same sex. He believes that if a child chooses the parent of the opposite sex, behavior disorders will almost certainly develop. This point of view is open to question. Studies have shown that young children are much more likely to identify with the mother than with the father. To be sure, in preadolescence and adolescence it is probably desirable for the greater identification to be with the parent of the same sex.

According to Diamond, the process of identification goes on throughout life, although it is a more powerful force during infancy and early childhood. Diamond does not stress the significance of empathic relationships during the first year of life as much as does Sullivan. Certainly the deep interpersonal relationships that in adult years are experienced with one's wife or husband or children modify to a considerable extent the image of one's self.

It should be kept in mind, of course, that the most significant persons in an individual's life at any one period may not be the members of his immediate family. This fact is sometimes overlooked. Sullivan, for example, tends to make the mother almost all-important. Older children, and especially adolescents, frequently modify their perceptions of themselves because of observation and emulation of their peers rather than of their parents. Allison[21] investigated the relationship between parent and delinquent-child attitudes as compared with the relationship between delinquent-child and peer–

[19] F. M. Jourard and R. M. Remy, "Individual Variance Score: an index of the degree of differentiation of the self and the body image," *Journal of Clinical Psychology*, XIII (1957), 62–63.

[20] Diamond, *op. cit.*, p. 239.

[21] S. G. Allison, "Parent and Peer–Group–Friend Attitudes as They Relate to the Self-Concept of the Juvenile Delinquent," *Dissertation Abstracts*, XVII, 1957, 3086–3087.

group–friend attitudes. She found that the delinquents imitated more of the self-attitudes of their friends than they did of the self-attitudes of their mothers.

Diamond has expounded a dynamic theory of the development of the self. He never even suggests the existence of a static true self. Rather, one is constantly changing, although the changes take place gradually, since the individual while changing is at the same time defending the self against change. To Diamond the self *is* the person.

Combs and Snygg

Combs and Snygg present a phenomenological view of the nature of the self and of its development. The reader will recall that reference was made to these authors in Chapter Two, where their explanation of motivation was given. In that chapter the terms "phenomenal field" and "phenomenal self" were defined. Some elaboration is now called for in order to obtain a better understanding of the point of view of the phenomenologist.

First, the individual's phenomenal environment includes all of his perceptions, including those about himself and those about the not-self. This is his total field of awareness. Within this phenomenal field, and part of it, is the phenomenal self. This self includes everything that the person has set apart as being characteristic of him. "The phenomenal self is the self in a given situation."[22] Obviously, it changes from time to time, even from moment to moment, as figure becomes part of ground and as certain portions of ground become figure. Within and at the center of the phenomenal self is what Combs and Snygg call the self-concept. The self-concept is made up of those perceptions about the self which are of great importance to the individual. These perceptions constitute the essence of "me," whose loss is regarded as personal destruction.

That which is a part of the not-self for one person may be a characteristic of the phenomenal self for another and an important aspect of the self-concept for a third. For example, if a person's attention is drawn to the glasses another is wearing, this becomes for the moment a part of his phenomenal field, but it is a not-self characteristic of that field. If, however, he thinks about glasses that he him-

[22] A. W. Combs and D. Snygg, *Individual Behavior,* rev. ed. (New York: Harper & Row, Publishers, 1959), p. 127.

self is wearing and has worn for several years, he is now probably concerned with a part of his phenomenal self. Occasionally, inanimate objects may even be a part of the self-concept. A wedding would be an example. Ideas, beliefs, and convictions are important to human beings. Sometimes these are aspects of the phenomenal environment, sometimes of the phenomenal self, and sometimes of the self-concept. For instance, religion may be so unimportant for one individual that it is not considered as part of the phenomenal self but is rather in the not-self area of his life; for another, religion may be relatively important but not important enough to be considered as part of the self-concept; for a third individual, religious convictions may be so deep-seated, so central to the individual's perception of himself, that they constitute a significant characteristic of his self-concept—any threat to his beliefs is a very serious matter for him.

Combs and Snygg believe that almost simultaneously with the birth of the child the self begins and continues to develop slowly as the infant differentiates the "me" and the "not me." As he explores his body and his external environment he discovers, for example, that his fingers are a part of him but his blocks are not. "Bit by bit as experience increases, the self becomes more and more clearly differentiated from the remainder of the phenomenal field."[23] With the development of language the process is considerably accelerated, for "language provides a 'shorthand' by which experience can be symbolized, manipulated, and understood with tremendous efficiency."[24]

Combs and Snygg believe that the self is basically a social product arising out of experience with other human beings. In their emphasis on the importance of social interaction these authors are in agreement with Sullivan, Allport, and Diamond. They are also in agreement with these theorists that the earliest years are the most important and that the family provides the child with his most lasting self-definitions. Such important self-perceptions as adequacy or inadequacy have their main source in the family group.

Combs and Snygg point out that two of the major characteristics of the phenomenal self are consistency and stability. The self is not a collection of unrelated perceptions; rather, these perceptions are organized to a high degree. This organization results in considerable consistency in self-perceptions and in behavior. The self enters each new situation with the unique oranization of all of its past and,

23 *Ibid.*, p. 133.
24 *Ibid.*, p. 134.

as has been pointed out before, strives to maintain that organization. However, each new situation alters the self to some degree. This, of course, is essential to the survival of the individual as he continues to live in an ever-changing world of external reality. These changes take place most easily, of course, in areas relatively unimportant to the self. In adult years modifications of the core of the self or the self-concept are difficult to make. Combs and Snygg state that changes in the perceived self appear to be dependent on at least three factors: "(1) the place of the new concept in the individual's present self-organization; (2) the relation of the new concept to the person's basic need; (3) the clarity of the experience of the new perception."[25] The first of these relates to the significance of the new experience to the behaver. As was mentioned earlier, the peripheral concepts of self are more easily changed than those which are central. The second factor relates to selectivity. New ideas, new experiences which reinforce the individual's present image of himself are easily incorporated into his personality structure, but experiences which are threatening to his existing concepts of self are likely to be rejected. "The absence of threat increases the mobility of the self concept."[26] The third factor, dealing with the clarity of the new experience, is obviously important. The more vivid the experience the more likely it is that a change in perception will take place. Consequently, direct experience is more important than that from secondary sources. Occasionally, a direct experience may be so vivid and fraught with emotion that it is traumatic for the individual and can in a very brief period of time cause a considerable change in the perceived self.

The presentation by Combs and Snygg of the nature of the phenomenal self and how it develops is excellent, although these authors make somewhat more general statements than Sullivan, Allport, and Diamond. They do not explain in any detail what takes place during the first year of life when the foundations for later perceptions of the self are being laid. Also, there is not enough emphasis on what the biological organism brings to the world of experience or, for that matter, what this organism with its infant experiences brings to new situations after language has been acquired. It is entirely possible that the impressions about the self which have been experienced before the development of language are the most difficult to alter because they were unverbalized.

25 *Ibid.,* p. 163.
26 *Ibid.,* p. 164.

The emphasis by Combs and Snygg on the social aspects of the individual's environment is good; the body of perceptions which we call the self is the product of the individual's complex experiential background. Whitman stated this truth in poetic form back in the 19th century.

A CHILD WENT FORTH

There was a child went forth every day,
And the first object he look'd upon, that object he became,
And that object became a part of him for the day. . . .
Or for many years or stretching cycles of years.
The early lilacs became part of this child. . . .
And the old drunkard staggering home from the tavern. . . .
And all the changes of city and country wherever he went.
And the friendly boys that passed, and the quarrelsome boys. . . .
The mother at home quietly placing the dishes on the supper table
The father, strong, self-sufficient, manly, mean, anger'd, unjust
The blow, the quick loud word, the tight bargain, the crafty lure
The family usages, the language, the company, the furniture,
the yearning and swelling heart. . . .
The doubts of day-time and the doubts of night-time. . . .
Men and women crowding fast in the streets. . . .
The streets themselves and the facades of houses, and
goods in the windows. . . .
The light falling on roofs and gables of white or brown. . . .
These became part of that child who went forth every day,
and who now goes, and will always go forth every day.

FACTORS IN SIGNIFICANT CHANGES IN PERCEPTIONS OF SELF

There are periods in the lifetime of an individual when his perceptions of himself may change more readily and more rapidly than at other times. It would be difficult to list all of these. The three which appear to be most important are: (1) changes in the course of usual growth and development; (2) changes as a result of crisis or catastrophe; (3) changes through psychotherapy. Each of these will be discusssed briefly.

Developmental Changes

Strang says "changes in the individual's self concept may occur at any time during his life, but especially at the beginning of each developmental phase."[27] She lists seven developmental phases: when the child begins school; preadolescence; early adolescence; late adolescence; when the individual marries; when one's children no longer need constant care; and finally when one reaches retirement age.

As was pointed out earlier, Allport believes that the child achieves self-identity when he becomes four or five years of age. This, of course, is not a sudden development. It probably begins at about two and a half years of age when he characteristically goes through a period of negativism. This early insistence on his rights as a person constitutes his first declaration of independence. If he is allowed a certain amount of self-assertion, he develops a feeling of worthwhileness. As time goes on he achieves to some extent a give-and-take relationship with his parents. To be sure, he is still very dependent, but he is at the same time beginning to perceive himself as an independent member of the family group. He is at least partially prepared for his venture into the new and exciting world of school.

School in our culture is the second major developmental change for the child. Sullivan writes of this period:

> The interpersonal factors between teacher and pupil in [the] school situation may work good or evil effects on the growth of personality. Where, for example, there has been an eccentric parent . . . gradually, gradually, the self may expand somewhat . . . the experience of the school may head the self-dynamism in another direction which will make for much greater opportunity for contented living, for mental health . . . . On the other hand, harsh cruel teachers . . . may affect the child from a happy home who has been taught to expect friendliness and a receptive and inquiring attitude, may teach him gradually by reiterated pain and humiliation, that the world into which he has moved is an unfriendly and cruel world . . . may start revery processes in him, the goal of which is to return to the home from which he has unhappily been expelled, apparently for no reason other than that he has gotten older.[28]

The first few weeks or, for that matter, even the first few days of school have a considerable impact upon the child's perception of

[27] R. Strang, *The Adolescent Views Himself* (New York: McGraw-Hill Book Company, 1957), p. 78.
[28] Sullivan, *op. cit.*, pp. 39–40.

his self. The teacher for several hours a day, five days a week, becomes a substitute mother. Her attitudes toward him, as Sullivan points out, are very important, She is another significant person who vitally affects his appraisal of himself. His relations with his classmates are also vital to him. Do they like and accept him, or do they ridicule and reject him? One indication of the significance of this period is that adults frequently have rather vivid memories of their first few days in school. It is the responsibility of teachers and, to some extent, parents to do all they can to make these memories pleasant ones.

The third major developmental phase is preadolescence when the child is developing the capacity for intimate friendships with others of the same sex. For the first time in his life his strongest emotional ties are with persons of his own age rather than with adults. This is frequently a difficult period for the child since there may be many conflicts between the standards of his friends and the standards of his parents. Moreover, it is time when conformity is almost brutally enforced by the peer group. During this period a certain amount of individuality is lost and the child perceives himself more than he ever has before as a member of a group.

The next change occurs with the onset of adolescence. Rather rapid physical changes are taking place in height, weight, body build, sex organs, and voice. The individual during this phase must consequently make major modifications in his body image. If these changes take place too early in the life of the child, acceptance of the new body image is difficult. For example, if the girl's menstrual periods begin when she is only ten or eleven she may be frightened and embarrassed. Conversely, those who mature late, perhaps as late as sixteen or seventeen years of age, may develop feelings of physical inadequacy because they have lagged behind their peer group.

Early adolescence is a difficult period for many, perhaps for most. There is not only a shift away from emotional ties with parents but also, to a lesser degree, from emotional ties with others of the same sex. There is a vague, half-understood, new desire to establish physical and emotional relationships with persons of the opposite sex. There is an impelling wish to be accepted and loved. At the same time some doubts are harbored as to whether or not that acceptance and love will ever come, because many children in early adolescence find it difficult to see their new selves clearly and to accept themselves as they now are. Eager to reach out, they find it hard to do so. This attitude is expressed poignantly in the following poem by a fourteen-year-old girl:

AN APPEAL

Here I am.

      LOOK!

Eyes and mouth and bone like anyone,

And with a soul like anyone,

And with a heart like anyone

            that beats fast.

Yet

    no one sees me or

      they look and look away and go away

and I sleep inside.

It is a deep sleep with no friends to dream about

              and no enemies

              and nobody.

If I could smile and you would smile back with your eyes—

If I could whisper and you would listen—

If I could touch your wrist and you would lead me—

                I would wake up then.

                But somehow I cannot smile or touch or whisper.

                I don't know why.

                I don't know.

                      Somebody tell me why.

                      Hello, somebody. Here I am.

                            LOOK!

In late adolescence, growth has been achieved; the young person is relatively competent but as yet usually has no specific role in the adult world. He no longer has the privileges and security of childhood—unless he is being overprotected. Neither does he have the full privileges of adulthood. In middle- and upper-class families he is usually still economically dependent upon his parents and may chafe at that dependence without knowing what to do about it. If he is a college student he is in a somewhat protected environment. It may be that in our society adolescent attitudes and perceptions are continued too long. In the America of the 18th and 19th centuries, it was customary for young people in their late teens to assume adult responsibilities.

Many studies show that the self-concepts of adolescents seem to be in a constant state of flux. In one of these, Roff[29] attempted to compare two dimensions of the self—self-satisfaction and identification with mother—in three developmental periods: pre-puberty, early puberty, and late puberty. She selected three ages to correspond to these developmental periods: eleven, fourteen, and seventeen. When she found that the seventeen-year-old group responded in much the same way as the fourteen-year-old group, she added a fourth group made up of twenty-year-old young people and retested her hypotheses. Roff found that self-satisfaction declines continuously through the adolescent period until about twenty years of age when it rises slightly. Her conclusions suggest that the self-concept is most severely shaken at about the age of seventeen. Self—mother identification declines continuously throughout the entire adolescent period and is at its lowest at the end. Ideal-mother identification remains high until the end of adolescence when it declines sharply.

The assumption of the relationships and responsibilities of marriage usually follows rather closely upon the conclusion of the adolescent period. This requires new modifications of the perceptions of one's self. The woman learns to perceive herself as a satisfactory or unsatisfactory wife, as a good or poor homemaker or manager of the family budget. Moreover, the time may soon come when she is a mother, a role that brings many more changes in her self-image. The young man who such a short time before saw himself as free and independent must now learn, with all the adjustments which it involves, to perceive himself as a husband. He must also learn to take on the responsibilities of the head of a family. Later he will probably have to perceive himself as a father. These and related changes in perception are frequently difficult for young people. In spite of marriage some remain perpetual adolescents.

The next major developmental phase is middle age. It is difficult to define this period in terms of chronological years since it varies so widely with individuals. The term is most applicable to

29 C. Roff, "The Self Concept in Adolescent Girls," *Dissertation Abstracts*, XX (1959), 385.

women in their forties and to men in their fifties. It appears to be somewhat more difficult for women than for men to make the necessary changes in self-perceptions during this period. A few fail rather completely and develop a severe behavior disorder called involutional melancholia. The great majority, however, succeed in seeing themselves as less attractive than they were. They are able to accept the fact that their children, no longer small, are not now as important a part of their phenomenal selves as they were. A great many men who in earlier years were ambitious and confident are now faced with the necessity of perceiving themselves as nearing the end of a mediocre career. They must also adjust themselves to the fact of waning physical vigor.

Middle age is characteristically harder for women than for men, but retirement age is harder for men than for women. Given adequate health, women in their middle and late sixties (unless they are career women) can continue with their social life, their community activities, and their household responsibilities. For them there is no abrupt break. Men, on the other hand, upon reaching retirement age suddenly lose much that was important to them. They are no longer doing the work which for a man becomes an important part of his phenomenal self. All of their basic needs are frustrated to some extent. Many men learn to adjust to these situations by satisfactorily modifying their perceptions of themselves. Those who succeed in doing this find many rewards in the retirement period.

Changes Because of Life Crises

There are, of course, crises in the life of an individual which are not necessarily associated with a developmental phase. It is impossible to make a list of such crises because that which is a catastrophic experience for one individual may be a neutral one or perhaps even bring relief to another. There is the story of the man whose wife had died a few days before and who upon being extended sympathy by a friend replied, "Don't be concerned about me. This is the first time I have had any peace in forty years." To be sure, the loss of a husband or wife results in changes in self-perception for many. Other experiences which may seriously affect the self-concept are economic losses, crippling accidents, and loss of health. However, in every instance it is only the individual himself who knows what a specific experience means to him.

Any experienced therapist knows that seemingly obvious life crises may not be crises at all. Nevertheless, a wide variety of crisis situations do come to pass for most persons. Because a traumatic experience by definition is intense, it always results in some change —perhaps even a great change—in the self. It should be remembered that a crisis can be positive as well as negative. A great gain has as much emotional impact as a great loss.

Changes Resulting from Psychotherapy

Psychotherapy will be discussed at some length in the last chapter, "Regaining Mental Health." However, it must be considered in a chapter on the self since the principal goal of psychotherapy is to bring about changes in the perception of the self and of others.

There is nothing miraculous about psychotherapy. It is primarily a learning situation with the emphasis on the emotions rather than on the intellect. The client comes into therapy with a relatively rigid and derogatory perception of himself. He yearns for a more positive self-concept, but his growth process is impeded by conflicts, anxieties, or abnormal defense mechanisms. His great need at the beginning of psychotherapy is to be fully accepted by the therapist. He needs complete understanding of his feelings, whatever they may be.

Rogers[30] has delineated seven stages in the process of psychotherapy, assuming that the client who has come for help is very seriously disturbed. Such a client would have "little or no recognition of the ebb and flow of the feeling life within him. He construes his experience rigidly in terms of the past. . . . The individual at this state represents stasis, fixity, the opposite of flow or change." There is so much rigidity present that the client finds it almost impossible to communicate with others or with himself. He is, in truth, as Sullivan put it, "a caricature of what he might have been."

If the client is "fully received" and is able to experience this understanding and acceptance, then there is a slight loosening of the self-structure and he gradually goes into the second stage. In this stage feelings may be expressed but they are not owned. "Experiencing is bound by the structure of the past." If the psycho-

[30] C. R. Rogers, "A Prcoess Conception of Psychotherapy," *The American Psychologist,* XIII, No. 4 (1958), 142–49.

therapeutic process is successful, the client slowly works his way through the third and fourth stages. In the fifth stage, with increasing freedom of expression concerning the self, there is also an increased ownership of the feelings expressed and a dawning of understanding of what the real self is like. Experiencing is no longer remote. Rogers says:

> This phase is several hundred psychological miles from the first stage described. Here many aspects of the client are in flow, as against the rigidity of the first stage. He is very much closer to his organic being, which is always in process. He is much closer to being in the flow of his feeling. His constructions of experience are decidedly loosened and repeatedly being tested against referents and evidence within and without. Experience is much more highly differentiated, and thus internal communication, already flowing, can be much more exact.

In the sixth stage, the client is living in the present rather than in the past. He is experiencing subjectively with a sense of process rather than of fixity. The self is no longer primarily an object. It is rather feelings and experiences which the individual is having. The self is more integrated, more confident. It is expanding.

The seventh stage, according to Rogers, is rather easily achieved by the client who has successfully reached the sixth. "The self becomes, increasingly, simply the subjective and reflexive awareness of experiencing. The self is much less frequently a perceived object and much more frequently something confidently felt in process." The client will now "be a continually changing person, experiencing with freshness and immediacy in each new situation, responding to its newness with real and accepted feelings, and construing its meaning in terms of what it is, not in terms of some past experience."

It is obvious that the process of psychotherapy results in considerable changes in the self. Excessive rigidity, excessive fear, excessive anxiety are no longer present. The individual has been freed from these and can now experience fully and harmoniously. He is a changed person but not a new person.

Certain aspects of the process of psychotherapy may be clearer if an actual case is presented.

When Mrs. R. came to the author she was not in the first stage but she was seriously restricted by a number of fears and anxieties. She was afraid of the interiors of large buildings, especially if a considerable number of people were present. This fear was so intense that she could not go to movies or attend church. She was especially afraid of riding on a train. She was also afraid of small places, such as an elevator. At the time she came for psychotherapy a new fear was beginning to develop; namely, that of riding in an automobile. In spite of the fact that her fears were relatively specific they had only partially channeled her anxiety. She was excessively concerned about the safety of her husband and her small son. Burdened as she was with these fears and anxieties she was, of course, very tense and unhappy.

In the therapeutic interviews much time was spent on her feelings about herself and her family. In the permissive relationship which existed, Mrs. R.'s concentration on her fears gradually lessened and she talked more and more freely about her present and about her past. Eventually much repressed material was admitted into consciousness. She recalled, for example, all of the details of what had been for her a very difficult experience when she was eighteen years of age. Before that time she had evidently been a relatively well-adjusted girl. Upon finishing high school she went to work in a mental hospital quite a distance from her home. She was deeply distressed by what she saw there. The large rooms filled with patients were closely related to her present fear of the interiors of large buildings filled with persons. In fact, the entire surroundings were more than she could tolerate. After a few days at the hospital she told the superintendent that she could stand it no longer but he insisted that she remain for at least another week. At the end of that time she returned home. The whole experience had been a crisis in her life and an important cause of the neurotic reactions which developed later on.

Since Mrs. R.'s childhood had been a healthy one the psychotherapeutic process was rapid. The excerpt which follows is a transcription of part of the fifteenth and last interview. By now the tension was almost gone and the fears and anxieties were practically eliminated. What Mrs. R. has to say in this fifteenth interview represents the changes in the self expected in the sixth stage described earlier. After this interview she was able to complete the process by herself.

*C. I understand Bob and I think that means a lot.

*P. Oh, yes, it does.

C. Well, before I never could understand him. I wouldn't want to listen to him. I wouldn't want to hear his excuses or anything about it.

P. That must be very gratifying. How much clearer you now see not only yourself but also your relationship with Bob.

C. Well, and my boy, too.

P. And your boy, too.

C. I can see the change in my boy. I can. Even within the last week, I can see a change in Donald. Now, when he used to go out to play he'd say he was going to somebody's house down the road. I wouldn't let him go. I was afraid. I'd think—oh, what if a car hit him, what if he got hurt!

P. Yes.

C. The other day Donald said, "Mummy, I'm going over to Albert's." When I saw him going down the road a little ways, I wasn't afraid; I wasn't afraid thinking if he got hit. The only thing I thought of was that my little boy has got to play like other little boys and that's the way I look at it now.

* * *

C. I went up to Dr. Sawyer's. Remember, I told you I was going to see him about Linda. Last Saturday afternoon Bob and I went up. I went toward that office and as I walked along the street I said to myself, "This is heaven, not to be afraid." And I knew that if I did feel a little upset, I would know why I was upset.

P. Yes.

C. And I sat in that office and I felt a little nervous, but believe me never like I did before. There were people in that office and above all I had to wait at least an hour. I guess it was an hour and fifteen minutes, and it was the waiting that used to bother me. The funny part of it is, when I used to get nervous before, I'd get a book and I'd try to relax that way, but I would still be so tense and nervous. Last Saturday when I was up there I took a book and looked at it once or twice. Then I looked at the people in the room. I looked at them and I thought to myself, "They don't understand that I feel a little nervous." And I thought, "I know why I've been afraid." The more I thought of it the less nervous I was . . . . Well, as I said, I knew I wasn't going to get over it in the snap of a finger, but as time went on and I did these things more and more without being afraid . . . the funniest thing is, when I get up in the morning, it used to be that I was more

* C—Client; P—Psychologist.

upset when I got up in the morning. The first thing in the morning and the last thing at night. This morning I got up and it seemed so odd to me to get up and not feel the way I used to. It seems wonderful but it entered my mind, "Gee! it's wonderful not to feel the way I used to feel." It seems unbelievable, I'll put it that way, that I don't feel the way I used to feel.

P.   You'll feel a little strange for a while as you get used to your new way of looking at things.

C.   Well, it seems wonderful. That's all I can say. It really does.

P.   This is what we have been working for, isn't it?

DISTORTION AND FULFILLMENT

It is clear from the preceding material in this chapter that a person's perceptions of self are the product of his environment achieved within the limitations set by his biological inheritance. What his past has been determines to a considerable extent what his future will be. Since there is an almost infinite variety of experiential backgrounds it follows that there is an almost infinite variety of personalities. Some distortion and some fulfillment, some negative perceptions and some positive perceptions, some feelings of inadequacy and some feelings of adequacy exist within each personality. It is impossible to make a sharp division between those who live twisted lives and those who have achieved a high degree of self-actualization. Inadequacy and adequacy, as Combs and Snygg point out, is on a continuum ranging from "little feeling of adequacy" to a "high degree of adequacy."[31] At the lowest level on the continuum are the psychotics who have lived under so much threat that they have been forced to extreme forms of adjustment in their efforts to maintain any kind of self at all. Above this group on the adequacy continuum are the neurotics who, though they have distorted perceptions of themselves and of their environment, are in most cases still trying to grow. In the majority of people, positive perceptions are stronger than the negative perceptions, although the latter are present to some extent. Above these are the still more adequate ones. Members of this group have found life to be challenging and relatively happy. They are continuing to reach out for new experiences and for greater growth. At the extreme right of the continuum are those who have achieved

[31] Combs and Snygg, *op. cit.*, p. 266.

the greatest degree of self-actualization. These are the extremely fortunate ones. Threat for them is at a minimum.

Although adequacy is on a continuum, there is some value in comparing the dynamics and characteristics of those who are well below the median and those who are well above it, of those who have a very negative self-concept and those who have a very positive self-concept. These will be labeled "distorted personalities" and "self-actualized personalities."

Distorted Personalities

Persons with distorted personalities should excite sympathy rather than condemnation. They have become what they are because of circumstances beyond their control. They could not decide upon the characteristics of the organism which they inherited, and some of these characteristics or potentialities may have made inadequacy inevitable; for example, severe mental retardation. They had no choice of experiences during the first year of life; the reader will recall how much Sullivan emphasized the importance of this period. If Allport's point of view is accepted, then by the age of four or five a real self exists, a self produced by the interaction of the inherited body with the personal and impersonal environment. If the experiences before the emergence of self have been preponderantly negative, then the perceptions of self will be negative with all that that implies. The individual sees himself as unworthy, as weak, as incapable of dealing with life. Small problems become major crises. He feels that he is surrounded by threats with which he must cope in order to preserve and enhance his phenomenal self, but he is not equipped with effective weapons for the battle.

One important response to threat is anxiety. Anxiety, as was noted in the preceding chapter, is repressive and inhibits new learning. The threatened person defends himself in part through the denial of new perceptions. He insists on their nonexistence even though at the time he knows that they are present; however, the denial may eventually be carried to the point where the new perceptions are completely repressed. Now only the awareness of threat itself remains. One of the main purposes of psychotherapy is to help the disturbed person, in an atmosphere that is free from threat, to recall the denied experiences, to examine them, and to incorporate them into the self-structure.

Threat, of course, is not limited to inadequate personalities. Everyone experiences it to some extent. It is the degree or the extent of the threat for a certain individual that is important; also important are the techniques used in dealing with threat. The adequate person makes little use of denial.

The threatened (and therefore anxious) person is inhibited in learning new perceptions. He must concentrate on maintaining his rigid personality structure through constant attention to his defenses. One of these defenses is distortion, through which he makes the new event or experience more acceptable to the self. This kind of defense involves the excessive use of the adjustment mechanisms to be discussed in the following chapter. For example, such a person may rationalize extensively, substituting acceptable reasons for real reasons for his failures, or he may escape into a world of fantasy where for a time he can feel successful and important. Once these distorted perceptions have become a part of the self the individual struggles to maintain them, even though at the same time he would like to be reaching out and growing.

It appears to be rather well established that the distorted person who cannot accept himself cannot accept others either. This accounts to a considerable extent for the loneliness that characterizes those who are inadequate. They feel apart from the real world and from other human beings. They long for close personal contacts but are unable either to give or to receive.

The most serious forms of denial and distortion resulting from threat are found in psychotic patients. Those suffering from schizophrenic reactions, for example, have learned to defend themselves through such mechanisms of adjustment as hallucinations and delusions. They have escaped from the real world, which was too much for them, into an unreal, at least partially satisfying, world.

Self-Actualized Personalities

Those who satisfy their needs adequately and who achieve a high degree of fulfillment or self-actualization are far removed from the distorted persons just described. Usually, if not always, their biological inheritance is normal. Also usually, if not always, the experiences of infancy and early childhood were positive. Because their needs, especially the need for emotional security, were satisfied during the first few years of life, they were off to a good start. To be

sure, at a later period severe crisis situations may shake this foundation, but at least the foundation is there providing the individual
with a high threshold of resistance. Perhaps it should be mentioned
again that a reverse situation exists for children with inadequate
personalities. As a result of developmental changes, or of positive
crisis situations, or through psychotherapy some of them, too, become adequate.

Combs and Snygg list three major characteristics of the perceptual fields of adequate persons: "(1) Adequate persons perceive
themselves in general positive ways. (2) Adequate persons are more
capable of accepting and integrating their perceptions in the phenomenal field. (3) Adequate persons are capable of wide identification of self with others."[32]

A positive self-concept usually indicates realistic self-appraisal
and good mental health. A person possessing this positive picture of
himself is relatively free from threat. Consequently, anxiety is at a
minimum, and there is no need to set up elaborate defenses against
it. There is very little denial of the realities of life; instead, difficult
experiences are accepted and incorporated into the self-structure.
There is also relatively little distortion, because the confident person
feels much less need to twist and turn than the timid person. He
feels sure that he has the resources to deal with whatever life may
bring. He feels free to reach out, to explore. He is flexible. He knows
how to "roll with the punch."

Positive perceptions of the self indicate mental health if they are
based on a realistic appraisal of the self. Friedman[33] studied the
self-attitudes of three groups: normal persons, neurotics, and paranoid psychotics. The members of these groups were asked to describe
themselves in two ways: how they felt they were and how they would
like to be. The instruments used in this study were the Q sort and
the thematic apperception test. Friedman found in general that
normal subjects had positive attitudes toward themselves on a realistic basis, that neurotic subjects had negative self-attitudes based
upon realistic perceptions of disturbances within their selves, and
that the paranoid subjects had positive self-attitudes which, reflective
of self-enhancing defenses, were based on unrealistic self-appraisal.

---

[32] Combs and Snygg, *op. cit.*, p. 240.
[33] I. Friedman, "Phenomenal, Ideal, and Projected Conceptions of Self,"
Journal of Abnormal and Social Psychology, LI (1955), 611–15.

It was mentioned earlier that Combs and Snygg believe that adequate persons are capable of wide identification with others. The use of the term "wide identification" is open to question. Many highly intelligent persons frequently find it impossible to establish close relationships with a considerable number of other individuals. Their circle of intimates is often a small one, yet in spite of this they are able to achieve fulfillment.

In recent years there has been considerable interest among psychologists in those persons who have actualized themselves to a very high degree. The studies which have been made are admittedly not very scientific. Less is known about the very well adjusted than about the very maladjusted, partly because they are so individualistic in their flexibility that it is difficult to study them objectively.

Maslow[34] has done some excellent work in this area. He selected a group of self-actualized persons made up largely of public and historical figures, although he did include a few contemporary persons who were not widely known. Maslow states that from his study only composite impressions can be offered with respect to the characteristics of self-actualizing persons. Among several which he gives are the following:

More efficient perception of reality and more comfortable relations with it

Acceptance (self, others, nature)

Spontaneity

The quality of detachment; the need for privacy

Autonomy; independence of culture and environment

Continued freshness of appreciation

Gemeinschaftsgefühl

Philosophical, unhostile sense of humor

Creativeness

Self-actualizing persons are spontaneous. Their behavior is simple, natural, and direct. They dare to be themselves because of their confidence in and acceptance of themselves. They are not concerned about making an impression. They know who they are and are not

[34] A. H. Maslow, *Motivation and Personality* (New York: Harper & Row, Publishers, 1954), Ch. 12.

ashamed. In discussing spontaneity, Maslow makes a rather surprising statement. He says:

> The motivational life of self-actualizing people is not only quantitively different but also qualitatively different from that of ordinary people. It seems probable that we must construct a profoundly different psychology of motivation for self-actualizing people . . . the motivation of ordinary men is a striving for the basic need gratifications that they lack. But self-actualizing people in fact lack none of these gratifications; and yet they have impulses. They work, they try, and they are ambitious, even though in an unusual sense. For them motivation is just character growth, character expression, maturation, and development; in a word self-actualization.[35]

It seems highly unlikely that self-actualizing persons are qualitatively different from all others. Everyone has the drive for growth. To be sure, many are warped by their environment, but they are still trying to preserve and enhance themselves as they see themselves. It is difficult to believe that the self-actualizers are not also products of their environment. They, too, have experienced frustrations and at times feelings of guilt, but they are equipped by nature and by early experience to deal with these effectively. Their positive characteristics are as much adjustment mechanisms as are the behavior characteristics of those who are neurotic or psychotic. They are fortunate in that they have learned to use mechanisms which have led to fulfillment rather than to distortion.

An interesting characteristic of self-actualized persons is the quality of detachment. Since they are at peace with themselves, they not only can enjoy solitude and privacy but also on many occasions actually prefer it. They have the ability to be objective and calm in situations where others would be threatened and so lose their poise. Self-actualized persons do not need others nearly as much as most individuals do. They are self-sufficient, sometimes to an irritating degree.

The seventh characteristic on the list, Gemeinshaftsgefühl, needs some explanation. This refers to the feelings for mankind which self-actualized persons have. Even though, as was pointed out in the preceding paragraph, they do not need others to the extent that normal persons do, they nevertheless identify deeply with the

[35] *Ibid.*, pp. 210–11.

human race and usually have a strong desire to help their fellows. They have a "social conscience" in the best sense of the term.

Self-actualized persons are creative. Maslow states that this is a universal characteristic. This creativeness "being an expression of healthy personality, is projected out upon the world or touches whatever activity the person is engaged in."[36] In view of their flexibility, their spontaneity, their naturalness, it is easy to see why this is so.

Self-actualized persons are not perfect. They are not always good and wise as goodness and wisdom are defined by their contemporaries. Maslow points out they can be extremely ruthless, which is to be expected considering the strength of their personalities. They are also characteristically nonconformists; they may not make good organization men. Since they care very little about the opinions of others, they frequently antagonize. Even their emotions are by no means wholly unruffled; they too have conflicts; they too can experience deep sadness as in the case of Lincoln (one of Maslow's subjects). They are not supermen but they do serve as examples of the realization of human potentialities at a very high level.

SUMMARY

The self-concept is learned. This is a fact of great importance to the individual and to those persons who are responsible for his development during the early years of his life when the foundations of his self-structure are being laid. Everything that one knows about one's self comes from experience, social experience being of major importance. During infancy these social experiences are largely confined within the limits of the family circle. Members of the family group are usually the significant persons in the infant's world. From these significant persons, especially the mother, the infant establishes the basis of his concept of his self. It may even be that very early in life, before the ability to use and understand language has developed, a feeling about the self is learned through empathy. Certainly by the time the child is three or four or five years of age the self-concept has become to some extent organized, although it is still fluid and can be altered rather easily.

As time goes on, the child becomes more and more conscious of the appraisals made of him by others, and his concept of self in turn

---

[36] *Ibid.*, p. 223.

becomes a reflection of these appraisals. If the appraisals are in the main derogatory, then the child learns to look upon himself as inferior. On the other hand, if the appraisals are preponderantly positive, then he learns to look upon himself as worthy. There is no point in an individual's life when the self-concept becomes completely established in the sense that it is no longer subject to change. Actually, it is continuously being modified as the result of constant interaction with the environment. However, these changes are of course made much less frequently during adult years than they are during childhood.

Even though the self is subject to change as it adjusts to environmental pressures, it is at the same time striving to maintain itself. There is marked consistency in the behavior of individuals, especially of adults. Resistance to change with accompanying rigidity in behavior is increased when the individual perceives himself as threatened. Conversely, in a relatively nonthreatening environment the individual reaches out for new experiences. He is in a much better position to make adequate differentiations and to learn more about himself and his environment, thus achieving a more complete self-actualization.

EXCEPTIONAL CHILDREN

All children are exceptional in the sense that no one child is exactly like any other. Some children, however, deviate so markedly from that which is typical that they deserve special attention in a book on mental hygiene. These extreme deviations appear in all human characteristics: intellectual, physical, emotional, and social. As was pointed out in Chapter Four, whenever a characteristic is measured in a large representative sampling of the population, the scores will usually be found to follow the normal probability curve. This means, of course, that the extreme deviates are relatively few in number. For example, it will be recalled that while 68 per cent of the general population fall within a Stanford-Binet IQ range of 84–116, only about 1 per cent rate as high as 140 and about 2 per cent fall below 60. A similar situation exists with respect to physical abnormalities, a majority falling within a normal range with respect to hearing, sight, and so on. However, there are many who have extreme physical handicaps.

Within the limits of a single chapter on this subject, it is obvious that all the groups of exceptional children cannot be considered. The writer has, therefore, selected three of the most important: intellectually gifted children, feebleminded or mentally retarded children, and physically handicapped children. Since physical handicaps are so numerous, the discussion of this group will be limited to a consideration of the problems of those who are crippled, those who have impaired hearing, and those who have impaired vision. All these groups have special adjustment problems, especially in their relationship with others, resulting from the fact that they are very exceptional in at least one important area.

INTELLECTUALLY GIFTED CHILDREN

Children with Stanford-Binet IQs of 140 or above are designated (rather arbitrarily, to be sure) as intellectually gifted. Such children possess the potentialities for high achievement. However, it does not follow that they will inevitably succeed, for eminence is multi-determined. Those who are in the top 1 per cent with respect to intelligence might well be divided into two groups, with the term "genius" being limited to those who rate an IQ of above 170. These extreme deviates usually have considerable difficulty in adjusting to an environment dominated by individuals much less intelligent than they. Although geniuses are few in number, they carry great responsibility for the advancement of humanity. Society should do everything possible to nurture them.

Intellectually gifted persons or geniuses differ in degree, rather than in kind, from those who are average in mentality. They merely have more of the same thing. They have so much more, however, that the differences appear to be qualitative. Everyone has the capacity to learn. The dull individual learns slowly and achieves mastery over relatively simple materials only. The brilliant individual learns rapidly and achieves mastery over relatively complex materials. He sees and understands relationships which the dull individual would never see or comprehend. It is important to keep in mind that though the precocious child or the adult genius appears to be very different, actually his nature and abilities are basically the same as those possessed by his fellows. In common with everyone else, he needs success, he needs recognition, and he needs affectional ties.

Intellectually gifted children have been studied rather extensively during the last quarter of a century. The most complete report concerning them is contained in the five volumes of *Genetic Studies of Genius* by Terman and others. Research studies reveal, among other things, that gifted children tend to be born of gifted parents, that they come from the higher socioeconomic levels, and that race and sex exert some influence on their incidence. The studies have provided us with a number of facts concerning the scholastic achievements and physical characteristics of very superior children but are inconclusive concerning their social and emotional characteristics. There is need for more research on the question of the relationship between emotional stability and very superior mentality or genius.

Mental Characteristics

Intellectually gifted children usually manifest their mental superiority at a very early age. By the time he has reached his first birthday, the average child is likely to have a vocabulary of two words; it is not unusual for a very gifted child to have a vocabulary of from ten to fifteen words at that age. The best single criterion of mental superiority during the first two years is size of vocabulary. It would be expected that the gifted child, since his verbal intelligence is so high, would learn how to read much earlier in life than do average children. Approximately one half of those who are in the top 1 per cent in intellect learn to read before they enter school. Terman reported that 20.5 per cent of the California group that he studied learned to read before the age of five, 6.1 per cent before the age of four, and 1.6 per cent before the age of three.[1] It is rare for such a child to be forced to learn how to read. He usually develops the ability without formal instruction.

Having learned how to read at a very early age, the gifted child frequently turns to such subjects as history and geography, so that by the time he enters the first grade, he may already have gathered a great deal of information that is customarily taught in the middle grades. Since arithmetic is more difficult to learn by independent study than is reading, the preschool gifted child is not likely to become so proficient in that subject.

Scholastic Achievement   As mentally precocious children go on through school, they tend to do very superior work in their subjects. Their educational quotients, however, are likely to be somewhat lower than their intelligence quotients. The differences between

[1] L. M. Terman *et al.*, *Genetic Studies of Genius* (Stanford, Calif.: Stanford University Press, 1926), I, 272.

educational quotients and intelligence quotients are probably almost wholly the result of the failure of the school to adjust course
content to the abilities of these brilliant children.

There is not only a marked difference in scholastic achievement
between gifted children and average children, but also a difference
between those at the upper levels of giftedness and those at the
lower levels of giftedness. Children with intelligence quotients of
over 170 experience an even greater handicap with respect to
educational opportunities than do those with intelligence quotients
between 140 and 150.

Family Adjustments

Terman[2] grouped the fathers of 560 of the gifted children whom he
studied into the Taussig five-grade classification with the following
results:

Professional		31.4 %
Semi-professional and business		50.0 %
(a) Higher group	31.2%	
(b) Lower group	18.8%	
Skilled labor		11.8 %
Semi-skilled to slightly skilled		6.6 %
Common labor		0.13%

It is fortunate that approximately one third of gifted children,
as indicated by Terman's study, are born and reared in homes where
the fathers are professional men. In such a setting the chances are
excellent that the children will have the intellectual companionship
that they seek. A considerable number, however, are born to parents of average or below-average mentality. In such instances, both
the parents and the child may feel frustrated. Being human, such
parents are likely to experience a confused emotional reaction to
their gifted child; the more precocious he is, the greater the confusion. Pride in his achievements is mixed with resentment that he
knows too much. It is difficult for any adult to accept a ten-year-old
child who knows more than he does. Moreover, the average or below-
average parent frequently believes that precocious children come to
no good end.

Any gifted child who is wholly or partially rejected by his par-

2 L. M. Terman, op. cit., I, 64.

ents senses early in life that there is something about him that is not liked. As he grows older he begins to suspect that it is his high intelligence. He is no more to blame for his excellent mentality than another child is for superior physical equipment, yet it may be a barrier between him and his family. This situation is brought out very well in Eve Curie's biography of her mother, Madame Curie. The writer tells of an experience which the four-year-old Marie had when she presumed one day to read aloud to her family from an elder sister's reader.

> One morning, while Bronya (an older sister) was faltering out a reading lesson to her parents, Manya (Marie) grew impatient, took the book from her hands, and read aloud the opening sentence. At first, flattered by the silence which surrounded her, she continued this fascinating game; but suddenly panic seized her. One look at the stupefied faces of her parents, another at Bronya's sulky stare, a few unintelligible stammers, an irrepressible sob—and instead of the infant prodigy, there was only the baby of four, crying through her tears:
>
> "Beg—pardon! Pardon! I didn't do it on purpose. It's not my fault—it's not Bronya's fault! It's only because it was so easy!"
>
> Manya had suddenly conceived, with despair, that she might perhaps never be forgiven for having learned to read.[3]

Many gifted children learn to accept such situations as this. They sublimate their family frustrations through concentration on intellectual activities. Some, however, resort to less acceptable mechanisms of adjustment. They withdraw or become negativistic. A frequent reaction is to become ashamed of the intellect which has been the cause of the partial or perhaps complete loss of parental love. Many highly intelligent college students are so ashamed of their good minds that they cannot achieve to capacity.

The relationship of an intellectually gifted child with less intelligent brothers and sisters is frequently unsatisfactory to both. Instead of the gifted child's feeling superior, he is likely to be made to feel inferior by aggressive siblings who inwardly envy him but outwardly despise him. The precocious child may be forced to adjust by pretending that his intellect is much less than it is. This is

[3] E. Curie, *Madame Curie* (Garden City, N. Y.: Doubleday & Company, Inc., 1937), p. 9.

not good mental hygiene, for every individual should accept himself with all his assets and liabilities, then proceed to capitalize on his assets. This is difficult for a young genius whose greatest gift is not one which meets with general social approval.

School Adjustments

The gifted child often experiences considerable difficulty in adjusting to the typical school situation. The scholastic achievements of mentally superior children are far superior to average children of the same chronological age. For example, a child with an intelligence quotient of 150 is capable of doing third-grade work when he is six years of age. Usually he is forced to go through the routine of the first grade. When he reaches the age of ten he is capable of mastering the subject-matter customarily taught during the freshman and sophomore years of high school, yet he is mired in the fourth or fifth grade. The writer recalls a boy of ten who was referred to him because he was doing poor school work and had become a disciplinary problem. On testing the boy, it was found he had a Stanford-Binet IQ of 165. In an interview, the boy stated that he had become so disgusted with being drilled on arithmetic problems that he had been able to solve years before and with copying spelling words thirty or forty times each—words which he had been able to spell as long as he could remember—that he had given up. He was weary of going through meaningless motions.

Probably the majority of our very gifted children in America are caught in a trap, insofar as school is concerned. It is a difficult problem to know how to get them out of that trap. Acceleration does not seem to be the answer; to place them with children of like mental age is to take them away from children whose social, emotional, and physiological ages are comparable to theirs. A ten-year-old child in high school would have his need for achievement satisfied, but this would be more than offset by the frustrations he would experience with respect to status and emotional security. It may be that the answer lies in special opportunity classes, although there are strong social arguments against this form of adjustment. Theoretically, the best way to deal with the problem is to leave gifted children in heterogeneous classes and then adjust the course content and methods of instruction to their needs and abilities. Practically, this is very difficult. Teachers are often incapable of making such adjustments; moreover, even when they could do so, they usually have such large classes that they cannot find the needed time.

There is little doubt that many gifted children develop behavior disorders because of the school's failure to meet their intellectual and emotional needs. The rationalization that "the gifted can take care of themselves" is merely a defensive attitude. These children need guidance. They need a kind of education that will make it possible for them to develop to the full extent of their capacities.

Adjustment to Peers

When the average human being comes in contact with those who are so superior to him intellectually that he cannot understand them, he reacts with fear, or ridicule, or both. If the gifted individual is to avoid being feared or ridiculed, he must have or develop abilities which will compensate for the high intelligence which is usually a social handicap. Gifted children as a group appear to be adept in making such adjustments. Investigations by Terman, Hollingworth, and others reveal that gifted children at the lower levels of the top 1 per cent make as good, or slightly better, social adjustments than average children. Moreover, they are somewhat more likely than average children to become school leaders. The situation is quite different, however, for those at the upper limit of the gifted group.

It would seem that the child with an intelligence quotient of 145 or so is close enough to those with average mentality to be able to learn to talk their language and to play their games. He is helped in making the necessary adjustments by the fact that he is likely to be physically as well as mentally superior to others of his own age, although his physical superiority is considerably less than his mental superiority. This moderate physical superiority makes it somewhat easier for him to play the games which are liked by his own age group or by somewhat older children.

Gifted children are also helped in their social adjustment problems by the fact that they are likely to be accelerated in school by from one to two years. By playing with other children they are enabled partially to bridge the gap which exists with respect to mental ages. The difference in mental ages, however, between extremely gifted and average children is so great that normal social adjustments are difficult, if not impossible, to achieve. Such children are likely to lead lonely lives, seeking their satisfactions in solitary play or in the creation of imaginary companions. In such instances, the child's personality is temporarily—sometimes permanently—marred. No child, not even a genius, can remain unaffected by failure to be accepted by his peer group. It is not surprising that many of these highly gifted children become ashamed of the high intelligence which has been the principal cause of the frustration of their status and security needs.

Emotional Stability

The mental superiority of gifted children and adult geniuses produces adjustment problems of a kind which average individuals never have to face. Are these problems so difficult to resolve that the individuals experiencing them become emotionally unstable? There have been only a few studies of this question, and these are rather inadequate. The most widely quoted investigation is the one made by Terman, who gave a modified form of the Woodworth-Cady Emotional Stability Questionnaire to 284 gifted boys and 258 control boys and to 248 gifted girls and 275 control girls.[4] He found a difference between the means for the boys of 4.4 and for the girls, 5.1. The difference between the two groups for the sexes combined was 4.7. In each instance, the difference was reliable.

Terman also asked the teachers of the gifted group and of the control group to rate the children on nervous disturbances. He summarized the results as follows:

> Indications of "nervousness" are reported by the school for 13.3 per cent of gifted and for 16.1 per cent of control. Stuttering, including mild cases, is reported for 2.6 per cent of the gifted and for 3.4 per cent of control. Only two cases gave a history of chorea. "Excessive timidity" and "tendency to worry" were reported with about equal frequency in the gifted and control groups.[5]

Although, as Terman points out, indications of "nervousness" were noted less frequently in the gifted group, "excessive timidity" and "tendency to worry" were noted more frequently for the gifted. The teachers reported "excessive timidity" for 7.4 per cent of the

4 L. M. Terman, op. cit., I, 511.
5 Ibid., I, 212.

512 gifted children and 7 per cent for the 472 control children. With respect to "tendency to worry," the difference was somewhat greater, being noted in 10.4 per cent of the gifted group as compared with 9 per cent of the control group.

The methods used by Terman for evaluating the emotional stability of gifted children are open to question. Paper and pencil tests of neurotic tendency possess relatively little validity unless one is certain that the individual tested has answered the questions honestly. Moreover, Terman has undue confidence in the ability of teachers to know whether or not a child is maladjusted. This is rather surprising in view of his remark, "If one would identify the brightest child in a class of 30 to 50 pupils, it is better to consult the birth records in the class register than to ask the teacher's opinion."[6] If teachers have so little success in identifying those children in their classes who have the best minds, how can they be expected to know which ones are emotionally unstable? Emotional conflicts are much less obvious to casual observers than mental capacity. Terman's study of the emotional stability of gifted children proves nothing conclusive. It merely indicates the possibility that superior children are at least as stable emotionally as average children.

Studies of the relative prevalence of serious behavior disorders among very gifted adults are inconclusive and few in number. Lange-Eichbaum, in a questionable study of geniuses, found that a large number of them had been psychotic. He says:

> But among geniuses (considered to the number of from three to four hundred individuals) we find that from 12 to 13 per cent have been psychotic at least once during their lifetime. Confining our examination to the "very greatest" names, numbering seventy-eight in all, we find that more than 37 per cent have been psychotic once during their lifetime; that more than 83 per cent have been markedly psychopathic; that more than 10 per cent have been slightly psychopathic; and that about 6.5 per cent have been healthy. The proportion of diseased persons becomes a little greater still, if we select thirty-five persons who are regarded as "the greatest geniuses of all": the psychotic number 40 per cent; the psychopathic, more than 90 per cent; the healthy, 8.5 per cent.[7]

6 *Ibid.*, I, 33.

7 Wilhelm Lange-Eichbaum, *The Problem of Genius* (New York: The Macmillan Company, 1932), p. 112.

In a follow-up study of the California group of gifted children, published in 1959, Terman and Oden arrived at conclusions very different from those presented by Lange-Eichbaum. Their gifted subjects, now in early middle age, had been identified in early childhood. The principal sources of the new information concerning the mental health of this group were "personal conferences by the research staff with the subjects, their parents, and their spouses; letters from the subjects or members of their families, or other qualified informants; and responses to questionnaires filled out by the subjects and, in the earlier years, by their parents also."[8] Such sources of information as the preceding are rather unsatisfactory in view of the fact that there is a strong tendency for most individuals and their families to avoid admitting the existence of emotional disturbances. It would have been desirable, although perhaps impossible, for each person in the group studied to have been interviewed by a qualified psychiatrist or clinical psychologist.

On the basis of the data they had gathered, Terman and Oden classified their subjects into three categories: satisfactory adjustment; some maladjustment; serious maladjustment. Those who were seriously maladjusted were divided into two subgroups, those who were hospitalized and those who were not. Terman and Oden had sufficient information to rate 98 per cent of the 1,196 living subjects with whom they had kept in contact for approximately thirty-five years. In terms of percentages these gifted adults were classified as follows: satisfactory adjustment, 68.8 per cent of the men and 65.9 per cent of the women; some maladjustment, 22.3 per cent of the men and 25.1 per cent of the women; serious maladjustment without hospitalization, 6.2 per cent of the men and 6 per cent of the women; serious maladjustment requiring hospitalization, 2.7 per cent of the men and 3.0 per cent of the women.[9]

Terman and Oden point out that, among the subjects who had died before this follow-up study was made, five men and four women had been patients in mental hospitals. When this group is included among the living subjects, the percentages of those with a history of hospitalization are increased to 3.1 for men and 3.4 for women.[10]

[8] L. M. Terman and M. H. Oden, *The Gifted Group at Mid-Life*, Genetic Studies of Genius (Stanford, Calif.: Stanford University Press, 1959), V, 35.

[9] *Ibid.*, p. 37.

[10] *Ibid.*, p. 39.

According to the Goldhamer-Marshall expectancy rate for the general population, 3.4 per cent of all men and 3.0 per cent of all women have been hospitalized for mental and emotional disturbances by the age of forty-five. The average age of the gifted subjects at the time of the Terman-Oden follow-up study was 44, so the two groups are comparable with respect to age. The data, then, show "the incidence among gifted men to be slightly below the expectancy for the male population of comparable age, and among gifted women, slightly above the expectancy. Probably neither sex differs greatly from the generality in the frequency of mental disease."[11]

It is entirely possible that intellectually gifted individuals do not differ appreciably from the general population with respect to the frequency of mild or serious behavior disorders. Certainly, because of their high intelligence they are better equipped to deal with emotional crises as they arise. On the other hand, their problems are more complex than those experienced by average persons and their perceptions of the threatening aspects of their environment are more acute. Moreover, men and women with superior mentality, such as those in the Terman-Oden study, are characteristically living at a socioeconomic level which makes it possible for them to seek and to obtain private professional treatment in time to avoid actual hospitalization. There may be important psychological differences which affect the degree of adjustment or maladjustment between those who are merely intellectually superior and those who are both intellectually superior and creative. The majority of the Terman-Oden subjects belong in the first group; the majority of the Lange-Eichbaum subjects in the second.

Creativity   There has been almost no research on the nature of creativity or the relationship between creativity and emotional disturbances. As Guilford points out, this may be attributed to the general adoption by psychologists of the stimulus-response model. "There is no questioning of the advances that psychology has made with this conceptual model but when we come to the higher thought processes, particularly to problems of creative thinking, the limitations of the model become very apparent."[12] Since facts are not

---

[11] *Ibid.*, p. 43.

[12] J. P. Guilford, "Traits of Creativity," in *Creativity and Its Cultivation*, ed. H. H. Anderson (New York: Harper & Row, Publishers, 1959), p. 144.

available it is necessary to depend upon theories. The psychologists, whose addresses at the Inter-disciplinary Symposia on Creativity held between April 1957 and July 1958 are printed in *Creativity and Its Cultivation,* take the point of view that, in order to be creative, one must have good mental health. The editor, H. H. Anderson, says:

> There is essential agreement among those authors who comment on these topics, and no disagreement among them, that mental health and high utilization of one's creative potentials are closely associated. The whole volume is an attempt to define the positive qualities and characteristics of a healthy life process, a way of life, the activity and relating of a fully functioning person, the self-actualizing individual, the person of courage and integrity who is also at peace with his neighbors. The consensus of these authors is that creativity is an expression of a mentally or psychologically healthy person, that creativity is associated with wholeness, unity, honesty, integrity, personal involvement, enthusiasm, high motivation, and action.
>
> There is also agreement that neurosis either accompanies or causes a degraded quality of one's creativity. For neurotic persons and persons with other forms of mental disease, such assumptions as the following are offered: that these persons are creative in spite of their disease; that they are producing below the achievements they would show without the disease; that they are on the down grade, or that they are pseudo creative, that is, they may have brilliant original ideas which, because of the neurosis, they do not consummate.[13]

These authors may be right, although there is no certainty that neurotic persons are actually producing "below the achievements they would show without the disease." It may be that creative persons are driven to achieve by what might be called "productive anxiety." It is difficult to see why a complacent, self-satisfied person at peace with himself and with the world would expend the effort needed to write a novel or to compose a symphony. Is he not forced to do so by doubts and uncertainties within himself? Does he not find release from tension and anxiety in intensive concentration on self-expression and communication with others through his chosen medium? Such activity for intellectual giants might even be thought of as a form of occupational therapy.

[13] H. H. Anderson, "Creativity in Perspective," in *Creativity and Its Cultivation,* ed. H. H. Anderson (New York: Harper & Row, Publishers, 1959), p. 248.

INTELLECTUALLY RETARDED CHILDREN

At the opposite extreme from intellectually gifted children are those who are mentally retarded. These individuals have difficult adjustments to make because of the low level of their intelligence. Those at the lowest levels are so handicapped that it is impossible for them to meet the requirements of society. In most instances such persons are institutionalized, although a few are cared for in the home.

It is very difficult to give a definition of feeblemindedness or mental retardation. Law stresses the capacity of the individual to understand, to be responsible for his acts, to know the difference between right and wrong. Medicine stresses the physiological basis of mental deficiency and is especially interested in secondary amentia. Psychology emphasizes the importance of mental age and of IQ as determined by an individual intelligence test. Sociology gives considerable weight to the ability of the individual to adjust to the social and economic requirements of society. No one of these is complete by itself. Doll states:

> A satisfactory criterion of feeble-mindedness involves four essential attributes, namely, social (including occupational and educational) inferiority, intellectual retardation, developmental arrest, and constitutional deficiency or defect. No one of these criteria may be omitted without weakening the concept. Thus, mental deficiency in the limited sense of low mental test performance which is not accompanied by social incompetence is not synonymous with feeble-mindedness in its traditional and legal definition. . . . Similarly, developmental deficiencies which are not primarily mental in nature and do not result in social inaptitude cannot be considered as the genuine feeble-mindedness with which the term *mental deficiency* has long been associated.[14]

Mentally retarded children are customarily divided into three subgroups. Until recently these groups were called idiots, imbeciles, and morons. During the last few years, however, there has been a trend away from these labels because of their unfavorable connotations. As would be expected during a period of transition, there is difficulty in finding new terms which are satisfactory. Perhaps the

[14] Leonard Carmichael, ed., *Manual of Child Psychology* (New York: John Wiley & Sons, Inc., 1954), p. 847.

best of those which have been suggested are: severely retarded, moderately retarded, and mildly retarded. These will be used in the present discussion.

The severely retarded are those persons with intelligence quotients ranging from 0 to 25 and with mental ages from zero to three years. Mental growth usually does not continue beyond the chronological age of eight or nine. The severely retarded person has so little intelligence that he must be cared for even in maturity as though he were a child. He can never learn to read or write and uses speech on the infant level. He can, however, establish some degree of elementary habit training and conditioning. His social intelligence is characteristically slightly higher than his abstract intelligence. He is in need of supervision in all areas of living but may be able to participate in planned activities. He is always inferior physically and in nearly every instance possesses physical stigmata.

The moderately retarded group fall within an IQ range of 25 to 50 and a mental age range of from three to six or seven. Moderately retarded persons can master simple routine tasks and with much patient instruction can learn to do simple kinds of work. They can learn self-care, and they have the capacity for taking an interest in themselves, including their personal appearance. Although they can never acquire sufficient occupational skill to be self-supporting, they can, with adequate training, achieve some degree of personal independence and can even be economically useful in a sheltered environment. Mental growth rarely continues beyond a chronological age of twelve. Moderately retarded persons at the upper level of the group can sometimes learn to write a few simple words and when they are near or have reached mental maturity they can read a little at the primer or sometimes at the first-grade level.

The mildly retarded group fall within an IQ range of from 50 to 70, although some psychologists have set the upper limit at 75—occasionally at 80. Their mental age range is from six or seven to ten or eleven. Social and emotional criteria are important determining factors with respect to this classification. Mildly retarded persons can profit from a specially planned academic program. Frequently they are able to become economically independent, to marry, and to support their families. There is a reasonable expectation that at maturity they will be capable of making adequate social adjustments.

Various estimates of the number of retarded persons in the United States have been made in recent years. These estimates vary considerably, largely because of disagreement as to the dividing line between the retarded group and the normal group. Moreover, a great many emotionally disturbed persons have been inaccurately classified as mentally retarded. The United States Office of Education estimates that 2 per cent of the school population in the United States fall within the retarded or feebleminded classification. The National Association for Retarded Children, on the other hand, states that 3 per cent of the population are mentally deficient. There are no severely retarded children and only a few moderately retarded children in our public schools. However, there is a very considerable number—from 2 to 3 per cent—of school children who are mildly retarded. They present educational problems which have been only partially solved. Moreover, as school children, they may experience frustrations which will have disrupting effects on their personalities.

Adjustment Problems

Mentally retarded children and adults have the same basic needs as persons with a better mental endowment. Because of their handicap, their needs—especially the need for emotional security—may be even more pressing. If these needs are severely frustrated and an emotional disturbance results from the frustration, the retarded person is at a special disadvantage. He does not have sufficient intelligence to develop a variety of adjustment mechanisms to help him to resolve emotional problems. More than any other intellectual group he must rely upon a healthy personality to meet the crisis of everyday living.

Retarded children are not only mentally handicapped but they are also much more likely than normal children to be physically handicapped, the frequency of physical defects found in their group being about twice as great as those found in a comparable number in the general population. Since a retarded child is poorly equipped mentally to deal with a physical handicap, it constitutes a greater personal problem for him than it does for brighter children. Certain physical stigmata may make social contacts difficult and so accentuate his feelings of being different from others. On the positive side, if the physical defect is one in which society has become interested and if the mental retardation is not too extreme, he may find himself more acceptable in the community because of his deformity and in spite of his intellectual inferiority. Just as society is more accepting of physical illness than it is of mental illness, so is it more accepting of physical handicaps than it is of mental handicaps.

The School   The child whose intelligence is markedly below average usually has a very difficult time in the classroom. If, for example, he has an intelligence quotient of 67, he is developing mentally at a rate of eight months for each calendar year. Therefore, if he enters school at the age of six he has a mental age of only four. He may be expected to be able to learn to read, yet he cannot do so. His teacher may stress his backwardness before the class. At the end of the year he may be told that he must repeat the grade, or he may be sent on into the second grade. He is now seven years of age but is still mentally incapable of reading even simple material. He goes on through grade school, struggling year after year with material that is too difficult for him. At the age of twelve he has a mental age of eight. He is now capable of doing third-grade work, but probably finds himself in the fifth grade. If he is in a typical school, his need for achievement is being constantly frustrated. At fifteen or sixteen years of age he may be graduated from grade school. If he attempts high school, he finds the usual curriculum too difficult, for he now has a mental age of only ten.

There are two good solutions for the school problems of mildly retarded children, most of whom should be in school rather than in institutions for the mentally handicapped. In large school systems the special class is desirable. In the special class it is relatively easy to adapt the curriculum content and the methods of instruction to the needs and abilities of the children being taught. The subject matter should not only be individually appropriate; it should also be socially useful. Functional, rather than academic, values should at all times be emphasized in the education of retarded children.

In small school systems, where it is difficult or impossible to segregate retarded children for instructional purposes, differentiation within the heterogeneous class can go far in helping the mentally handicapped child to develop his potentialities, limited though they are. The difficulties involved in adapting the subject matter and the teaching methods to the needs and abilities of this very slow group are much greater when it is a part of the larger class representing a cross section of the school population than when dealing with a segregated group. Nevertheless, much can be done. The teacher must, of course, not only be aware of the necessity of making the adjustments, but she must also be acquainted with the needs and abilities of the retarded group and know how to teach them.

Family Adjustments   The relationship of the retarded child with his parents is fully as important—if not more so—than is the relationship of the intellectually normal child with his parents. His personality, including his emotional stability or instability, is to a considerable extent a reflection of the personalities and stability of his parents. Chamberlain and Moss say: "After handling hundreds of children in our schools, we have come to the conclusion that children bring to school the emotional and social problems of the home. They reflect to a much greater degree than do normal children the emotional attitudes of their parents."[15]

The parents of a retarded child are in a difficult situation. Because of the attitude of society they may feel ashamed of their offspring, and the feeling of shame may result in overt or covert rejection. Many families drastically alter their way of life because of the presence of a mentally deficient child in the family circle and withdraw from community activities almost completely. In such a situation, the retarded child is likely to have a half-formed, uneasy realization that he is to blame for this.

Fortunately, not all parents respond negatively to the presence of a retarded child in the family circle. There is some evidence that poorly educated parents from the lower socioeconomic groups are more successful in helping their mentally retarded children than are well-educated parents from the higher socioeconomic groups. Although it is by no means always true, well-educated parents tend to look upon a retarded child of theirs as a threat. Consequently, they may reject him or refuse to accept his intellectual limitations and try to force him to achieve on a level well beyond his potentialities.

The parents of a retarded child should accept his handicap and help him to adjust to it. On the one hand they should avoid setting goals that are too high for him to attain, and on the other hand they should realize that there is much they can do to help him satisfy

[15] N. H. Chamberlain and D. H. Moss, *The Three "R's" for the Retarded* (New York: National Association for Retarded Children, 1953), p. 6.

his need for achievement within his limited fields of activity. Even though he cannot do well academically, there are many occupational and personal skills he can master. If he feels secure in his family relationships, if he knows that his parents care deeply for him, and if he and they are satisfied with his small achievements, he will be helped greatly in the adjustments he must make to the outside world. Acceptance of the fact of limited mentality is the principal key to the mental health and social adequacy of all retarded children but especially of the mildly retarded.

Institutionalization   The question as to whether or not mentally retarded children should be institutionalized is difficult to answer. Certainly there is justification for the statement that *not all* retarded children should be institutionalized. The majority of those who are mildly retarded can become useful members of the community. Even many of the moderately retarded can make adequate adjustments within the family circle if they are accepted by parents and siblings. Usually the severely retarded are better off in institutions.

Four criteria should be considered before reaching a decision concerning the institutionalization of a retarded child: Is an institution the only place in which he can obtain the special training which he needs? Is institutionalization essential for his own protection or for the protection of others? Is a greater amount of physical care required than can be provided by the home? Is the retarded child a serious strain upon the financial or emotional situation in the home?

If the home community does not have adequate facilities for the training of retarded children, it is often, although not always, desirable to place these children in an institution where specialized instruction is given. Such training frequently makes it possible for the mildly retarded to make a good adjustment to society. Some retarded children, either because of a very low level of intelligence or because of serious behavior disorders, must be institutionalized in order that they themselves as well as other persons may be protected. Any person who is a menace to others must be segregated, regardless of his intellectual capacity. Most of the severely retarded children and adults need more physical care than can be provided in the home. Institutionalization is essential for this group. The fourth criterion is the most difficult to evaluate. If the expense of keeping the retarded child at home constitutes such a drain upon the family's economic resources that all are made to suffer by it, it is probably better that the handicapped child be placed in an institution. Often the members of the family of a retarded child find it impossible to accept his handicap. His presence constitutes a continuous threat to their emotional security. It is probably best in this unfortunate situation to have the child cared for in an institution.

A great deal needs to be done in our institutions for mentally retarded persons. Such institutions are usually handicapped by lack of funds, a situation which results, in many instances, in their merely providing custodial care at a relatively low level. These institutions should have adequately trained personnel and a rehabilitation program designed to return many of these handicapped persons to their communities with enough training and enough emotional stability to be self-supporting and responsible members of society.

Emotional Stability

Intellectually retarded persons are somewhat more susceptible to behavior disorders than are those who have normal mentality. These disorders range from relatively mild maladjustments, such as lack of emotional control which would be expected in view of their mental ages, to advanced psychotic states. Although there is disagreement concerning the actual incidence of psychotic reactions among persons who are mentally deficient, it is generally agreed that they appear more frequently than in the intellectually normal population. From the studies that have been made it would appear that psychotic reactions are about three times as great among those who are mentally retarded as would be expected on the basis of their relative numbers. This is not surprising in view of their difficulties in adjusting to their environment. As with the normal population, in the retarded group neurotic reactions are found more frequently than psychotic reactions.

Although therapy with retarded children and adults presents many problems, the situation is by no means hopeless. Some form of environmental therapy is usually essential. This involves the manipulation of the environment in ways that will help the handicapped person in his efforts to overcome his emotional difficulties. Occupational therapy has often proved to be very useful. The retarded person sometimes makes his first social contacts outside the family circle through an occupational therapy group. Group therapy which deals more directly with emotional problems is still in the experimental stage but it seems to be a specially valuable method in helping mentally retarded persons with their emotional problems. Individual therapy has worked successfully with many cases. Psychotherapy will not increase the native mental capacity of the retarded person but will, if successful, make it possible for him to function more adequately within his intellectual limitations by reducing his emotional disturbances.

Pseudoretardation

Pseudoretardation is fear of trying or an escape from trying. Instead of low mentality being one of the important causes of the emotional instability which is present, the emotional instability is the principal cause of the apparent stupidity. A person who has been persistently frustrated in his need to achieve and who has, because of those frustrations, lost most of his self-respect and ambition, may resort to stupid behavior as a defense mechanism. In this way he avoids responsibility; he is no longer expected to perform difficult tasks. Having reduced his tension by this device, he continues to behave as though he were feebleminded.

It is frequently very difficult to differentiate those persons who are actually retarded because of low mental capacity from those with normal capacity who are utilizing many of the behavior patterns of those who are retarded as a basic mechanism of adjustment. It is even more difficult to discover how much the intelligence quotient of a retarded person is the result of actual mental capacity and how much is the result of emotional disorders. Diagnosis in this situation becomes very important, since emotional disorders can be treated successfully but mental deficiency cannot be appreciably improved. There have been many attempts to explain why the number of feebleminded individuals in our society is about double the statistical expectation. Perhaps the principal reason for this discrepancy is that large numbers of individuals have been classified as mentally retarded when actually they were emotionally disturbed.

Yepsen has listed fifty statements relating to mental retardation and has then indicated whether these statements are true or false and why. The writer has selected seven from this pamphlet as a means of emphasizing some of the points made in the preceding discussion.

1. *Many mentally deficient persons can be trained to be self-supporting citizens.*

TRUE

Their social and economic adjustment may not be at a high level but many of them need not be totally dependent upon the community. There are thousands of mentally deficient persons in the community who are successful graduates of classes for the mentally subnormal and the state training schools for the mentally deficient. They may require some supervision from time to time in order to increase their effectiveness, however.

2. *Mental deficiency can be cured.*

FALSE

There is absolutely no evidence that mental deficiency can be cured. In the light of today's knowledge there is no known medical treatment or training program which can give a truly mentally deficient individual normal intelligence or enable him to function at a normal level. Training and treatment will, however, help him to reach his full potential and permit him to accomplish many things he would not otherwise be able to accomplish without such training. In instances where there has been an apparent "cure" it is likely that the child was not mentally deficient in the first place. He may have appeared to have been mentally deficient and a false conclusion reached because of inconclusive or inappropriate examinations.

3. A mentally deficient child is not capable of loving its parents.

FALSE

The mentally deficient child responds to love and affection perhaps even more than does the normal child. His is primarily an emotional and not an intellectual life.

4. *Mentally deficient children need specialized training, not merely a "watered down" regular course of study.*

TRUE

The most successful training programs are those which are devised to meet the individual and particular needs of the mentally deficient child. The program should be one essentially of "clinical teaching." The mentally deficient child is an outstandingly slow learner and, therefore, must have the material presented to him at the moment which is psychologically appropriate in steps which are small. Small steps provide for the elimination of gaps in the teaching process. All learning must be highly motivated.

5. *Special types of training can make a person more intelligent.*

FALSE

This point of view is strongly adhered to by some persons. It has not been shown, however, that training does make the individual any more intelligent. It may be true that the child or the individual, after training, may appear more intelligent but it is likely that what has happened is that the individual has more nearly reached his full potentials. Basically, the growth of intelligence is not the result of training. If it is possible through training to make a mentally deficient child anywhere near normal, then it ought to be possible to make a normal child a genius. One must differentiate between an act which is performed as the result of training and an act which is performed because of the individual's basic intelligence. Either the potentials for high intelligence are there or they are absent. In the mentally retarded they are absent.

6. *Childhood schizophrenia (a mental illness) may be mistaken for mental deficiency.*

TRUE

It has been but a few years that it has been widely recognized that young children could become mentally ill. Such mental illness may be mistaken for severe mental deficiency. A study of the growth curves together with the use of highly specialized techniques by the examining team should enable the diagnosticians to differentiate between incompetence due to lack of normal development and disturbed mental function.

7. *Placement in a state institution is the worst thing a parent can do for a child.*

FALSE

It is grossly unfair, in many instances, to the child, the family and the community to take this point of view. Sometimes it is the best thing that can be done. The child finds in a state residential school a world to his liking and one in which he can compete on more nearly equal terms and find happiness.[16]

16 L. N. Yepsen, *Facts and Fancies About Mental Deficiency* (Trenton, New Jersey: Department of Institutions and Agencies, State of New Jersey, 1954).

PHYSICALLY HANDICAPPED CHILDREN

A person's physique is an important factor in the formation of body image and in the development of the concept of the self. If the physique varies markedly from the norm, with an attendant sensory or motor inadequacy, such deviation will influence to a considerable degree the form of the self-image. The way in which the individual integrates this emerging concept of self with all the other significant variables in his life will determine the harmoniousness or disharmoniousness of his adjustment. It should be kept in mind that even a serious physical disability does not necessarily result in a distorted personality.

The Crippled

The psychological effects of orthopedic disabilities are not clear-cut and direct. Instead they are determined to a considerable extent by the interpersonal relationships which the handicapped person has experienced. In other words, the *attitudes* of his family and of the other significant persons in his environment exert great influence on the behavior reactions of the individual to a physical handicap. The attitudes of these important persons in his environment will be, in turn, largely a reflection of the attitudes of the cultural groups to which they belong.

The attitudes of the public toward those who are physically disabled have been investigated to some extent. The results of these studies indicate that verbalized attitudes toward disabled persons tend to be mildly favorable, but an appreciable minority is openly negative. Deeper unverbalized attitudes are more frequently hostile.

Occasionally a marked physical handicap excites ridicule. Children can be ruthless in dealing with one of their kind who is a variant. There are many examples in literature of the suffering experienced by children because of persecution by those of their own age group for some very noticeable physical defect. An excellent example is found in Somerset Maugham's *Of Human Bondage*. The boy Philip has a clubfoot.

Philip saw a boy running past and tried to catch him, but his limp gave him no chance; and the runners, taking their opportunity, made straight for the ground he covered. Then one of them had the brilliant idea of imitating Philip's clumsy run. Other boys saw it and began to laugh; then they all copied the first; and they ran round Philip, limping grotesquely, screaming in their treble voices with shrill amusement, and choked with helpless merriment. One of them tripped Philip up and he fell, heavily as he always fell, and cut his knee. They laughed all the louder when he got up. A boy pushed him from behind, and he would have fallen again if another had not caught him. The game was forgotten in the entertainment of Philip's deformity. One of them invented an odd, rolling limp that struck the rest as supremely ridiculous, and several of the boys lay down on the ground and rolled about in laughter; Philip was completely scared. . . .

At night when they went up to bed and were undressing, the boy who was called Singer came out of his cubicle and put his head in Philip's. "I say, let's look at your foot," he said.

"No," answered Philip.

He jumped into bed quickly.

"Don't say no to me," said Singer. "Come on, Mason."

The boy in the next cubicle was looking round the corner, and at the words he slipped in. They made for Philip and tried to tear the bedclothes off him, but he held them tightly.

"Why can't you leave me alone?" he cried.

Singer seized a brush and with the back of it beat Philip's hands clenched on the blanket. Philip cried out.

"Why don't you show us your foot quietly?"

"I won't."

In desperation Philip clenched his fist and hit the boy who tormented him, but he was at a disadvantage, and the boy seized his arm. He began to turn it.

"Oh, don't, don't," said Philip. "You'll break my arm."

"Stop still then and put out your foot."

Philip gave a sob and a gasp. The boy gave the arm another wrench. The pain was unendurable.

"All right. I'll do it," said Philip.

He put out his foot. Singer still kept his hand on Philip's wrist. He looked curiously at the deformity.

"Isn't it beastly?" said Mason. . . .[17]

[17] S. Maugham, *Of Human Bondage* (New York: Doubleday & Company, Inc., 1915), pp. 40–43.

The Family   The emotional climate in the family is, as has been said many times in this book, very important in the personality development of any child. Because of the special dependence of the crippled child on parental love and protection, his relationship with his parents and siblings is even more important than it is for the normal child. The mother's reaction to the child's handicap, her attitude, and her efforts to help and assist will profoundly affect the quality of the child's character and personality. In many instances the parents are reluctant to admit that the child does have a handicap. This reluctance to accept the situation is often accompanied by self-blame or blame for the child. Eventually these attitudes may lead to rejection, the child having become a threat to the parents' need for self-enhancement.

Overprotection is a parental attitude that is probably more common than rejection. The parents, very much aware of the child's limitations and of his greater need for affection and security, are oversolicitous and display excessive anxiety in their desire to make compensation to the child for his defects. Through overprotection they may actually harm the child by frustrating his need for independence. They may even retard the child's attempts to develop his emotional and physical resources.

The basic principles of mental hygiene which were discussed earlier apply to the relationship between crippled children and their parents in much the same way as they apply to the relationship between normal children and their parents. Neither rejection nor overprotection is desirable. It is important that the parents accept the child as he is and help him to learn how to live with his physical handicap. There is much that he can do in spite of his limitations. Care should be taken, of course, not to exert pressure upon him to overcompensate for his defects. It does not follow that because he must necessarily have low goals in certain areas he should have abnormally high goals in others. As with normal children, he should be encouraged to strive for reasonable success in those activities in which he is most proficient.

Attitudes Toward Self   The attitudes of disabled children toward their handicap and toward themselves not only vary widely but also are not closely correlated with the degree of disability. In other words, there is no uniform set of perceptions which disabled persons of a given culture have of their handicaps. As was pointed out earlier, their attitudes are influenced by the larger social situation. Each physically handicapped child is an individual case with his own specific emotional needs, innate equipment, and experiential background. If he has had normal parental love, if he, along with his physical handicap, has been accepted by the significant persons in his environment, then the chances are excellent that he has learned to accept his disability and has worked out satisfactory ways of adjusting to it. On the other hand, if he has not had this fortunate environment, if he has been rejected or overprotected, his perception of his self will probably be highly colored by resentment or self-pity with accompanying personality distortions. Whether or not a physical disability becomes an important factor in the development of behavior disorders depends almost wholly on one's attitude toward it.

Impaired Hearing

Although there is some disagreement concerning definition of terms in differentiating the groups who have impaired hearing, the term *deaf* is usually limited to those in whom the auditory sense is nonfunctional. The *hard of hearing* are those whose auditory sense is more or less defective but still partially functional. There are no exact statistics available on the incidence of impaired hearing. However, it is estimated that there are about 100,000 deaf-mutes in the United States. The estimates as to the number of those who are hard of hearing range from one and a half million to fifteen million. This wide range is the result, of course, of the variety of criteria used in setting limits.

Attitudes Toward Those with Impaired Hearing   Persons who are deaf or hard of hearing are somewhat more likely to be disliked than are those who are crippled or blind. This is probably due in part at least to the fact that those who have impaired hearing appear to be like everyone else. Therefore, their behavior in a social situation is more irritating because it is difficult for both the group and the handicapped person to accept the situation. Persons with normal hearing often assume that those with impaired hearing are inferior, because the deaf and those who are hard of hearing ask many questions and have difficulty in understanding what has been said.

As with all children, parental influence is an important factor in determining the attitudes of the deaf child toward his handicap and toward his self. As with crippled children, parents of deaf children frequently resort to rejection or overprotection. Obviously it is desirable—even essential—that parents help their deaf child in every way possible to accept his handicap and adjust to it.

Impaired hearing is not in itself emotionally crippling. The important factor in personality development is what the handicapped person himself thinks about his situation, and what he thinks and feels concerning his deficiency is largely a reflection of what others think. Since the attitudes toward the deaf on the part of those who have normal hearing are somewhat negative, it is not surprising to find that deaf persons are somewhat more unstable emotionally than those who are not deaf. Barker[18] has summarized the results of experimental investigations on the personalities and degree of adjustment of persons with impaired hearing. In this summary, he states that children with impaired hearing are "more poorly adjusted, more unstable emotionally, and more neurotic than children with normal hearing." Some of his other conclusions are:

> Deaf children appear to behave more rigidly than physically normal children on tests of level of aspiration and restructuring by classification.
>
> Children with impaired hearing tend to have more fears than children with normal hearing.
>
> Data regarding wishes suggest that the desire to hear and speak better is directly expressed less frequently than desires for other satisfactions. There is some evidence, however, that on unconscious levels the desire to communicate effectively is strong and sometimes assumes the character of an autonomous need.
>
> Better adjustment tends to be associated with intelligence, full use of residual hearing via amplified sound, and with the presence of other deaf members in the family.

Earnest Elmo Calkins, who was internationally famous as an advertising agency executive, became partially deaf at the age of six—presumably, he says, as an aftermath to measles. There was a steady increase in the loss of hearing, and eventually he became completely

18 R. G. Barker, *Adjustment to Physical Handicap and Illness: A Survey of the Social Psychology of Physique and Disability* (New York: Social Science Research Council, 1953), pp. 233–34.

deaf. He writes of the period immediately following his sixth year as follows:

> A sort of mist seems to veil the next three or four years. The reason for the mist was that the Boy was growing deafer. School seemed more futile because he heard less of it. The world-old conflict between heredity and environment was henceforth to be influenced by a new element whose effect could not be foreseen. Deafness introduced complications that required new adjustments, like deuces wild in a poker game. . . . He was at least ten years old before his condition was realized, even by himself. His fits of abstraction and oblivion were laid to inattention by the higher powers, both at home and abroad.
>
> He supposed that all the world was a little deaf, that hearing was the reward of special exertion, the result of "paying attention" on which the teacher harped so often, and that he was for some reason incapable of paying enough attention. He sat in a seat near the front, as much in recognition of his well-deserved reputation for mischief as of his auditory shortcomings. There he heard what the teacher said, but seldom the responses of the class, for he was not allowed to turn around in his seat, so recitations took on the one-sided character of an overheard telephone conversation.[19]

Emphasizing the same point that has been stressed in these pages, Calkins says:

> To begin with the first lesson and the hardest, it is imperative to admit that one is deaf—admit it to one's self and tell the world, and accept the penalties, as well as the compensations. The compensations outweigh the penalties, as you will see. Deafness of the kind known as hard of hearing—and how hard it is!—grades from a defect scarcely noticeable to total eclipse of sound from the outer world. Somewhere along that line one must give up the struggle of trying to pass as a normal hearing person. Most of us wait too long, buoyed up by the same false pride that makes people wear wigs . . . the deafened are happiest once they renounce the innocent pose of hearing and proceed to accept all the drawbacks, but also all the benefits of being deaf.[20]

[19] E. E. Calkins, *And Hearing Not—*(New York: Charles Scribner's Sons, 1946), pp. 67–68.
[20] *Ibid.*, p. 308.

Diagnosis and understanding of the many types and degrees of deafness is difficult at best, but the child (or adult) who appears to be deaf but who seems to have absolutely no physical basis for deafness is indeed a puzzle for clinicians and teachers. Some cases fall within the neuroses fitting the description of conversion reaction or malingering. However, both these syndromes are associated with primary and secondary gains. What of the cases which fit none of the known categories?

A new body of literature points to an increasing interest in the possibility of early temporary sensory deprivation interfering with normal development and causing deviant behavior in later years. Eisen[21] says the child who "has had hearing difficulties early in life, during those crucial stages in which one learns to listen to the speech of others, to pay attention, to respond with speech and to develop relationships with others, may never learn to do these things in a normal or adequate manner. . . . In school he may have difficulty learning to read. . . . Speech . . . may not become the easy basis for interpersonal relationships that it is for most people. If this is the case, we would expect the more complex and integrated aspects of behavior dependent on normal relationships—social behavior, emotional responsiveness—to develop in [an] atypical fashion."

Eisen makes it clear that several factors must interact before this type of deafness is brought to the attention of the psychologist.

A. PREDISPOSING FACTORS

1. Biological

   a. Infection or other disease leading to hearing loss during crucial stages of preverbal and early verbal development. This clears up at a later stage.

2. Psychological

   a. A family background leading to faulty personality development—at least a lowered tolerance for stress or competition.

   b. Familial reaction to the hearing difficulty so as to intensify the lowered stress tolerance.

[21] Nathaniel Herman Eisen, "Some Effects of Early Sensory Deprivation on Later Behavior: The Quondam Hard-of-Hearing Child," *Journal of Abnormal and Social Psychology*, LXV, No. 5, 338–42.

B. PRECIPITATING FACTORS

In most instances, the stresses and strains of adjustment to school peers and other social factors that the child encounters as he leaves the more sheltered environment of the home.

This and other reports like it may prove very helpful for many cases. However, considerably more research needs to be done on this subject.

Blindness

The incidence of blindness in the United States has not been accurately determined. One of the reasons why reliable statistics are unavailable is that there is little agreement on a definition of blindness. If a central visual acuity of 20-200 is taken as a criterion, then approximately a quarter of a million persons in this country are blind. A person with this amount of vision can read large type (more than fourteen points). If the criterion is "light perception only," the incidence would probably drop to around 130,000.

The attitude of the general public toward the blind is much more favorable than it is toward the deaf. Blindness is a handicap immediately obvious to all who see. The public attitude is reflected in federal and state laws. Blind persons, for instance, are granted special deductions in computing their income taxes. In many states they are given exemption from poll and even from property taxes. Reduced postage rates are provided for reading and writing materials used by the blind. Welfare organizations for the blind are numerous and well financed. Evidently, blindness excites sympathy in others. This sympathy, however, may be resented by the blind person himself.

The attitudes of the blind toward themselves vary widely and are largely reflections of the attitudes of the significant persons in their environments. Since frequently within the family there is either overt or covert rejection, blind persons are somewhat more maladjusted than seeing persons. Moreover, with so many of the usual channels of both perception and behavioral expression closed to them, blind persons have a marked tendency to turn inward a great many of their aggressive impulses. However, even though blind persons are somewhat more maladjusted than seeing persons, it is a very significant fact that severely impaired vision is not associated with severe behavior disorders in the great majority of persons.

Marginal Cases

Is it easier to be totally blind than it is to be partially blind? Is it easier to be completely deaf than it is to be hard of hearing? Is it easier to be obviously crippled than it is to have a minor disability? Although there is very little evidence on such questions as these, probably an unambiguous handicap is more readily accepted and adjusted to than is a marginal situation. The person who can see a little or hear a little is expected by others to see more and to hear more than he is capable of seeing or hearing. This places him in a situation where he has to try to play two roles: one, that of a handicapped person; the other, that of a normal person. This is disturbing and unhealthy.

The problem of marginality exists in many areas. An idiot or an imbecile probably finds life easier than does a person with borderline intelligence. An adolescent girl may be much more embarrassed by an unsightly birthmark than she would be by a leg crippled by polio. A young man may be more concerned over poor muscular coordination than he would be about an obvious physical handicap which could be accepted. A professional man may find it more difficult to adjust to poor muscular control of the eyes with accompanying extreme sensitivity to light than he would to actual blindness.

Where the handicap is extremely clear and sharply defined there is a tendency for the individual and his associates to accept it and to realize that certain goals and certain forms of behavior are inaccessible. Where the barrier is cloudy and uncertain there is a tendency for the individual and his associates either to ignore it or to try to do so. The goals and behavior patterns of more normal persons are still considered to be accessible. Resulting frustrations are difficult to tolerate and may lead to severe behavior disorders.

SUMMARY

Intellectual deviates frequently experience difficulty in satisfying their needs in a society dominated by those who are at or near the norm in mentality. The basic needs which are most likely to be frustrated are security and status. Highly gifted children are likely to be rejected by average children and frequently even by members of their own family. Human beings tend to envy, distrust, and dislike those who are intellectually superior. Mentally retarded children, also, are likely to find that they are unacceptable to those of normal mentality. They are frequently ridiculed or pitied, and neither pity nor ridicule satisfies one's need for status. Gifted children, because they have more resources to draw upon, are more likely than feeble-minded children to work out satisfactory adjustments in later years. Physically handicapped persons have special adjustments to make. If their handicap is accepted by the significant persons in their environment and by themselves, then they are no more subject to behavior disorders than those who are not so handicapped. If, however, acceptance is not achieved, then the physical impairment becomes an important predisposing factor in the development of emotional disturbances. Individuals with marginal handicaps are especially in need of a clear understanding of their limitations as well as of the activities which are comfortably accessible to them.

NEUROTIC
ADJUSTMENTS

A man complains of pain in the region of his heart. He visits a doctor and the physician tells him that he finds no organic cause of the pain. A soldier about to go into battle suddenly finds that he has lost control of his right arm. It hangs limply at his side. He has not been physically injured in any way, yet his arm is, in effect, paralyzed. Is it possible that psychological factors can so affect bodily functions?

A person who seems to be normal faints at the sight of blood. Another becomes almost frantic with fear when he finds himself in an elevator or in a very small room. Another cannot walk across a bridge or look out of a ten-story window. What causes them to be afraid in situations which typical individuals do not find fear-producing?

A woman mails a letter and feels compelled to return to the box three or four times to be certain that the letter has dropped inside. Another woman feels forced to pick up a pin whenever and wherever she sees one. Another is driven to wash her hands dozens of times every day. What lies in back of such irrational behavior? Could they not behave more normally if they wished?

Behavior patterns such as those just mentioned are usually neurotic adjustments. Such adjustments are more serious and less frequent than minor emotional maladjustments and less serious and more frequent than psychotic adjustments. Like the minor emotional maladjustments, they represent ways of dealing with frustrations and conflicts and the anxiety which has resulted from those frustrations and conflicts. A person resorts to neurotic behavior, then, in order to reduce anxiety, but at the same time he has done little or nothing toward eliminating inner conflicts that produced the anxiety in the first place. Thus, as Mowrer points out, the neurotic adjustment

> . . . is at one and the same time both self-perpetuating and self-defeating. It is self-perpetuating because it is reinforced by the satisfaction provided through the resulting anxiety reduction; and it is self-destructive in that it prevents the individual from experiencing the full force of his anxiety and being modified by it in such a direction as to eliminate the occasion for the anxiety.[1]

In the discussion of anxiety in Chapter Seven it was pointed out that neurotic anxiety involves repression. Consequently, a person who utilizes neurotic adjustments in an effort to reduce his anxiety does so without any clear understanding of the relationship between his basic emotional conflicts and the behavior that is merely symptomatic of those conflicts. He clings to his phobias, his compulsions, or his physical difficulties because they provide him, to a greater or lesser extent, with an escape from the intolerable tension which accompanies neurotic anxiety.

Neurotic adjustments, like normal adjustments, are learned. The results of many experiments with both humans and lower animals support this statement. For example, Masserman[2] trained a cat to manipulate an electric device which flashed a light, rang a bell, and deposited food in the food box. After a period of several months during which the cat thoroughly learned this means of obtaining food, the animal was subjected to an air blast across its mouth or a shock through its paws as it was about to eat the food it had earned. In response to the shock the cat dropped the food, retreated from the food box, and became hesitant about manipulat-

---

[1] O. H. Mowrer, *Learning Theory and Personality Dynamics* (New York: The Ronald Press Company, 1950), p. 535. Copyright 1950 by The Ronald Press Company.

[2] J. H. Masserman, "Experimental Neuroses," *Scientific American*, 182, No. 3 (March 1950), 38–43.

ing the electric device again or even approaching the food box. When it did try once more, it was allowed to eat several times before it was shocked again. "After from two to seven repetitions in as many days of such conflict-inducing experiences, the animal began to develop aberrant patterns of conduct so markedly like those in human neuroses that the two may be described in the same terms."

In his extensive experiments with cats Masserman found that those which had learned to be neurotic as a result of disruptive frustrations exhibited many of the physiological manifestations, such as rapid heartbeat, high blood pressure, and trembling, that are found in humans experiencing neurotic anxiety. They were easily startled and responded with fear to such stimuli as air currents, caged mice, and even food itself. Many developed reactions comparable to hysteria in humans. Many resorted to compulsive behavior. "In short," says Masserman, "the animals displayed the same stereotypes of anxiety, phobias, hypersensitivity, regression, and psychosomatic dysfunctions observed in human patients. The neurotic patterns of behavior continued indefinitely unless the animal was treated by special therapeutic techniques."

Before a description of some of the more frequent neurotic reactions is given, it is well to take a brief look at some of the ways in which they differ from more severe behavior disorders. First, there is no relevant organic pathology present. Neurotic behavior is psychologically caused, although it may eventually result in organic pathology or may be associated with it. Second, there is no severe disorganization of personality, such as is found in psychotic reactions. The person remains relatively well integrated. Usually he is not in need of the care and restraints of a mental hospital. Third, there is no marked distortion of external reality. A neurotic person's perception of his environment is characteristically within the normal range. For example, he does not have hallucinations or delusions. Fourth, there are no deep and lasting disturbances of affect. He may at times be depressed, but the depression is not accompanied by such psychotic characteristics as severe agitation or stupor. Fifth, his intellectual potentialities remain unaffected, although the neurotic condition, especially in the case of diffuse anxiety, may for a time inhibit to a considerable extent the use of those potentialities.

CLASSIFICATION

Any classification of neurotic reactions must necessarily be more or less arbitrary since so much overlapping of symptoms occurs that it is usually difficult to label with a specific term a pattern of neurotic adjustments. A neurosis is not a disease entity; it is a behavior disorder—a response to the frustrations and conflicts which the individual is experiencing or has experienced. There is some practical value in classifying these responses or reactions or adjustments if we keep it constantly in mind that the categories are flexible.

In the following classification, familiar psychiatric terms are used:

Anxiety reaction.
Dissociative reaction.
Conversion reaction (hysteria).
Phobic reaction.
Obsessive-compulsive reaction.
Depressive reaction.

Each of the above will now be considered briefly. Conversion reaction or hysteria will be emphasized somewhat more than the others, since a conversion reaction is a clear manifestation of the close relationship between psychological and somatic factors.

ANXIETY REACTION

In an anxiety reaction, the anxiety is diffuse or free-floating. It has not been channeled into relatively definite outlets as is the case with other neurotic reactions, such as phobias. It is characterized by extreme and generalized apprehension, by indecision, by a feeling of helplessness, and by resentment. The individual fears the future with all its responsibilities and dangers. This dread of the future casts a heavy shadow over all the person's activities and frequently engulfs him in an anxiety attack.

The anxious individual is always uncertain. He is fearful of making mistakes. He experiences difficulty in reaching definite decisions. He prefers making no decision at all to making a wrong one.

He is very sensitive to failure, especially to moral failure. When he has brought himself to the point of acting, he is likely to regret what he has done. Even harmless acts may precipitate anxiety attacks.

The overly anxious personality is characterized by a feeling of helplessness. He does not know which way to turn. He is sure that anything he attempts will result in failure. He is dependent on others, but he does not like to be dependent, so resentment wells up within him. This resentment eventually results in aggression toward others or toward the self. The person with an anxiety neurosis is likely to strike out in anger against those upon whom he is dependent, but he rarely has the courage to carry through. How does he dare to speak in this way to those who provide him with the only security which he has? Then there is the quick reversal to aggression against the self—to marked self-condemnation.

DISSOCIATIVE REACTION

Dissociative reactions have so caught the popular fancy that there is a widespread belief that this form of neurotic behavior is very frequent. Actually it is quite rare. The three dissociative reactions of psychogenic origin are amnesia, fugue, and multiple personality. The central feature of each of these disorders is a loss of personal identity.

In amnesia the individual forgets temporarily all those experiences which are associated with the kind of self which he wishes to forget. Much of his learning is obviously retained. For example, he still continues to speak the language which he knows. He may remain in a state of amnesia for just a few minutes, for hours, or for days. If the loss of identity continues for a long period of time, it is called a fugue. He may live in a state of fugue for several years.

Amnesia or fugue represents a neurotic escape from an intolerable situation. Although the onset is characteristically sudden, there is nearly always in the background a history of neurotic anxiety growing out of severe conflicts. This neurotic anxiety becomes unmanageable as a result of a crisis in the individual's personal life or as the result of an overwhelming external situation. Loss of identity is then utilized as a solution. Most persons have experienced the desire to get away, to "take off," to forget the past and start all over again. The neurotic person who resorts to amnesia experiences this desire as a compelling wish and, when pushed far enough, succumbs to it.

Occasionally dissociation appears in the very extreme and very rare form known as multiple personality. In multiple personality, loss of the original personal identity is replaced by two or more new self-systems which apparently function independently. Multiple personality is developed basically in the same way that amnesias and fugues develop. There is a need to escape from the conflicts of the past and from the threat of the present; the emphasis in the development of multiple personalities is probably on the conflicts of the past. In counseling sessions, the author has frequently heard individuals who were functioning well within the normal range make the statement that they did not know what their real selves were; that they were acting out a part. Evidently the person who has developed a full-fledged multiple personality has made a complete escape from his real self and has developed the two or more parts which he once consciously played into actual separate self-concepts.

CONVERSION REACTION OR HYSTERIA

In the following discussion, the terms *conversion reaction* and *hysteria* are used interchangeably. They mean the same thing, hysteria being the older term. Occasional references will be made in this section to the disorders which are sometimes classified as psychophysiologic rather than as neurotic reactions. Because of the difficulty in distinguishing between conversion reactions and other physical manifestations of tension, the best criterion for deciding whether or not a physical reaction is neurotic is to ask the questions: Do the physical manifestations fulfill a neurotic purpose? Do they represent a conversion of conflict, this conversion bringing some relief from anxiety?

Hippocrates described hysteria in *De Virginibus*. He considered it to be a physical affliction limited to women and believed that it was caused by a wandering uterus. Although Hippocrates did not speak specifically of sexual causation in hysteria, he did recommend marriage as treatment. Galen did not accept the thesis that hysteria was caused by a wandering uterus, but he believed that it was as-

sociated with that organ. He recommended stimulation of the clit-
oris and the neck of the uterus as treatment. Evidently Galen, like
Hippocrates, had a vague idea that sex and hysteria were somehow
associated.

During the Middle Ages, persons suffering from hysteria were
treated as heretics, for their behavior was supposed to be the direct
result of their sins. The sufferers were presumed to be possessed of
devils, and exorcism was frequently used in an attempt to drive the
evil spirits from their bodies.

Late in the 19th century, new approaches to hysteria were made
—first by Charcot and later by Janet and Freud. Charcot believed
that hysteria was a disease entity. He maintained that one of the
major characteristics was cutaneous anesthesia. He observed three
characteristics of these anesthesias: first, they were rarely noticed by
the patient; second, they never caused the patient any hardship;
third, they followed the patient's concept of anatomy. Later it was
demonstrated by Babinski that the manifestations of the presumed
cutaneous anesthesia resulted from suggestions unwittingly given by
the physician. Charcot recommended rest and isolation as the method
of treatment.

Janet, a student of Charcot's, rejected most of Charcot's conclusions. Janet believed that hysteria began with exhaustion, which
in turn brought on depression which caused a retraction of the field
of consciousness, which in turn limited the patient's ability to carry
on complex mental operations. This inability to perform complex
tasks resulted in dissociation. In other words, Janet believed that hysteria was a failure to maintain integration of the personality. The
most significant fact in Janet's theory of hysteria is his belief that
the physical manifestations of the disorder were mental in origin. It
was the mental processes, not the physical complaints, which were
basic.

Freud's approach to the study of hysteria was very different. He
maintained not only that the symptoms had a psychic cause but
also that the origin of the symptoms was hidden from the patients
and that the reason for the patient's inability to recall the causes
was that the memories were unpleasant and associated with guilt
feelings. The patient could not forget but instead repressed these unpleasant memories into the unconscious. Some outlet, however, was
necessary, so an indirect one was used in the form of bodily com-

plaints. This is why Freud used the term "conversion hysteria." Early in his career Freud used hypnosis as a method of treatment, but later he turned to free association.

For a rather long period of time following Charcot, Janet, and the early work of Freud, relatively little advance was made in the understanding of hysteria and related disorders. During the last two or three decades, however, there has been considerable progress. Karen Horney emphasized the cultural factor in the development of hysteria and the other neuroses. She stressed anxiety and hostility, such as grow out of cultural conflicts, as important causes of neurotic behavior. The anxiety of which Horney speaks is a feeling of helplessness experienced by the individual in the face of a hostile world.

Hysteria, then, is a behavior disorder in which psychological conflicts are converted into physical symptoms. It represents a learned reaction to frustration. The physical symptoms resorted to are manifold, and vary considerably in intensity. They can be grouped under three main headings: (1) physical disorders without any observable pathological condition of the organ or organs involved; (2) exaggeration of actual organic symptoms; (3) organic pathology resulting from psychological tension.

It is a well-known fact that we react physically to psychological stimuli. If a man suddenly came face-to-face with a tiger, his fear reaction would be automatic and instantaneous. His autonomic nervous system would immediately take over in an attempt to meet the emergency situation. His blood pressure would rise, his rate of heartbeat would increase, his digestive processes would stop, and he would stand rooted to the spot, poised for fight or for flight, depending on which seemed the better alternative. The tiger has not touched him, but the sight of the tiger has resulted in definite physical reactions.

Another man is walking down the street, relaxed and comfortable. He is a veteran who saw service with the Third Army in France and Germany. Suddenly he becomes extremely tense. His blood pressure rises, his heart begins to beat fast, his digestive processes cease, and he breaks out into a cold sweat. He does not know what has caused this sudden physical reaction. It may be that the man walking on the other side of the street had some mannerism or facial characteristic that reminded him, though not consciously, of an officer under whom he had fought. He was afraid of the officer, and he was afraid of going into battle. Now all the old fear is instantly aroused through a process of redintegration by the sight of a man across the street.

A student is asked to speak for fifteen minutes before a large class. No one has done anything to him physically, yet the fear of appearing before that class results in definite physical reactions not unlike those experienced by the man facing the tiger. If this student has a hysteric personality, he may find that his stomach aches. There is no pathological condition present, yet it really does ache and may continue to pain him for hours afterward.

A child of six is asked to take his first pill. The psychological conflict is clear-cut. On the one hand, he wishes to please his mother; on the other hand, he is fearful of swallowing the unknown substance. The psychological conflict has a direct effect upon the musculature which controls swallowing. Try as he will, he cannot get the pill down. There is nothing organically wrong with the boy's throat. Physical tension resulting from psychological factors merely makes it impossible for certain of his organs to carry out their normal functions. Give the boy a piece of candy, and the difficulty immediately disappears. The altered psychological condition makes it possible for him to swallow without difficulty.

It is obvious from the foregoing examples and from experiences common to every individual that bodily functions can be inhibited or otherwise affected by psychological stimuli.

Conversion reactions are frequently superimposed upon a relatively slight pathological condition of the organ involved. Thus, an individual who has an actual eye defect, for example, converts his emotional difficulties into physical symptoms based on the organic handicap. If he has a minor heart disorder, he may build an hysterical superstructure on this foundation. The hysteric individual is eager that his escape mechanism shall appear reasonable to his fellows. By combining his hysterical reaction with an actual physical difficulty, he is more likely to meet this need and to avoid criticism.

It is often difficult to discover in such instances the relative potency of psychological and physical factors. The doctor is likely to concentrate solely on the physical basis, and the psychologist on the psychological basis. In such cases the two should work together in an attempt to evaluate adequately the factors involved.

Psychological tension frequently causes an actual organic pathology. This tension is usually a predisposing cause rather than a precipitating cause of pathological conditions. For example, stomach ulcers are directly caused by the presence of acid digestive juices acting upon a stomach whose muscles have been inactivated. This condition results from the interaction of the hypothalamus and the cerebral cortex which have been stimulated by persistent and intense fear or anger experiences. Thus fear and anger, psychological in origin, carry in their wake a whole train of physiological effects which eventually, in this instance, result in stomach ulcers.

A similar situation exists with respect to functional heart disorders. When an individual is emotionally calm his heart normally pumps three and one half quarts of blood each minute through the arteries. Under emotional stress, such as fear or anger, the heart responds to the emergency by pumping from five to six quarts per minute into the arteries. If the intense emotional state continues for a long period of time, with the accompanying excessive demands on the heart, that organ may eventually show the results of the strain.

Examples of Symptomatic Manifestations

Anxious individuals who resort to conversion reactions or psychophysiologic disorders utilize a rather large number of outlets, a few examples of which will be discussed briefly. All these are responses to needs and to tension. They are considered neurotic only if they meet the criteria mentioned earlier in this chapter.

Motor Disorders   Motor symptoms of the muscles which are under voluntary control are frequent in hysteria. Perhaps the most common of these is tremor or shaking. Sometimes the individual trembles all over, but more often just the lips or the hands are affected. Tics are also fairly common. A tic is a spasmodic twitching of a small group of muscles, usually in the face.

Another motor manifestation of hysteria is paralysis, usually of the arms or legs. A limb becomes useless and so makes it possible for the individual to escape from what is to him an impossible situation. If the condition remains for a long period of time, the bodily tissue may be affected.

The so-called occupational neuroses are usually motor symptoms of hysteria. The stenographer finds that her fingers will no longer respond to the demands made upon them in typing; the machinist is no longer adept with his hands; the singer has difficulty in controlling his vocal cords; the writer develops writer's cramp. A change in occupation and a readjustment of goals is often all that is needed to eliminate the muscular disturbance.

Hysterical Seizures   An hysterical seizure or convulsion is a generalized muscular disturbance which, in many respects, simulates epilepsy. The individual falls and may become unconscious. Although he may throw himself around, he does not bite his tongue, as usually happens in epilepsy, and he is nearly always careful not to injure himself. The seizure is usually experienced when others are present, the person seeming to obtain satisfaction from the attention which he receives because of his behavior.

Anesthesia   In anesthesia there is a partial or total loss of sensation. It is interesting to note that in anesthesia the loss of sensation appears in a functional unit rather than according to the anatomical distribution of sensory nerves. Anesthesias appear most frequently in the hands, wrists, forearms, feet, and legs. Anesthesia represents a wish fulfillment; the individual does not want to feel. The condition can be brought about by suggestion, as in hypnosis.

Visual and Auditory Manifestations   It is a fundamental principle that whenever possible we concentrate on that which interests us most. Through concentration we are able to shut off that which is irrelevant or noninteresting. We see what we wish to see, and we hear what we wish to hear. If two novelists, one an idealist and one a realist, were living in the same community and writing about the people around them, their books, though equally good and perhaps equally true, would contain sharply variant character studies of individuals in that community. Each writer would, to a considerable extent, present what he expected and wished to see and hear.

In hysterical visual and auditory disorders there is merely a more extensive blocking-off of things that are not to be seen or heard. In hysterical blindness, for example, the individual see little, if at all, even though the eyes and the optic nerves are normal. Hysterical blindness is occasionally caused by a traumatic visual experience which so shocks the individual that he no longer dares use his eyes for fear of what he may see.

Visual and auditory illusions and hallucinations are occasionally associated with hysteria and frequently with the functional psychoses. Illusions are always based on certain elements in a given experience, but the interpretation is erroneous. Hallucinations are perceptions which have no basis in the facts of a given experience. A little child may lie awake during the night before Christmas and experience the auditory illusion, or perhaps even hallucination, that he hears Santa's sleigh bells. The auditory perception represents a deep-seated wish. An adult may hear voices telling him that he is Napoleon, or God. In this instance also the auditory hallucination represents a deep-seated wish. In the little child, such faulty perceptions are normal. In the adult, they are manifestations of mental derangement.

Speech   A frequent conversion reaction is difficulty in swallowing and poor control of the tongue. Even though the person is hungry he has difficulty in "getting his food down" and at times, when he is eating, he bites his tongue. Speech is a form of motor expression which depends to a considerable extent upon the proper functioning of the mouth and tongue. Speech defects constitute one of the most common of the motor manifestations of hysteria.

It is estimated that from one to two per cent of the total population in the United States are stutterers. In a few cases the disorder is the result of physical abnormalities. In the majority it is a manifestation of hysteria. The individual, eager to say the right thing but fearful that he will say the wrong thing, sets up inhibitions which interfere with the normal functioning of the speech organs. In such individuals the stuttering is merely a manifestation of tension resulting from conflicts. Treatment of the manifestation will do little good. It is necessary to deal directly with the psychological factors which have caused the tension.

Respiratory Disorders   When an individual is in a state of emotional excitement he may note that he breathes very rapidly or that he experiences some difficulty in breathing at all. Occasionally hysteria manifests itself through a contraction of the bronchial muscles. If this muscle spasm is extreme, asthma results. Asthma is not always caused by emotional tension. In many instances it has a definite organic basis. Frequently the organic and the emotional work together, the psychological factors intensifying the asthmatic attack.

Visceral Difficulties   Visceral disorders are one of the most frequent, perhaps the most frequent, manifestations of anxiety. These disorders are varied, ranging from a slightly uncomfortable feeling of distension to swellings or even growths. Comment has already been made on the speed with which the digestive system responds to a strong emotion. An individual who is in a constant state of resentment or anxiety may have a perpetual stomach-ache. From this, as was stated earlier, peptic ulcers may develop. Colitis is another manifestation of emotional strain. The condition may take one of two forms: spastic or atonic. In spastic colitis the colon becomes very tense, thus inhibiting bowel movements. In atonic colitis the colon is completely relaxed, making control of bowel movements difficult. Atonic colitis is occasionally accompanied by lack of control of the sphincter muscles.

Nausea is often present in the anxious individual. Although the malfunctioning of the digestive system is the immediate cause of the nausea, the real causes may be psychological factors. A certain student, for example, came to the writer with the complaint that he had felt nauseated for several weeks. He found it difficult to walk across the campus or down the street because any unclean object which he saw precipitated waves of nausea. Food had the same effect upon him, and he experienced great difficulty in eating. A study of the case brought out strong homosexual urges and marked masochistic desires. The boy was caught in an attraction-revulsion conflict, and the conflict was manifesting itself through nausea.

Causation

A conversion reaction, like all other functional disorders, represents learned behavior. It is inherited only in the sense that the individual was endowed with a bodily constitution which was susceptible to hysterical or other psychoneurotic reactions.

In the histories of hysterical individuals there will always be found considerable frustration of one or more of the four major needs. The hysteric personality is usually in great need of status. His desire in this respect is so strong that it can rarely, if ever, be satisfied. Consequently he is being continually frustrated. The tension which results from his frustration and conflict forces him to find a way of escape.

The steps in the development of hysteria conform to the learning sequence presented in Chapter Two. The individual finds himself in a difficult, perhaps intolerable, situation from which he wishes to escape. He is at the trial-and-error stage and is ready to try any procedure. Illness presents itself as a possibility. In this connection he may recall previous pleasant experiences associated with illness. Perhaps as a child he succeeded only when ill in obtaining the attention and understanding which he craved from his family. He may step directly, as a result of this suggestion, into an hysterical reaction, or he may wait until he experiences some minor accident or illness. While in this state of indecision he may actually desire to be injured in an accident in order that he may have an excuse to retreat from reality. Many accidents are actually wish fulfillments.

Having temporarily escaped from a difficult situation through injury or illness, he does not wish to get well, for that would make it necessary for him to return to his previous status with all the tensions that it involved. Having much to gain by remaining ill, he remains ill. As time goes on he exaggerates his symptoms. He is actually experiencing pain, but the physical discomfort is much easier to bear than the emotional strain which he experienced when he was attempting the carry the responsibilities of a healthy individual. He is not malingering. The distinction between hysteria and malingering is this: in hysteria the motivation is wholly or almost wholly unconscious; in malingering, it is conscious. In hysteria the individual succeeds in deceiving himself. In malingering no self-deception is involved—the individual is trying to deceive others.

If the person has been rewarded through resorting to hysteria, it is difficult to persuade him to adopt more adequate adjustment mechanisms. He wished to escape from the tension of an active life; hysteria provided him with that escape. He was eager for attention and sympathy; hysteria provided him with that attention and sympathy. Why should he give up the means by which he has obtained what he wanted most?

The Hysteric Personality

The hysteric personality is characterized by extroversion, egocentrism, suggestibility, sensitivity to criticism, ambition, emotional immaturity, and need for praise. Being essentially an extrovert, he enjoys people and would like to express himself freely; but, being tense, he usually cannot do so. Therein lies one of his frustrations. He is self-centered, though not in an introverted sense. He is not so interested in liking people as he is in making people like him. He tends to refer everything to himself and to interpret all social experiences in terms of his own personality.

Eager to please, the egocentric person is suggestible. His strong drive to make people like him causes him to be rather naïve in his responses to what they say. It is this suggestibility which makes it relatively easy for him to believe that he is really ill. Possessing great need for status, especially social status, it is not surprising to find that the hysteric individual is very sensitive to criticism. Even minor criticism makes him irritable and resentful and intensifies the physical symptoms of his hysteria. He is ambitious—usually extremely ambitious—but lacks either the ability or self-discipline, or both, to achieve the high goals that he has set. He is usually not interested in achievement for its own sake, but rather for the status that accompanies success. He desires praise and adulation, but he expects to purchase it cheaply. He is an emotionally immature individual who has never grown to sufficient stature to accept adult responsibilities with equanimity.

PHOBIC REACTION

A phobia is an intense fear reaction to a specific situation or object. Even though the person realizes that no actual danger exists, he is, nevertheless, afraid. He usually experiences the fear only when in the specific situation or when he sees the specific object. At times, however, a phobia is associated with an obsession. In such instances the person responds to the obsessive thoughts as he would to the actual situation.

No one is wholly without fear. Probably most people have specific fears. Such specific fears become a matter of concern only when they are so intense as to interfere with the person's normal activities and to affect his mental health.

The list of phobias is a long one. The most common types are the following:

Acrophobia, fear of high places.
Agoraphobia, fear of open places.

Algophobia, fear of pain.

Claustrophobia, fear of closed places.

Hematophobia, fear of the sight of blood.

Hydrophobia, fear of water.

Mysophobia, fear of contamination.

Nyctophobia, fear of darkness.

Photophobia, fear of strong light.

Toxophobia, fear of being poisoned.

Zoophobia, fear of animals.

There are three principal causes of phobias. (1) a traumatic fear experience which in most instances has been forgotten; (2) a conditioned response to a fear-producing situation usually experienced during early childhood; (3) the projection or symbol of a general fear or of a conflict. In nearly all cases the real cause of the phobia is either unknown to the sufferer or so repressed by him that he cannot recall it.

Reference has already been made to selective forgetting. We tend to inhibit recall of unpleasant experiences, or of thoughts or fears which we have had that are not socially approved. Repression frequently results in distorted expression. It is probably true that many phobias are the distorted expression of thoughts or experiences associated with a feeling of guilt. For example, a man came to the author with the complaint that he was afraid of hands. He was very religious but found it difficult to sit through a church service because of his emotional reaction to his minister's hands. In the course of the interviews it was eventually learned that during adolescence the man had experienced a marked feeling of guilt concerning sex habits. He had repressed to a considerable extent the memory of what he considered to be abnormal sex behavior. At the time, he had been greatly disturbed emotionally because his acts did not conform with his religious ideals. As time passed, hands became the symbol of the conflicts which he had had. It was significant that his minister's hands caused him more distress than the hands of any other person, for the minister represented religion.

Although phobias which have persisted for a long period of time are highly resistant to therapy, they are often reduced in intensity or even eliminated when the causes are thoroughly understood.

If the individual is generally fearful and manifests considerable emotional rigidity, the chances of eliminating the phobia are slight. The situation is often made very complex by the association of phobias with obsessions, compulsions, anxieties, and other neurotic symptoms.

OBSESSIVE-COMPULSIVE REACTION

An obsession is the persistent recurrence of unwelcome and disturbing thoughts. Even though the individual realizes that these thoughts are irrelevant if not actually abnormal, he is, nevertheless, unable to rid himself of them. Obsessions in minor degree are common to the experience of everyone. They manifest themselves in indecision, in difficulty in concentrating, in absent-mindedness, and, at times, in sleeplessness. An obsession becomes a serious problem when the possessor, realizing its strength, tries unsuccessfully to rid himself if it and, having failed, feels dominated by it.

Individuals who suffer from obsessions are usually persons who are convinced of their own worthlessness. They have lost their self-respect. The fact that they cannot throw off obsessive thoughts intensifies their lack of self-confidence and their belief in their own weakness. Persons so afflicted are usually perfectionists—the religious individual who desires to lead an ideal life and yet is tormented by persistent thoughts which he knows to be evil; the mother who earnestly wants always to do the right thing for her children and yet is obsessed by thoughts of injuring them, the uncertain adolescent with inflexible moral standards who cannot tolerate lapses in himself or in others and yet is deeply disturbed by obsessive ideas not in accord with his principles.

In crisis situations the individual with obsessions reacts in two principal ways. Hostility is likely to come first, followed quickly by self-degradation. Expecting hostility from others, he is overready to strike the first blow. However, since he is convinced of his inability to handle the situation, he is likely to crumple when the blow is returned. He expects to be humiliated, and he is.

Compulsive acts are forms of behavior which the person feels compelled to carry out in spite of the fact that they are unreasonable, or even criminal Minor compulsions are harmless and appear frequently in the behavior of well-adjusted individuals. Included among these would be such experiences as checking the alarm clock three or four times to be sure that it has been wound, or returning to be sure that the door has been locked, or following a ritualistic sequence of positions in bed before going to sleep. Such patterns of behavior are unnecessary. The person knows that the alarm clock has been wound or that the door has been locked, but he feels uncomfortable unless he acts upon the compulsion.

In more serious compulsions the doubt is not eliminated by one or two repetitions. The individual feels forced to return to his house again and again to be certain that his door is locked, or he develops an elaborate ritual which he must follow in detail. Perhaps the most common of the compulsive acts is handwashing. This may be a manifestation of a deep-seated fear of disease, or it may be a symbolic attempt to wash away a feeling of guilt. The most famous literary example of the latter appears in Shakespeare's *Macbeth.* Lady Macbeth gives expression to her feeling of guilt by trying to cleanse her hands of imaginary blood spots in her sleep.

Enter *Lady Macbeth,* with a taper.

> *Gentlewoman:* Lo you! here she comes. This is her very guise; and, upon my life, fast asleep. Observe her; stand close.
>
> *Doctor:* How came she by that light?
>
> *Gentlewoman:* Why it stood by her: she has light by her continually; 'tis her command.
>
> *Doctor:* You see, her eyes are open.
>
> *Gentlewoman:* Ay, but their sense is shut.
>
> *Doctor:* What is it she does now? Look, how she rubs her hands.
>
> *Gentlewoman:* It is an accustomed action with her, to seem thus washing her hands. I have known her to continue in this a quarter of an hour.
>
> *Lady Macbeth:* Yet here's a spot.
>
> *Doctor:* Hark! she speaks. I will set down what comes from her, to satisfy my remembrance the more strongly.
>
> *Lady Macbeth:* Out, damned spot! out, I say!—One; two; why, when 'tis time to do't.—Hell is murky!—Fie, my lord, fie! a soldier, and afeard? What need we fear who knows it, when none can call our power to account?—Yet who would have thought the old man to have had so much blood in him.
>
> *Doctor:* Do you mark that?

Lady Macbeth: The Thane of Fife had a wife: where is she now?—
What, will these hands ne'er be clean?—No more o' that, my lord, no
more o' that: you mar all with this starting.

Doctor: Go to, go to; you have known what you should not.

Gentlewoman: She has spoke what she should not, I am sure of that:
Heaven knows what she has known.

Lady Macbeth: Here's the smell of the blood still: all the perfumes of
Arabia will not sweeten this little hand. Oh! oh! oh!

Doctor: What a sigh is there! The heart is sorely charged.

There is a group of compulsions, some of them of a criminal
type and all of them very disturbing to the individual unless carried out, that are called the manias. Included among these are
coprolalia, the impulse to utter obscene words, with which Samuel
Johnson was afflicted; kleptomania, an irresistible impulse to steal;
pyromania, an urge to set fires; and, most serious of all, homicidal
mania, a compulsion to kill.

An individual suffering from kleptomania does not steal because
he needs the articles which he takes. He does so, in part, in order to
compensate for his feeling of helplessness. The thefts provide him
with a temporary sense of power. This desire of an essentially weak
person for power is also a causal factor in pyromania and in homicidal mania.

In compulsive disorders, as in all other behavior disorders, it
does little or no good to treat the symptoms. It is necessary to discover the individual's basic frustrations and conflicts and to attempt
to reduce them. A person who suffers from serious compulsions is
usually a fearful, repressed individual who feels impelled at times
to assert himself.

Obsessive-compulsive reactions appear occasionally during childhood. The following is a brief case description of a ten-year-old
boy who was referred to the author for psychotherapy.

Larry had several compulsive forms of behavior. While working on arithmetic problems he was compelled to fill in very carefully
all numbers which had closed loops or circles, that is, 0, 6, 8, and 9.
It is significant that he was accelerated one year in school, even
though his intelligence was at the low normal level. Whenever he
turned in papers in the classroom, he felt forced to return to the
teacher's desk and tap the papers at least once. There were also

compulsive behavior patterns at home. When getting dressed in the morning he had to put on his shoes three times. He could never go downstairs without going back up and down again. Certain objects in his room had to be lined up in perfect order.

Larry had many anxieties that were only partially relieved by his neurotic escape. He was afraid to be alone in his room, especially at night. He was very concerned about dying and at times was sure that someone would break into the house and take him away and kill him. Much of the time he was just anxious without knowing what he was anxious about.

In the course of the interviews, Larry began to talk more and more about his severely retarded sister, who was three years younger than he. In the past he had wanted her to play with him, but she was incapable of doing so. His mother had tried to explain the situation to him, but he failed to understand. At times, after his parents had retired, he would get up, take his sister from her bed, and try to force her to play games. Occasionally, he hurt her unintentionally causing her to cry out. Once the mother heard the cries and punished the boy, who not only felt guilty but also was sure that he had inflicted serious harm on the little girl.

Eventually the parents decided to have their daughter institutionalized. Larry was overwhelmed by the decision, largely because he was convinced that he was to blame for her present condition. After a few months at the state institution, the girl died. Larry was sure that she had been killed and at the same time was not certain that she had died at all. This doubt was intensified when his parents refused to let him go to the funeral.

The boy's guilt-laden associations with his retarded sister were the principal causes of his anxiety and of the obsessive-compulsive reactions that represented an attempt to escape from that anxiety. When his experiences, many of which had been repressed, were fully expressed and understood, Larry began to improve.

DEPRESSIVE REACTION

For practical purpoes, a neurotic depressive reaction can be considered as being about halfway between normal discouragement and grief and psychotic depression. The behavior resorted to by normal persons who have experienced a deep personal loss is well known, since it has been rather frequently observed in one's self and in others. For example, the death of a loved one is usually responded to by weeping, restlessness, sleeplessness, recurring denial of the facts, and a feeling of hopelessness concerning the future. However, in normal grief and depression, the passage of time with the new interests it brings lessens the despair. Life is worth living once more. At the other extreme is psychotic depression which will be described in some detail in the next chapter. Some of the symptoms of this extreme depressive reaction are delusions, hallucinations, extreme feelings of guilt, strong suicidal desires, and marked retardation of the thought processes.

A neurotic depressive reaction would be viewed by an objective observer as excessive. However, from the point of view of the sufferer it is not, because characteristically he blames himself for the loss and this self-reproach adds greatly to his grief. This consciousness of guilt so intensifies his anxiety that he is forced to relieve it, at least in part, through extreme self-criticism and relatively long-continued depression. In other words, the depression fulfills a neurotic purpose.

The following is an example of the kind of situation which could result in normal grief, in a neurotic depressive reaction, or could even be the precipitating cause of a psychotic depressive reaction.

A young couple had been married for about a year when the husband died of poisoning from canned food he had eaten at home. In such a circumstance his widow might have experienced normal grief, but she was convinced that she was to blame for his death. She had prepared the dinner. She reproached herself for using canned food. Since she had used it, had she been careless in checking its freshness? Such thoughts intensified her grief to the point where she had to find a partial escape through a rather long-continued period of depression.

SUMMARY

Neurotic reactions are ways of dealing with persistent anxiety. They are purposive adjustments that have been learned. Although they are not disease entities, there is some value in classifying them on the basis of the salient behavioral characteristics manifested. An anxiety reaction or adjustment is diffuse; it has not been channeled into a relatively specific behavioral pattern. It has sometimes been called free-floating in that it attaches itself to almost all the person's present activities and to his future expectations. A dissociative reaction is a form of running away from one's self as in amnesia or, much more rarely, in the development of a multiple personality. In a conversion reaction, the individual achieves a partial escape from his anxiety through the development of functional physical symptoms. A phobic reaction represents a displacement of anxiety from the experience or experiences which caused it to a relatively specific fear. Obsessions and compulsions are grouped together under the heading obsessive-compulsive reaction since an obsession is really a compulsive return of disturbing thoughts. In compulsive behavior the individual is compelled to carry through with certain acts even though he himself realizes how unreasonable or even antisocial they are. A depressive reaction, and the name implies, involves a rather long period of depression accompanied by extreme self-criticism.

Neurotic adjustments are amenable to treatment, although the period of therapy is often a long one. Often the neurotic behavior is so rewarding that there is no felt need present to change to more constructive adjustment mechanisms.

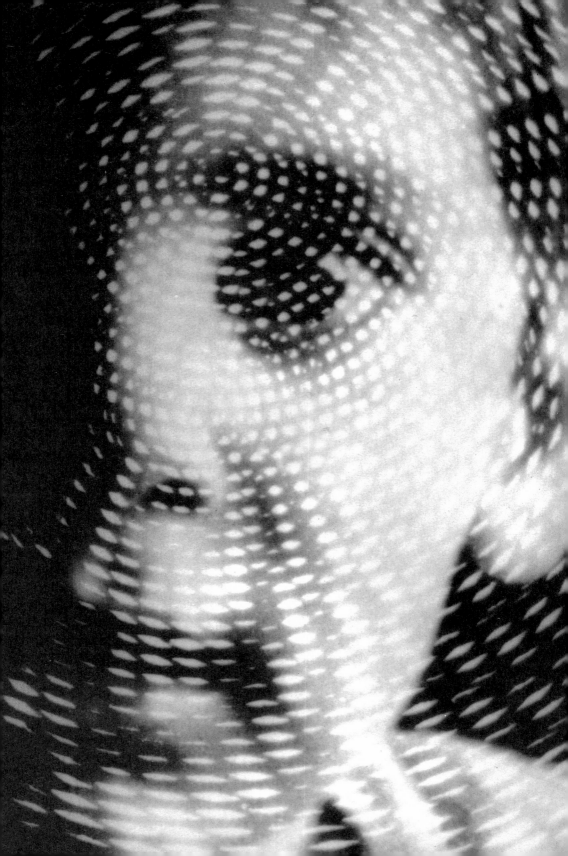

PSYCHOTIC ADJUSTMENTS

chapter 14

A detailed study of the psychoses is not justified in a book on mental hygiene. Brief consideration of these serious behavior disorders, however, is valuable in that it provides the student with a point of reference which is useful in evaluating the more normal adjustments. A student who is beginning his study of mental hygiene and psychopathology frequently makes the mistake of interpreting minor maladjustments as symptoms of insanity. He can achieve a much better perspective if he is familiar with the salient characteristics of psychotic behavior.

CLASSIFICATION

The psychoses are customarily classified into two main groups, the organic and the functional. In an organic psychosis, a pathologic condition of the body can be demonstrated as a significant cause. The central nervous system is the part of the organism most likely to be affected, as in cerebral tumor. Discussion of the organic psychoses does not come within the scope of this book.

The functional psychoses have no observable physical basis. They are generally considered to be learned behavior patterns.

Objection to the term *functional* has been frequent because it suggests a mind-body dichotomy. All learning has a physical basis, although, as was pointed out earlier, it is not known exactly what that physical basis is. In an organic psychosis, observable organic defects are present which can be shown to be an important cause, perhaps the sole cause, of the impaired behavior. In a functional psychosis, no such organic defects can be found.

In this chapter, as in the preceding one, the usual psychiatric nomenclature will be followed. There are four groups of psychotic disorders that are psychogenic in origin. These, together with their principal subgroups, are.

Schizophrenic reactions
    Simple type
    Hebephrenic type
    Catatonic type
    Paranoid type

Affective reactions
    Manic-depressive reactions
      Manic type
      Depressed type
      Other

Paranoid reactions
    Paranoia
    Paranoid state

Involutional psychotic reaction

SCHIZOPHRENIC REACTIONS

The psychotic reactions known as *schizophrenia* account for slightly more than one fifth of the annual admissions to mental hospitals in the United States and for slightly more than one half of all the patients in mental hospitals at the present time. Year after year, these figures remain about the same. Schizophrenia leads all the psychoses, functional and organic, in frequency.

At first glance, there may appear to be an inconsistency in the reference to the *one fifth* of first admissions and the *one half* of resident patients. The first figure results from a longitudinal view of the situation; the second, from a cross-sectional view. Many patients entering a mental hospital remain for a relatively brief period of time. They either get well, as is the case with many suffering from manic-depressive reactions, or die, as is the case with many suffering from organic psychoses. Schizophrenia, on the other hand, frequently develops rather early in life and continues for a long period of time. Consequently, the duration of hospital residence of schizophrenic patients is characteristically longer than that for any other group. About one third of them remain for at least fifteen years, and a few for as long as forty-five years or more.

What is this behavior disorder which is so serious and so widespread that approximately one fourth of all the hospital beds in the United States are occupied by persons suffering from it? The confusion concerning the exact nature of schizophrenic reactions is reflected in the difficulty that has been experienced in selecting a truly definitive name. In 1883 Kraepelin designated the disorder as *dementia praecox*. He used this term because he believed that the disorder began during adolescence and that it was always characterized by a progressive behavioral deterioration. This term came into disrepute when it was discovered that this form of psychotic behavior was not limited to youth but appeared in adult years as well. Moreover, later studies uncovered the fact that mental deterioration does not necessarily accompany the disorder. In view of the inappropriateness of the term *dementia praecox,* Bleuler recommended that *schizophrenia* be substituted for it. Schizophrenia means literally *splitting of the mind.* This term is also misleading, since to the general public *splitting of the mind* means a split personality similar to the amnesia and multiple personality discussed in the preceding chapter. Actually the *splitting* means in this case a marked separation of the self from reality.

Retreat from or lack of interest in reality, together with disorganization of personality, constitutes the core characteristics of schizophrenic reactions. White says "the feature that best distinguishes schizophrenia from the other psychoses, and is at the same time common to the several subgroups, is a peculiar attitude toward reality, *a lack of interest in adjustment to reality . . . his interest in adjusting to reality has become secondary to other interests.*"[1]

[1] Robert W. White, *The Abnormal Personality* (New York: The Ronald Press Company, 1948), pp. 527–28.

Cameron and Magaret say "schizophrenic disorders are syndromes of disorganization and desocialization, in which delusions and hallucinations are prominent and in which behavior is dominated or determined by private fantasy."[2]

For purposes of diagnosis—and presumably, also, for treatment —schizophrenic reactions are subdivided into the several types listed earlier in this chapter. These subdivisions are made rather arbitrarily on the basis of the salient characteristics of the disorder. The four major types will now be discussed briefly.

Simple Type

The distinguishing characteristic of a simple schizophrenic reaction is an attitude of indifference or, in advanced stages, of extreme apathy. The disorder usually develops very gradually. It manifests itself first in a decreased interest in the normal activities of life. At the outset, this decreased interest may be slight; the adolescent may, for example, prefer solitude to the athletic, social, or intellectual pursuits of his age group. He finds that by withdrawing he escapes from the tensions which are present when he attempts to participate in the life around him. The effort which has to be exerted for such participation is too much for him. What is the use? It is more comfortable not to try. It is much easier to obtain his satisfaction through daydreaming.

As time passes, he gives more and more time to this daydreaming and less and less to the demands of his environment. Eventually he sinks into an apathetic state, from which he may be aroused only with great difficulty. He really does not care at all now. There is nothing to wish for, nothing to fight for. He has escaped from realities that were too difficult for him.

Persons who develop simple schizophrenic reactions are introverted individuals who are timid, nonsuggestible, and relatively unemotional When attacked they will retreat instead of fighting back. They have no confidence in their ability to hold their own with aggressive persons. Besides, why bother? It is not worth the effort.

This kind of person is not susceptible to suggestion because suggestion usually implies trying something that is new, and he is fear-

2 Norman Cameron and Ann Magaret, *Behavior Pathology* (Boston: Houghton Mifflin Company, 1951), p. 494.

ful of facing the unknown. Eventually the feeling of fear disappears, and he becomes wholly uninterested in attempting anything that is different.

It is not possible to say whether the individual who develops simple schizophrenia was originally highly emotional or not. Probably there was always some emotional insufficiency present and this lack became more pronounced as the disorder developed. Simple schizophrenia frequently remains unidentified until it has reached an advanced stage of development, largely because the individual suffering from the disorder usually manifests no marked peculiarities in behavior, and almost never experiences delusions or hallucinations. On the contrary, a child with schizoid trends is frequently praised for his shyness, for the fact that he keeps out of the way. He rarely causes any trouble. He is often the classroom teacher's idea of a model child.

Hebephrenic Type

A hebephrenic schizophrenic reaction comes much closer than the simple type to the layman's conception of insanity. The disorder is characterized by silly behavior, including smiling and laughter which appear seemingly without cause, by hallucinations, by disorganized delusions, and usually by progressive deterioration. This behavior develops gradually, frequently beginning in adolescence.

Hebephrenia represents withdrawal in an extreme form. The hebephrenic patient is no longer interested in the world around him. He lives almost completely within himself. The emotional outbursts, such as weeping or laughing, to which he is subject, result not from external stimuli but from stimuli from within the imaginary world in which he lives.

A large number of bizarre hallucinations are found among hebephrenic patients. They frequently hear voices; at times these voices tell them pleasant things, but more frequently revile them. Auditory hallucinations in hebephrenia are often literally the voice of conscience. Persons suffering from hebephrenia frequently feel that foreign objects are inside of them. One college girl was sure that little moles were running about inside her head. Another thought that little devils were playing discordant music on violin strings strung from her hips to her shoulders.

The delusions found in hebephrenia are neither logical nor

persistent. Occasional feelings of grandeur may appear, but they never attain the strength of those found in paranoid schizophrenia. Mild delusions of persecution are also sometimes present.

In hebephrenic schizophrenia there is always a considerable amount of personal disintegration which involves regression to childish behavior. At times the regression is so extreme that the person behaves in many ways like an infant. After such regression has taken place, nothing can be done for him. He continues to exist on the infant level in the strange world which he has created.

Catatonic Type

Students visiting a mental hospital are usually very much interested in observing the patients who sit or lie immovable in some strange position, or who engage in such senseless and repetitive behavior as walking endlessly up and down the ward, so many steps in one direction and so many steps in the other, or repeating the same phrase over and over. These are the persons who are suffering from a catatonic reaction.

Catatonic schizophrenia is characterized by extreme fluctuations in emotional behavior—between stuporous depression and wild excitement. During his periods of stupor, the patient may lie without moving for days or weeks, or, in some instances, even longer. Even though he is conscious, he takes no part in the activities which go on around him. At times this state is characterized by waxy flexibility, the individual remaining in any position in which he is put. On the other hand, he may respond negativistically to any interference.

The periods of wild excitement to which the catatonic patient is subject nearly always result from the inner struggles of the individual rather than from environmental stimuli. During such periods the individual may shout, throw himself around, attack another, or attempt suicide. The violence of the catatonic patient is unbridled.

Catatonia develops from severe conflicts and repressions. The phrases which the patient so often repeats again and again and which seem so senseless to the listener are actually never senseless in the light of the patient's conflicts and repressions. The stereotyped physical activity is also undoubtedly symbolic of the conflicts which the individual has experienced or is experiencing.

Catatonic patients frequently experience hallucinations—often of a paranoid type involving ideas of grandeur and of persecution. Sometimes echolalia and echopraxia are also present. *Echolalia* is the automatic repetition of words said by another; *echopraxia* is mimicry or imitation of what others do.

Indications of developing catatonia are seen in the very repressed, introvertive individual who at times appears extremely sullen or sits motionless in his room for long periods of time. He is of unstable temperament, breaking out into fits of uncontrolled anger. Any type of conflict may be a source of this functional psychosis. Sex frustrations and feelings of guilt concerning sex desires or sex behavior are frequent.

Paranoid Type

The principal characteristics of a paranoid schizophrenic reaction are delusions of persecution and of grandeur. The disorder develops rather slowly and is likely to appear somewhat later in life than the other schizophrenic reactions.

The individual who develops paranoid schizophrenia is usually a very ambitious person who sets unobtainable goals and then blames others for his failure to achieve them. Frustrated in his abnormal need for achievement and status, he adjusts by convincing himself that others are trying to keep him from succeeding. Suspicions of others gradually grow into ideas of reference, and ideas of reference, in turn, become delusions of persecution. No person can afford to be wholly naïve. He must necessarily entertain some distrust of the motives of others. The paranoid personality carries this defense to extremes. He distrusts everyone, especially those who are closest to him—such as members of his family—and distrusts them so deeply that he is sure they have designs against him. At times he may believe that they wish to destroy him, so he destroys them first in order to save himself.

Early in the development of the disorder, the paranoid individual usually feels unworthy. Ths may be the result of his failure to achieve on a high level, or it may grow out of guilt feelings over sex desires or sex behavior. Homosexuality usually appears in the history of paranoid patients. This feeling of inferiority is uncomfortable for the individual, and, as time passes, he escapes from it to a considerable extent by blaming others, as has already been shown, and by convincing himself of his own great importance.

Occasional withdrawal and occasional periods of excitability occur in paranoid schizophrenia. The patient may develop the fear that he will be poisoned and so refuse to eat; or he may avoid the company of others because he is certain that he will be attacked. He usually experiences hallucinations of the auditory type, and often of other types as well. Deterioration of personality, including regression, may take place, although this is not so likely to happen in paranoid schizophrenia as in the other kinds of schizophrenic reactions.

Causation

There are many questions concerning the causes of schizophrenic reactions which as yet have not been fully answered. Are the reactions caused by hidden lesions or by malfunctioning of one or more of the endocrine glands? Are they inherited? Are they related to body build? Are there predisposing constitutional factors? Are environmental factors fundamental causes? Are frustrations of personal needs the principal source of behavior disorders? Are they learned?

The claim that schizophrenia is inherited is based almost wholly on the fact that the disorder tends to run in families, a number of studies having definitely established the importance of family line. For example, Kallmann traced the family histories of 1,087 schizophrenics who were admitted to the Herzberge Hospital in Berlin between 1893 and 1902. The members of the several families included the mates and parents of the schizophrenic patients, 3,384 direct descendants, 3,920 nephews and nieces, and 3,920 siblings and half-siblings. Garrison, in a discussion of Kallmann's studies, presents a number of conclusions, the most significant of which follow:

> In families where one parent had schizophrenia, 16.4 per cent of the children developed schizophrenia. This is in contrast to a sample taken from the general population which showed that 0.85 per cent of the population developed schizophrenia. . . .
>
> When both parents were schizophrenics, 68.1 per cent of their offspring developed schizophrenia, which is about 80 times normal expectancy. . . .

Schizophrenia occurred about five times more frequently among grandchildren and nephews and nieces of schizophrenics than it does among the general population. . . .

Although 10 per cent of the parents of the schizophrenic patients had schizophrenia, only 15 per cent of the patients' brothers and sisters developed the disease. Therefore, 85 per cent of the siblings shared some part of a very similar early home environment of the schizophrenic patients without themselves succumbing to the disease.

The general meaning of the genetic explanation of schizophrenia is that a true schizophrenic psychosis cannot be developed under usual life conditions unless a particular predisposition has been inherited. Whether or not a psychosis occurs when the innate predisposition is present depends on the intricate interactions of varying genetic and environmental influences. . . .[3]

Demonstration of the fact that schizophrenia runs in families does not, of course, prove that it is inherited. It would be as logical to argue that because a boy born of French parents could speak French, the language that he used had been genetically transmitted. However, it may be that a predisposition to develop serious behavior disorders is transmitted through the genes as is the capacity for speech. It is significant that in the Kallmann studies there was only 85.5 per cent relationship rather than a 100 per cent relationship with respect to schizophrenia in identical twins. If schizophrenia itself, rather than merely the predisposition, is inherited, then its emergence in one identical twin would always be accompanied by its emergence in the other identical twin, for identical twins have identical heredity.

There is definitely a possibility that the predisposition is inherited. Every individual has his breaking point, but the threshold of resistance is relatively low for some. In a specific case it is usually very difficult to determine just what constitutional factors may be involved. Malfunctioning of the adrenal cortex may be a significant causal factor in schizophrenia, but is certainly not the sole cause. Hoagland reports the following results in a study in which normal persons and mental patients were contrasted in both physiological and psychological stress situations:

[3] Mortimer Garrison, Jr., "The Genetics of Schizophrenia," *Journal of Abnormal and Social Psychology*, XLII (1947), 123–24.

Among normal individuals we find that, within limits, the greater the stress the greater the hormonal output; and we have been able to correlate measurements of the degree of fatigue in the pursuitmeter test with adrenal-cortex secretions. Patients suffering from psychoneuroses . . . generally exhibited adrenal responses similar to those of normal persons, although often in a somewhat exaggerated form.

The schizophrenic group showed a striking inability to respond to these tests with enhanced steroid output as measured by our blood and urinary indexes, despite the fact that their hours of rest was little different from that of the general population. A schizophrenic does not have an underproductive adrenal cortex, as does the sufferer from Addison's disease, but the organ is generally unresponsive to stress and cannot change its activity with changing situational demands.

What then do these findings mean in terms of schizophrenia? They certainly do not imply that adrenal stress-response failure is the one and only "cause" of the psychoses, although it is probably one of the important factors involved.[4]

Kety in a review and evaluation of current theories and research used in support of the biochemical hypothesis points out that research is difficult because of the large margin of error. Diagnosis and evaluation of progress are hazardous, partly because there is not a common etiology underlying the many forms of schizophrenia. However, some recent findings may hopefully shed light on these problems.

The hypothesis that a disordered amino acid metabolism is a fundamental component of some forms of schizophrenia remains an attractive though fairly general one.

The theory which relates the pathogenesis of schizophrenia to faulty metabolism of epinephrine is imaginative, ingenious, and plausible. It postulates that the symptoms of the disease are caused by the action of abnormal, hallucinogenic derivatives of epinephrine. . . . . By including the concept of an enzymatic, possibly genetic, defect with another factor, epinephrine release, which may be activated by stressful life situations, it encompasses the evidence for

---

4 Hudson Hoagland, "Schizophrenia and Stress," *Scientific American*, CLXXXI (July 1949), 46.

sociological as well as constitutional factors in the etiology of the schizophrenia.[5]

The presence of lesions in cerebral tissue has sometimes been advanced as the principal cause of schizophrenic reactions, despite the fact that there is no experimental evidence to support this point of view. White says:

> The course and character of schizophrenia is hardly consistent with gross histopathology, that is with large changes in cerebral tissue, such as come from infection or degeneration . . . whenever it has been possible to compare normal and schizophrenic brains holding constant such factors as age and general health and the nature of the terminal illness it has proved impossible to tell the two brains apart.[6]

In summary, nonpsychological causal factors appear to be relatively unimportant in the development of schizophrenia. The evidence which has been advanced to support histopathology or endocrine pathology is contradictory and very inconclusive. The most that can be said for the part that heredity plays is that the individual may inherit a predisposition. No reputable medical man or psychologist would maintain that there is proof that such a complex pattern of behavior as schizophrenia is directly inherited. It is difficult to say just what is meant by an inherited predisposition. Certainly, as was pointed out earlier, individuals vary widely in their thresholds of resistance to the development of schizophrenic reactions, but even the threshold of resistance is determined only in part by genogenic factors. It is influenced also by the prenatal experiences of the organism, by the birth experience, and by those experiences, especially in infancy and early childhood, which the person cannot recall but which have profoundly influenced his personality.

Learning Schizophrenic Reactions   Within the last few years the evidence in support of the point of view that schizophrenic reactions are learned has steadily accumulated, with the result that at the

[5] Seymour S. Kety, "Biochemical Theories of Schizophrenia," *Science*, CXXIX (1959), 1528–32.

[6] Robert W. White, "Abnormalities of Behavior," *Annual Review of Psychology*, IV (1953), 546–48.

present time this is the most generally accepted causal theory. Persons who become schizophrenic are motivated by the same needs, learn in the same way, and resort to the same adjustment mechanisms as do normal individuals. Their behavior differs only in degree, but it is so extreme that it gives the impression of being different in kind. Case studies of schizophrenic patients indicate clearly the struggle they go through to preserve their selves. This struggle usually begins in infancy or early childhood in response to an overtly or covertly threatening family environment. Anxiety is learned in an atmosphere of continued insecurity, and, in attempts to reduce that anxiety, certain adjustment mechanisms are utilized in extreme forms. Fantasy and withdrawal rate high as avenues of escape. In time these defensive barriers against intolerable realities become so wide and so high that the person who has built them can no longer see around them or over them. He has cut himself off from the real world by his own individual iron curtain. Certainly he feels safer in his private world backstage; it is impossible to know whether or not he feels happier.

Schizophrenic reactions usually develop slowly and gradually. Many authorities believe that the origin can be found in experiences during infancy. Harry Stack Sullivan, for example, maintains that the first year of life is the most important period with respect to the initiation of such disorders. Fromm-Reichmann says:

> Traumatic experiences in . . . [infancy] will damage a person more seriously than those occurring in later childhood such as are found in the history of psychoneurotics. The infant's mind is more vulnerable the younger and less used it has been; further the trauma is a blow to the infant's egocentricity. In addition early traumatic experience shortens the only period in life in which the individual ordinarily enjoys the most security, thus endangering the ability to store up as it were a reasonable supply of assurance and self-reliance for the individual's later struggle through life. Thus is such a child sensitized considerably more towards the frustrations of later life than by later traumatic experience. Hence many experiences in later life which would mean little to a "healthy" person and not much to a psychoneurotic, mean a great deal of pain and suffering to the schizophrenic. His resistance against frustration is easily exhausted.[7]

[7] Frieda Fromm-Reichmann, "Transference Problems in Schizophrenics," *Contemporary Psychopathology*, ed. Silvan S. Tomkins (Cambridge, Mass.: Harvard University Press, 1946), p. 372.

There is considerable question as to whether or not traumatic experiences (emotional shocks) are essential as early causes of later schizophrenic behavior. An accumulation of a large number of frustrations and the threat which accompanies these frustrations is presumably much more significant. Such a series of frustrations may be experienced during the first year of life; they may also be experienced in later childhood or even in adult years, with much the same results. In childhood, as was indicated earlier, the threat is most likely to come from the parents themselves. The child who has found it difficult, if not impossible, to establish a satisfactory relationship with his parents experiences great difficulty later in establishing and maintaining mutually satisfying relationships with other people. Standish, Mann, and Menzer[8] point out that, generally speaking, the patient could turn to neither parent for affection and security because the parent was either too distant and rejecting or too close and threatening. This relationship provokes feelings of anger and bitterness in the child. "Does anyone love me? Is there somebody I can love? Whom shall I be like?" The child never gains an emotional understanding of these questions. In such a situation intense anxiety arises, seemingly in relation to the struggle for self-preservation. "The cumulative effect of lack of love, plus the threat to the child's identity, gives rise to tremendous anxiety, anger, and revengeful, destructive fantasies." These feelings set up a fear of equally destructive retaliation on the part of the seemingly omnipotent parent-figures. Thus the schizophrenic dilemma becomes, "If somebody loves me, will he eventually destroy me? If I love someone, will I eventually destroy him?" These ambivalent feelings influence all the individual's attempts at interpersonal relationships.

There have been a number of studies which support the point of view that the parents, especially the mothers, are potent contributors to the development of schizophrenic reactions. In a study of the mothers of 25 hospitalized schizophrenics, Tietze came to the following conclusions:

All mothers were overanxious and obsessive, all were domineering —ten more overtly and fifteen in a more subtle fashion. All mothers were found to be restrictive with regard to the libidinal gratification of their children. Most of them were perfectionistic and over-

8 Christopher T. Standish, James Mann, and Doris Menzer, "Some Aspects of the Psychopathology of Schizophrenia," *Psychiatry*, XIII (1950), 439–45.

solicitous and more dependent on approval by others than the average mother. Two of them verbally expressed absolute rejection of
the schizophrenic child. Rejection was a conspicuous component in
the relationship of seven otherwise solicitous mothers, and its presence in most other cases can be surmised.

It is the subtly dominating mother who appears to be particularly
dangerous to the child. Her methods of control are subtle and therefore do not provoke open rebellion as undisguised domination may.
The children exposed to this form of subtle domination under the
disguise of maternal love and sacrifice are deprived of any outlet
for their aggressive impulses. All schizophrenic patients who were in
good enough contact with reality and who formed a reasonably
good relationship with their psychiatrist expressed a feeling of rejection by their mothers.[9]

Tietze herself points out that criteria for selecting the mothers,
while making it possible for the study to be carried out, precluded
securing a representative sample of all parents of schizophrenics.
These criteria were. (1) the mothers had to be sufficiently intelligent
to cooperate usefully, and (2) they had to agree to keep appoint-
ments and to live near enough to the hospital for regular visits.

An interesting report by McCord[10] suggests that schizophrenia
has its origin in the familial situation. McCord used material from a
study of delinquency gathered in the childhood of men who later
became psychotic. These men had been delinquents in their youth
and as such had been used in a large study on the causes of delinquency. For the present study their early life data were re-analyzed
for similarities and differences in their life histories which might
shed light on causes of psychosis. The analysis of material revealed
a common history of dominant mothers, fathers absent or passive,
mothers who were overprotective and forced sons into dependence
on her and fathers who were deviant and ineffectual. According to
the study, the course of psychosis is as follows: the child is encouraged, even forced, to become dependent. There is no stable
masculine model. This existence fosters a feeling of inadequacy and
a lack of ability in human interaction. As an adult "such a person is

[9]Trude Tietze, "A Study of Mothers of Schizophrenic Patients," *Psychiatry*,
XII (1949), 64–65.

[10] W. McCord; Judith Porta, and Joan McCord, "The Familial Genesis of
Psychosis," Psychiatry, XXV (1962), 60–71.

forced by the nature of the society, to undergo a series of severe dis-locations. Eventually, by death or other separation, he is deprived of his dominating mother, and he is unlikely to find a satisfying replace-ment for her. He is confronted with a number of situations—dating, marriage, military service, career—for which he is ill-trained. His response in the face of these demands for independence, responsibil-ity, and masculinity is, presumably, a compound of confusion and fear. It would seem only natural, therefore, that such a person would attempt to recapture the dependent relationship, either in actuality or fantasy."

In their review of 79 cases of schizophrenia found in single case reports in the literature, Reichard and Tillman[11] found that the parents could be divided into three clear-cut categories. In all three, one parent was dominant and the other submissive and inadequate. They found no examples of a democratic give-and-take between parents and observed that, while the dominant parent had played the more traumatic role, the weaker parent had contributed to the patient's difficulties through inability to give support. A breakdown of their findings follows:

76 per cent of cases (N—60)—mother dominant; father quiet, in-effectual, withdrawn.

13 per cent (N—10) of these mothers overtly rejecting.

63 per cent (N—50) of these mothers covertly rejecting.

15 per cent of cases (N—12)—fathers overtly rejecting, cruel; mothers dared not defend child against father.

9 per cent of cases (N—7)—no clear pattern.

In the first two categories, the pathogenic agent is the mother, a domineering and aggressive woman married to a quiet and ineffec-tual man whom she despises. Reichard and Tillman divided these women into two groups: those who were overtly rejecting and those who were coverting rejecting.

Category 1. The Overtly Rejecting Mother   This kind of mother was found rather infrequently. Characteristically, she conceived un-willingly and rejected the child from birth on. She was cold and

[11] Suzanne Reichard and Carl Tillman, "Patterns of Parent-Child Relations in Schizophrenia," *Psychiatry,* XIII (1950), 247–57.

sadistically critical, making excessive demands for cleanliness and neatness on the part of the child. She also attempted to force the child to be excessively polite, to observe social forms meticulously, and to fulfill her own unfulfilled ambitions. She destroyed her child's self-confidence by constant nagging, disapproval, and complete non-acceptance of him as a person.

Category 2. The Covertly Rejecting Mother   This kind of mother was as domineering as the overtly rejecting mother, but in a more subtle way. She masked her rejection by overprotection. She reacted to the child not in terms of his welfare but in terms of her own projected needs. The child, however, was not deceived. Unfailingly he recognized the lack of love. Reichard and Tillman found this to be by far the most common pattern of parent-child relationships in the reports of schizophrenic patients which they studied.

Category 3. The Overtly Rejecting Father   Although the role of the overtly rejecting father in the home was that of a sadistic parent, his domination appeared to be a camouflage to cover up his basic weaknesses. In most cases he was actually ineffectual, unsuccessful, and more or less of a failure in life. He was quite dependent on the mother and extremely demanding of her time and attention. He reacted to his children like a jealous sibling, resenting any attention which the mother gave them. The mother in such cases was characteristically passive, dependent, and ineffectual. She clung masochistically to her husband, rarely opposing him or defending their children against him. She frequently resorted to a conversion reaction as an escape from the situation.

An example of the third kind of relationship referred to in the study by Reichard and Tillman is the case of C.S. who came to the author for counseling. In the course of thirty-four interviews the sources of his self-concept and the attendant difficulties gradually came to light. Basic among these was his relationship with his parents. As far back as he could remember C.S.'s father had treated him with contempt, and at times sadistically. In the father's eyes, everything that the boy did was wrong. He was frequently ridiculed, and even more frequently punished. Each mealtime, when the father was present, was an ordeal. C.S. was required to sit beside his father who carried on a running criticism of his table manners. Often when he made a mistake his father would hit him a heavy blow, or, at times, even put his hand on his head and force his face into his food.

This kind of treatment went on for years, with the boy becoming more and more confused and broken. Deep resentment against his father grew with the years, but he was powerless to do anything about it. When he reached adolescence he did make one effort. One day he struck back at his father; as a result he was severely beaten.

The mother could have helped the boy during these years, but she took the attitude that the father was the head of the family, and that anyone who disagreed with him was wrong. She consistently refused to give the boy any support. In this situation he gradually came to the conclusion that it was he who was all wrong—that he was no good. During the early interviews he frequently made the statement, "I am worthless; I am nothing." When C.S. reached high-school and college age, he made a few attempts to establish himself. There was a period during which he did a great deal of stealing, another period when he tried to prove himself through excessive fighting, and then, later, a period when he tried to find security in sexual relations with girls. The satisfactions gained from such activities were, however, temporary. At the time he came to the author, he was on the verge of escaping into a world of fantasy where life would not be so frustrating and chaotic. The following two excerpts from a tape recording of the first interview indicate C.S.'s anxiety and tension and his strong desire to escape.

*P. Would you like to tell me where your thoughts go when you daydream?

*C. In my daydreams I usually think of some place or some way in which I can have more success and recognition. It seems to all boil down to the need for success. The distressing thing is that things alternate so. I resolve that now I'm going to make a change, yet even the changes I recommend to myself—I realize they are not reasonable. I'm so convinced that I want to make it logical. I want to have a consistent program. Therefore I don't want to change. I don't want to come back to being normal, so to speak, so I get these long, extended plans of some kind of work that I could do that would give me some satisfaction.

P. Then you do feel sometimes that you're not quite sure whether you would like to remain as you are, or whether you would like to be wholly normal in your behavior.

* P—Psychologist; C—Client.

C. I want to run away, but I realize personally it would be hard on my wife. It wouldn't work, but sometimes it gets so strong that I want to make it real. I say, "I *will* make a break. Sure it will be difficult for someone for a time"; so I concentrate all my efforts on saying, "This is the real thing," but I realize that I'm only daydreaming, in a way, so I can't take myself seriously even—I can't reason about it. I say, "You're being unreasonable. There's no reason why you should ever be other than this," and yet within twenty-four hours I'll be contemplating evasion, an escape from my present situation.

P. Things are in such an even balance that you can't take action one way or another.

C. Yes. Yes. Of course in my longest stretches of being reasonable I say, "Don't be absurd," and yet when I get into a state of depression, I pursue this daydreaming to such a relentless—such a force to make it a reality—that . . . uh . . . uh . . .

P. Your daydreaming means a great deal to you.

P. Would you like to tell me about some of the things in the present that make you unhappy?

C. I guess this is basic. The idea of being remote—of not being alive, of participating in normal activities with other people. That seems to me to be the most unpleasant. In everything, I do things separately, yet at the same time, while not wanting to be separate I'm not very reasonable. My idea—which is just the opposite—this emotional thinking—I want to be at the top of the heap. I want to be getting all the attention, yet I fail to get that. Even if I should get it I wouldn't want it. It would be very uncomfortable.

P. Then you feel very much alone.

C. Yeah.

P. In your daydreams, are you sometimes on top of the heap?

C. Yeah. There's always a tendency for me to think that I am on top of the heap. I think about how I might run for senator, or be President, or be a great writer. Then after a while I realize how absurd it is. Then I come right back to guilt complexes.

P. Would you like to talk about those for a bit? I know there are some things that are hard to face.

C. Yes, that's true. I can't recall many of them off-hand. The guilt complexes are always there. There's one social guilt complex I have. These world problems—I blame myself for my attitude of indifference.

Treatment and Recovery

Although schizophrenic reactions have been studied for more than a century, knowledge concerning treatment is still limited. In a book on mental hygiene, it would be undesirable to explain in any detail such medical therapies as psychosurgery, insulin shock, and electro-shock. The value of such physical approaches to behavior disorders that have presumably been learned is highly questionable. It will be remembered that the principal characteristic of the behavior of persons suffering from schizophrenia is withdrawal; therefore, it would appear to follow that the principal ingredient of treatment should be relationship. The authors of *Action for Mental Health* point out that, since the time of Hippocrates, the first responsibility of the physician is *"to attend the sick,* to give them confidence and comfort, *and to do* nothing to harm them." The same principle holds for psychotherapists working with psychotic patients. Quoting from *Action for Mental Health* again, "In treating the functional psychoses, we believe that this primary approach is scientifically sound; the available evidence indicates it is possible to double or triple the spontaneous remission rate and achieve improvement or recovery in the majority of cases so approached."[12]

In support of the thesis that the personal relationship between the seriously disturbed individual and his therapist is very important, the authors of *Action for Mental Health* present data from a mimeographed report by Dr. John C. Whitehorn of the Henry Phipps Psychiatric Clinic of Johns Hopkins Hospital. Whitehorn and Betz studied the results of individual psychotherapy for 100 schizophrenic patients who were treated by several psychiatrists. It was noted that some psychiatrists consistently did better than others.

> . . . there was a 75 per cent improvement rate in 48 patients treated by seven doctors (Group A) and a 27 per cent improvement in 52 patients treated by another seven doctors (Group B).
>
> Whereas patients treated by Group A and B doctors did not seem to be different at the beginning of treatment, judged by the usual clinical criteria, the A group's patients showed greater trust in their doctors and communicated their personal problems more freely than did the B patients.

[12] *Action for Mental Health,* Final Report of the Joint Commission on Mental Illness and Health (New York: Basic Books Inc., Publishers, 1961), p. 55.

The investigators turned their attention to other psychiatrists and their patients. Again, choice of therapist loomed as a significant factor in results obtained.

Following up five or more years later, Whitehorn and Betz found that whereas 80 per cent of Group A patients were improved at time of discharge, 77 per cent were improved five years later. Among Group B patients, 31 per cent were improved at discharge and 65 per cent were improved after five years. Some had been discharged unimproved but improved later with or without treatment elsewhere.

The investigators now scrutinized the A and B doctors intensively, not only as to the way they worked with patients but also as to their vocational interests. From the results of this scrutiny they found that they could predict which doctors would do well with schizophrenics and which would not. They noted that, in psychotherapy, Group A doctors expressed their personal attitudes toward the patients' problems rather freely, and set limits on the kind and degree of obnoxious behavior they would permit, but did not seek to interpret or instruct. The Group B doctors, in contrast, were either passively permissive or pointed out, in an instructional style, the patients' mistakes and misunderstanding.[13]

It is clear from the data in the preceding material that a considerable number of schizophrenic patients do recover.

The late nineteenth century medical dictim that schizophrenia is a hopeless, incurable disease requiring the person to be removed from human society for the rest of his life is baseless. The one in five chance for spontaneous recovery without individual treatment refutes the incurable dictum; the fact that an additional two or three out of five patients can improve sufficiently as a result of proper treatment to lead useful lives in the community further refutes it.[14]

It should be noted that the above results are achieved as a "result of proper treatment." If persons suffering from schizophrenia are merely institutionalized and provided with custodial care of an authoritarian kind, the prognosis is not nearly so good. Schizophrenics are human beings. Like normal persons, they respond negatively to punitive treatment and positively to warmth and understanding.

13 *Ibid.*, pp. 36–37.
14 *Ibid.*, p. 52.

When the word "improvement" is used, the question is immediately raised as to what is meant by it. It does not necessarily mean "cured," since the person who has been partially or almost wholly incapacitated by his schizophrenic reaction may have only learned how to live with some of his limitations. The three criteria for improvement, all of them to a considerable extent subjective, are: (1) the therapist's observation that positive changes have taken place; (2) the patient's sincere statement that he feels better; (3) the patient's ability to function socially and occupationally within a normal range. To be sure, psychological scars usually remain, but this is not surprising. The same situation exists with respect to many physical disorders. A person who has had a major operation may never again regain the excellent health which he once had, but he is much better off than he was just before the operation. How do we know? The surgeon observes that he has improved, the patient himself knows that he feels better, and the patient is able to resume social and occupational activities, although these activities may be somewhat limited by the effects of the operation.

Will the psychological disorder return? It may. An odd characteristic of the thinking of the general public with respect to serious behavior disorders such as schizophrenia is that the "disease" must be all or none: that the person must be completely psychotic and incurable or that he must be made, through treatment, completely sane. We do not think in such dichotomous terms with respect to physical disorders; neither should we with respect to behavior disorders. There are varying degrees in both the seriousness of the disturbance and the extent of the recovery.

AFFECTIVE REACTIONS

Psychotic affective reactions are characterized by a marked disturbance of mood so severe that it affects seriously the thought processes and general behavior of the individual. Loss of control of the emotions occurs, often accompanied by a misinterpretation of reality, with attendant hallucinations, or by great exaggeration of relatively isolated facts in reality. Persons suffering from affective reactions differ from those with schizophrenic reactions in some respects, although there is a great deal of overlapping of symptoms.

One important difference is the relationship which the patient maintains with reality. In schizophrenia, retreat from reality is the basic form of adjustment, but in an affective disorder, the reaction—especially in mania—is a fighting one. The individual appears to be desperately trying to do something about the situation. Even in depression there is an element of aggression.

Affective reactions are not nearly so frequent as schizophrenic reactions. The percentage of those entering mental hospitals each year under this classification is at or close to seven; in other words, this kind of psychotic behavior is about one third as frequent as schizophrenic disorders. Patients in this category are much less likely than schizophrenics to remain hospitalized for a long period of time. More than half of them are discharged in good health after a few weeks or a few months in the hospital.

Manic-Depressive Reactions

Normal individuals experience changes in mood. A person may be very happy for a time; everything is going well; all's right with the world. This mood may be followed by a period of slight discouragement; the person feels a little blue; the future looks a bit dark. After a while the pleasant mood returns again. No individual is happy all the time or unhappy all the time. When these feelings are moderately extreme, the person is said to be moody. It is difficult to predict how he is going to behave. He may be a little too elated or a little too depressed. These swings, or cycles, vary widely in intensity, but the differences are probably wholly differences of degree. In extreme form, they characterize the behavior of an individual suffering from a manic-depressive psychosis. When in the manic stage, he may become so extremely elated that he talks very rapidly in incoherent phrases. His physical activity may be so uncontrolled that he will smash the furniture in the room, attack other persons who may be near, or perhaps destroy himself. When in the depressed stage, he may be extremely unresponsive, either failing to answer questions altogether, or waiting for a long time before he replies. He may weep for long periods of time. He may long for death.

It used to be thought that manic-depressive cycles were always characteristic of a manic-depressive psychosis, even though it was granted that a considerable length of time—several years, in some instances—might elapse between the manic stage and the depressive stage. In recent years, however, it has been clearly shown that a person may have one or more manic attacks or one or more depressive attacks without ever experiencing a manic-depressive swing. In other words, some persons experience only a series of elations, others only series of depressions, while still others go through the classical manic-depressive cycle. Clifford Beers, in his book, *A Mind That Found Itself,* describes very effectively his emotions, thought processes, and general behavior in both manic and depressive stages.

Manic-Depressive Reaction, Manic Type   The prominent characteristic of mania is excessive excitement which manifests itself in overresponsiveness to emotional stimuli in rapid, though disorganized, thought processes and in excessive physical activity. Manic reactions are classified into three subgroups: hypomania, acute mania, and hyperacute mania.

Hypomania is a mild form of excitement which manifests itself through restlessness, or what is commonly called nervousness. The individual is compelled to be constantly on the move. He cannot sit quietly while others are talking. He drums with his fingers or keeps his feet in motion. He may get up and pace about the room. When participating in conversation, he talks rapidly. He must be doing something, anything, and doing it at high speed. A person suffering from hypomania usually does not need to be hospitalized. As a matter of fact, hypomania in an intellectually gifted person is often an important factor in the achievement of eminence. In such instances, the restlessness becomes a source of drive, and the individual finds it not only easy but essential to work for long hours. If he has the physical constitution to stand the strain, he may contribute much more to society than if he were relatively complacent.

The essential difference between acute mania and hypomania is one of degree. In acute mania the restlessness is more marked, the elation more extreme. The patient is overconfident and very talkative. His conversation is at times scintillating, although disorganized. He finds it difficult, if not impossible, to follow through with a thought process. At times he may become so excited that he loses what little self-control he has. During such periods he will strike out violently against inanimate objects or against persons. His behavior represents the bursting forth of the repression of the extrovert who needs to be outgoing and who needs to dominate others. An individual suffering from acute mania resents any form of restraint or criticism. If he is restrained or criticized, his mood may shift quickly from one of extreme happiness to one of extreme anger. The manic patient, with his strong desire for dominance, resents authority. He openly expresses his antagonism toward those who have some control over him, and on occasion will attempt to do them bodily harm. He frequently has delusions and hallucinations, although these are not well organized. They are usually of the grandeur type and are resorted to as a means of increasing his feeling of self-importance. They often contain religious elements. The acute manic patient is always a case for hospital care.

Hyperacute mania is the most extreme form of mania. The patient is delirious. In his wild excitement he has completely lost touch with reality. His delusions and hallucinations are much more real to him than his immediate environment. He is dangerous both to himself and to others. A person who is suffering from hyperacute mania has to be isolated in a room where it will be impossible for him to injure himself or someone else.

Manic-Depressive Reaction, Depressed Type   In general, depressive reactions may be considered as the opposite of manic reactions. The patient feels discouraged and sad. He shows relatively little interest in his surroundings. He may moan or sigh; he is convinced of his unworthiness; his thought processes are slowed; he seems to have difficulty in summoning enough energy to think. He talks slowly and hesitantly or not at all; he lacks interest, also, in physical activity. The effort needed is too great. He may sit quietly for hours, or lie inert.

Depressive reactions often include delusions and hallucinations. These are always related to feelings of guilt. The patient may hear accusing voices reminding him of the sins that he has committed. An intense feeling of guilt is always present in depression.

Depressive reactions are often classified under three subheadings: mild, acute, and depressive stupor.

A state of mild depression is characterized by inability to concentrate, discouragement, and fatigue. The patient is unable to carry on with his customary activities. He is tired and listless; he does not sleep well; his appetite is poor; he is pessimistic about the future. Individuals suffering from mild depression usually have a difficult time if they are not hospitalized. Their behavior is likely to be misunderstood by their families and friends. They are accused of being lazy and told to "snap out of it." This they cannot do. Often the feeling of hopelessness is so great that the person commits suicide.

Acute depression differs from mild depression in degree. The listlessness is more marked. Speech is difficult, responses to questions coming only after considerable delay, or not at all. Physical activity is at a minimum. In acute depression the patient sleeps very little and his appetite is poor—so poor, in fact, that often he has to be spoon-fed. He is frequently concerned about bodily functions. His contact with reality is at times very tenuous. Delusions and hallucinations associated with guilt feelings are nearly always present. The desire for death is so strong that suicide is likely if the opportunity presents itself. Often self-destruction is carefully planned.

Depressive stupor is the most extreme form of depressive reaction. The patient will neither eat nor speak. He lies inert. He has completely given up trying even to satisfy his physiological needs. He is impervious both to cajolery and to threats. Completely discouraged, feeling wholly unworthy, he abnegates himself insofar as he possibly can and still live.

Manic-Depressive Reactions, Other   This classification covers those manic-depressive reactions which are neither primarily manic nor primarily depressive, but a mixture of the two. In the mixed type, manic manifestations may appear more frequently than depressive manifestations or vice versa, but each group of symptoms does appear. In the so-called circular type there is a continuous, almost rhythmic alternation between manic and depressive attacks. This type, once thought to be the most frequent, is actually the least frequent.

Causation   The question of the causation of manic-depressive reactions has not yet been fully answered. A predisposition may be inherited, but in manic-depressive disorders, as in schizophrenia, the evidence for it is contradictory. A number of studies have established the fact that mania and depression, either separately or combined, tend to run in families somewhat more frequently than is the case with schizophrenia. However, this is by no means proof of inheritance. As was pointed out earlier, not only is anxiety learned, but the patterns of behavior resulting from anxiety are also learned. If one or both of the parents of an anxiety-ridden child have found an outlet for their own tension in manic or near-manic outbursts or in periods of melancholia or depression, it is reasonable to assume that the child might utilize similar forms of adjustment.

Histogenic and chemogenic conditions have been offered as important causes in the development of manic-depressive reactions. The first of these, however, can be discarded, since no evidence has been produced demonstrating a causal relationship between lesions of the central nervous system and manic-depressive behavior. Some facts have been gathered in support of the thesis that chemogenic factors are important since they are frequently present in manic-depressive cases. However, they do not seem sufficient to account for the complex changes which take place.

Psychogenic factors appear to be by far the most significant in the development of manic-depressive disorders, although the causation of affective reactions has not been studied nearly so extensively as the causation of schizophrenic reactions. English[15] has reported on six patients who had been treated intensively through psychotherapy. Four of these were depressive; two were manic. The age range was from twenty-five to forty years. English found marked frustration of the need for emotional security in the childhood experiences of these patients. He says that there had been "a minimum of happy experiences in the past; that is, experiences such as fondling, cuddling, being played with and shown appreciation as a baby or child in a way that would leave positive impressions." And "the manic-depressive with his lack of love in early life feels a greater need for love expressed on a childish level than the average." The lack of affection during the early years of life resulted in anxiety, and the anxiety in turn resulted in an overly strong desire for affection with accompanying hostility. These attitudes, in turn, resulted in the impoverishment of human interrelationships. One patient said, "I hear all the negative things said about me but I cannot seem to hear the more positive things which raise my self-esteem!" . . . Another patient said:

[15] O. S. English, "Observation of Trends in Manic Depressive Psychosis," *Psychiatry*, XII (1949), 125–34.

Mother had two different personalities. One I liked and the other I didn't like. The one I liked was when she was dressed up and out in public. Then she was pleasant and amiable. When she was at home she wore old clothes, was unpleasant, nagging, and pessimistic. I guess she was home too much, for that part of her personality seems to have had a profound effect on me.

Persons who utilize manic-depressive adjustments have more ego strength than those who resort to schizophrenic reactions. They retain real values which they feel are worth fighting for. Clifford Beers is an excellent example of this. In *A Mind That Found Itself,* we see a man striving to make concrete contributions to the world of reality. Obviously, this ego strength contributes greatly to the high incidence of recovery of manic-depressive patients.

It was noted earlier that the person who eventually becomes schizophrenic characteristically withdraws gradually from the world of reality. In mania and depression, on the other hand, although there is a long, slow accumulation of frustration and repressed hostility, the actual onset of psychotic behavior is characteristically sudden. In a manic attack, for instance, the outburst is violent. For a while the individual is free; he is himself. Often this extreme form of catharsis has such a beneficial effect on the patient that he does not have another attack for years; he may never have another. Temporarily, he has experienced full expression.

PARANOID REACTIONS

Paranoid reactions are relatively rare, accounting for 1 to 2 per cent of the annual admissions into mental hospitals. Paranoid reactions are subdivided into two groups: paranoia and paranoid state. Paranoia, sometimes called *true paranoia,* is very rare. This disorder develops slowly and is characterized principally by highly systematized delusions of persecution and of grandeur. There is little or no general personality disorganization present. A paranoid state is not so logical or complex as true paranoid behavior; neither does it have the schizophrenic features found in paranoid schizophrenia. A person may remain in a paranoid state for a brief period, then recover. Paranoia, on the other hand, is continuous and incurable.

The delusional system in paranoia is almost unassailable. It is very logical, and the paranoiac will defend it most convincingly. It follows from this that one must have high intelligence if he is to develop paranoia. The causes of paranoia are similar to those which were mentioned in the preceding discussion of paranoid schizophrenia. Excessive ambition is always in the background. Failure always accompanies excessive ambition, and the person who develops paranoia adjusts to this state by utilizing the mechanism of projection. Freud, in emphasizing the importance of projection, as well as the significance of homosexuality as an etiologic factor, gives this formula: "I don't love him, I hate him, I don't hate him, he hates me."

In paranoia, feelings of resentment run deep. The patient adjusts to these feelings of resentment through aggression. Since he is usually a very well-controlled individual, he may plan aggression against another with great care and cunning. A paranoid patient is dangerous.

The paranoid individual is very well integrated, and usually remains so throughout his life. In fact, he is better integrated than normal individuals. His poise is so unusual that it is abnormal. He is cool, calculating, and ruthless. He knows who his enemies are, but he does not fear them. He is sure that he can destroy them before they are able to destroy him. He is unshakable in his belief that he is a great man, capable of meeting any emergency.

A brief biographical sketch of a man who will be called John may be helpful in understanding paranoia. His mother was ambitious for her children but there were so many of them and the father's income was so small that when John finished grade school he was unable to go on to high school, since it was necessary that he go to work. This was a difficult situation for an ambitious boy with an intelligence quotient of approximately 150. Gradually his bitterness grew toward society in general and toward his parents in particular. One day he returned home from his job in another town and threatened his mother with a shotgun. Soon after that he disappeared. When he was located several months later he was living in a city in another state under an assumed name. During this period he had become very religious and had decided that he must go into the ministry. In the meantime, the conflicts which he had been experiencing for several years increased in intensity. He had strong sex desires which pushed him into promiscuity, behavior which was antithetical to his sincere religious convictions. He tried to solve the problem by marrying at the age of nineteen. However, he and his wife had several children during the next few years and this financial burden made it difficult for him to continue his study for the ministry. He was frustrated at every turn and always blamed others for his situation.

Eventually John was ordained and was called to serve in a small parish. He was a brilliant preacher and was sure that in a short time he would have a big church. However, this did not come about and his delusions of persecution developed rapidly. Eventually he became convinced that the entire Catholic hierarchy from the Pope down was keeping him from succeeding. Why? Because he was such a great preacher that he would lead a religious revolution and destroy the Catholic Church. In order to get support, John joined the Masons, but it was not long before he concluded that the Masons were working with the Catholics to destroy him. He was now in his early thirties and the delusions of grandeur and of persecution had become fixed. Except for the delusions, John appeared normal. There was no deterioration of his intellectual powers and he exercised remarkable self-control.

When he was in his middle thirties John was arrested because of sexual advances to a twelve-year-old girl. He was sent to a mental hospital for a psychiatric examination and was found to be paranoid. He was hospitalized for the rest of his life, dying in his middle sixties.

The adjustment sequence as explained in Chapter Two and the mechanism of projection as explained in Chapter Three are directly applicable to John. He had to find some escape from his frustrations and conflicts and the responses which he made were delusions of grandeur and systematized delusions of persecution.

Paranoid trends or paranoid conditions are frequently found in the general population, including college students. These individuals always lack flexibility and are difficult to get along with. Their rigidity manifests itself not only in their ways of thinking but also in their bodily posture and carriage. The writer has interviewed a number of such students in his work as a clinical psychologist. One boy searched the office for a hidden dictaphone each time he came in for an interview. Another was convinced that he was a great musician, even though at the time he was failing in his music courses. A girl came in one day and talked for nearly an hour in an effort to prove that a group of individuals on campus were making an organized attempt to have her forced out of the university. Another girl was convinced that the people with whom she had worked during the summer had united to work out a plan to destroy her reputation.

Individuals with such paranoid trends or paranoid conditions may remain *in status quo,* or they may become completely psychotic and have to be institutionalized. It is very difficult to know at just what point a paranoid individual should be considered a menace to society.

INVOLUTIONAL PSYCHOTIC REACTION

An involutional psychotic reaction is one more form of depression, rather arbitrarily set off from the other forms in that it appears during middle age—in the forties for women and in the fifties for men—in persons without an earlier history of extreme depressive behavior. Often the depression is accompanied by paranoid ideas; at times the paranoid characteristics are dominant.

Until quite recently it was believed that the physiological change which takes place in women during the menopause was the principal cause of what was for a long time called involutional melancholia. However, in neither the research laboratory nor the clinician's office has it been possible to establish changes in body metabolism as the sole cause or even the most important single cause of an involutional psychotic reaction. The same basic psychogenic factors are working here in much the same way as we found them working in the other nonorganic psychoses. Middle age is a period of stress for all; for some this stress is too great to bear. In the forties a woman is called upon to face a number of disturbing facts: she is no longer so attractive to men, she can no longer bear children, her children are growing up or have already left home, her physical stamina is decreasing. A man in his fifties is beginning to realize that he is getting old. He has to face the facts of decreasing physical energy, of declining sexual vigor, and the challenge of younger men in his field of activity. In a few short years he will no longer be needed. Where once he was pushing on to new heights, he is now becoming conscious of the fact that his days of climbing are over.

The majority of persons, of course, make the necessary adjustments to the demands of middle age. Some, however, because of environmental stress as well as personal anxieties which perhaps go back for several years, become depressed. This depression may be sufficiently severe to be called an involutional psychotic reaction.

SUMMARY

Although there is still considerable controversy concerning the etiology of functional psychotic adjustment, the evidence strongly indicates that environment is the principal causal factor. The fact that functional psychoses tend to run in families is not in itself proof that the disorders are biologically inherited. It may be, however, that a predisposition is inherited. Individuals vary widely in the extent of their resistance to behavior disorders. A low threshold of resistance may be the result of an inherited predisposition or it may be caused by such factors as prenatal influences, the birth trauma, or experiences during infancy and early childhood which cannot be consciously recalled. Although psychotic reactions of psychogenic origin do not constitute disease entities, it is customary to classify them for practical purposes. The labels given are schizophrenic reactions, affective reactions, paranoid reactions, and involutional psychotic reaction. Schizophrenia alone accounts for a little more than one fifth of the annual admission into mental hospitals.

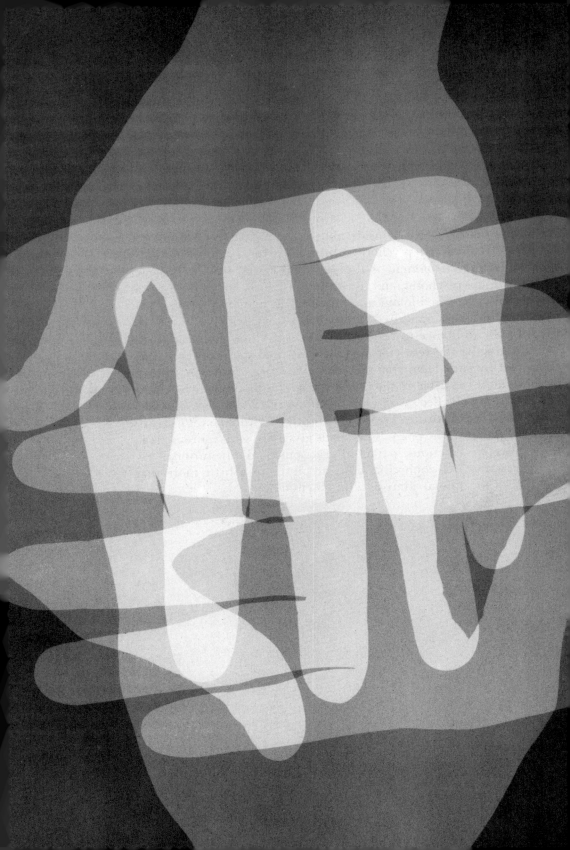

REGAINING MENTAL HEALTH

chapter 15

Serious behavior disorders are not unusual. One person out of every ten, as the data in Chapter One show, suffers at some time or other during his life from a psychotic condition. A much larger number experience at least a temporary neurosis. Where can such individuals, as well as those whose difficulties are less serious, go for help? To whom should they turn for treatment?

The answers to these questions are easy to give and hard to abide by. Obviously one who is suffering from a behavior disorder should be treated by a professionally trained person. Such professionally trained men and women can be found in hospitals, in clinics, and in private practice. There are, however, two obstacles in the way of this direct approach, obstacles which do not block the path of those who seek treatment for physical ills. The first is the lay attitude; the second, the lack of facilities and personnel adequate to meet the needs.

Although the attitude of society and of individuals is changing slowly, there is still a widespread belief that neither the person involved nor his family and friends should admit the presence of behavior disorders. It is still considered something of a disgrace for one to need help with his emotional problems. Actually, of course, a person is no more responsible for psychological ill health than he is for physical ill health. He should feel as free about seeking treatment for the former as for the latter. He has not chosen to be neurotic any more than he would choose to have pneumonia. When this point of view becomes generally accepted, it will be possible to deal much more effectively with abnormal behavior.

Unfortunately, when a person does make a decision to seek treatment, he may find that it is not available. There is a lack of personnel resources. This dearth of trained personnel causes many persons with behavior difficulties to turn to quacks. The need is obviously there, and since neither medicine nor psychology has as yet provided adequate means of satisfying that need, it follows that untrained persons will attempt to do so. The best way to prevent quacks from practicing is for schools of medicine and psychology to produce enough psychiatrists and clinical psychologists to meet the demand. Progress toward this end is being made by these two groups.

WHO ARE QUALIFIED THERAPISTS?

There is need for a much wider dissemination of information concerning the qualifications of the therapist. The public lacks knowledge of what his training should be and of the nature of the treatment used. The field seems to be shrouded in mystery.

Professional Qualifications

Nearly every adult at one time or another has served as a counselor. Parents try to help their children solve their problems, teachers give advice freely, clergymen regard the personal problems of their parishioners as their responsibility, and friends help one another in working through difficult situations. This sort of counseling will, of course, continue, whether for good or for ill.

Formerly the general medical practitioner often served as a practical psychologist. He made use of three techniques: suggestion, reassurance, and catharsis. Finding that many patients with no discoverable physical disease felt better for taking simple medication, the general practitioner did not hesitate to prescribe it. He helped by encouragement those who were worried and anxious and often listened with patience and understanding while the patient told him about his problems. All this was good, but was not enough.

Few doctors have time to deal with their patients' psychological problems. Few are familiar with modern techniques for dealing with emotional disorders, therefore they are no better equipped to treat a neurosis or functional psychosis than is any intelligent lay individual.

As an undergraduate student, a doctor has taken the premedical program in which emphasis is (as it should be) on the biological and physical sciences. The premedical student rarely takes more than six semester hours of psychology and has little or no training in this field; he usually has no psychology credits at all. If he does take courses in this field—and usually there is time for no more than two —their content, as would be expected, is weighted heavily with material on the organic psychoses. There is usually no instruction in such important areas as motivation, individual differences, learning, and psychotherapy. With this background, in which the emphasis has been almost exclusively upon organic disorders, the practicing physician naturally looks for a physical basis for a behavior disorder. Finding none, he may dismiss a case with such comment as, "It's all your imagination," or "What you need is a good rest."

Assisted by three collaborators, Dr. O. L. Peterson found that patients' emotional problems were in large degree an enigma to some of the physicians surveyed in North Carolina. Twenty-nine per cent surveyed were unable to recognize emotional problems, let alone treat them. Fifty-four per cent realized that emotional problems were present, but either treated the physical symptoms or showed a marked lack of sympathy. Only seventeen per cent of the physicians were able to recognize emotional problems and to treat them with some competence.[1]

The Psychiatrist   The psychiatrist is a physician who had specialized in mental illness. If, as an undergraduate student, he already planned to go into psychiatry, he probably took several courses in psychology. In medical school he received almost the same basic

[1] O. L. Peterson, R. S. Spain, L. P. Andrews and B. G. Greenburg, "An Analytical Study of North Carolina General Practice, 1953–1954," *Journal of Medical Education,* XXXI: Part II (Special supplement to December 1956 issue), 1–165.

training as that given to other prospective doctors, but he took as much related work in psychology as he could. The greater part of what he knows about behavior disorders is learned from his experience as an intern. His internship is usually in a mental hospital. The psychiatrist, with his training in the biologic and medical sciences, is well prepared to treat the organic psychoses and the psychoneuroses, such as hysteria, which are accompanied by somatic complications. Many psychiatrists, however, notably the neurologists, are not equipped by training or experience to treat functional behavior disorders through the use of psychotherapy.

Until recently, psychiatry has shared with psychoanalysis the responsibility for treating individuals who have become neurotic or psychotic. The M.D. degree carries a great deal of prestige in America; individuals who are mentally ill usually feel less hesitant about going to a psychiatrist than to a psychoanalyst or to a clinical psychologist. He is another kind of *doctor,* and they have learned to have confidence in doctors. Psychiatrists have done a great deal of excellent work. Many of them have succeeded in synthesizing the organic and dynamic points of view. They constitute one important professional group to whom the seriously disturbed individual can turn with confidence. This is especially true if the disturbance is organically caused, or if it is accompanied by physical manifestations.

The Psychoanalyst   Psychoanalysis has its roots in clinical practice rather than in the laboratory. Its principles have been derived from observation of human behavior rather than from experimentation. Although interested in developing its distinctive methods of investigation, it is primarily concerned with therapy; the individual constitutes the central problem and an individual cannot be understood without the use of subjective evaluation and insight.

The founder of the psychoanalytic movement was Sigmund Freud, who began his career as a medical practitioner but later specialized in neurotic disorders. In 1885 he went to Paris to study under Charcot. As a result of this association he became very much interested in the use of hypnosis in the treatment of hysteria and other neuroses. Eventually he discarded this technique and developed certain methods in wide use today, not only among psychoanalysts, but also among psychiatrists and clinical psychologists. Included among these are catharsis, free association, transference, and dream analysis. Of these, catharsis is now basic in all psychotherapy. It will be discussed further in a later section dealing with the interview. Free association was used as a technique for bringing into consciousness painful experiences that had been repressed into the unconscious. Transference is one of the fundamental procedures in psychoanalytic therapy. The patient transfers his deepest emotions to the analyst, the analyst becoming the love object or the hate object. Freud's theories concerning dreams evolved slowly, as did all of his theories. After years of clinical practice he became convinced that a person's dreams are very significant, providing invaluable clues to repressed desires and conflicts. Dream analysis is an essential part of psychoanalytic methodology.

Analysis is a long, tedious procedure. The time usually required in a single case is from two to five hours per week for a period of at least two years. The first task of the analyst is to reconstruct in detail the life history of the patient in order that he may obtain clear understanding of the dynamics of the individual's personality. This necessitates going back to the experiences of childhood and of infancy. Freud and his followers are largely responsible for present understanding of the importance of childhood experiences upon adult behavior. When the life history of the patient has been reconstructed, his present maladjustive behavior, bizarre though it may be, appears wholly reasonable. It is the inevitable result of the experiences he has had. After the life history has been completed, an analysis is made. If the treatment has been successful, the patient will have acquired sufficient insight to make the needed adjustments.

A neurotic individual can go to a psychoanalyst with confidence, providing he selects one who meets the requirements of the American Psychoanalytic Association. Most psychoanalysts in good standing have an M.D. degree. In other words, they are psychiatrists who have specialized in analysis as a method of treating behavior disorders. Persons with psychological difficulties should use care in selection of an analyst, because a number of men and women without adequate training in either psychology or medicine are practicing in this and related fields.

The Clinical Psychologist   Largely because of experiences gained during World War II and because of the present great demand for clinicians, clinical psychology, is rapidly establishing itself as an important profession. Moreover, it is coming to be accepted on an equal footing by medicine and psychiatry. As early as 1946, Miller had the following to say concerning the status of clinical psychology:

> Although there still are exceptions, the attitude of the medical profession in general and psychiatrists in particular toward clinical psychologists has changed profoundly. At one time a definite "pecking order" existed, the psychologists submitting to the superior authority and training of the physician. Disaffection between the two professions was widespread, engendered by their different training and goals, as well as by the unfortunate sense of inferiority resulting from the hierarchy. But now it is commonly agreed that each profession has its characteristic tasks with a vague region of overlapping functions in some areas. The concept of the psychiatric team composed of neuropsychiatrist, clinical psychologist, and psychiatric social worker, each with his complementary activities, is generally accepted.
>
> Clinical psychology did much during the war to improve the practice of psychiatry by making available to the psychiatrists old and new procedures for diagnosing personality and mental disease. Furthermore, it is probable that a majority of military clinical psychologists carried on psychotherapy in certain types of cases. Almost always this was under the direction of, or in collaboration with, psychiatrists or medical officers who attended to the somatic problems involved, but nevertheless, in the military situation, working together as a team, both professions did nearly similar tasks for patients without somatic involvement or serious mental abnormality. This was therapy and it was called "therapy"—recourse was rarely had to the euphemism "counseling."
>
> At the same time that these developments were occurring in the armed forces, the psychological profession received further recognition by legislation in certain states to permit them to practice. It is clear that in the future psychotherapy will be explicitly among the usual tasks of clinical psychologists, but it is essential for the protection of both patients and psychologists that this practice be conducted in the medical framework with no trespassing into fields of surgery, diet, the use of drugs, or similar procedures which are proper precincts for the medical profession.[2]

The training of clinical psychologists varies from university to university, as would be expected. Characteristically, however, it

---

[2] J. G. Miller, "Clinical Psychology in the Veterans Administration," *The American Psychologist*, I, No. 6 (June 1946), 181–82.

is now as follows: an undergraduate major in psychology with related work in the social and biological sciences; a graduate program of four years, the first two years being given to concentrated study in such areas as personality dynamics, learning, psychometrics, neurology, mental hygiene, and clinical therapy. During the third year the student serves as an intern, usually in a clinic, often in a mental hospital, where he works under supervision with both psychiatrists and psychologists. During his fourth year he concentrates on his dissertation and on psychotherapy. Eventually the successful candidate receives a Ph.D. degree. In many universities, during this four-year graduate program he takes related work in either the social or the biological sciences, or both.

The clinical psychologist has a number of advantages over the psychiatrist and the psychoanalyst insofar as the treatment of functional disorders is concerned. In the first place, he is likely to be more eclectric in his point of view and in the methods which he uses. He is acquainted with psychoanalytic techniques but does not limit himself to analysis. He understands directive therapy, but he is also familiar with the nondirective approach. He selects the method best suited to the patient. In the second place, he is thoroughly trained in the use of tests, an area in which both the psychiatrist and the psychoanalyst are relatively weak. In the third place, and this is the most important, he possesses a thorough knowledge of the learning process. Since the functional behavior disorders are learned, this knowledge is essential to sound therapy.

A person who decides to go to a clinical psychologist for treatment should remember that a Ph.D. degree in psychology is not in itself a guarantee that the person possessing it has had adequate training in the techniques of psychotherapy. Psychology has many branches; clinical psychology is but one. The principal check that should be made on the training and experience of the psychologist is to find out whether or not he is a diplomate in clinical psychology. If he is, it means that he has the stamp of approval of the Board of Examiners of the American Psychological Association.

Personal Qualifications

Psychotherapy is not a science; it is an art. Although many techniques used are based on scientific investigations, their success in actual practice depends upon the skill of the practitioner. Moreover, psychotherapy involves a close relationship between two persons, the therapist and the patient. In such a relationship the personality of the one who is conducting the treatment is inevitably a potent factor. Individuals who do not have the necessary personality traits, regardless of their professional training, should be discouraged from entering the profession. A scholar is not necessarily a good therapist.

The qualifications which are essential for the successful therapist are discussed in detail in most books on clinical psychology. The following are among the most important:

1. Sensitivity to human relationships.
2. A sincere interest in and respect for others.
3. Willingness and ability to listen.
4. The psychological rather than the moralistic point of view.

Sensitivity to human relationships is the most important characteristic of social intelligence. A person who possesses this sensitivity in marked degree quickly senses the feelings and attitudes of others. He depends not so much on what others say as upon how they say it. He obtains his cues from the inflections of the voice, from facial expressions, from gestures, and from posture. He is adept at understanding the sign language so important in human intercourse. A person who has considerable understanding of the behavior reactions of others is often referred to as "intuitive." That understanding which appears on the surface to be intuitive is actually the result of years of close observation of the behavior of human beings. It is an ability which every really good novelist possesses. It involves understanding not only of the patient in an interview situation but also of the relationships among individuals in a social group. This ability is invaluable to the therapist, who must avoid saying or doing anything in an interview which would retard the progress of therapy.

The therapist would find the arduous work of interviewing an intolerable burden if he were not deeply interested in the problems of others and sincerely desirous of helping them to solve them. He, like the successful physician, must be interested in human welfare. He practices the art of mental healing in order that those with whom he works may lead happier and more useful lives.

During interviews the good therapist spends far more time in listening than he does in talking. He is an attentive listener, always keeping in psychological contact with his patient. He is responsive to everything that the patient says, even though his responses are seldom put into words. When they are, his statements are brief. The therapist who prefers talking to listening usually experiences considerable difficulty in maintaining rapport and nearly always retards the progress of therapy.

The therapist is never a moralist in the sense in which the term is customarily used. He never blames the patient, no matter how serious his offense may have been. He is not even interested in persuading the patient to conform to the accepted code of moral and social behavior as an end in itself. Rather he is interested in giving the patient an opportunity to consider the effect that running counter to group standards may have upon his own happiness and success. His goal is to help the patient to develop patterns of behavior which will be most satisfactory for him now and in the future.

COUNSELING AND PSYCHOTHERAPY

Mental hygiene, as has been stated before, is concerned primarily with prevention. It seeks to further the development of attitudes which will help individuals to make healthy adjustments to problem situations as they arise. It is concerned, also, with the creation of the kind of environment which will reduce the number and intensity of frustrations and conflicts for individuals functioning in that environment. Consequently, there is little justification for giving much attention in a textbook on mental hygiene to therapeutic procedures. However, the general student who does not expect to take advanced courses in abnormal or clinical psychology is usually interested in knowing at least a little about the methods of treatment which are used; therefore, the following material is included. It should be read with the realization that justice obviously cannot be done to so broad a field in so few pages.

Counseling

In our schools, colleges, and universities the men and women who have been appointed to help students with their problems are usually called counselors. This title resulted from the earlier attitude that the principal function of such persons was to counsel children and young people on educational and vocational problems. These are still important areas of activity. Many otherwise well-adjusted students need guidance in such matters as study habits, reading and speaking disabilities, the selection of a college, and getting a job. Providing information and giving advice on such practical matters probably should continue to be called counseling. However, problems in these areas are often indications of emotional difficulties. Poor study habits may be basically the result of emotional conflicts. Underachievement and overachievement are frequently manifestations of emotional disturbance, and inability to hold a job is usually symptomatic of a behavior disorder. Consequently, counselors cannot always function at the comfortable superficial level of passing out information and of giving advice, even though for many of their clients this is all that is needed. They must have sufficient training to be able to identify emotional problems and then to refer them, if they themselves do not have adequate training, to qualified psychologists and psychiatrists. A large number of counselors are adequately trained to handle emotional problems as well as educational and vocational problems. The good counselor works in accordance with the following principles:

1. Counseling should rarely be forced on a student.
2. The counselor should always view the counselee as a total personality.
3. The counselor should respect the personalities of all counselees.
4. Counseling should be positive rather than negative.
5. The counselor should aid the counselee to understand and accept himself.
6. The counselor should do more listening than talking.
7. Final decisions must be made by the counselee.
8. The counselor should understand the limitations as well as the values of the instruments and techniques which he uses.

Students should go to counselors on their own volition and should retain the privilege of breaking off the counseling relationship at any time they choose. This statement holds even when students are referred by faculty advisors or supervisors. In this situation the student should be asked if he would like to talk with one of the counselors, but in most cases he should not be required to do so. There are a few exceptions to this rule. Obviously, students must consult periodically with their advisors about their registrations for courses and, in cases of very severe emotional maladjustments, it is necessary that the student be required to see the clinical psychologist or the consulting psychiatrist. Counseling and especially psychotherapy is made very difficult if the counselee is present under duress. A felt need on his part is almost indispensable.

Since behavior is a function of the whole individual, it is important that counselors view their counselees as total personalities. In other words, emphasis should be on the person rather than on the specific problem. This is especially true of counselees with emotional difficulties. Emotional difficulties can never be taken out of context. They do not exist as entities. They have meaning only as they are related to the total personality of the individual and, of course, to his experiential background.

Respect for the personalities of one's counselees is one of the most important of the principles of counseling and psychotherapy, for it affects almost every aspect of the counseling relationship. It involves the ability to like and to accept the counselee regardless of his personality characteristics and his behavior. This principle is especially essential in dealing with individuals who have emotional problems. The good counselor never blames a counselee. He realizes that if emotional problems are present the counselee already has deep feelings of guilt and that intensification of these will do much more harm than good. It means, too, that there is never any threat in the counseling relationship. The atmosphere should always be one of permissiveness. It also means that all personal revelations will be kept strictly confidential. The information that a counselor cannot be trusted soon becomes generally known. Once this confidence has been lost, it is almost impossible to regain it. Good counselors never show dislike for any of their counselees. Neither do they ever take advantage of them in any way. They like them and respect them for what they are.

Counseling should be positive rather than negative. For some reason or other, it is easier for most persons to tell a person what he ought not to do than it is to tell him what he should do, or—to put it in client-centered terms—it is easier to think that he will probably make wrong decisions than it is to have confidence in his ability to make right decisions. Even severely maladjusted individuals possess considerable capacity for growth and adjustment. A specific application of the importance of stressing a positive approach can easily be made in the field of vocational counseling. If a battery of interest inventories and aptitude tests has been given, it is much better to stress the vocation or vocations in which the counselee is likely to succeed. A similar application can be made in helping a student in choosing a major. Even being dropped from college can be made a positive step if the counselor helps the student to see that it is now possible for him to get into a line of work where he will probably be successful.

The counselor should aid the counselee to understand and accept himself. This principle is especially important in personal counseling. It is impossible for the counselor to tell the student what he is like. No counselor can be that omniscient. He reflects and to some extent interprets what the counselee has to say, thus helping him to a better understanding of himself. Out of the insights gained comes a changed perception of the self with resultant changes in behavior.

Closely related to the fifth principle is the sixth: the counselor should do more listening than talking. It is probable that the student with problems has been told what to do since early childhood. What he needs now is not more advice but an opportunity to think through with a sympathetic, understanding listener the adjustment difficulties which he is experiencing. The listening done by the counselor is active rather than passive. He is, insofar as possible, projecting himself into the thoughts and feelings of the counselee.

In all forms of counseling—educational, vocational, and personal —final decisions should be made by the counselee. The counselor may provide factual information and, if his orientation is directive, he may make recommendations; but the counselee retains the right to make his own choices. It is to be hoped, of course, that before he makes these choices he considers all the evidence carefully. In educational and vocational counseling with students who do not have any serious emotional problems it is relatively safe to offer advice, since the well-adjusted individual is able to weigh recommendations and then accept or reject them. The emotionally disturbed student, on the other hand, is likely to profit more by a nondirective or client-centered approach. In fact, so long as they are short of an actual psychosis, the greater the client's emotional difficulties, the more nondirective the counselor should be.

The counselor should understand the limitations as well as the values of the instruments and techniques which he uses. During the last fifty years, psychologists have devoted a great deal of time and energy to the construction of tests. Psychological tests are valuable instruments when used by a person who has been thoroughly trained in psychometrics. Such a person not only understands the positive characteristics of tests but is also fully aware of the hazards involved in attempting to evaluate human behavior quantitatively. For example, he knows that an intelligence quotient represents a range rather than a specific point on a scale and that it has different meanings for different tests. He knows that vocational aptitude tests and interest inventories provide helpful information for one who is trying to decide what line of work he will follow but that they do not provide a final scientifically established criterion of what he should do. He knows that personality tests of the pencil and paper variety are occasionally valuable, but he also knows that the examinee can distort his responses in such a way that the scores earned are misleading. He knows that certain of the projective techniques are helpful in diagnosis and to some extent in therapy, but he also knows that the scoring methods used are highly subjective. Tests are valuable as supplementary tools, if the person using them constantly keeps in mind that the scores which the counselee earns are subject to many reservations and qualifications.

Psychotherapy

More than a hundred years ago Nathaniel Hawthorne summarized in a single paragraph in "The Scarlet Letter" some of the basic characteristics of psychotherapy, although he did not call it that. The passage follows:

> Few secrets can escape an investigator, who has opportunity and license to undertake such a quest, and skill to follow it up. A man burdened with a secret should especially avoid the intimacy of his physician. If the latter possess native sagacity, and a nameless something more,—let us call it intuition; if he show no intrusive egotism, nor disagreeably prominent characteristics of his own; if he have the

power, which must be born with him, to bring his mind into such affinity with his patient's, that this last shall unawares have spoken what he imagines himself only to have thought; if such revelations be received without tumult, and acknowledged not so often by an uttered sympathy as by silence, an inarticulate breath, and here and there a word, to indicate that all is understood; if to these qualifications of a confidant be joined the advantages afforded by his recognized character as a physician,—then, at some inevitable moment, will the soul of the sufferer be dissolved, and flow forth in a dark, but transparent stream, bringing all its mysteries into the daylight.[3]

Psychotherapy is a difficult term to define. In a broad sense it includes all psychological or mental methods of treating behavior disorders. The term might very well be limited to the methods used by the therapist in his psychological relationship with the patient or client for the purpose of promoting growth toward better mental health. It is a learning situation in which the client is provided with an opportunity to make corrective adjustments in his perception of himself and of his environment.

In psychotherapy, much greater emphasis is placed upon the emotions than upon the intellect. The client needs corrective emotional experiences more than intellectual understanding. Consequently, in modern psychotherapy such approaches as forbidding, exhortation, asking for pledges, verbal reassurance which is not in accord with the client's perceptions, and direct advice which goes beyond the client's own insights have been largely discarded. Most clients, long before they come to a psychotherapist for help, have directly experienced the use of such methods by well-meaning persons, such as parents, friends, or untrained clergymen and physicians. Because of that experience they usually expect the therapist to follow similar procedures and are surprised to find that, actually, the therapeutic relationship is different from any that they have ever before experienced.

How is it different? The psychotherapist is not a parent substitute (excepting for a phase in orthodox psychoanalysis). He is not emotionally involved in the way that a parent characteristically is. The psychotherapist does not function like a clergyman. He does not represent God. He is not deeply concerned, in this situation,

---

[3] N. Hawthorne, *The Scarlet Letter* (New York: Dodd, Mead & Co., 1948), pp. 125–26. (First published in 1850.)

with strict standards of right and wrong behavior. The psychotherapist does not function as the family physician. It is not his role to examine the client, diagnose, and then to prescribe treatment. The psychotherapist does not function as a friend, since friendship involves a mutual exchange of confidences. The psychotherapist does not even function as a teacher in the usual meaning of the word, even though psychotherapy is a learning process. The teacher is thought of as a person who tells the student what he ought to know and measures the extent to which he has achieved. The teacher gives information, directs, lectures. The psychotherapeutic relationship is not like any of the preceding. It is unique.

A good psychotherapist, regardless of his orientation, is deeply interested in his client but is, at the same time, detached. He reflects and understands, but he does not love or hate, he does not rejoice or despair. He is objective without being coldly scientific. He uses his knowledge of the dynamics of human behavior and of the learning process to help the client to resolve his conflicts, to bring repressed material into consciousness, and to make needed adjustments. He creates a relationship in which the client feels free to relive emotional experiences which heretofore he has been unable to face. It is the kind of relationship in which the client, perhaps for the first time in many years, can be himself without fear of condemnation. It is the kind of relationship in which the client can discover what he has been, what he is, and what he would like to be.

Parloff[4] defined good relationship as one in which there is comfort, effectiveness and objectivity. Then, using a group therapy setting, attempted to determine whether an association does exist between a good relationship and outcome of therapy. As might be expected, he found that those who benefited most had established better relationships with the therapist and those who had terminated therapy prematurely perceived the relationship as unsatisfactory.

Although the process of psychotherapy has been intensively studied since the early days of Freud, our understanding of it is still far from complete. A great deal of research is needed to evaluate the many theories that have been advanced and the numerous techniques that are in general use or have been proposed. One very important

[4] M. B. Parloff, "Therapist-Patient Relationship and Outcome of Psychotherapy," *Journal of Consulting Psychology,* XXV, No. 1 (1961), 29–38.

reason why progress in treating behavior disorders has been so slow is that the problems involved are extremely complex. Obviously it is much easier to remove a diseased appendix than it is to remove an obsession or a delusion. In psychotherapy the total personality is the object of concern and each personality has its own unique experiential background, its own unique reactions to its present environment. The problems involved in reducing such intangibles to manageable, and at the same time meaningful, research studies are almost overwhelming. It is not surprising that science began with astronomy. The distant galaxies are more amenable to scientific study than is human behavior.

Since there are still so many unanswered questions concerning the process of psychotherapy and the nature of the learning which takes place during that process, it would be expected that divergent points of view would develop. The two major systems of theory and methodology are psychoanalysis and nondirective or client-centered psychotherapy. There would be little justification for the inclusion in a textbook on mental hygiene of a detailed presentation and critical evaluation of these and other procedures. Instead, the writer will try to present a brief statement of the therapeutic process from the client-centered point of view. It should be kept in mind that, regardless of differences in orientation, studies have shown experienced psychotherapists to be surprisingly alike in the principal techniques which they use.

When a person comes to a psychotherapist for help, he usually looks upon himself as an unworthy individual unable to live in peace with himself or with his fellows. He is in need of a situation in which he can talk freely. The interview provides him with this opportunity. Sometimes he is so inhibited that he finds it difficult to put his feelings into words. The experienced therapist, however, knows how to help him break down the barriers.

What is the value of catharsis? Why does it help the individual to regain mental health? Catharsis may be considered as a form of emotional reconditioning. It will be remembered from the discussion in Chapter Two that a fear can be reconditioned by associating the feared object with a series of pleasant experiences. A person goes to a therapist because he is troubled by guilt feelings concerning certain experiences. Because of those experiences he has lost his self-respect; he may feel that if anyone learns of his behavior he will be punished. He tells the therapist about these experiences, and the punishment that he expected and feared does not come. Instead, while he is verbalizing the behavior that to him seems so despicable, he finds that the therapist is not critical but understanding. Instead of being punished for his behavior, he finds that it is accepted and explained. The consequences are not at all what he had anticipated.

In this permissive atmosphere the client, during the early interviews, characteristically becomes increasingly critical of himself. The therapist reflects and accepts the expression of these negative attitudes. Moreover, during the early stages of the therapeutic process, the client talks a great deal about his symptoms and, while he usually blames himself in part for his behavior, he also expresses a great deal of hostility toward others, especially toward members of his family. Frequently his hostility is also turned toward the broader aspects of his environment. As time goes on, he gives less attention to his symptoms and his generalized hostility decreases. Increasingly, he concerns himself with an examination of his self. Initially, this self-examination is tentative and fearful. He not only does not understand himself but is afraid of what he will find when he begins to explore. One of the author's clients, a college student, stated it this way: "There is a dark room which I am afraid to enter. I know it is filled with horrible things, but I have no idea what they are." When the author suggested opening the door together, ever so little, to try to pierce the darkness, he replied, "I can't, because the room in which I live is so filled with heavy shadows that I could not find the knob to the door which leads into this other room." That, briefly stated, is what repressed material means to the person who is deeply disturbed emotionally.

Gradually the client is able to come to grips with himself and examine with increasing objectivity the desires and the experiences which were once so threatening. This progress results from the skillful use of the interview situation by the therapist. The warmth, the permissiveness, the acceptance, the ever-present understanding has made it possible for the client to lower his defenses, to be more relaxed, to be free to explore his self. Going along with him on this fearful journey is another human being, the therapist, who, although he does not know all the bypaths, is an indispensable alter ego.

As the therapeutic process continues, the client makes more and more positive statements about himself and his environment. At first these positive statements are tentative and relatively few, but as time goes on they become more numerous than the negative statements. These positive statements are accompanied or preceded by insights. An insight is a new way of preceiving one's self; it is the integration of old experiences into a pattern; it is an understanding of the relationship between present attitudes and emotions and past experiences. While insight itself usually comes suddenly, the process leading up to the achievement of insight is typically slow. Often, too, the new perception or insight is unwelcome to the client, who at first rejects it because it does not conform to the earlier perception of the self. Slowly, however, this perception of the self is changed and eventually the client sees himself in a different light. His self-respect increases markedly; he no longer feels worthless. He looks upon his value system as based upon his own experiences rather than imposed upon him by others. His hostility decreases. He faces life with confidence. Rogers has summarized these changes in self-perception as follows:

> The essential elements would appear to be that the individual changes in three general ways. He perceives himself as a more adequate person, with more worth and more possibility of meeting life. He permits more experiential data to enter awareness, and thus achieves a more realistic appraisal of himself, his relationships, and his environment. He tends to place the basis of standards within himself, recognizing that the "goodness" or "badness" of any experience or perceptual object is not something inherent in that object but is a value placed on it by himself.[5]

Changes in self-perception result inevitably in changes in behavior. Positive actions are tried and, if not retarded by failure, are repeated. With each success there is less fear in making decisions. The client's confidence grows apace. The basic motivating force throughout this entire process of therapy is the fundamental need of the individual to preserve and enhance his self. Rogers says:

> In the service of this basic tendency the pre-therapy self operates to meet needs. And because of this deeper force the individual in therapy tends to move toward reorganization, rather than toward

[5] C. R. Rogers, *Client-Centered Therapy* (Boston: Houghton Mifflin Company, 1951), p. 139.

disintegration. It is a characteristic of the reformulated self which is achieved in therapy that it permits a fuller realization of the organism's potentialities, and that it is a more effective basis for further growth. Thus the therapeutic process is, in its totality, the achievement by the individual, in a favorable psychological climate, of further steps in a direction which has already been set by his growth and maturational development from the time of conception onward.[6]

The Case of Ruth   In order to clarify what is meant by the concepts discussed in the preceding pages, a few excerpts from recorded interviews between the author and a client will now be presented. The client, who will be called Ruth, was a married woman with two children. She had experienced emotional problems since childhood. When she came for psychotherapy she was very depressed. Some schizophrenic trends were present, but she was not actually psychotic. Short excerpts will be taken from four of the interviews. The following are from the first part of the second interview. It should be noted that Ruth spends most of her time in negative catharsis. This was true throughout the first eight or nine interviews. It should also be noted that the psychologist does not deny the feelings expressed; neither does he give advice. He responds to her feelings no matter what they are. The printed word can only suggest the nature of these responses since voice inflections, rate of speaking, and general attitude toward the client are very important aspects of the overall atmosphere.

*C. As far as this week has gone, there were a few days when I felt very bad, and there would be another day when I would feel a little bit better, but still not really good.

*P. Do you want to try to put those feelings into words?

C. Well, as I mentioned to you before I do have a lot of anxieties. It seems the days I feel the worst I have more anxiety and I have it longer and it will last longer and I feel as if I am walking in a fog more or less; it is just a black cloud.

P. The black cloud is all around you, and you can't see your way ahead.

C. It just doesn't make any sense in living at all, and time just seems to go by and there is nothing that I do that seems to matter. It is just

---

[6] *Ibid.*, pp. 195–96.
* C—Client; P—Psychologist.

a way of marking time for nothing, really, and it just seems impossible to go on when I feel like that.

P. This fog that you speak of and the cloud around you affect you a lot.

C. Yes, it does. I think what bothers me more than anything is that I do feel the way I do and, it just seems impossible to go on and that of course is very frightening; and sometimes I feel it can't be me that feels like this. It doesn't seem right or fair.

P. It is almost as though you were cut off from what you want to be or what you were.

C. Yes, that's right. And I hardly remember what that was like, and it has cut me off pretty much from everyone, and of course I get angry with the children at times, and that makes me feel bad, too. It is just a horrible feeling. There are no two ways about it.

P. Being angry with the children and not knowing quite why you are angry with them and feeling guilty because you are angry with them.

C. Yes, that's right. And all the time so depressed, and it worries my husband too, I know. He will feel a little depressed and it will get him down. I can't blame him for that. He will feel bad. Of course that bothers me. It is a funny thing between us. Sometimes I think that I need him and I love him, and other times I think that I just don't, that I can't stand him, and why that is I don't know, but I do.

P. You can't understand why you change back and forth in your feelings toward him.

C. That's right.

P. There are times when you love him very much.

C. Yes, when I feel close to him.

P. Then other times you almost hate him.

C. That's right.

* * *

C. When I think of having a baby I would much prefer a girl. I can remember before my little boy was born, I didn't want a boy at all. I thought if I had a little boy, I wouldn't know how to love him. I did not want one, I know; I didn't want a boy.

P. Are you having similar feelings in connection with the new baby?

C. Well, no. I know that I would much prefer to have a girl, but I think that if I had a little boy like my little girl who is affectionate and all that, I would love him.

P. Then when your first child was born you definitely did not want a boy.

C. No, I definitely did not; but of course my little boy has been very difficult always. All his life he was just one of those children who was very, very hard.

P. It is an awfully difficult thing for a mother.

C. It is. I get mad at him and I think of all the trouble I have had since he was born and then I take it out on him.

P. You blame him for it for a while and then feel badly afterwards because you have.

C. Yes, very bad.

P. Do you want to tell me some of the things he does?

C. Well, for one thing he is abnormally loud. He talks loud, he is always very loud. You can get mad at him, and things go right over his head until you just get violently mad, and then it will sink in and he will begin to cry. Well, I can understand that. I take him in my arms and I just comfort him and I just tell him that I am sorry, that mommy doesn't mean it, because that is normal, and I can understand that. I would like to talk to my mother and father about it and about a lot of other things, too. I would like them to know what I think. I'd like to stand on my own two feet and not let them talk me down.

P. So many times they have talked you down.

C. Well, my mother has. My father was never that interested or around that much, I guess. If I could ever get past that domination it would do me a lot of good, but she has a heart condition now and that's bad. I don't know what would happen to me if my mother died because there is still a lot of feeling there.

P. You still feel tied to her pretty closely.

C. Sometimes I feel that I need her very much, and at other times I feel that I hate her. It is quite a mixed-up feeling.

P. That is much harder than a clear-cut feeling, isn't it?

C. It is very much harder.

P. You are pulled toward her, and at the same time you are pulled away from her.

In the preceding excerpts Ruth has in general expressed a feeling of helplessness. She says it is like "walking in a fog." She has ambivalent emotions toward her son and toward her mother. She speaks very little of her father. In the following excerpt, taken from the eighth interview, her relationship with her father is explored in depth. The insights which she achieved from this exploration represented the first major turning point in her therapy. From this point on she began to improve.

C.   Of course with my father I can't understand him at all. I often think I just don't care about him at all and yet there is an emotional tie with him. There has to be for me to be so upset when he says things.

P.   That's good understanding. If there weren't any emotional tie you wouldn't be upset.

C.   I wouldn't care.

P.   You wouldn't care, but you are upset.

C.   Mm-hmm.

P.   And you feel that you have missed so much there and wish even now so much that there could be a warm relationship between the two of you.

C.   Yes, that's certainly so.

P.   You see, Ruth, you are naturally a very warm, emotional person, but you have had your feelings pushed back so many times. As you've said in our earlier talks, you don't quite know how to express them.

C.   Mm-hmm, that's true.

P.   When you were a child growing up I'm sure you were warm and emotional, but you couldn't be really free and spontaneous.

C.   No, I couldn't.

P.   You probably never got any affection from your father.

C.   He's not affectionate at all; I can't remember any affection.

P.   You never recall his even ever putting his hand on your head.

C.   Oh, no. No. What I can remember when I was very, very small, just a little, that he used to call me doll or something. Probably that was before my sister was born.

P.   Yes.

C.   I can remember that; that's the only thing.

P.   The only time that you can remember that he showed you any affection at all.

C.   That's right. He was very affectionate with babies, but not when they got older.

P.   Very affectionate with babies, not affectionate with older children; so perhaps, Ruth, a feeling on your part that if you hadn't grown up maybe he would have continued to show you a little bit of affection.

C.   Of course I can't really see that now, but I can see that as a child I must have. I was three when my sister was born. He must have given me all of the affection in the world then, and when she was born, completely ignored me. He would do that completely.

P.   And how that must have hurt a three-year-old girl.

C.   Yes, that must have been terrible and he paid all of his attention to my sister.

P.   Maybe there was a feeling on your part that there was something wrong about you; otherwise he would have kept on showing you affection.

C.   Yes, at that age it must have been so.

P.   Yes, at that age of course you didn't think it through.

C.   I could just imagine it. He wasn't like the average—really thinking more of babies but trying to pay attention to the older children. He wouldn't; it would be complete withdrawal.

P.   Yes.

C.   He would just baby the baby and ignore me completely. I've seen him do that.

P.   And you can still remember it.

C.   I can't remember it very well, but I can imagine it.

P.   Probably he paid a lot of attention to your sister for three or four years.

C.   Well, she was a year-and-a-half old when my brother was born.

P.   Then maybe he shifted his affections to your brother.

C.   I don't know, I think my sister was always his favorite. My mother often said that dad just idolized Linda when she was born. My aunt thought little boys were wonderful. She loved my little brother so much, so my mother said that she loved me more because no one else did. She said, "I tried to pay a lot of attention to you because I felt so sorry for you, my first-born, and your father completely ignored you." I know I remember her saying that.

P.   That's charged with an awful lot of meaning, Ruth. Here's your father who thought that your little sister was wonderful and your aunt who thought that the boy was wonderful and then your mother saying, "I tried to love you." Not that she really did, but she tried to make it up to you, which perhaps indicated to you as a child that she really preferred the others, too.

C.   Yes, and I often wondered when I was growing up about how my mother was so all-important to me. She just had to love me. I couldn't exist if she didn't, and when she'd tell me she didn't—oh, I would just cry and cry! I wonder now, as I think about it, if my father's neglect didn't make me turn to my mother. I had to have her love. I didn't have my father.

P.   That's wonderful understanding, Ruth.

C.   I didn't have my father. He had gone and all that was left was my mother.

P.   And you had to have her.

C.   I had to have her, so I couldn't displease her, and of course in growing up, things that I did . . . .

P.   Displeased her?

C.   Yes.

P.   But you still had to have her.

C.   Yes, and just thinking about that . . . (*begins to cry*).

P.   That means we're getting close to a sore spot, Ruth.

C.   Nobody really loved me.

P.   I know it hurts, Ruth.

C.   I never thought of it before, but it's true.

P.   Of course it's true, and it hurts. I know it does.

C.   I can see it; I had to have her love me.

P.   You did, you really did.

C.   Because he wasn't there.

P.   He wasn't there, and you had to have her.

C.   So I think as I grew up when she wasn't there I tried to turn to him and he was never there.

P.   He was never there.

C.   And I'm probably still doing it (*short laugh*).

P.   I know it hurts, but in time this will mean a lot to you.

C.   Yes I know, but it upset me just thinking of it.

P.   Just thinking of it, but you broke through to something that means a lot to you.

C.   I never saw it that way before but I can see it and I can imagine it.

P.   Yes.

C.   And I'm still doing it.

P.   Still doing it.

C.   I'm looking to him when I think she fails me, and I know he's not there.

P.   He's not there.

C.   I must have always done that all the time I was growing up and then she was so dominating and told me she hated me, I can see now what that would do.

P. Telling you she hated you when she was all you had and you were really desperate.

C. Yes, I really was. I can remember I had to have that.

P. Absolutely had to have it.

C. It was like the whole world leaving me when she said she didn't love me. I can understand it all somehow now and that's probably the reason why I feel the way I do about my father. I never made the connection before.

In the preceding dialogue it can be seen how Ruth relives a deeply emotional experience in a permissive relationship. As a result she achieves new insights, new understanding of the relationship between her past experiences and her present difficulties. Even though it was painful to accept the fact that her father was "never there" and that her mother probably did not really love her, she achieves a feeling of relief once these emotions have been expressed.

In the interviews which followed the breakthrough which Ruth achieved in the eighth interview, there was the usual exploration of personal relationships and increasing attempts to broaden her understanding of herself. After a few weeks had passed her father unexpectedly died of a heart attack. The death of a significant person is usually of great importance for a disturbed person, resulting in either marked improvement or in intensification of the behavior disorders. The following excerpt is from the twenty-first interview, which was held shortly after Ruth's return from her father's funeral.

P. Was there any feeling as you went through it either of relief on the one hand or great frustration on the other?

C. No, I wouldn't say so. The only feeling I had and I was really ashamed of it was that now actually mother won't be going away. I know I shouldn't have felt like that.

P. Try to tell me just what your feelings were.

C. Well, I guess the feeling that I really had was that I'd always been a little jealous of my father and wanted my mother more to myself.

P. Yes.

C. And what was kind of an eye-opener, too. Well, just let me think. I did feel terribly but not as bad as I felt I should.

P.   You did feel terribly but at the same time you didn't feel as bad as you felt you ought to.

C.   There was one thing that I was very glad about. I never did tell him how I felt about it. It is much better to talk to you; much better, because I thought if—oh, if I had I never would have forgiven myself. Now, I don't have to reproach myself and I'm ready very happy about that.

P.   And so there was relief that you didn't tell him and also relief now that you don't have to.

C.   That's right; that's true.

P.   You have a feeling now that you don't have to tell and that you will be able to work it out.

C.   Yes, and even at the funeral I had that feeling of being left out. Of course, I was so exhausted. For two and a half days I had to be there from early in the morning until late at night. The second night I was so exhausted and had such a terrific headache and such an awful feeling that I was being left out. I looked over at my father. Somehow he didn't seem dead but alive and I said to myself—well, now you wouldn't have let them hurt me—and yet then I thought—yes, you would. It was mixed up, the feelings, and I said—I know I'm tired and I'm not thinking clearly. He would have.

P.   You're facing this beautifully.

C.   It was a mixed-up feeling.

P.   So mixed-up, the feeling that he wouldn't let you be hurt and yet at the same time knowing that he would. Going way back and remembering so many times when you wanted him to support you and knowing that he didn't.

C.   That's right. I can see it and there's another thing that I know, that I realize. I do accept fully that my mother really loves me down underneath. I don't worry about that now. She is there and she does love me, but my brother and sister, they can hurt me very much.

P.   Yes.

C.   (Pause) . . . I wonder what would happen if something happened to my mother. I guess that's why I feel so anxious when she leaves. I wonder if I will ever see her again, so it's much worse when she leaves than when she comes.

P.   Still that strong tie with her.

C.   Yes, that very strong tie.

P.   So difficult to bring it to an adult level.

C.   My mother still comes first and she shouldn't. My husband and children really should come first but she does. There's too much of a tie there,

there's no two ways about it. I am realizing it more and more, just how much there is and as I said my father had much more power to hurt me for some reason, because I did expect him to stand up for me and protect me the way he should and yet I realize now that he couldn't do it. He wanted to but he couldn't do it.

P. He wanted to but he couldn't.

* * *

C. Oh, another thing that I thought of when I was there, that, I don't know, it was so difficult for me growing up in that family. When I considered that my father was a very brilliant man, there's no two ways about it, and my mother is a brilliant woman. She is and my sister was second in her graduating class in college and was valedictorian in high school and my brother—I was looking at his IQ and it was oh so high and I said to myself—oh, good Lord, I'm just normal and I've grown up in a family that were almost geniuses and here I thought I grew up in a family with a normal IQ and I'm not particularly smart, and, I thought, good heavens what that could do, just that alone.

P. Just that alone. Terrific pressure was brought to bear on you.

C. (Pause). . . . I think, too, that it has helped me to appreciate Dick more, which is good. When I got home I thought, "Oh, how childish I've been, how ridiculous I was, being worried about his looks, when he is really such a wonderful person."

P. He really is.

C. He is. It just struck me how stupid that idea I had was.

P. That's a wonderful change.

C. Yes. How important he really is to me, and I never realized it before. I think with my father's going it kind of woke me up. I thought, "What would I do without him and how much he does mean to me."

P. And how much you really think of him.

C. I really do. I really do love him and how silly I've been, kind of an awakening, actually.

P. You see Dick in a different light now.

C. I do. I actually do and I hope it stays because I do see him differently.

P. That can mean so much to you through the years to come.

C. Well actually the feelings about his looks and all was a childish feeling, a very childish feeling. I couldn't help it but oh it was so silly. It wasn't important at all.

It can be seen from the preceding excerpt that Ruth experienced a feeling of relief because of her father's death although she was somewhat ambivalent about it. Her relationship with her mother remains a major problem. She is still somewhat confused as to what it is and to what it ought to be. However, she is achieving a better understanding of herself and of her relationship with her husband. The death of her father had altered her interpersonal environment and, in time, was a positive complement to psychotherapy.

In succeeding interviews, Ruth made considerable progress in her understanding of herself. To be sure, there were frequent relapses. It may be said that in psychotherapy the client takes two steps forward and one step backward as he works toward the regaining of his mental health. The following excerpt is taken from the thirtieth interview. The reader will note in Ruth's statements many changes in her perception of herself and of the members of her family. In this interview she demonstrates that she is nearing the end of psychotherapy.

C.   Actually Jimmy [her son] is better-looking than most boys. He's an extremely good-looking boy now. He was a very homely baby. I think he'll be the best-looking of my children. People say, you know, that real homely babies turn out to be the best-looking people, and evidently that's true because he is really very good-looking—extremely. I really get a lot of fun out of keeping him well dressed, even more than I do with Sally because when he is well dressed he looks really outstanding. I am proud to be with him. But Sally, of course—she really is very cute.

P.   Yes.

C.   And it's important to me that she look nice and clean and well dressed.

P.   Yes.

C.   And it seems to me that the cleaner they are the healthier they are.

P.   But you don't have the feeling now that you're trying desperately to make everything right.

C.   Oh, no. I can't say that I ever really did. I'm just not that type of person.

P.   Mm-hmm.

C.   Really, I'm not. I like to have things in their place, of course.

*   *   *

P.   And now would you like to tell me how you feel toward your husband?

C.   About the same as I have been feeling in recent weeks; just about the same.

P.   Any recurrence of the old feelings that you used to have about him?

C.   No, not yet! Of course, we're both getting older. It's something I've begun to face in a way. I've decided I'm just not going to worry so much about how I look. Actually I have other things that are much more important to be concerned about.

P.   Then the old anxiety about losing your youth doesn't bother you as much now as it did.

C.   No, I'm just determined not to worry about it. I like to look as nice as I can, of course.

P.   You're accepting the fact, then, that you're now nearly thirty and you can't expect to look as you did when you were twenty.

C.   With children you just can't; it's impossible. These ads that I see just give me a laugh. It's ridiculous. With a husband and children, I've got all I can do to take care of them. I don't have time to be fixing up myself all the time. If you worry too much about yourself you're really in for trouble.

P.   Mm-hmm. Then you're realizing now that there are other things than your personal appearance that are important.

C.   And I think it helps me more to accept Dick. It does.

P.   Of course it does.

C.   Of course, there is the difference in our ages. It used to bother me, but as I get older it doesn't bother me much now.

P.   When you were first married it did make more of a difference then; now it doesn't bother you nearly as much.

C.   Well, it's that; and of course when I was younger I had so much attention from other men. And I think about when I could have chosen any one of them, which I could have at the time.

P.   Yes.

C.   But now Dick is older and I'm getting older, and we've got to learn to get along together. I really don't have that conflict any more. In a way it's hard, and in a way it's easier.

P.   In a way it's hard, but in a way it is really easier.

C.   Yes, in a way it's easier.

P.   That's one of the things you have needed—to have things get easier. Life has been pretty hard for you.

C.   Yes, and as for Dick—I think what a good husband he actually is.

P.   He is.

C. I've had so many women—countless, honestly—tell me how lucky I was. Oh, so many, and they've said that they would give anything for a husband like Dick.

P. And you couldn't accept that.

C. No, I couldn't accept it. And, of course, my mother, too; so many times she has said that he is just exceptional. She says she's never seen a man who will do the things for you that he has done.

P. And you're beginning to feel that yourself.

C. Yes, I am. Of course, with Dick I'm on a pedestal. I know I am, which is exceptional. He loves the children very much, but I come first and probably will always come first, no matter how terrible I look. For some reason I look wonderful to him.

P. You do all the time.

C. All the time. It's phenomenal, but it's true. No matter how I look or where I go he thinks every man is envying him, and it is not an act.

P. No, it isn't.

C. He has an illusion, and when I'm really looking bad, he thinks I look good. I think he wants to or something.

P. It comes from the fact that he thinks so much of you. You always look wonderful to him.

C. It must be and it really is something. I know. It just amazes me.

P. And it must make you feel very good to know that that is the way he feels.

C. Yes, it does. It gives me more confidence in myself actually. And we get along very well. We rarely argue now. I think the last argument we had was months and months ago.

P. That's unusual.

C. So many months ago I can hardly remember, which is good.

P. You're not nearly so likely now to be critical.

C. No. No, I'm not at all. And, as I said before, I'm getting older too.

P. You're getting older, and you're getting much better able to live with your family.

C. Well, I certainly do see them in a very different light, which is good.

P. Yes.

C. And Jimmy has stopped that blinking, overnight, just like that. He stopped it.

P. And you worried about that for a long time.

C. And he brought home his report care yesterday. He's passing everything. The teacher said how well he's getting along with the other children.

The reader should compare the preceding excerpt with the two from the second interview. In this, the thirtieth interview, most of Ruth's statements are positive in nature. She sees her son as a very good-looking boy and accepts the fact that he is not getting high grades in his school work. Her perception of her husband and of her relationship with him has changed considerably. She has also achieved a much better understanding of herself. The discrepancy between her ideal self and her real self is not nearly so great as it was in the early interviews.

There were six more interviews before psychotherapy was ended. These were, in many respects, similar to the thirtieth. Ruth gained an increased understanding of herself and took several steps which represented positive action. Included among these was a greatly increased social life which she enjoyed and in which she felt confident. Her relationship with the members of her immediate family was excellent. In summary, she had considerably modified her perception of herself and of her environment.

SUMMARY

Persons suffering from behavior disorders should seek treatment from professionally trained men and women. This trained personnel is usually found in psychiatry and clinical psychology. Psychotherapy is a verbal approach to behavior problems; it is basically a learning process. The main objective in psychotherapy is to bring about changes in the client's perception of himself and of his environment. In successful psychotherapy these changes in the perceptual field are accompanied and followed by positive changes in behavior. Since mental health, once lost, is difficult to regain, every effort should be made to prevent behavior disorders through the maintenance of healthy conditions in the community, in the school, and in the home.

QUESTIONS FOR STUDY AND DISCUSSION

Chapter One

1. What is meant by the term *mental hygiene?*

2. How extensive is the mental health problem in the United States?

3. What is the attitude of normal persons toward those who are emotionally disturbed? What are the reasons for this attitude?

4. What is the mental hygiene point of view?

5. Why is respect for one's own personality and for the personalities of others an essential part of the mental hygiene point of view?

6. Why is it desirable to recognize limitations in ourselves and in others?

7. What is meant by the moralistic attitude toward adjustive difficulties?

8. What is meant by the psychological attitude toward adjustive difficulties?

9. Does every human being possess a drive for self-actualization?

Chapter Two

1. Is all behavior motivated?

2. What is meant by the term *instinct?* Is there any justification for believing that any human behavior is instinctive?

3.   Are the terms *motive, need,* and *drive* synonymous?

4.   What does Freud mean by Eros or the life instinct?

5.   Does man have any instincts which are not modifiable?

6.   What is meant by the pleasure principle and the reality principle?

7.   What are some of the weaknesses of Freud's theory of motivation?

8.   Is there a basic similarity between Adler's theory of motivation and that presented by Combs and Snygg?

9.   Is all behavior completely determined by and pertinent to the phenomenal field of the behaver?

10. Are childhood experiences important motivating factors in adult behavior?

11. Is a person's social inheritance as significant for him as his biological inheritance?

12. Should a differentiation be made between the terms *frustration* and *conflict?*

13. Do all conflicts fall into three categories?

14. What are the major manifestations of emotional tension?

15. Why do response, tension reduction, and effects involve learning?

16. What is a conditioned response?

17. Is need reduction essential for the continuation of a conditioned response?

18. What is meant by insight?

19. What are the essentials of trial-and-error behavior?

20. When is a response a good response?

21. Is the law of effect as stated by Thorndike early in the 20th century acceptable today?

Chapter Three

1.   What is an adjustment mechanism?

2.   Is it desirable to use adjustment mechanisms?

3.   What are the several ways in which individuals use compensation as a mechanism of adjustment?

4.   What are some of the values derived from the use of identification?

5.   Is rationalization really rational?

6.   What are the three principal ways in which projection is used?

7.   What distinctions can be made between normal and abnormal utilization of projection?

8.   Why do persons resort to attention-getting? Is this adjustment mechanism more normal for young children than it is for adults? Why is it so frequent among adolescents?

9.   What are some of the reasons why a child or an adult is occasionally negativistic?

10.   Should intellectualizing be considered an adjustment mechanism?

11.   What are some of the ways in which persons escape into verbalizing?

12.   What are some of the degrees in the use of isolation as an adjustment mechanism? Is it inconsistent to say that a person needs to be alone and also to say that isolationism is a danger signal?

13.   Is daydreaming really a form of relaxation?

14.   What are some of the different types of daydreaming?

15.   What are some of the causes of regressive behavior?

16.   Why is repression the least satisfactory of the adjustment mechanisms?

Chapter Four

1.   How is success defined?

2.   What is perfectionism?

3.   Why is knowledge of the facts of individual differences essential to an understanding of adjustment problems which have their source in achievement needs?

4.   What is a measure of central tendency?

5.   What is a measure of variability?

6.   How should correlation coefficients be interpreted?

7.   Should a person always take into consideration his relative position in the group of individuals with whom he is competing?

8.   Do individuals differ in kind or in degree?

9.   What are the principal causes of individual differences?

10.   What is the present point of view concerning the relative potency of heredity and environment in the determination of an individual's intelligence?

11. What should be the relationship between one's goals and one's abilities?

12. Can a person do anything if he will only work hard enough?

Chapter Five

1. Is it possible for the status drive to be much stronger than the achievement drive?

2. Are individuals in our culture expected to adjust to a series of group codes?

3. What is meant by role-taking?

4. Does the individual have as many selves as there are different social groups with which he is associated?

5. What are some of the causes of the conflicts between roles?

6. What are some of the conflicts experienced by college students in role-taking?

7. What are some of the changes in roles which result from growing older?

8. What are some of the ways in which the desire for prestige expresses itself?

9. What is meant by role lag?

10. What are some of the hazards of role-taking in fantasy?

11. How are status needs satisfied through identification with organizations or institutions?

12. What is the relationship between leadership and the need for status?

Chapter Six

1. What is meant by homeostasis?

2. Is homeostasis the only need of man?

3. Are the organic urges modified by learning?

4. What are some of the psychological and sociological implications of the hunger drive?

5. Can overeating be psychologically caused?

6. Do sex conflicts arise during adolescence only?

7. Are autoerotic practices harmful?

8.   What are some of the causes of homosexual behavior?

9.   Do parental fixations frequently result in abnormal sex adjustments?

10. Should sex education be left entirely to the home?

11. Are fear and shame good incentives for proper sex conduct?

12. What are some of the factors which retard heterosexual adjustment during adolescence?

Chapter Seven

1.   In what ways do the autonomic nervous system and the central or somatic nervous system differ?

2.   What is meant by the term *emotional security*?

3.   Why is a rather high degree of emotional security essential for physical and mental health?

4.   What are the sources of emotional security? Should additional ones be added to the four discussed in this chapter?

5.   Is it desirable to assume that the behavior of the monkeys in the Harlow study is comparable to what can be expected in human beings?

6.   Why is security in personal relationships so important during infancy and early childhood?

7.   What are some of the problems of adolescents in their search for security through interpersonal relationships?

8.   Is there a greater variety of personal associations during adulthood than during any other period in life? If so, why?

9.   Are personal relationships less significant and intense in old age?

10. Why is it desirable that the impersonal environment be rich in possibilities for a variety of attachments?

11. Is there any relationship between chronological age and the importance of attachment to inanimate objects?

12. What significance do memories have for emotional security?

13. Should future prospects be considered to be a source of emotional security?

14. What are the principal differences between normal anxiety and neurotic anxiety?

15. How is anxiety learned?

16.   What is the association between anxiety and repression?

17.   Why does anxiety inhibit new learning?

Chapter Eight

1.   In what ways is the home a unit?

2.   Why is it so important that the home provide an atmosphere in which the child feels secure?

3.   How is the infant's need for emotional security satisfied?

4.   What are some of the reasons why parents reject their children?

5.   In what ways can overprotection harm a child?

6.   Why does quarreling between parents make the child feel insecure?

7.   Should parents select their children's goals?

8.   Are the relationships which the child has with his brothers and sisters significant factors in personality development?

9.   What are the essentials of a satisfactory marriage?

10.   What is meant by maturity?

11.   Will love transcend all the differences which may exist between the married couple?

Chapter Nine

1.   What is the principal goal of education in grade school and high school?

2.   What are some of the arguments for and against the use of intelligence tests?

3.   Are percentage grades ever justified?

4.   What are some of the major objections to the use of personality tests or inventories?

5.   Does personality testing constitute an invasion of privacy?

6.   What should be the teacher's attitude toward problems in discipline?

7.   Are school behavior problems symptoms of frustration?

8.   What are the characteristics of effective teachers?

9.   How can the teacher make the mental hygiene point of view functional in the classroom?

10.   Should counseling in the schools be done solely by professional personnel or by teacher-counselors and psychologists working together?

11.   Are the twelve underlying concepts presented by Hobbs limited to the reeducation of emotionally disturbed children or are they applicable to all classrooms?

Chapter Ten

1.   Why did earlier societies look upon abnormal behavior as mysterious?

2.   What was the relationship between witchcraft and the attitude of the public toward persons suffering from behavior disorders?

3.   Why has there been so much more hostility toward mentally ill persons than toward physically ill persons?

4.   What are the current attitudes of the public toward persons who are suffering from behavior disorders and toward the professional groups who are responsible for their care and treatment?

5.   What is the mental hygienist's attitude toward religion?

6.   How can the church contribute to the mental hygiene movement?

7.   How can the attitudes of the community toward problems of mental health be reflected in the schools?

8.   How can parent-teacher groups contribute to a mental health program in a community?

9.   What are the contributions that can be made to prevention and to treatment by child guidance clinics?

10.   Is a child guidance or mental health clinic preferable to the organizational approach described by Hobbs in the preceding chapter?

Chapter Eleven

1.   How does Sullivan explain the development of the self-system?

2.   What does Allport mean by the term *proprium*?

3.   According to Diamond, in what ways is the self discovered?

4.   Why do many persons believe that the self has a specific location within some organ or part of the body?

5.   Why do Combs and Snygg make a distinction between the phenomenal self and the self-concept?

6.   In what ways are the theories presented by Sullivan, Allport, Diamond, and Combs and Snygg alike and in what ways are they different?

7.   Why do changes in the perception of the self come about as a function of chronological age?

8.   Can a psychological crisis in the life of an individual drastically modify his perception of himself?

9.   Does a new self-structure emerge as a result of successful psychotherapy?

10.   What is meant by the statement that adequacy is on a continuum?

11.   How do distorted personalities develop?

12.   How do self-actualized personalities develop?

Chapter Twelve

1.   Who are gifted children?

2.   Do the attitudes of parents and siblings frequently create special adjustment problems for the gifted child?

3.   Why does the gifted child experience difficulty in adjusting to a typical classroom situation?

4.   Is a high level of intelligence insurance against emotional maladjustments?

5.   What is meant by feeblemindedness or mental retardation?

6.   Should curricula and standards be modified to meet the needs and abilities of mentally retarded children?

7.   What should be the point of view of parents toward their mentally retarded child?

8.   Are retarded children and adults more susceptible to behavior disorders than those who have normal mentality?

9.   What should be the attitude of parents toward a physically handicapped child?

10.   How should a physically handicapped person view his defect?

11.   Why is impaired hearing more socially unacceptable than impaired vision?

12.   Why is it frequently more difficult to adjust to a marginal handicap than to a more severe defect?

Chapter Thirteen

1.   What is a neurotic adjustment?

2.   What are some of the major ways in which neurotic adjustments are different from psychotic adjustments?

3. When would psychophysiological disorders be classified as conversion reactions?

4. How is it possible for a person to develop amnesia?

5. What is meant by conversion reaction?

6. How can stomach ulcers be psychologically caused?

7. Are speech defects usually caused by psychological factors?

8. What are the characteristics of the hysteric personality?

9. What are the characteristics of a phobia?

10. What are the principal causes of phobic reactions?

11. Are normal individuals occasionally troubled by obsessive thoughts?

12. What is a compulsion?

Chapter Fourteen

1. What is the principal distinction between an organic psychosis and a functional psychosis?

2. What is meant by the term *schizophrenia*?

3. What are the four major groups of schizophrenic reactions?

4. What behavior patterns are characteristic of each of the four groups?

5. Is schizophrenic behavior inherited or learned?

6. What is the difference between inheriting a predisposition and inheriting a complex pattern of behavior?

7. What is the distinction between predisposing factors and precipitating factors?

8. How do manic-depressive reactions differ from schizophrenic reactions?

9. Is there frequently a great deal of overlapping in symptoms between manic-depressive reactions and schizophrenic reactions?

10. Are manic-depressive reactions inherited or learned?

11. What are the principal characteristics of paranoia?

12. What are some of the causes of involutional psychotic reactions?

Chapter Fifteen

1. What are some of the reasons why a person hesitates to go to a psychiatrist or clinical psychologist for help with his adjustment difficulties?

2. Why are the facilities for the treatment of behavior disorders so inadequate?

3. Is the typical medical practitioner qualified to function as a therapist?

4. What are the qualifications of the psychiatrist as a therapist?

5. What are the qualifications of the psychoanalyst as a therapist?

6. What are the qualifications of the clinical psychologist as a therapist?

7. What are the personal qualifications of a successful therapist?

8. What is the difference between counseling and psychotherapy?

9. What are some of the basic principles underlying good counseling?

10. Why and how does an individual achieve insight through catharsis in a permissive relationship?

11. What basic changes take place in the individual in successful psychotherapy?

12. In the case of Ruth, what caused the changes in her perception of her self and of the members of her family?

13. What responses did the psychologist make which helped Ruth toward a better understanding of herself and of her personal environment?

SELECTED LIST OF BOOKS

ACKERMAN, N. W., *The Psychodynamics of Family Life.* New York: Basic Books, Inc., Publishers, 1958.

ADLER, A., *Understanding Human Nature,* trans. W. B. Wolfe. New York: Greenberg Publishing, Inc., 1927.

ALLPORT, G. W., *Becoming.* New Haven, Conn.: Yale University Press, 1955.

ANDERSON, C. M., *Beyond Freud: A Creative Approach to Mental Health.* New York: Harper & Row, Publishers, 1957.

ANDERSON, HAROLD, *Creativity and Its Cultivation.* New York: Harper & Row, Publishers, 1959.

ANSBACHER, H. L., and R. R. ANSBACHER, *The Individual Psychology of Alfred Adler.* New York: Basic Books, Inc., Publishers, 1956.

AXLINE, VIRGINIA, *Dibs: In Search of Self.* Boston: Houghton Mifflin Company, 1965.

BEERS, C., *A Mind That Found Itself,* 7th ed. Garden City, N.Y.: Doubleday & Company, Inc., 1948.

BENDA, C. E., *The Image of Love.* Glencoe, Ill.: Free Press, 1961.

BLAINE, GRAHAM B., and C. C. MC ARTHUR, *Emotional Problems of the Student.* New York: Appleton-Century-Crofts, 1961.

BLAIR, G. M., and R. S. JONES, *Psychology of Adolescence for Teachers.* New York: The Macmillan Company, 1964.

BONNEY, M. E., *Mental Health in Education.* Boston: Allyn & Bacon, Inc., 1960.

BOWER, ELI M., *Early Identification of Emotionally Handicapped Children in School.* Springfield, Ill.: Charles C. Thomas, Publisher, 1960.

BRUNER, JEROME S., *On Knowing.* Cambridge, Mass.: Harvard University Press, 1962.

BURNHAM, W. H., *The Wholesome Personality.* New York: Appleton-Century-Crofts, 1932.

COFER, C. N., and M. H. APLEY, *Motivation: Theory and Research.* New York: John Wiley and Sons, Inc., 1964.

COLEMAN, J. D., *Abnormal Psychology and Modern Life,* 3rd ed. Chicago: Scott, Foresman & Company, 1964.

COMBS, A. W., and D. SNYGG, *Individual Behavior,* rev. ed. New York: Harper & Row, Publishers, 1959.

CROW, L. D., and A. CROW, *Mental Hygiene for Teachers.* New York: The Macmillian Company, 1963.

DEUTSCH, A., *The Mentally Ill in America,* 2nd ed. New York: Columbia University Press, 1949.

DEUTSCH, J. A., *The Structural Basis of Behavior.* Chicago: University of Chicago Press, 1960.

DIAMOND, S., *Personality and Temperament.* New York: Harper & Row, Publishers, 1957.

DINKMEYER, DON C., *Child Development: The Emerging Self.* Englewood Cliffs, N.J.: Prentice-Hall, Inc., 1965.

————, and RUDOLPH DREIKURS, *Encouraging Children to Learn: The Encouragement Process.* Englewood Cliffs, N.J.: Prentice Hall, Inc., 1963.

DOLLARD, JOHN; N. E. MILLER; L. W. DOBB; O. H. MOWRER, and R. R. SEARS, *Frustration and Aggression.* New Haven, Conn.: Yale University Press, 1939.

EBLE, K. E., *A Perfect Education.* New York: The Macmillan Company, 1966.

ERIKSON, ERIK H., *Insight and Responsibility.* New York: W. W. Norton & Co., Inc., 1964.

————, *Youth: Change and Challenge.* New York: Basic Books, Inc., Publishers, 1964.

FARNSWORTH, D. L., *Mental Health in College and University*. Cambridge, Mass.: Harvard University Press, 1957.

FELIX, ROBERT H., *Mental Illness: Progress and Prospects*. New York: Columbia University Press, 1967.

Final Report of the Joint Commission on Mental Illness and Health, *Action for Mental Health*. New York: Basic Books, Inc., Publishers, 1961.

FREUD, S., *An Outline of Psychoanalysis*. New York: W. W. Norton & Company, Inc., 1949.

————, *The Problem of Anxiety*. New York: W. W. Norton & Company, Inc., 1936.

FROMM, ERICH, *May Man Prevail*. Garden City, N.Y.: Doubleday & Company, Inc., 1961.

GAGE, N. L., *Handbook of Research on Teaching*. Chicago: Rand McNally & Co., 1963.

GARDNER, JOHN, *Self Renewal*. New York: Harper & Row, Publishers, 1964.

GLASSER, WILLIAM, *Reality Therapy*. New York: Harper & Row, Publishers, 1965.

GRAY, SUSAN, *The Psychologist in the Schools*. New York: Holt, Rinehart and Winston, Inc., 1963.

GREEN, HANNAH, *I Never Promised You A Rose Garden*. New York: Holt, Rinehart & Winston, Inc., 1964.

GURIN, G.; J. VEROFF, and S. FELD, *Americans View Their Mental Health*. New York: Basic Books, Inc., Publishers, 1958.

HODGINS, E., *Episode*. New York: Atheneum, 1964.

HOFFMAN, MARTIN L., and LOIS WALDIS HOFFMAN, eds., *Review of Child Development Research*. New York: Russell Sage Foundation, 1964.

JAHODA, M., *Current Concepts of Positive Mental Health*. New York: Basic Books, Inc., Publishers, 1958.

JERSILD, A. T., *In Search of Self*. New York: Teachers College, Columbia University, 1952.

JOHNSON, W., *Stuttering and What You Can Do About It*. Minneapolis: University of Minnesota Press, 1961.

KAPLAN, BERT, ed., *The Inner World of Mental Illness*. New York: Harper & Row, Publishers, 1964.

KAPLAN, L., *Mental Health and Human Relations in Education*. New York: Harper & Row, Publishers, 1959.

KARDINER, A., *Sex and Morality*. Indianapolis: The Bobbs-Merrill Co., Inc., 1954.

KASSANIN, J. S., *Language and Thought in Schizophrenia*. New York: W. W. Norton & Company, Inc., 1964.

KATZ, B., *How to Be a Better Parent*. New York: The Ronald Press Company, 1954.

————, and L. P. Thorpe, *Understanding People in Distress*. New York: The Ronald Press Company, 1955.

KINSEY, A. C., *et al.*, *Sexual Behavior in the Human Male*. Philadelphia: W. B. Saunders Co., 1948.

————, *Sexual Behavior in the Human Female*. Philadelphia: W. B. Saunders Co., 1953.

KRUMBOLTZ, JOHN K., ed., *Revolution in Counseling*. Boston: Houghton Mifflin Company, 1965.

LEVINSON, H., *et al.*, *Men, Management and Mental Health*. Cambridge, Mass.: Harvard University Press, 1963.

LUCAS, F. L., *Literature and Psychology*. Ann Arbor, Mich.: University of Michigan, 1957.

MC CANDLESS, B. R., *Children and Adolescents*. New York: Holt, Rinehart & Winston, Inc., 1961.

MC KENZIE, NORMAN, *Dreams and Dreaming*. New York: Vanguard Press, Inc., 1965.

MAIER, N. R. F., *Frustration*. New York: McGraw-Hill Book Company, 1949.

MASLOW, ABRAHAM; CARL ROGERS; ARTHUR COMBS, and EARL KELLY, *Perceiving, Behaving, Becoming*. Washington, D.C.: Association for Supervision and Curriculum Development, 1962.

MASLOW, A. H., *Motivation and Personality*. New York: Harper & Row, Publishers, 1954.

————, *Toward a Psychology of Being*. Princeton, N.J.: D. Van Nostrand Co., Inc., 1962.

MAY, R., *Man's Search for Himself*. New York: W. W. Norton & Company, Inc., 1953.

————, *The Meaning of Anxiety*. New York: The Ronald Press Company, 1950.

MEDNICK, S. A., *Learning*. Englewood Cliffs, N.J.: Prentice-Hall, Inc., 1964.

MILLER, B. J., and ZELMA MILLER, *Good Health: Personal and Community*. Philadelphia: W. B. Saunders Co., 1960.

MILLER, DANIEL R., and G. E. SWANSON, *Inner Conflict and Defense*. New York: Holt, Rinehart & Winston, Inc., 1960.

MOUSTAKAS, CLARK E., *Loneliness*. Englewood Cliffs, N.J.: Prentice-Hall, Inc., 1961.

————, et al., *The Self*. New York: Harper & Row, Publishers, 1956.

MURPHY, LOIS BARCLAY, and associates, *The Widening World of Childhood: Paths Toward Mastery*. New York: Basic Books, Inc., Publishers, 1962.

MUSSEN, P. H.; J. J. CONGER, and J. KAGAN, *Child Development and Personality*. New York: Harper & Row, Publishers, 1963.

NATIONAL SOCIETY FOR STUDY OF EDUCATION, Fifty-fourth Yearbook, *Mental Health in Modern Education*, Part II. Chicago: University of Chicago Press, 1955.

NEWMAN, H. H.; F. N. FREEMAN, and K. J. HOLZINGER, *Twins: A Study of Heredity and Environment*. Chicago: University of Chicago Press, 1937.

OPLER, MARVIN K., ed., *Culture and Mental Health: Cross-Cultural Studies*. New York: The Macmillan Company, 1959.

PARKER, BEULAH, *My Language is Me*. New York: Basic Books, Inc., Publishers, 1962.

RIBBLE, MARGARET, *The Rights of Infants*, 2nd ed. New York: Columbia University Press, 1965.

ROGERS, C. R., *On Becoming a Person*. Boston: Houghton Mifflin Company, 1961.

ROKEACH, MILTON, *Three Christs of Ypsilanti*. New York: Alfred A. Knopf, Inc., 1964.

ROLO, CHARLES, ed., *Psychiatry in American Life*. Boston: Little, Brown and Company, 1963.

SCHEFF, THOMAS J., ed., *Mental Illness and Social Processes*. New York: Harper & Row, Publishers, 1967.

SEXTON, ANNE, *To Bedlam and Part Way Back*. Boston: Houghton Mifflin Company, 1960.

SHRODES, C.; J. VAN GUNDY, and R. W. HUSBAND, eds., *Psychology Through Literature: An Anthology*. New York: Oxford University Press, 1943.

SOUTHWELL, EUGENE A., and MICHAEL MERBAUM, *Personality: Readings in Theory and Research*. Belmont, Calif.: Wadsworth Publishing Company, 1964.

SROLE, L., et al., *Mental Health in the Metropolis, the Midtown Manhattan Study*. New York: McGraw-Hill Book Company, 1962.

STONE, ALAN A., and SUE SMART STONE, *The Abnormal Personality Through Literature*. Englewood Cliffs, N.J.: Prentice-Hall, Inc., 1966.

STRANG, R., *The Adolescent Views Himself*. New York: McGraw-Hill Book Company, Inc., 1957.

STUART, H. C., and D. G. PRUGH, eds., *The Healthy Child*. Cambridge, Mass.: Harvard University Press, 1960.

SULLIVAN, H. S., *Conceptions of Modern Psychiatry*, 2nd ed., New York: W. W. Norton & Company, Inc., 1953.

TERMAN, L. M., and M. H. ODEN, *The Gifted Group at Mid-Life*. Genetic Studies of Genius, V. Stanford, Calif.: Stanford University Press, 1959.

TYLER, LEONA, *The Work of the Counselor*. New York: Appleton-Century-Crofts, 1961.

ULLMANN, L. P., and L. KRASSNER, *Case Studies in Behavior Modification*. New York: Holt, Rinehart & Winston, Inc. 1965.

WRIGHT, BEATRICE A., *Physical Disability—A Psychological Approach*, New York: Harper & Row, Publishers, 1960.

WYLIE, RUTH, *Self Concept*. Lincoln, Nebr.: University of Nebraska Press, 1961.